The Dream Is Lost

THE
DREAM
IS LOST

Voting Rights and
the Politics of Race
in Richmond, Virginia

Julian Maxwell Hayter

 UNIVERSITY PRESS OF KENTUCKY

Scholarly publisher for the Commonwealth,
serving Bellarmine University, Berea College, Centre College of Kentucky, Eastern
Kentucky University, The Filson Historical Society, Georgetown College, Kentucky
Historical Society, Kentucky State University, Morehead State University, Murray
State University, Northern Kentucky University, Transylvania University, University
of Kentucky, University of Louisville, and Western Kentucky University.
All rights reserved.

Editorial and Sales Offices: The University Press of Kentucky
663 South Limestone Street, Lexington, Kentucky 40508-4008
www.kentuckypress.com

Library of Congress Cataloging-in-Publication Data

Names: Hayter, Julian Maxwell, author.
Title: The dream is lost : voting rights and the politics of race in
    Richmond, Virginia / Julian Maxwell Hayter.
Description: Lexington, Kentucky : The University Press of Kentucky, 2017. |
    Includes bibliographical references and index.
Identifiers: LCCN 2017003551| ISBN 9780813169484 (hardcover : acid-free
    paper) | ISBN 9780813169507 (PDF) | ISBN 9780813169491 (ePub)
Subjects: LCSH: African Americans—Civil rights—Virginia—Richmond—History—
    20th century. | African Americans—Suffrage—Virginia—Richmond—History—
    20th century. | African Americans—Virginia—Richmond—Politics and
    government—20th century. | Civil rights movements—Virginia—Richmond—
    History—20th century. | Richmond (Va.)—Race relations—History—20th
    century. | Richmond (Va.)—Politics and government—20th century.
Classification: LCC F234.R59 N446 2017 | DDC 323.1196/0730755451—dc23
LC record available at https://lccn.loc.gov/2017003551

ISBN 978-0-8131-7846-2 (pbk. : alk. paper)

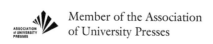

To Mom, Dad, Cate, and Evelyn, with love.

Rest in peace, Steve.

Journey well, Pops.

Evils which are patiently endured when they seem inevitable, become intolerable when once the idea of escape from them is suggested.

—Alexis de Tocqueville,
Old Regime and the Revolution

Contents

Abbreviations

BMC	black-majority council
CCC	Citizens' Crime Commission
CETA	Comprehensive Education and Training Act of 1973
CRD	Civil Rights Division (U.S. Department of Justice)
DOJ	U.S. Department of Justice
HB	House Bill (Virginia General Assembly)
NAACP	National Association for the Advancement of Colored People
RCA	Richmond Civic Association
RCC	Richmond Civil Council
RF	Richmond Forward
RMA	Richmond Metropolitan Authority
RPD	Richmond Police Department
RPS	Richmond Public Schools
RRHA	Richmond Redevelopment and Housing Authority
SCLC	Southern Christian Leadership Conference
TOP	Team of Progress
USCCR	U.S. Commission on Civil Rights
VRA	Voting Rights Act of 1965
VUU	Virginia Union University

Introduction

Richmond, Virginia, is seldom central to the narrative of the American civil rights movement or pointed out in studies of twentieth-century urban history. Yet in June 1980 *Ebony* magazine featured the Commonwealth of Virginia's capital in an article entitled "Richmond: Former Confederate Capital Finally Falls to Blacks." The column documented the arrival of black governance in what was once the industrial capital of slave-based tobacco production and the home of the Confederacy. Richmond activist Curtis Holt Sr. was at the center of the *Ebony* article. In 1971, Holt, armed with a tenth-grade education, walked into a federal office in Richmond and filed a suit against the city under the authority of the Voting Rights Act (VRA) of 1965. According to Holt, Richmond's white leaders had in 1969 purposefully diluted the collective power of the city's black voters by annexing portions of Chesterfield County, a primarily white and affluent suburb contiguous to Richmond. Vote dilution, Holt charged, cost him a seat on the city council during the election of 1970. Few knew it at the time, but Holt's contentions would transform municipal politics in Richmond. His lawsuit was part of a much larger voting rights revolution that changed the meaning of representative democracy in America.[1]

In 1972, Holt's suit led a federal district court to use the VRA's preclearance clause in section 5 to place a moratorium on Richmond City Council elections. This moratorium lasted until the U.S. Supreme Court and the U.S. Department of Justice (DOJ) determined whether the annexation of Chesterfield County had indeed diluted—the process of diminishing a group's ability to elect candidates of their choice—blacks' votes by adding nearly 44,000 white suburban residents to the city. The suspension of the city council elections lasted for roughly seven years. Although the Court eventually upheld the annexation, it demanded in return that Richmonders abandon at-large elections and implement an electoral system that allowed African Americans, who represented more than 50 percent of Richmond's total population prior to the boundary expansion, to vote within almost exclusively black districts. Racial redis-

1

tricting led immediately to the election of a five-to-four black-majority council (BMC) in 1977 and the appointment of a nationally celebrated civil rights lawyer, Henry L. Marsh III, to the mayoralty.[2]

Roughly twelve years after Congress passed the VRA, the former capital of the Confederacy had fallen again. African Americans seemed to have political control over a city whose foremost tourist attraction, Monument Avenue, was and continues to be a street lined with statues honoring Confederate leaders. By the early 1980s, the commonwealth's capital was one of thirteen U.S. cities with populations greater than 100,000 to be controlled by a black city council, mayor, and administration. *Ebony* argued that Holt, a resident of Richmond's Creighton Court housing projects who was generally unkempt and "misplaced infinitives and mispronounced words," seemed an unlikely candidate to transform a city's political landscape—especially a city that had played such a pivotal role in perpetuating oppression of African Americans. But Holt, the historical record demonstrates, had not done it alone.[3]

Richmond, Virginia, founded in 1737 by William Byrd II on the James River fall line, was fundamental to the formation of both American liberty and American slavery. On one hand, Richmond is inextricably linked to the establishment of American independence. Patrick Henry delivered the celebrated "Liberty or Death" speech atop Church Hill at St. John's Church in 1775. Lawmakers signed Thomas Jefferson's *Virginia Statute for Religious Freedom* at Richmond's temporary state capital building in 1786. Some of the loudest cries for American liberty and home rule during the revolutionary era came not only from New England and Pennsylvania but from Virginia as well. Ambivalent political and economic traditions also characterize Richmond's history. English colonials eventually transformed Richmond and the Tidewater Region of Virginia into a tobacco-producing powerhouse during the eighteenth and nineteenth centuries. As European demand for tobacco increased, local tobacco growers and manufacturers came to rely almost exclusively on the process of slavery, and slavery made a handful of Virginians extremely wealthy. These Virginians, historian Edmund Morgan contends, "bought their independence with slave labor" and tobacco production.[4]

Slavery and segregation shaped Richmond's development well into the twentieth century. During the antebellum period, industrial slavery in

Richmond gave rise to limited freedoms for blacks, and these freedoms had a profound influence on future generations of black Richmonders. Not only was Virginia central to domestic slave trading, but Richmond's tobacco factories, flour mills, pig iron production, railways, and canal systems also represented "the most advanced economic developments in the antebellum South." Many of these industries relied almost exclusively on slave labor by the mid–nineteenth century. A considerable number of the city's slaves worked in tobacco factories—a multi-million-dollar industry by 1860—on or near the James River's canal system. There were so many black tobacco workers, historians now know, that employers were often forced to provide "board money" for slaves' lodging. Slaves' accommodations, which were often near the point of production yet apart from slave owners, nurtured personal and communal autonomy. These areas eventually gave rise to strong church-based, economic, and family ties that survived both the Confederacy's impressment of slave labor during the Civil War and the incremental rise of Jim Crow segregation. In 1901–1902, white powerbrokers countered blacks' demands for independence by drafting a new state constitution that authorized the use of poll taxes and literacy tests. Poll taxes worked—wealthy whites were overrepresented in Virginia's governing bodies until the mid–twentieth century. Nearly a century after the Civil War, around 1956, an organization of well-heeled black professionals called the Richmond Crusade for Voters set out to secure black Richmonders' rights as American citizens by paying these levies. Curtis Holt may have been the centerpiece of the *Ebony* article in 1980, but the Crusade was the engine that drove racial politics in Richmond.[5]

No civic organization did more to democratize local politics in twentieth-century Richmond than the Crusade. The story told in this book describes more than thirty years of national and local politics. It explains how local suffragists pressed federal officials to strengthen the VRA and redistribute southern political authority along racial lines. The rights embodied in the VRA cannot be explained by separating the mobilization of black voters on one hand and federal policy directed toward race on the other. Richmond's African Americans, who watched segregationists use municipal government and New Deal programs to raise whites' standard of living (often at the expense of black communities), skipped the protest portion of the freedom struggle and went straight to politics. They eventually seized political leadership from gradualist African American ministers in the late 1950s, registered thousands of black voters, and challenged white elites' ascendancy over local politics during the early 1960s. The Crusade, led by men and women alike, influenced local politics nearly a decade before the VRA and decades before the Supreme Court mandated the city's majority–minority district system. These types of pre-VRA suffrage crusades—not just civil disobedience and mass protests—raised political consciousness in black communities across America and eventually generated the momentum necessary for Congress to pass the VRA. The VRA may have given rise to dramatic changes in American political culture, but it also fell short of eliminating, according to Supreme Court justice Ruth Bader Ginsburg, "all vestiges of discrimination against the exercise of the franchise by minority citizens." The Crusade ushered in a period of profound political promise, but it also witnessed the rise of an era characterized by new political restrictions.[6]

This book is not merely a triumph narrative about Richmond's contribution to the long struggle for black freedom but also a cautionary tale about a city coming to terms with the continuation of racist political trends in American life after 1965. The VRA had unintended consequences. As the members of groups such as the Crusade transitioned from protest to politics after 1965, their white counterparts embarked on a Machiavellian crusade of their own: vote dilution and political obstructionism. White leaders, who had grown accustomed to restricting and granting freedoms, remained convinced that African Americans lacked the intellectual capacity to manage municipal affairs. As black elected officials assumed control over America's city halls, they often had to resolve social problems left over from the racist policies of the mid–twentieth century. The Crusade, its representatives, and black communities across the United States had inherited what political scientist H. Paul Friesema in 1969 called a "hollow prize." If annexation led immediately to the district system in 1977, the very forces that made Richmond's majority–minority district system possible—an increase in African American populations in densely packed enclaves, unremitting residential segregation, white flight, and an unmistakable pattern of urban retrenchment—were the same forces that brought about deepening marginalization and dispossession in black communities during the twilight of the twentieth century. Although African Americans maintained a city council majority throughout the 1980s, *Ebony* could not have written a triumph narrative about black governance in Richmond in 1985. White resistance to black governance crested at the very moment that black-majority cities in America were overcome by deepening demographic and economic crises. By 1985, preoccupation with poverty and public safety impinged upon the Crusade's strictly political approach to black equality. African Americans, who circled the race wagons in the 1960s, no longer agreed on how to solve their communities' problems.[7]

In telling the story of the civil rights movement in Richmond, this book connects three subjects: (1) how middle-class African Americans used politics as a means to empower their communities; (2) how local people helped influence national voting rights policy during the civil rights movement; and (3) how race and racism shaped policy and politics in Richmond well into the twentieth century. This account of Richmond's role in the civil rights movement is first and foremost about politics: it explains how people used civic organizations, electoral politics, litigation, media, and other tactics to influence public policy and reclaim black citizenship from the clutches of white supremacy. It also explains the unintended consequences of that reclamation. After decades of studying the ways everyday people shaped the quest for civil rights, experts now have a much firmer understanding, as historian Emilye Crosby contends, of "*what* and *who* we think" are important to the freedom struggle. In connecting local and national matters, this story's chronology demonstrates that pre–*Brown v. Board of Education* (1954) voter mobilization and national enthusiasm for integration gave rise not only to massive resistance but also to a specific type of civil rights activism in Richmond. Recent accounts of the American civil rights movement demonstrate that national and international events profoundly influenced not merely the movement, but public policy. These accounts also confirm that local people worked within the context of local circumstances to create the conditions necessary to challenge Jim Crow. Black Richmonders were ruthlessly committed to the political aspects of the freedom struggle. African American women, working poor, public-housing residents, and middle-class technocrats spent the mid- to late twentieth century defining and redefining the meaning of American citizenship.[8]

The Richmond Crusade for Voters did not emerge from thin air: its members inherited a drawn-out struggle against Virginia's culture of racist civility. Three specific factors gave rise to the Crusade: Richmond's legacy of gradualist leadership, growing momentum for voting rights mandates before 1965, and Virginia's history of racist paternalism. John Brooks, Lola Hamilton, Dr. William Ferguson Reid, Ethel T. Overby, and Dr. William S. Thornton created the Crusade in 1956 to combat massive resistance to public-school integration. The Crusade had immediate roots in African American gradualism and the National Association for the Advancement of Colored People (NAACP). Before the mid-1950s, limited interracial cooperation characterized Richmond's color line—the story of how black leaders collaborated with a handful of moderate white elites to hammer out solutions to various grievances is now well known. Although whites often dictated the terms of racial improvements, they relied on a "better class of black leaders to counsel prudence and ensure that change" occurred within the context of white paternalism. Yet even within this context of racist civility, African American leaders continued to challenge the boundaries of racial segregation in Richmond. Richmond not only elected Oliver W. Hill to the city council in 1948 but also—roughly one hundred miles south of the nation's capital—became a "beehive" for the NAACP's desegregation lawsuits during the early 1950s. As whites manufactured massive resistance to public-school integration, the Crusade revolted against poll taxes and black ministers who supported only moderate racial reforms. The Crusade believed that the racial polarization brought on by the *Brown* decision called for more robust political organization. It not only had the financial resources to create a self-sustaining network of precinct-based groups but also mobilized to pay others' poll taxes, registered thousands of black voters, and raised political consciousness with the help of the area's black newspaper, the *Richmond Afro-American & Planet*. By 1964, the Crusade facilitated the election of an African American, B. A. "Sonny" Cephas, to the city council and was instrumental in shaping local policy.[9]

The maelstrom that followed the *Brown* decision and the rise of direct-action demonstrations often overshadows the story of African Americans' "re-enfranchisement." The Crusade was part of—and essential to—the larger voting rights movement taking place below the Mason–Dixon line before 1965. The idea that African Americans were not voting at all in the South prior to 1965 is a popular misconception about the freedom struggle. This notion also belies the data. In 1956, one million of the South's roughly five million African Americans had registered to vote. In their search for the civil rights movement's origins, scholars have demonstrated that black Americans in cities such as Atlanta, Louisville, Wilmington, and as far south as Sunflower County, Mississippi, not only drew from organizing traditions that often predated the 1930s but also parlayed the urgency from World War II and *Brown* into voter mobilization movements. It is difficult to understand how local people and organizations such as the Crusade changed national voting rights policy without examining the voter mobilization campaigns that predated 1965. After Congress passed the Civil Rights Act of 1957, which was largely about voting rights, both the Southern Christian Leadership Conference (SCLC) and the NAACP committed themselves to voter registration.[10]

The Crusade's voter mobilization campaigns force us to reimagine the *Brown*-to-Selma narrative of the civil rights movement. Not only did national civil rights organizations such as the SCLC and NAACP capitalize on indigenous political movements, but the struggle between black mobilization and vested white political interests also provided the basis for what became the VRA. The NAACP's executive secretary, Roy Wilkins, made Crusade member John Brooks the national organization's voter registration director in 1958. Brooks and a handful of southern organizers single-handedly orchestrated the NAACP's "Miracle of 1960"—a campaign to register three million African Americans before 1960 that has received scant attention from historians. Martin Luther King Jr., the SCLC, and the events that culminated in Selma, Alabama, during the summer of 1965 certainly motivated President Lyndon B. Johnson to *sign* a voting rights bill. Yet Attorney General Nicholas Katzenbach and federal policy makers in fact wrote the provisions of the VRA to preclude the types of disenfranchisement that Brooks, organizations such as the Crusade, and national civil rights organizations had encountered during the late 1950s and early 1960s. In telling the story of black Richmonders' pursuit of the ballot, this book demonstrates that local people inspired national civil rights organizations to lobby for voting rights.[11]

The Crusade's struggle for political power would not have been possible without the organizational and political will of Richmond's black women. The historical record on women's involvement in the Crusade's founding is not commensurate with the historical reality: women and gender were fundamental to the organization's formation and preservation. "History of the Crusade: Report of the Historian"—in particular the section on the Crusade's founding—is guilty of the same "sin of omission" that too often characterizes what the late Julian Bond called "the master narrative" of the civil rights movement. Recent community studies of the freedom struggle have dismantled this master narrative by demonstrating the myriad contributions women made to the movement as both secondary figures *and* leaders. Women, we know now, were more than matrons of the movement. In their recent examinations of race in Richmond, scholars such as Lewis Randolph, Gayle Tate, and Caroline Emmons demonstrate that women played a critical yet unsung role during the fight for voting and civil rights. The Crusade's first meetings took place in Ethel T. Overby's home, and by the late 1950s Overby and the Crusade transformed people's homes into a type of cottage industry for voter mobilization activity. This story of racial politics in Richmond is not just about men's and women's roles but also about how expectations of manhood and womanhood shaped the struggle for civil rights in Richmond.[12]

Black women held positions of *actual* influence within the Crusade, helped transition from protest to politics, and led the way into elected office. The Ethel Overbys of the movement—Overby was the first black public-school principal in Richmond, led the fight against whites' massive resistance to integration and equal political rights, cofounded the Crusade, and was its finance chair—existed on a long continuum of black women in Richmond specifically and Virginia generally (i.e., Maggie Walker and Barbara Johns) who initiated the fight against segregated transportation and education well before the late 1950s. Much has been made of the ways patriarchy, masculine histrionics, and the politics of moral suasion informed civil rights leadership. We know now that the movement's men often relegated women to secondary work. Middle-class civil rights organizations, historian Barbara Ransby argues, "emphasized the primacy of women's domestic roles." National stories of black voter mobilization often emphasized male leadership because men were often the movement's most visible representatives. Men were often political spokespersons and the first elected officials. But community studies of the civil rights movement shed light on a different story. Women struggled with patriarchy and secondary roles. While a great number of middle-class women in the Crusade were what the anthropologist Karen Sacks calls "center-women"—women of status who took on the roles of informal leadership—a handful floated between the all too familiar binary spaces of leadership and followership. These women—for instance, Richmond's first black councilwoman, Willie J. Dell—were the Crusade's "bridge leaders." As African Americans moved into electoral politics, women—who often worked directly with vulnerable communities as social workers and activists—bridged the divide between vulnerable communities, grassroots organizing, and official political power. As poverty deepened throughout Richmond's black communities, these women also led the charge against middle-class political leadership.[13]

The ways white southerners controlled race relations also influenced the types of civil rights movements that emerged in Richmond and postwar America. On one hand, Virginia's poll tax, not threats of mob violence, dictated who voted in the commonwealth. Richmond's African Americans used voter mobilization to challenge Jim Crow because Virginia's white powerbrokers, under the auspices of Senator Harry F. Byrd and his reputed "machine," allowed some blacks to vote well before 1965. Byrd's Democratic machine also maintained segregation through paternalistic elitism rather than through violent rigidity. It is difficult to understand how Virginia's African Americans organized civil rights strategies without recognizing how the commonwealth's white elites, who embraced segregation but rejected maintaining the color line by force, sustained their age-old skepticism of broad-based democracy by practicing a regionally specific brand of racist civility and genteel paternalism. Before *Brown*, Richmond's white elites maintained segregation by handing out piecemeal concessions to gradualist black leaders. Byrd engineered racial solidarity around the issue of massive resistance to public-school integration, and the racial polarization brought on by massive resistance undermined both the commonwealth's "friendly" race relations and a significant number of gradualist black ministers (which is largely why professionals rather than ministers led the freedom struggle in Richmond). When it came to black voting, Byrd Democrats knew they could pay lip service to limited black political participation without conceding substantive political power. Yet even Byrd understood that if more blacks paid poll taxes, they might swing the balance of power in local elections because the levies also suppressed large white voter turnout. The Crusade eventually confirmed Byrd's fears.[14]

Massive resistance to public-school integration may have brought an end to the practice of maintaining segregation by promoting friendly race relations, but it did little, this book demonstrates, to extricate white elites from positions of entrenched power. Richmond's white establishment maintained its paternalistic proclivities well into the 1980s. The VRA and the abolition of state and local poll taxes in *Harper v. Virginia Board of Elections* (1966) not only reenergized the Crusade but also crystallized white resistance.[15] Crusade members and their allies on the city council spent the late 1960s fighting against police brutality, urban-renewal projects, and the construction of two expressways. In time, white officials came to associate the Crusade's demands with the Black Power movement. After 1965, white leaders advocated for interracial cooperation while secretly devising color-blind structural barriers (i.e., annexations) that prohibited blacks from assuming real political power. These barriers affirmed some Virginians' belief that good government was still synonymous with elite whiteness. Federal policy makers and the Supreme Court disagreed.

This book also examines the complex coalitions and litigation that emerged during the late 1960s as African Americans fought to preserve the VRA. American cities labored to negotiate the friction between their history of oppressing blacks and their openness to progressive political reforms. After 1965, Richmond was part of a much larger revolution in voting rights. Curtis Holt's claim that annexation diluted blacks' votes ran Richmond right into a national voting rights revolution. This so-called reapportionment revolution, which local litigants started, Earl Warren's Court accommodated, and Warren Burger's Court strengthened, went beyond safeguarding access to the suffrage. As whites devised structural barriers to dilute the voting power of recently enfranchised African Americans, federal officials began to protect a minority group's right to elect preferred representatives in a manner that was commensurate with their total voting-age population. The Supreme Court, using an employment-based affirmative-action remedy known as "disparate-impact analysis," eventually recognized that the discriminatory *effect* of electoral laws mattered just as much as the discriminatory *intent*. Although the Court struggled to find a solution to vote dilution, it found that a "presence of factors," known as the "totality of circumstances" test, made it difficult for minority voters to elect more than a handful of public officials. White officials combined white and black districts, relocated polling places to white neighborhoods, threatened economic reprisals against black voters and candidates, switched to at-large election systems, and, in the Deep South, continued to intimidate voters with violence. National policy makers and the Supreme Court, which acknowledged that resistance to the VRA might be characterized as undemocratic, came to prefer majority–minority districts as a solution to vote dilution. Racial redistricting not only protected a minority group's right to elect candidates but also allowed minority voters to elect preferred candidates free of white interference.[16]

The political abuses of electoral reforms have been a continuous and unfortunate feature of U.S. political history, and politics following the VRA was no exception to this rule. The United States, experts contend, often sways back and forth between greater political access and more political restrictions. We know a great deal about the personal motives of high-ranking political figures who were integral to passing and strengthening the civil rights bills. Recent assaults on key provisions in the VRA and the reemergence of direct disenfranchisement have forced scholars to move beyond portraying voting rights mandates as a triumph narrative. If officials implemented majority–minority districts during the 1970s to counteract machinations such as Richmond's annexation of Chesterfield County, they also designed these districts to "redress present, institutionalized manifestations of historical injustices against blacks as a group." The story of how Washington preserved the spirit of the civil rights bills is outlined in the pages to come, but it has also been well documented by scholars and historians of voting rights.[17]

Institutional political stability between Congress, the Supreme

Court, and the federal executive branch became critical to the preservation of the Second Reconstruction. In many ways, white resistance to the VRA and the documentation of that opposition by the U.S. Commission on Civil Rights had an unintended consequence. As African Americans transformed the civil rights movement from "protest to politics," from right to reality, whites continued to design rules, such as annexations, that appeared on their face to deny no one the right to vote. Majority-minority districts—the crowning achievement of the so-called reapportionment revolution—gave rise to an unprecedented, albeit brief, period of explicitly defined racial politics in the United States. This racial democracy, by diversifying southern and American politics, seemed at that time to represent a durable shift in American governing authority.[18]

Washington's commitment to preserving the civil rights bills also had unintended consequences for the future of African American associationalism. The federal government's protection of Great Society legislation during the late 1960s and 1970s convinced men such as Curtis Holt, for better or worse, to hedge their bets against institutional bigotry with the liberal state. Black southerners knew that state and local governing bodies were, as historian Thomas Sugrue argues, "the key architects of racial inequality" and executors of Jim Crowism. In many ways, "the smaller the government, the more black support for it eroded." As President Johnson championed an "equality of results" standard—the belief that civil rights laws needed to engender a proportional share of results such as employment, office holding, resources, and so on—African Americans came to believe that the federal government was "a positive agent for social change." After 1965, many civil rights advocates defended the value of their hard-won right to vote not by protesting or demonstrating but by working quietly within the democratic system. As we shall see, sustained resistance to the VRA led the freedom struggle to revert to the legal and political strategies that helped define the movement before the Montgomery bus boycott. During the late 1960s and 1970s, a deluge of litigation (fifty cases or more) concerning vote dilution inundated state and federal court systems. Civil rights laws, according to leading scholars of Black Power, moderated the movement by convincing African Americans to lodge their grievances against racism in Washington. This transition away from extrainstitutional forms of community mobilization toward a greater reliance on federal protections was evident not just in the War on Poverty, as experts have demonstrated, but also in the case of voting rights. For people such as Curtis Holt, the reapportionment revolution was evidence that federal officials had finally embraced the centrality of race in American politics.[19]

As black governance supplanted registration drives, contention over racial politics and redistricting was often most pronounced at the local level. Racial politics after 1965 was not a southern matter exclusively. As scholars expand the field of twentieth-century urban history, we know now that few cities with sizeable black populations were immune to rising anxiety over Black Power. The fear of a black takeover rose in cities that witnessed actual racial unrest in the late 1960s, and whites often accused blacks of extremism even in cities where African Americans had few connections to the Black Power movement. Black Richmonders, who elected three African Americans to city council in 1966, took an almost strictly political approach to the freedom struggle. By 1968, working-class and working-poor African Americans as well as the new generation of young activists (drawing from Richmond's sit-in movement of the early 1960s) were exhausted by the pace of racial reforms. The annexation of Chesterfield County confirmed their weariness. Not only was annexation a panic reaction to the possibility that blacks might assume control over city hall in 1970, but many white elites also came to believe that black governance was synonymous with government for blacks only. Racial redistricting and the BMC exacerbated these anxieties. White opposition to voter protections grew even more intense as districts guaranteed black representation at city hall, and black representatives struggled to negotiate the tension between rising expectations in their communities and managing municipal affairs. Richmonders soon found out something that policy makers and voting rights experts have known for some time—Washington often fixes one problem at the expense of creating another.[20]

Ultimately, this book describes how public policy shaped Richmond's development. If the first part of this story (chapters 1 and 2) focuses on municipal politics in Richmond prior to annexation within the context of the black freedom struggle, the second part (chapters 3, 4, and 5) follows the unintended consequences of majority–minority districts and questions more broadly what became of the civil rights movement. The latter chapters also trace how Jim Crow–era policies shaped life in Richmond well into the 1980s. The facts that mid-twentieth-century disinvestment characterized many of Richmond's black neighborhoods and that many of these areas still nurtured poverty even at the end of the twentieth century should surprise few experts. That so little has been written about this portion of Richmond's history—particularly given the city's key role in domestic slave trading, industrial slavery, the Confederate cause, and massive resistance—is disquieting.[21]

By the 1970s and 1980s, years of well-orchestrated disinvestment and social engineering had taken its toll on a significant number of predominantly African American cities. Richmond, like most American cities, in fact used federal and state tax money—from New Deal programs to the block grants of the 1970s—to underwrite resegregation after the 1930s. Prior to World War II, not only did private lenders use money from the Federal Housing Administration to reinforce existing patterns of residential segregation, but white elites also invested this money in their own communities at the expense of black neighborhoods. By the 1950s, Richmond's African American neighborhoods struggled to keep pace with their white counterparts. These neighborhoods were severely blighted, lacked sewage drains and indoor plumbing, and suffered from poor educational facilities. As Richmond tapped the wellspring of federal largess to clear its slums during the social engineering campaigns of the 1950s and 1960s, city officials compressed a large number of African Americans into a handful of public-housing divisions. These divisions incubated poverty, were in earshot of one another, and were in close proximity to downtown. As manufacturing jobs relocated to Richmond's outlying counties and the city transitioned toward semiprofessional, professional, and service employment, growing disparities in education and economic access were most apparent throughout black Richmond.[22] Much of the economic vulnerability that emerged during the 1980s was by design.

There was nothing exceptionally southern about mid-twentieth-century infrastructure building in Richmond. By the 1970s and 1980s, years of systemic neglect had given rise to glaring economic vulnerability, and this vulnerability characterized most American cities with sizeable black populations. Local policy makers relied on many of the same urban policies and planners that other cities employed. In fact, Richmond took the Robert Moses approach to urban redevelopment in the attempt to address automobile congestion, slum clearance, and public housing. Richmond's master plan eventually displaced tens of thousands of African Americans and compacted them—thanks to restrictive covenants—into smaller and smaller enclaves. Holt may have personified African Americans' triumph over the forces of disenfranchisement, but the public-housing resident was also emblematic of an intensifying economic crisis. In 1970, one year prior to Holt's suit, the poverty rate for Richmond's African American families stood at nearly 25 percent (roughly 15 percent higher than the national average), and only 16 percent of African Americans over twenty-five years old completed high school. Black neighborhoods in the capital city were more segregated by class and race in 1980 than they were in 1960. Although the grind of twentieth-century urban history was not inevitable, if you were poor and black in Richmond, it may have appeared so by the mid-1980s.[23]

Racial redistricting may have ensured that minorities could elect black candidates, but districts also intensified racial animosity at city hall. Shortly after 1977, black politicians in Richmond, led by Mayor Henry Marsh, sought to redirect service deliverables to communities that segregationists had purposefully neglected. They also tried to secure their positions on the city council by redrawing safer district boundaries and firing white administrators. As African American council members rejected their position as political cue takers, however, whites argued that mayors such as Marsh, Marion Barry, and Maynard Jackson were race leaders rather than city managers. Richmond's BMC found out about diplomacy the hard way—if black politicians were to implement substantive policy changes and bring material resources to struggling communities, they first had to fight their way through white skepticism. They also needed to work with colleagues from white-majority districts. These colleagues were the very white leaders who detested racial redistricting and were often unconvinced that blacks could do the job. African Americans may have taken control of city halls, but they often lacked the types of private–public relationships that, according to leading urban-regime theorists, cities need to thrive.[24]

By the 1980s, the era of possibility was in deep jeopardy. Districts were the price that African Americans initially paid to counter white backlash against the voting rights revolution. When it came to accessing the full panoply of resources needed to govern metropolitan Richmond, this price undeniably proved to be high. By following black mobilization to its logical conclusion, electoral empowerment and governance, we see not only that white resistance to black governance continued to be a defining feature of black-led city halls but that the Reagan rollbacks exacerbated forces such as white flight and concentrated poverty. Historian Robert O. Self argues that the struggle over postwar economic growth and metropolitan expansion in predominantly black cities represented "more than a transition from an era of possibility to an era of limits." These struggles personified what was at stake for America's cities after World War II.[25]

Between 1978 and 1982, members of Richmond's city council white minority not only threatened to bring downtown revitalization to a standstill but also carried on the politics of paternalism and obstructionism by refusing to share power with members of the BMC. As the Reagan administration scaled back aid to cities in the early 1980s and middle-class residents relocated to outlying counties, a cascade of results-oriented economic pragmatism washed away black officials' civil rights–based optimism, and these elected officials had to come to terms with a stark political reality. City hall needed to deal with powerful business interests to address the sharp limitations on its own authority. Even more ominously, Virginia's rules governing city–county independence (i.e., Dillon's Rule) meant that Richmond had no official authority to work with its surrounding counties without an explicit mandate from Virginia's still largely white and increasingly Republican General Assembly. Richmond's BMC was no exception to the rule when it came to meeting the challenges of urban revitalization. Black mayors and their regimes attempted to lure investors back into their cities by emphasizing high-profile politics—they argued that shopping malls, convention centers, and hotels would resurrect the dying city center. Richmond's black politicians spent the better portion of the 1980s manufacturing their own silver-bullet strategies. Both Henry Marsh (in the form of Richmond Renaissance) and Richmond's second black mayor, Dr. Roy West (in the form of affirmative-action contracts), believed that revitalizing downtown would reinvigorate Richmond's tax base, create jobs, and alleviate poverty.[26]

As the BMC struggled to build its way to a better Richmond, the problem of class became more apparent within the black body politic. Although Richmond's intra-racial class struggle is not emblematic of the entire story of black governance, it contains essential qualities that enhance our understanding of race and American political development on the local level. If voting became a means to an end—a way to gain community control—by the early 1980s African Americans were no longer in agreement about how to solve their communities' problems. The story of late-twentieth-century urban history is replete with examples of technocratic black mayors who supplanted civil rights–era mayors. There was nothing particularly unique about the ways Richmond's black politicians met the challenges of urban retrenchment, declining tax bases, white flight, high crime, deepening poverty, and fledgling schools during the 1980s. Because cities are more limited in their ability to tax than state and federal governing bodies, public–private coalitions take special precedent in municipal politics. Mayors such as West, Tom Bradley, and Wilson Goode built private and public interracial coalitions by promoting efficient government and moderating appeals to racial favoritism. Once these middle-class black leaders, J. Phillip Thompson argues, "accepted the practical limitations on advocacy and policy change required by their new, often fragile, coalitions with business and white liberal reformers," they struggled to address the needs of vulnerable communities. Roy West may have become the cause célèbre for Richmond's growing black middle class when he secured 30 percent set-asides for minority contractors, but these contracts were evidence of a more ominous rift. West, who conspired with white council members to appoint himself mayor in 1982 and had no history of civil rights activism in Richmond, met the challenges of municipal politics in the 1980s by working exclusively from a white power base. The forces of intensifying black poverty and a growing black middle class, the sociologist Eric Brown argues, "meant that the experience of racism was not as common as it had been before" and during the civil rights era.[27]

Black women led the charge against pragmatic governance. During the 1970s, Curtis Holt and a Yale-educated lawyer named Jeroyd Greene had warned public officials that heightened residential segregation and deepening poverty were destroying Richmond. Women, who were continuous fixtures in Richmond politics, not only became the most vocal spokespersons against the black political establishment but also led the way in what Laurie Greene calls the "politics of protection." Richmond's murder rate per capita was second only to that of Detroit, Michigan, in 1985. Black women such as Willie Dell, who became the first female African American councilperson in Richmond in 1973, began to couch the struggle against economic vulnerability and residential isolation as civil rights violations. Dell and social activist Alma Marie Barlow spent the early 1980s intentionally politicizing the fight against crime and poverty and openly promoted the need for more pointed social welfare programs. As the black middle class raised its standard of living by securing affirmative-action-based set-asides, these women advocated for targeted policies that might move poor people into living-wage status. Women and their allies not only accused the Crusade of clandestinely supporting West but also contended that the middle-class leadership cared little about justice for *all* African Americans. Redistricting eventually did Dell in—Roy West defeated her in 1982 and 1984. And Dell's appeals to black unity drew fire from her district's middle-class residents, who were preoccupied with securing public deliverables. In mandating majority–minority districts, federal policy makers were victims of an ecological fallacy—they assumed that African American officials would inevitably represent their community's political interests most effectively.[28]

Disillusioned by a lack of economic progress and what appeared to be the return of control by white elites (despite the fact that blacks still held a five-to-four council majority), many black Richmonders came to believe that politics had failed to bring about the types of broad-based equality that African Americans had envisioned during the civil rights movement.

1

Strictly Political

Racial and Urban Politics and the Rise of the Richmond Crusade for Voters before 1965

Foundations for Improvement

America's age-old racial struggle between greater access and more restrictions peaked after World War II. Nearly a century after the Civil War, African Americans waged a second battle to secure their rights as citizens. These demonstrators insisted that the freedom struggle occur in public view. Civil rights advocates tapped the wellspring of time-honored organizing traditions and institutions: they activated the machinery of black churches, drew from traditions of labor activism, borrowed from the nonviolent social movements of the prewar era, and continued to challenge de jure segregation in the courts. The ways white southerners controlled race relations also influenced the civil rights movement. Racism, which differed sharply across the South, often dictated the ways civil rights advocates organized. Oliver W. Hill contended: "Richmond is as enlightened a community as there is in the South. On the other hand, it is still the 'Gateway to the South' and the former capital of the confederacy [*sic*]. Therefore, it furnishes the best laboratory for the demonstration of a positive approach to the ultimate solution of the dilemma created by a desire on the one hand to adhere to what is known as 'Southern traditions' and, at the same time, comply with the mandates of a constitutional democracy." The contention that Richmond was *the* "gateway to the South" became a referendum on the future of civil rights battles in the commonwealth's capital. Although Richmond was of the South, many of the city's leaders believed that they were more refined than southerners in general. A number of Virginia's white elites defended the philosophical underpinnings of black inferiority and de jure segregation yet forbade the violent racial rigidity that deep southerners often used to maintain the color line. As black folks' appeals for absolute equality grew louder over the course of the 1950s, the capital city labored to negotiate the tension between its history of institutionalized bigotry and its openness to progressive reforms. Richmond struggled to become Hill's "laboratory" for the future. In time, Virginia's culture of racist civility and black gradualism crumbled under the pressure of integration. Many of Richmond's African Americans used the franchise, not demonstrations, to wage their own war against segregation. These crusaders for electoral power sought nothing less than complete equality under the law.[1]

The mid-twentieth-century freedom struggle in Richmond drew from a history of African American protest traditions. Organizational life thrived in black neighborhoods at the turn of the century, and these communities often "turned within" to counter Jim Crow. In 1910, Richmond had the largest population of African Americans, close to 17,000, in the Upper South. The majority of them were working poor (e.g., factory workers, day laborers, laundresses, domestic servants, etc.), but a growing number of black entrepreneurs, business owners, and bankers joined the ranks of the middle class. Although tension often characterized the relationship between middle-class blacks, who often saw themselves as race leaders, and the black working poor, who struggled to earn living wages, both groups used community-based institutions to defend themselves against mounting encroachments on their citizenship.[2]

Maggie Lena Walker and John Mitchell Jr., two of Richmond's foremost Progressive Era race leaders, led the charge for respectability and equality. Walker, the daughter of a white abolitionist and a slave mother, came to prominence for her work as an educator and business owner and for her connection with Christian fraternal orders. She edited the Independent Order of St. Luke's newsletter, the *Saint Luke Herald,* and eventually gained national acclaim for being the first female bank owner—black or white—in the United States. Mitchell was part of the interracial politics that briefly characterized civic life in Virginia before the turn of the century. He served as Richmond's alderman from 1892 to 1894 and was the last African American public official to represent the city until the mid–twentieth century. It was his work as a newspaperman, however, that thrust him into the spotlight. As president of the National Afro-American Press Association and editor the *Richmond Planet* (the predecessor of the *Richmond Afro-American & Planet*), Mitchell earned a reputation as the "fighting editor." He, like Walker, used print media to promote uplift and to contest second-class citizenship. Walker and Mitchell were not merely counselors of prudence and race leaders; both built and maintained the types of institutions that enhanced black life in what was one of the most discriminatory periods of the Jim Crow era.[3]

Walker and Mitchell eventually parlayed their positions within the black community into action. Black Richmonders, who made up just more than 36 percent of the city's 46,733 residents in 1910, initiated one of the first broad-based boycotts against segregated public transportation in the United States. Roughly eight years after the Supreme Court mandated segregation in *Plessy v. Ferguson* (1896), Richmond's African Americans organized a mass protest against the Virginia Passenger and Power Company when the latter, following the General Assembly's lead, segregated the city's trolley car system in 1904. Under Mitchell and Walker's guidance, African Americans found alternative transportation or walked to their destinations for more than a year. Although the boycott faded in 1906 after the General Assembly authorized segregation in public transportation, the movement gained notoriety not for upending segregation but for its duration. Working-class blacks sustained the movement by staying off the system, and they eventually bankrupted the streetcar company. On one hand, Mitchell, Walker, and the boycott were emblematic of the ways black Americans united, regardless of status or station, to fight against the indignities of Jim Crow. On the other hand, Walker and Mitchell's insistence on respectability (despite the fact that the two disagreed on the degree to which poor African Americans were responsible for the race problem) left a lasting impression on black associationalism in Richmond. The boycott portended what became a long, drawn-out struggle against the forces modernity, the role of black leadership, the problem of poverty, and the persistence of racial segregation in the New South.[4]

The future of Richmond's freedom struggle had origins in both the respectability politics of the early twentieth century and the legacy of de jure residential segregation. If African American communities developed apart from their white counterparts during the early twentieth century and nurtured a sense of black independence, by the 1940s New Deal housing programs made residential segregation in Richmond worse. After the Great Depression, the federal government's New Deal programs subsidized the resegregation of many of America's cities. The Federal Housing Administration and the Home Owners' Loan Association Corporation eventually used race as a determining factor in assessing financial risk, granting mortgages, and doling out prolonged loans at low interest rates to potential homeowners. Because the Supreme Court forbade local governments from codifying racial zoning in *Buchanan v. Warley* (1917), local lenders and bankers became integral to the types of racial disinvestment that characterized housing discrimination after the 1930s. During the appraisal process, the Federal Housing Administration ordered local lenders to use its color-coded Residential Security Maps. Green and blue areas, populated by whites, were in good standing, but lenders considered yellow and red areas—often made up of Jews, immigrants, white laborers, and African Americans—high risk. Local lenders eventually designated all of Richmond's African American neighborhoods red regardless of their socioeconomic status. This process of denying loans to or jacking up interest rates on potential African American borrowers became known as "redlining." These policies eventually allowed a handful of whites to invest in their own communities, strengthen patterns of residential segregation, and systematically ignore the development of black neighborhoods. Private land developers and real estate agents in Richmond and throughout the United States underwrote resegregation with federal tax dollars. By the mid–twentieth century, this process of private withdrawal from black communities had grave consequences.[5]

By 1940, 45 percent of Richmond's census tracts were predominately African American, and almost all of the city's 61,336 African Americans lived within the redlined tracts. A majority of the city's African Americans *had* to reside in or near selected areas on the north side, East End, or southern portions of the city—namely, the Church Hill area, the Navy Hill neighborhood, the Carver area, Fulton, Randolph, Jackson Ward, and a handful of redlined neighborhoods on the city's south side, including the Bainbridge neighborhood. A considerable number of African

Americans lived in and around Jackson Ward, just east of Broad Street near downtown. Although African Americans had been in the Jackson Ward area prior to the Civil War, white officials formally created the district in 1871. In 1940, six census tracts in and around Jackson Ward were more than 90 percent African American.[6]

During the 1940s, Jackson Ward was the epicenter of black Richmond's cultural, political, and economic identity. Commonly referred to by contemporaries as the "Harlem of the South" or "Wall Street of the South," the area had become famous for its iconic redbrick Greek revival, Italianate, and late Victorian row houses. A majority of the city's black businesses, educational facilities, and churches were also in or near the Jackson Ward area. After a period of modest development in the 1930s, the neighborhood could claim nearly fifty black-owned businesses, three major insurance firms, a handful of real estate agencies, several banks, and a newspaper, the *Richmond Afro-American*. Richmond's historically black college and university Virginia Union University (VUU) sat just north of the Jackson Ward and Carver areas. Established in 1865 by the American Baptist Home Mission Society, VUU—then known as the Richmond Theological School for Freedmen—was originally located in Robert Lumpkin's slave jail in the Shockoe Valley. On the eve of World War II, it had grown from a Reconstruction-era seminary school into the focal point of African American intellectualism in Richmond. VUU also hired its first black president, Dr. John Malcus Ellison, in 1941 and opened the Graduate School of Theology in 1942. Three of the city's most prominent black churches were also located in or near Jackson Ward: Moore Street Baptist Church, Ebenezer Baptist Church, and First African Baptist Church. More often than not, these churches and educational institutions became synonymous with black Richmond's genteel and moderate approach to race relations.[7]

Gordon Blaine Hancock personified local leaders' deferential approach to community empowerment. Hancock, a native of Ninety-Six, South Carolina, received a master's degree in sociology from Harvard University and joined the faculty at VUU in 1921. He was also the head minister of Moore Street Baptist Church. Apart from teaching economics, sociology, and theology at VUU, Hancock published a nationally syndicated column for the Associated Negro Press, "Between the

Lines." During the 1930s, this column regularly urged African Americans toward frugality, respectability, and self-determination. Just prior to World War II, Hancock gained national recognition for what he called the "Double-Duty Dollar." He argued that supporting black-owned businesses served a "double" purpose—African Americans could cultivate both black employment and black communities by supporting their own businesses. Not only was building a distinct community of self-regulating and cooperative black consumers and producers, Hancock believed, commensurate with self-determination and community empowerment, but this community empowerment might also soften the blow of residential isolation and institutionalized bigotry. Hancock's Double-Duty Dollar was also in keeping with the economic-solidarity movements that often characterized the fight against racial inequality during the Great Depression, explicitly W. E. B. Du Bois's "group economy" and the "Don't Buy Where You Can't Work" campaigns of the 1930s. Although leaders such as Hancock and Du Bois opposed de jure segregation, they also understood that racial separation helped form the basis of black professional and business culture.[8]

Hancock and his close associate in Norfolk, Virginia, P. B. Young—editor and publisher of the *Norfolk Journal and Guide*—also worked pragmatically within the prewar context of Upper South race relations. Hancock's promotion of the Double-Duty Dollar may have fallen in line with black civil rights activism during the Great Depression, but he, as an integral member of the Virginia Interracial Commission, worked tirelessly toward racial reconciliation. During the early 1930s, the VUU professor helped found, with the help of white benefactors from Pennsylvania, the university's Torrance School of Race Relations. The Torrance School emphasized Hancock's belief in the power of moral suasion and deferential political activism; its mission statement emphasized that the school was committed to the discussion and study of reconciliation between blacks and whites. Hancock's dedication to the freedom struggle had a profound influence on future generations of black leadership in Richmond. A number of the Crusade's founding members were graduates of VUU—namely, William Thornton, Ethel Overby, and William Ferguson Reid. Richmond's first African American mayor, Henry L. Marsh III; future state senator and Virginia's first black governor L. Douglas Wilder;

and celebrated civil rights attorney Spotswood Robinson were also VUU alums.[9]

Virginia's white elites mistook Hancock's appeals for racial reconciliation as acquiescence. They firmly believed that Richmond's African American leadership had grown accustomed to a regionally specific brand of genteel paternalism that *Richmond News-Leader* editor Douglas Southall Freeman called the "Virginia Way." Led by newspapermen such as Freeman and *Richmond Times-Dispatch* editor Virginius Dabney, these white elites believed that blacks had willingly consented to racial separation, and so they promoted friendly relations with a so-called better class of black leaders. By the 1940s, white leaders had grown accustomed to racial paternalism. They restricted and granted freedoms under the pretext that they knew what was best for the commonwealth's African Americans. Yet as the push for full integration gained steam in the 1940s, racist paternalism, as J. Douglas Smith contends, "ceased to function as an effective means of managing race relations." Whites in the Old Dominion may have rejected strict racial oppression and promoted friendship with black leadership, but their emphasis on civility rather than on frankness often slowed the promise of effective racial reforms.[10]

Hancock's attempts to improve race relations peaked during a meeting in Durham, North Carolina, in 1942. Hancock, Young, and Virginia State College historian Luther P. Jackson brought together fifty-nine African American leaders in October 1942. This group also included Charles S. Johnson of Fisk University and Benjamin Mays of Morehouse College. Of the fifty-nine attendees, only five were women, and the authors of the meeting's final pamphlet referred to these women by their husband's names—Mrs. R. E. Clay, Mrs. J. G. Stuart, Mrs. Andrew W. Simpkins, and Mrs. D. K. Jenkins (Mrs. Zellar R. Boothe was also included in the list but was not physically present). The conference took place on October 10 at North Carolina A&T, and attendees released a statement of purpose ten days later, which became known as the "Durham Manifesto." The manifesto articulated a list of demands that addressed the state of bigotry in wartime America. It very cautiously denounced segregation and promoted stronger dialogue with racially progressive whites. Attentive to what blacks above the Mason–Dixon line might think, the tract also put forward what the conference attendees called the "articles of cooperation"—a set of guidelines they believed should govern the postwar South. They called for full participation and better safeguards in American politics, the military, southern agriculture, social welfare programs, education, and the service industry. These leaders, like thousands of African Americans who wanted more from the New Deal and southern leadership, believed that a combination of local good will, self-determination, and state action were crucial to black equality. Hancock, who authored the statement of purpose, personified what has become known as the "however" clause in the manifesto's preamble. He argued in section 3: "We are fundamentally opposed to the principle and practice of compulsory segregation in our American society, whether of races or classes or creeds; however, we regard it as both sensible and timely to address ourselves now to the current problems of racial discrimination and neglect, and to ways in which we may cooperate in the advancement of programs aimed at the sound improvement of race relations within the democratic framework."[11]

Hancock's call for racial cooperation drew criticism from less-moderate African Americans but praise from most white leaders. The *Baltimore Afro-American & Planet,* the lead paper of the Afro-American Corporation, referred to Hancock and his supporters as the "hush-hush boys"— the folks in Baltimore knew that the conference purposefully excluded civil rights leaders from the North out of fear of alienating southern white liberals, who associated northerners with radicalism and agitation. The *Richmond News-Leader,* in contrast, argued, "With at least 75 percent of the declaration, every reasonable white man probably will find himself in complete accord." Whites followed up with their own meeting on April 8, 1943, and this meeting led to an interracial meeting in Richmond between Durham and Atlanta delegates in June 1943. Reflecting on the Durham, Atlanta, and Richmond conferences, an editorial in the *Richmond Times-Dispatch* entitled "The Conservative Course in Race Relations" argued that the "Durham Statement . . . was a landmark in Southern race relations, and probably the most important document of the kind since the War Between the States. It set down the things which the Negroes of the South would like to expect from the whites of the region." Although the conference led to the creation of the Southern Regional Council in 1942, which replaced the Commission of Interracial Cooperation (est. 1919), Hancock walked away from these meetings believing that whites needed to do more than offer token promises. African Americans soon demonstrated that they wanted more than the Durham conference let on.[12]

Hancock and company hit the bull's-eye on one matter—World War II had indeed fanned the flames of rising expectations. The Durham Manifesto was evidence that African American leaders could exert some pressure on white officials during the 1940s, yet these breakthroughs in interracial dialogue often paled in comparison to the rising expectations brought on by African Americans' involvement in the war. Although men such as Hancock forged relationships with white powerbrokers, the realities of segregation during and after the war flew in the face of the fight against fascism. Approximately two million African Americans registered for the draft during World War II; one million of them fought bravely. On the home front, reports estimated that nearly 35,000 troops had visited Richmond every week while on leave. Veterans made up a sizeable number of the African Americans who participated in postwar civil rights struggles—including Oliver Hill and John Brooks. These were the men who wanted to put the "double-V" campaign, which challenged fascism abroad and racism at home, into action. They eventually recognized that white Americans had done little to contemplate the implications of pseudoscientific racism overseas and institutionalized bigotry at home.[13]

In terms of electoral politics, black veterans specifically and African Americans generally continued to face widespread disenfranchisement. They found only a few allies in Washington and the South after the war. By 1947, 5,069,805 African Americans resided in the twelve southern states. Of that number, only 645,000 were registered to vote—an increase of 545,000 from 1932. The defeat of fascism and racism abroad did little to engender electoral egalitarianism at home. Southern jurisdictions continued to use arbitrary tests and qualifications that made it extremely difficult for most Southern African Americans to register to vote. The Democratic Party prohibited southern African Americans "from a share in the nominating process by statewide rule or by rules of the county and city Democratic committees." After nearly a century of party-level disenfranchisement, in *Smith v. Allwright* (1944) the Supreme Court reversed these practices. The Court rejected the use of white primaries in Texas, where state officials oversaw the selection of county-level party leaders and governed primary elections under state authority. Although some southern states responded to *Smith* by divorcing the process of selecting party candidates from governmental action, and others continued the use of devices such as literacy tests, Washington began to show some support for the Court's ruling. In 1947, President Harry Truman's civil rights committee released its 178-page report *To Secure These Rights*. The report suggested that Americans might "guarantee equality of opportunity to all men" by removing voting impediments such as poll taxes, ending segregation in education, creating a permanent civil rights division in the DOJ, integrating the U.S. military, and eradicating the practice of lynching. *To Secure These Rights* was in many ways similar to the Durham Manifesto. While conservative Democrats scoffed at the Court and Truman's civil rights agenda, a handful of southerners ushered in a brief era of racial progressivism.[14]

As important as World War II was to the making of the modern civil rights movement, local people, historian Tomiko Brown-Nagin argues, created the circumstances needed to challenge segregation. After the war, a wave of modest interracial political progressivism swept up Richmond and the South. Southern politics witnessed a fleeting moment where the impulse for progressive reforms actually trumped the politics of race. These states had accumulated large surpluses from the war that they resolved to spend on internal improvements. For instance, W. Kerr Scott, who built a moderate constituency of North Carolina farmers, organized labor, and African Americans, changed the power structure in the Tar Heel State by increasing spending on rural electrification, local schools, and state roads. After his election to the governorship in 1948, Scott instigated a wave of racial progressivism and interracial dialogue that characterized places such as Charlotte and Greensboro until the late 1950s and the sit-in movements of the early 1960s. Big Jim Folsom did a variation of the same thing in Alabama. He won resounding victories in the Democratic primaries by promising roads, schools, state pensions, and the abolition of poll taxes. Folsom is also remembered for showing sincere friendship with Alabama's African Americans. These men, along with Estes Kefauver of Tennessee, Lyndon Johnson of Texas, Earl Long of Louisiana, and others, were testament to the ways that the politics of economic improvements, infrastructure building, and class overcame in short-lived moments some racial considerations. African Americans, it appeared, had a place in this newer and more modern South.[15]

Harry F. Byrd and his Democratic machine also shaped the future of racial politics in Richmond. Byrd, like the commonwealth's business elites, also championed a form of racist civility that not only restrained whites from deploying mob violence to control African Americans but also made room for modest African American voter registration. He believed mob violence impeded Virginia's business culture (local policy makers were particularly concerned that postwar largess from Washington, D.C., might flow into Maryland rather than Virginia). Byrd was born in Martinsburg, West Virginia, in 1887. He was also a direct descendent of Richmond's founder, William Byrd. Before his tenure in the U.S. Senate from 1933 to 1965, Harry Byrd served as the commonwealth's governor between 1926 and 1930. He assumed almost total control over state politics by the 1940s. His machine, which reached its height in the late 1940s, derived power by using poll taxes to eliminate voters, exploiting Virginia's circuit court system (the General Assembly appointed judges), and shaping a state constitution that made it difficult to reapportion the General Assembly's districts. Until the mid-1950s, when urban populations began to eclipse residents in the commonwealth's rural areas, rural Democrats (particularly from the heavily African American southwestern portion of the state) were disproportionately represented in the commonwealth's General Assembly. The organization also kept rolls of loyal Democratic workers and voters, and Byrd himself often personally supervised a network of patronage and fees within the assembly and court system. In terms of race relations, Senator Byrd replaced mob violence with legal injustice in Virginia, unlike in states beneath the Upper South that tolerated (and often encouraged) indiscriminate lynching practices. As the commonwealth's governor, Byrd passed antilynching laws through the General Assembly in 1928 as a means to control disorderly conduct and property damage. In effect, however, Virginians replaced lynching with capital punishment. Of the 236 executions performed in the Commonwealth of Virginia between 1908 and 1962, almost all (201) were of African Americans. Instead of using mob violence, Virginians used the letter of the law to legislate away African Americans constitutional liberties.[16]

If Byrd appeared to take a moderate stance on race, Virginia's poll tax kept most poor whites and African Americans out of politics. Not only did policy makers during the Constitutional Convention of 1901–1902 believe that African Americans lacked the intellectual capacity for politics and civic virtue, but poll taxes also affirmed their belief that good government was synonymous with elite whiteness. By excluding most working-class and poor voters, the levy created a small yet manageable electorate that made it extremely difficult for weaker parties and independent candidates to run for office. State law mandated that potential voters had to register for elections and primaries at least thirty days before an election. The annual $1.50 poll tax had to be paid at least six months prior to any particular election. Over time, these regulations ensured that Byrd's organization could pay lip service to limited black political participation without conceding substantive political power. As long as the poll taxes helped Democrats control who voted, it was the Byrd machine that determined whose votes counted.[17]

It was in this context that Rev. Dr. William L. Ransome organized the precursor to the Crusade for Voters, the Richmond Civic Council (RCC, est. 1946). Inspired by the political events taking place in Washington, throughout the South, and within the climate of the Old Dominion's race relations, Richmond's African Americans spent the late 1940s trying to consolidate biracial coalitions and elect an African American public official. Although African Americans lacked the organizational infrastructure necessary to back such aspirations, the raw material from which to mount such demands grew daily. Richmond's black population exploded between 1930 and 1950: in that twenty-year period, the number of African American residents increased by roughly 20 percent to approximately 70,000 (of 190,000 total residents). Many of these people had migrated to Richmond from outlying counties and the commonwealth's rural areas. In fact, Ransome was born in Nottoway County, roughly fifty miles southwest of Richmond, in 1879. He, like Hancock, taught at VUU for roughly twenty-two years and eventually became the senior pastor of Richmond's most prestigious African American church, First Baptist Church, where he remained until 1973. Although Ransome was also an active member of the NAACP—he was elected to the national board in 1939—his status as a local leader derived from his position at

First Baptist. Free African Americans had organized First Baptist (then known as First African Church of Manchester), the oldest independent African American church in Richmond, roughly forty-four years before the end of the Civil War. The church, which accommodated both free and enslaved African Americans, was renowned for its racial egalitarianism during slavery and community mobilization during Jim Crow. In 1946, Ransome hoped to use his position as First Baptist's leader to continue the legacy of community mobilization.[18]

The RCC was a loose confederation of church and community organizations. It acted as a type of umbrella organization—roughly eighty different black churches, civic orders, fraternal organizations, businesses, and educational groups made up the council. If African Americans were not affiliated with any of these groups, chances were that they were generally excluded from the RCC's voter mobilization activities and registration efforts. Yet in its first year the RCC used its position in the black community to raise the number of black voters from 6,587 to approximately 8,000. Ministers, including Dr. Joseph T. Hill, Rev. K. D. Turner, and Hancock, were largely responsible for coordinating the group's directives. The RCC was distinct from the Crusade in two particular and important ways: ministers led it, and it drew heavily from white support. Although this support helped the organization during the election of 1948 and during Richmond's charter reforms in 1947, it had grave implications for the future of voting rights in Richmond.[19]

The RCC's most notable attempt at interracial coalition building came during Richmond's charter-reform campaign in 1947. Richmond, like many American cities, initiated a series of postwar urban-renewal initiatives. No organization in Richmond had more to do with urban renewal and the charter-reform movement than the Richmond Civic Association (RCA). The RCA was a nominally interracial private political lobby made up of powerful politicians and businessmen. In time, these men came to believe that getting a charter reform through city council would be impossible without overhauling Richmond's burdensome ward system. Prior to the reform, Richmond had a thirty-two-member bicameral city council. Voters elected all thirty-two members of city council within individual wards—none of these elected officials was African American. The charter sought to replace the district system with an at-large, nine-member council that operated under a council–manager model. Under the new model, council members would be responsible for legislative functions such as creating policy, passing ordinances, voting on appropriations, and so on. Richmond's city manager would serve in an administrative capacity, much like a company's chief operating officer, supervising executive operations and day-to-day administrative and fiscal responsibilities. Under the proposed charter, the city council would appoint the mayor, and the mayor would have to be an elected member of the city council. The mayor would also serve primarily in a symbolic capacity only (whites would later charge that Henry Marsh specifically violated this section of the charter). Last, the charter proposal prohibited primaries in local elections—all local elections, should voters pass the charter reform, were to be nonpartisan in nature. Private political lobbies would supplant political primaries in all local elections. The last amendment to the city charter became essential to the Crusade's future ascendancy over local politics.

African American voters were essential to Richmond's charter reform. Although the reform resolution passed council, the RCA feared that voters would reject the referendum. Anticharter sentiment found its champion in a group called the Preservation of Our Democratic Form of Government. Preservation's members believed that the referendum had interracial overtones and feared that African Americans might be able to exert pressure on local government and help elect a five-to-four council majority. The "Virginia Way" had critics. Mounting fear of black political clout underlined resistance to the charter reform, but Preservation was not entirely wrong about majoritarian manipulation. The RCA eventually shored up votes for the referendum from white labor and the RCC. Using a political ploy from the Progressive Era playbook, it actively solicited African American voters to support the reforms, and Ransome, who served as a board member on the RCA, proved central to this process. Although there is no historical record to verify how Ransome mobilized black voters, it is highly likely that he used the power of the pulpit and the RCC's nascent organizational muscle to get black voters to the polls. Richmonders passed the charter reform by an unofficial vote of 21,561 to 8,068. In the end, roughly 73 percent of Richmond's voters supported the reform. Almost all of Richmond's African Americans voted in its favor.

In the end, the RCC hoped that its support of the charter reform might translate into the election of an African American councilman in the city council election of 1948.[20]

The best prospect for an African American city councilperson was a forty-one-year-old attorney named Oliver W. Hill, who had narrowly lost a bid for Virginia's General Assembly in 1947. Hill had grown up in Roanoke, Virginia, and Washington, D.C. He was an alumnus of the Howard University Law School, an integral member of NAACP's Legal Defense Fund, and a classmate and close companion of Thurgood Marshall. Upon returning from military service in World War II, Hill, like many black veterans, turned his attention toward the struggle for black equality. Hill and Spotswood Robinson—also a Howard Law School graduate—initiated a series of teacher salary equalization cases throughout Virginia during the late 1940s. In 1948 alone, Hill and Robinson brought approximately 124 cases against separate school jurisdictions throughout Virginia. Hill's equalization suits helped win the support of local labor leaders, African Americans, and racially moderate whites. Hill, with the RCC's backing, announced his candidacy for the Richmond City Council in March 1948. A month later, with the help of RCC's executive director, Amos C. Clark, he initiated a drive to register 20,000 black voters. In lieu of registering voters themselves, the RCC waged voting drives "through existing organizations by having each such group conduct an internal campaign to qualify" eligible voters. The organization also opened what it called "voting schools" at four locations in January to teach voters how to properly fill out ballots. Hill stressed that he intended to influence the way in which whites responded to the black community and that he wanted to urge white representatives to lift blacks out of the perils of segregation. The *Richmond Times-Dispatch* stated that Hill had the "best chance of getting elected. . . . [T]he general belief is that he will get enough supplemental votes from white citizens to win a seat."[21]

Three months after Hill announced his candidacy for the Richmond City Council, he became the first African American in the South to serve on a city council in the twentieth century. In Richmond, he was the first black councilman since E. B. Carter and four African Americans won council seats in 1888. Hill's election to city council revolutionized politics in Richmond. The council contest was also Richmond's first nonpartisan at-large election of the twentieth century. In a field of twenty-nine candidates, Hill finished ninth, receiving 9,097 votes. His campaign also reflected the politics of interracial cooperation laid down not only by the RCC but also by men such as Hancock. In fact, Hill garnered 4,095 votes in precincts that were at least 96 percent white. Nearly all of Hill's white votes came from the largely affluent and white West End, Westhampton, and north side. Yet the RCA failed to endorse Hill's candidacy. Although it had openly claimed that it needed black votes to pass the charter reforms, it argued at the last hour of the election that "no responsible official of the organization had promised the colored people any special rewards for their support." The Crusade never forgot the RCA's slight.[22]

Hill's election to the city council informed younger generations of young African American professionals. During the 1950s, these African Americans believed that they could challenge the politics of massive resistance by organizing and maintaining an economically autonomous black political organization. Although the RCC had little influence on public policy and failed to forge a functional coalition with the RCA, its involvement in politics demonstrated that African Americans could effectively register black voters. In the long run, Hancock's brand of leadership, the RCC's voter mobilization, and Hill's council victory paid huge dividends, even if they were not collected for decades.

No Special Restraints

On May 17, 1954, the Supreme Court delivered what at that time appeared to be the destruction of racial segregation. The Court held in *Brown v. Board of Education* (1954) that segregation in public schools deprived minority children of equal protection of the rights guaranteed by the Fourteenth Amendment. Chief Justice Earl Warren argued, "Segregation of white and colored children in public schools has a detrimental effect upon the colored children. The impact is greater when it has the sanction of the law, for the policy of separating the races is usually denoting inferiority." Motivated by the NAACP's full-on assault against southern segregation, Thurgood Marshall, Oliver Hill, Spotswood Robinson, and a battery of lawyers argued that the late-nineteenth-century

Court had misinterpreted the Equal Protection Clause in *Plessy v. Ferguson* (1896). Separate but equal, these attorneys contended, *did* constitute unlawful discrimination. The Court agreed. In a unanimous decision, the Court held separate was inherently unequal in terms of public education. Overt resistance to *Brown* characterized Virginia politics for nearly a decade.[23]

Virginia's governor, Thomas B. Stanley, urged the commonwealth toward restraint and compliance. In August 1954, Stanley appointed an all-white, thirty-two-member commission, commonly referred to as the Gray Commission because it was led by state senator Garland Gray, to examine the implications of the Supreme Court decision. Byrd Democrats made up a disproportionate number of the commission's members. Following a relatively brief meeting with Governor Stanley and Attorney General J. Lindsay Almond (Stanley's successor as governor and a staunch segregationist) on September 22, 1956, the Gray Commission released its findings to the public. The thirty-two-man commission put forward two recommendations for public-school integration, and these suggestions epitomized the initial bewilderment over *Brown*. The report gave local people and local governing bodies the power to resist the Court's ruling. First, local school boards were to be given discretion on the matter of pupil assignments. A state-level Pupil Placement Board would then review all applications by African Americans to white schools. These localities were to be given a wide area of choice in what action to take, ranging from integration to the complete closure of public schools. Next, lawmakers recommended that officials could not force students to attend integrated schools. This portion of the plan, which the commission argued was an "imperative recommendation," resolved to use state tax revenues to establish a system of tuition grants for students who wished to remain in segregated, private (parochial and Catholic) schools. This plan, which also proposed that the General Assembly lift compulsory-attendance laws, proved too relaxed for segregationists—even if black taxpayers were going to subsidize the sending of white children to private schools.[24]

Brown elevated race over the politics of interracial dialogue, but the issue of public-school integration simultaneously reinvigorated Byrd's political machine. Byrd Democrats saw resistance to *Brown* as an opportunity to shore up political support for what was at that point a fading political enterprise. By the mid-1950s, Byrd's machine had failed to meet the challenges of suburban population growth and floundering public schools. His "pay-as-you-go" approach to government finances and infrastructure creation avoided debt by dipping into the commonwealth's savings. This spend-as-needed approach to providing and creating services had severe consequences in the postwar era. Virginia had the lowest percentage of students attending high schools in the United States, and its local school boards had accumulated more than $200 million in debt collectively. Its cities had also undergone serious population decline as white residents moved to surrounding counties and suburbs. Between 1950 and 1960, Richmond's population declined by just a little more than 10,000, despite a nearly 20,000 increase in African American residents. White flight and bad fiscal planning eventually led to the Byrd machine's demise in the mid-1960s, but these forces had already taken their toll on the organization's political legitimacy just prior to massive resistance. By the time the Court ruled that schools needed to be integrated "with all deliberate speed" in *Brown II* (1955), the beginnings of vehement resistance to integration "had already begun to germinate" throughout Richmond and the commonwealth.[25]

Byrd Democrats manufactured racial unity around the issue of massive resistance. On February 24, 1956, Byrd abandoned his reserved approach to race relations and personally called for southern states to organize "for massive resistance" against integration. He found staunch allies in A. Willis Robertson (Democratic senator, native of Martinsville, West Virginia, and father of evangelist Pat Robertson) and *Richmond News-Leader* editor James Kilpatrick. Kilpatrick was almost single-handedly responsible for crafting the philosophical framework of massive resistance, and he gained widespread segregationist support by playing into southerners' proclivity to states' rights. He contended, "The whole concept of this Union . . . was the concept of dual sovereignty; in certain areas, the Federal Government would be supreme; in all other areas, the respective States would be supreme. . . . [U]nder the Tenth Amendment residual powers are reserved to the State respectively—not to the States jointly, but to each respective State in its . . . sovereign capacity." Two years after the *Brown* decision, nineteen southern senators, seventy-seven southern congressmen in Washington, as well as all of Virginia's General Assembly members signed or supported the Southern Manifesto, a polemic that vowed to use the power vested in state governments to resist integration. The manifesto, written by Strom Thurmond and edited by Georgia's Richard Russell, galvanized racial segregation as the issue of the day, forcing a significant number of moderate whites either to openly choose sides or to keep their integrationist inclinations to themselves.[26]

Virginia's General Assembly eventually saw the manifesto through by adopting a series of measures to forestall implementation of the Court's ruling. These segregationist tendencies crept into the state constitution during the General Assembly's twenty-seven-day session in 1956. In what was commonly referred to as the "Stanley Plan," legislators codified the Old Dominion's anti-integration course on September 22, 1956, at 2:11 a.m. Most notably, the plan enacted House Bill (HB) 68, creating a Pupil Placement Board that was directly controlled by the governor; HB77 gave the General Assembly and the governor the authority to "intervene [i.e., close], reopen, and operate local school systems" that integrated; and HB56 gave the governor control over school systems that had been closed by integration. HB2 authorized state money for tuition grants in cases where students objected to attending integrated schools, and HB3 provided localities the authority to tax residents (including African Americans) for tuition grants and to levy cash appropriations. The assembly also created the Commission on Constitutional Government. Led by Kilpatrick, the commission was nothing more than a cynical propaganda machine designed to defend massive resistance in the court of public opinion.[27]

Virginia, following Alabama's lead, also passed legislation that crippled the NAACP's litigation and community-mobilizing strategies. By the mid-1950s, eleven southern states had enacted laws that punished the NAACP for its part in *Brown*. Southern leaders argued that the NAACP provoked local plaintiffs toward litigation. In September 1956, Virginia followed the Deep South's lead by enacting a series of regulations that made it virtually impossible for the NAACP to operate within the boundaries of state law. In the final hours of the General Assembly sessions of 1956, delegate Harrison Mann of Arlington pushed forward HB59–64. These bills allowed a legislative committee to investigate the "activities of groups which encourage and promote litigation relating to racial activities." Although the bills did not specifically implicate the NAACP, the language was clearly directed toward it. HB60, for instance, required individuals and groups that solicited funds for racial matters and excessive litigation to register with the State Corporation Commission. The bills also stipulated that these groups provide information concerning finances and internal activities, including a list of branch members. In many ways, the South's anti-NAACP laws were also an indictment against the hundreds of local African Americans who were brave enough to sue segregated school systems. These men and women had brought hundreds of cases against public-school segregation in Virginia prior to the Court's *Brown* decision, and Oliver Hill, Spotswood Robinson, and the NAACP brought more cases against public schools in Virginia than had legal representatives in any other southern state during this era.[28]

If massive resistance to public-school integration sounded the death knell for ostensibly friendly race relations in Virginia, the push toward full integration devastated gradualist leadership in the black community. As even white moderates signed onto the massive-resistance campaign, black leaders such as Hancock and Ransome found few allies in the 1950s. In fact, as the push for complete racial integration gained traction on the national and international stage, Richmond's African Americans grew increasingly suspicious of gradualist leadership. The U.S. military integrated over the course of the Korean War, and this integration intensified the desire to end segregation at home. "There can be no end to second-class citizenship," the *Richmond Afro-American* argued, "if men who serve side by side in the Army must go their separate ways when they step outside the post." In 1952, Hancock retired from VUU after roughly thirty years. On June 14, 1952, the *Afro* bid Hancock a deferential farewell yet underhandedly referred to him as "a stormy petrel during the '30s on questions of the role of the colored American." If the push for integration at home and the fight against communism abroad confirmed that gradualists were anachronisms by the 1950s, developments in the courts also encouraged everyday folks that the fight against segregation had local implications.[29]

Few African Americans during the 1950s were willing to accept the political pragmatism that characterized gradualists' approach to race relations. Ransome came under intense scrutiny during the 1950s. Men like Ransome, who was in his early seventies by the 1950s, faced their greatest challenges as blacks embraced integration as the antidote to second-class citizenship. Ransome was still a member of the RCA's executive committee well into the 1950s, and his affiliation with that organization spoke volumes about his position on black equality. The First Baptist minister failed to get elected to the Richmond City Council in 1952, and his campaign advertisement that year exemplified his continued belief in white paternalism: "Many of his teachers were white instructors, rich in experience, and sane on the race question." Leaders such as Hancock and Ransome were integral in helping acquaint black Richmonders with the politics of mobilization and black political organization. The number of registered voters nearly doubled in Richmond between 1945 and 1948 from 6,734 to 11,127. These men's experiences in electoral politics and community mobilization paved the way for future generations of black leadership. However, they found it difficult to distance themselves from the very white moderates who had succumbed to the elixir of massive resistance.[30]

Middle-class black professionals led the movement for civil rights in Richmond because people had grown weary of ministers' cautious approach to segregation. As gradualist leaders struggled to stay relevant (Hancock eventually abandoned gradualism altogether in the 1950s), these black professionals began to encourage full integration. Oliver Hill was one of the few leaders in Richmond who saw around the corner. Howard University Law School dean Charles Hamilton Houston and his notion of social engineering deeply affected the type of lawyer and citizen Hill became. Houston stressed the imperative need for lawyers to challenge the constitutionality of segregation on strictly legal and political grounds. Hill argued, "He [Houston] kept hammering at us all those years that, as lawyers, we had to be social engineers or else we were parasites." By 1951, Hill and the NAACP, in the words of historian Jill Titus, "were no longer interested in filing suits to equalize segregated facilities." Hill's firm, Hill Martin, and Robison—later Hill, Tucker, and Marsh—began to vigorously file lawsuits against Virginia's segregated school system. Hill's suit *Dorothy E. Davis v. County School Board of Prince Edward County* (1952) eventually became one of four cases in the NAACP's omnibus *Brown* case. Hill also challenged segregation outside of the courtroom. He, along with two white attorneys (including future Richmond councilman Howard H. Carwile), purposefully defied a Richmond segregation ordinance by sitting with one another at the same table in police court. In October 1951, Hill threatened to sue Richmond if officials failed to integrate the city's public hall for the NAACP's annual state convention. It was this barrage of litigation that motivated the General Assembly's Stanley Plan yet electrified African Americans. No other national organization had a more profound impact on the nature of civil rights activism in Richmond than the NAACP.[31]

The Crusade ironically owed much of its immediate existence to anti-NAACP laws. Between 1956 and 1958, anti-NAACP laws successfully limited the NAACP's activities below the Mason–Dixon line and forced the organization to divert valuable resources from the battle against Jim Crow. According to historian Richard Valelly, the number of NAACP "branches dropped by about 17 percent, and membership by about 38 percent." Virginia's NAACP membership dropped from 23,000 to 17,300 in 1957 alone. African Americans, however, organized creative strategies to meet the demands of the Stanley Plan, and their strategies defy some of the data. Prior to the General Assembly's vote on the Gray Plan, Richmond's local chapter of the NAACP—which included founding members of what became the Crusade—formed an organization called the Committee to Save Our Public Schools. The committee was in everything but name *the* local branch of the NAACP. By banning the NAACP, white southerners unintentionally helped to reorganize black associationalism. Although the NAACP later successfully challenged the Stanley Plan in court, Virginia's attempts to prohibit the organization's litigation efforts had the unintended and immediate consequence of creating the Crusade for Voters. The Committee to Save Our Public Schools initially encouraged opposition to the Pupil Placement Board and urged blacks to vote against the referendum in January 1956. Voters passed the measure, however, and only half of Richmond's registered black voters showed up to the polls. That was the final insult, as far as the committee was concerned. William S. Thornton, William Ferguson Reid, John Brooks, Ethel T. Overby, and Lola Hamilton founded the Richmond Crusade for Voters. They eventually adopted the name under the suggestion of local Richmonder Christopher F. Foster Sr. By the late 1950s, these men and women challenged white leadership by registering as many blacks as possible and rendered the RCC obsolete by rallying around the idea of full integration.[32]

The Crusade's first meeting took place at Mt. Moriah Baptist Church on North First Street in Jackson Ward in the early months of 1956. Only Reid, Brooks, and Thornton attended. Born in 1925, William Ferguson Reid, a Richmond native, attended Armstrong High School. From Armstrong, he went on to VUU, where he received a bachelor's degree. After attending medical school at Howard University, he interned in St. Louis, Missouri. Following his service as a surgeon in the Korean War, Reid returned to Richmond to practice medicine. John Mitchell "Johnny" Brooks was a native of Braddock, Pennsylvania, whose family relocated to Richmond in 1931. Brooks eventually attended VUU and West Virginia State College. The U.S. military awarded Brooks the Bronze Star for his medical service during World War II. After the war, Brooks worked as a manager in Troy's Department Store and eventually became an active member in the local branch of the NAACP. William S. Thornton, a Richmond podiatrist, also grew up in Richmond, earned a degree from VUU, and eventually graduated from the Ohio School of Podiatry. Ethel Thompson Overby, also a graduate of VUU, eventually earned a master's degree from Columbia University in elementary education and supervision. A public-school teacher since 1912, Overby became the first African American female school principle in Richmond's history in 1933. The Crusade's first series of meetings actually took place in Overby's home. Less is known of Lola Hamilton's personal life, but she served as the Crusade's first office manager and organized its first Get Out the Vote campaigns.[33]

Although a great number of the Crusade's female members sustained the movement through secondary work, they also held positions of *real* influence. Many of these women were instrumental to the Crusade's leadership because they had been involved in the freedom struggle for decades. If Maggie Walker helped initiate organized campaigns against the city's segregated conveyances in the early 1900s, African American women in Virginia continued the fight against segregated education, transportation, and voting rights well into the mid–twentieth century. Many of Oli-

ver Hill and Spotswood Robinson's plaintiffs were women, most notably
Barbara Johns from Prince Edward County. Overby did more than celebrate the symbolism of her appointment as one of Richmond's first black
principles. She openly criticized the fact that whites paid black principles
"$80 less because the whites said it didn't cost as much for a Negro to
live." It was Overby, not the Hancocks and Ransomes of the movement,
who eventually discouraged black parents from enrolling their children
with Richmond's Pupil Placement Board. Her struggle against massive
resistance to integration and the General Assembly's prohibition of the
NAACP was central to the Crusade's establishment. In pioneering Richmond's preeminent civil rights organization, women such as Overby and
Hamilton demonstrate just how important black women were to changing the direction of civil rights leadership in the 1950s. In Richmond,
they helped lead the transition from protest to politics.[34]

Women not only helped establish the Crusade but were also essential to the organization's early survival. Although a disproportionate
number of Virginia's black women were still farm laborers and ser-
vice-industry workers in the 1960s, a slow but increasing number of
them moved into the middle class. Thirteen percent of Virginia's black
women were professional or technical workers, and 3 percent had completed four or more years of college. A sizeable portion of both groups
of women lived in Richmond. Although limited in scope, firms such as
Reynolds Metal Company in Richmond were instrumental in lower-
ing the occupational barriers that characterized economic life during
Jim Crow. By the 1960s, local businesses such as Reynolds integrated
so-called pink-collar employment by hiring black women as administrative assistants. Many of these middle-class black women—for example, teachers, service workers, administrative assistants—were active in
community groups and civil rights organizations such as the NAACP
and Richmond's chapter of the National Urban League. Overby, for
instance, had been active in the Urban League for years and worked on
teacher salary equalization in the 1940s. In fact, women in the Crusade did more than "community work"; they were also visionaries and
decision makers. Overby, who served as the chair of the organization's
finance chair until 1975, was singlehandedly responsible for maintaining its financial solvency. It was Overby who collected old newspapers

and sold them to raise money for the Crusade. These newspaper drives and community gatherings were often its "primary source of income." Overby also risked her position as a principle by secretly organizing parents to resist Pupil Placement Board enrollment. These women stressed electoral participation and, like Walker before them, laid the groundwork for women such as Willie Dell. It was Dell who parlayed her position as a social worker, Crusade member, and city employee into public office. She became the first black city councilwoman in Richmond's history—her election would have been difficult had women not been instrumental to the Crusade.[35]

Massive resistance prohibited the Crusade from relying on whites' resources and goodwill. The Crusade was "committed to increasing the Negro vote in Richmond, Virginia through year-round voter registration activity and to increasing political awareness of Negroes." This year-round activity included studying candidates' records, recommending potential candidates, voting almost exclusively as independents, and publishing job opportunities in municipal employment. These middle-class African Americans immediately distanced the organization's registration efforts from the politics and practice of white benefaction. The Crusade also avoided political support by staying staunchly independent of party affiliations. Free of white support, it organized in semi-military fashion, like nineteenth-century political parties. First, it appointed precinct-neighborhood captains. Then each of these captains sent out notices alerting people of regularly scheduled meetings, voter registration deadlines, and impending elections. Precinct captains often found that beauty salons and barbershops were the most effective places to register voters and hang lists of people who had and had not paid poll taxes. Precincts were their own self-contained units made up of officers, organizers, and workers. Each precinct captain recruited volunteers, kept track of registered/unregistered voters, and organized political activities of various sorts. Captains were also given the responsibility of appointing and instructing block leaders, who were ordered to organize homes and apartment complexes. Delegating these efforts to precinct captains and block leaders allowed the Crusade in time to penetrate not merely beyond the scope of black churches and civic associations but also more intensely into the class structure. These precinct-based groups were also essential fund-raising networks. The Crusade raised money by selling old newspapers, holding frequent block parties, picnics, fish fries, and hosting coffee and donut sessions. They then used event funds to keep the organization stable, help people pay poll taxes, and fund further voter registration drives. Once the Crusade recognized that winning local elections in Virginia hinged on organizing strategies to pay poll taxes, it began to register an unprecedented number of voters.[36]

The Crusade may have championed democracy, but it was not organized democratically. Although it worked diligently to register African Americans across class divisions, its decision-making process was almost completely in the hands of its middle-class members. The founders first established a citywide Crusade that appointed two delegates from each precinct. These delegates represented their precincts on a board of directors. The citywide Crusade also appointed two delegates from each of Richmond's black churches and civic groups. The organization's first president, Thornton, then established a six- to seven-person research committee that dictated policies, researched where candidates stood on issues, slated approved candidates, and strongly encouraged voters not to deviate from the agreed-upon slate. Black churches and the *Richmond Afro-American* became central to the slating process. The process of slating candidates, from the Crusade's creation into the mid-1980s, always remained independent of party affiliations. The research committee and the board of directors often cared more about where candidates stood on racial issues than about party allegiances. It was not abnormal for the Crusade to approve white candidates, Republicans, or independents for their slates.[37]

By the early 1960s, the Crusade had created an elaborate network of electoral activity. Each registered voter/Crusade member was responsible for adding at least one nonregistrant. During campaigns, the Crusade often worked hand in hand with the *Richmond Afro-American;* workers would field a battery of phones at the black-owned Slaughter's Hotel at 527–529 North Second Street, formulated plans at a popular, private bar called the 533 Club (next door to Slaughter's Hotel), mailed leaflets, and cruised Richmond's black neighborhoods in pickup trucks equipped with megaphones. Members disseminated 30,000 to 40,000 sample ballots marked with Crusade endorsements and handed out stickers that read, "Every member of our family is a voter." Voters were personally responsible for making sure that relatives paid poll taxes and that black preachers—who had by the late 1950s moved beyond gradualist strategies—pitched candidates from Sunday pulpits on the eve of elections. If that failed to work, the organization often dispatched children on bicycles to fetch voters who failed to show up on the day of elections. By the late 1950s, the Crusade's voter mobilization efforts began to pay huge dividends. Between 1956 and 1958, black registration in Richmond rose modestly by 25 percent, from 12,346 to 15,364. The organization began to exert influence on the city's African American communities almost immediately. It was the nature of the Crusade's organizational skills that inspired Earl Davis of the American Federation of Labor–Congress of Industrial Organizations to say, "The Crusade has the largest group of volunteer workers of any place that I have ever been." By the late 1950s, not only had the Crusade built an electorate of more than 16,000 registered black voters, but its leadership had a direct hand in the NAACP's national voting rights agenda.[38]

Balance-of-Power Strategies

Everyday African Americans were almost single-handedly responsible for changing the face of local politics and federal voting rights mandates. White policy makers thought they could forestall the freedom struggle by criminalizing the NAACP. In attributing the push for full equality to national civil rights organizations and other outside agitators, these officials severely misjudged the nature of black associationalism. By the late 1950s, the NAACP capitalized on indigenous political movements like the one taking place in Richmond. These organizations, however, did not get involved in voter mobilization for politics sake; they understood the relationship between representation and policy outcomes. In Virginia, where political machines controlled local and state government for most of the twentieth century, public opinion had little influence on the shape of public policy. The undemocratic nature of the commonwealth's political culture hit African Americans the hardest. Civil rights advocates had not only watched race relations deteriorate during massive resistance to integration but also knew that segregationists used federal funds to raise whites'

standard of living. Historian Thomas Sugrue argues, "Municipal governments were the key architects of racial inequality. Local control had kept
housing segregated, steered blacks into inferior schools, bulldozed black
neighborhoods in the name of urban renewal." The Crusade and thousands of voting rights advocates came to believe that black governance
could stem this tide of racist public policies and alleviate the problems facing their communities. By the early 1960s, these local and national voting
rights advocates were already transforming southern politics.[39]

Although organizations like the Crusade emerged before Washington passed the Civil Rights Act of 1957, it is difficult to separate pre-VRA
voter mobilization in the South from the passage of that act. Congress
approved the Civil Rights Act of 1957 in August, and President Dwight
Eisenhower, under national and international pressure from the public-
school events in Little Rock, Arkansas—as well as from the lynching of
Emmett Till—signed the act into law the following month. Apart from
the creation of the Civil Rights Division (CRD) of the DOJ, the act was
largely about voting rights. Although southern congressmen shaved the
bill down, the act eventually signed into law included a number of important voting rights provisions. First, it prompted modest investigation into
voting rights by creating the U.S. Commission on Civil Rights (USCCR).
Lawmakers gave the USCCR the power to investigate allegations of disenfranchisement. It also had the authority to examine and collect data in
situations where whites denied African Americans equal protection under
the law. In addition, the Civil Rights Act gave federal officials the authority to bring civil suits—not criminal suits—in cases where election officials denied, obstructed, or threatened the right to vote. In this way, the
act was more punitive than preventative. Data collection and litigation
in effect required that people take initiative. African Americans not only
had to register voters but also had to sue election officials in cases of disenfranchisement. While federal enforcement got off to a glacial start and
the data-collection process proved difficult (some southern registration
officials hesitated or refused to grant access to voting records), the bill
did convince local and national civil rights organizations that they had a
degree of suffrage support in Washington. On September 12, three days
after President Eisenhower signed the act, Roy Wilkins sent out a Western Union telegram to branch leaders of the NAACP, claiming, "Now

that the civil rights bill is law we believe there should be prompt movement to intensify our campaign to increase the registration and voting of Negro citizens."[40]

Wilkins, just three months after Washington passed the Civil Rights Act, arranged a conference in Atlanta to discuss the issue of voter registration. The Conference on Registration and Voting took place during the winter of 1957, November 15–17. Among those in attendance were W. Lester Banks of Richmond, Medgar Evers of Mississippi, W. T. Walden of Atlanta, Kelly M. Alexander of North Carolina, and W. C. Patton of Alabama. Of note, the conference led to the creation of the NAACP's Voter Registration Committee. The organization eventually appointed Kelly Alexander chairman of the committee and elected W. C. Patton to the position of field secretary. The NAACP's national office in New York City must have caught wind of the Crusade's activity in Richmond, so it made Johnny Brooks the committee's voter registration director, a position he held until 1975. In making the announcement, "Mr. Wilkins said that Mr. Brooks would head the Association's Southwide drive to reach a goal of 3,000,000 registered Negro voters in the region by 1960." Wilkins and company charged the new committee with four directives: promote a year-round program to increase registration, develop political awareness among black voters, teach black registrants the voting procedures, and study votes cast in previous elections to determine the strength of black voting. Wilkins and others were determined to shake Washington from its lethargy by prodding and probing southern election officials. The contention between this black mobilization and white resistance eventually helped policy makers draft the VRA.[41]

Encouraged by the number of people who were willing to register voters after the civil rights bill was enacted, the NAACP immediately began what it called the "Miracle of 1960" campaign. During the late 1950s and early 1960s, Brooks traveled extensively around the United States organizing and reorganizing registration programs. In 1959 alone, he conducted registration-awareness drives in nearly sixty cities. Of those sixty cities, Brooks reported that more than forty already had active voter registration programs, including Jackson, Mississippi; New Orleans; Spartanburg, South Carolina; Memphis; Asheville, North Carolina; and others. In the "Annual Report of Voter Registration," Brooks wrote, "In the

South, you will find 95% of the voter registration programs, regardless of the name, initiated and led by staunch NAACP leaders and members. Due to known reasons, many people will not get involved with a movement stamped NAACP. Change the name and they participate knowing full well the NAACP is promoting the program." It is often difficult to measure just how thoroughly the NAACP was involved in voter registration efforts because many local organizations remained loyal to the NAACP but were reluctant to use the organization's name. The NAACP found that local people were willing to work with the NAACP under the condition that they not be directly linked to the NAACP. To this end, the "miracle" campaign resolved to raise the number of black voters in the South from roughly one million in 1956 to three million by 1960, nearly 60 percent of voting-age black southerners. This was, by all measures, an ambitious endeavor given that there were 5,131,042 African Americans throughout the twelve southern states by 1960. In reality, the NAACP's Voter Registration Committee set out to raise political consciousness in black communities and bring national attention to the continuation of disenfranchisement.[42]

The pre-VRA wellspring of black political will was not specific to Richmond. In many cases, especially in the Upper and Outer South, Brooks simply provided guidance and resources to movements that already existed. By 1959, African Americans from Tennessee to North Carolina had long since initiated the transformation from protest to politics. In cases like Richmond's, black Americans skipped the protest portion of the movement. Locals elected a former NAACP branch president, Washington Butler, to the city council of Oak Ridge, Tennessee. Z. Alexander Looby, an NAACP attorney and board member, was reelected to Nashville's city council in the same year. North Carolina, where African Americans had built significant political momentum even prior to the NAACP's voter registration campaigns, elected six black municipal officials in 1959 alone. Most of these elected officials were card-carrying members of the NAACP—they had been and continued to be involved with the organization throughout their campaigns. During 1960, Brooks, Patton, and the NAACP organized seventy-eight voter registration drives and conducted two NAACP regional conferences, eleven NAACP state conference conventions, and two statewide voter registration workshops.[43]

Although the NAACP fell short of achieving the "miracle," it became a referendum on the capacity of civil rights activism. The USCCR, which spent the 1960s collecting data on southern voting, estimated that 1,361,944 African Americans were registered to vote at the beginning of 1961. The actual number of registered African American voters was probably higher than the commission's reports because officials often purged African Americans from registration lists, especially in Alabama and Louisiana. Voting rights campaigns in the South stalled for two particular reasons. First, the federal government, which committed itself to the data-collection portions of the Civil Rights Act, often failed to adequately protect African American voters from disenfranchisement. Second, the rise of the so-called classical phase of the civil rights movement may have also hindered the NAACP's voting registration efforts. As direct-action protests picked up traction in the late 1950s, the NAACP, the SCLC, and the Congress of Racial Equality began to rely on the same pool of community organizers. The SCLC also initiated a voter registration drive in February 1958 called the "Crusade for Citizenship." Yet Brooks noted to Wilkins in 1958 that the SCLC had in fact used NAACP staff, branch officers, and members to build this movement in the Deep South.[44]

As Brooks mobilized voters around the country, Richmond had its own problems. By the early 1960s, black neighborhoods began to suffer from the types of systematic retrenchment that often characterized segregation in mid-twentieth-century America. Organizations such as the NAACP, the SCLC, and the Crusade saw an inextricable link between voter mobilization and greater community control. Many of these organizers, who understood how New Deal programs and local politics helped raise whites' standard of living, believed that they could fight segregationists by electing African Americans to public office. African Americans ultimately realized that they needed to mobilize voters to address what Michael Harrington, in *The Other America* in 1962, called "an interlocking base of economic and racial injustice." Although Harrington was specifically referring to African Americans in Harlem, New York, his general observations about economic vulnerability were a discouraging reflection on the state of mid-twentieth-race relations. In 1963, 43 percent of non-white families in the United States were near or below the poverty line (households that survived on less than $3,000 annually). African Ameri-

Table 1.1. Household Income, Richmond, Virginia, 1960

	White (N)	Percentage of White Households	Nonwhite (N)	Percentage of Nonwhite Households
Households	51,983	100.0	28,801	100.0
Less than $3,000	15,508	29.8	16,303	56.6
$3,000–$4,999	11,217	21.6	7,101	24.7
$5,000–$6,999	9,152	17.6	3,169	11.0
$7,000–$9,999	8,259	15.9	1,625	5.6
$10,000 or more	7,847	15.1	603	2.1

Source: Data from U.S. Bureau of the Census, "Census 1960 Tracts Only Set," Social Explorer, tables, at http://www.socialexplorer.com/tables/C1960TractDS/R11289393 (accessed November 20, 2016).

can men earned 60 percent less than equally productive white men during the 1950s and 1960s. Richmond, unfortunately, was no exception to this rule. Between 1950 and 1960, Richmond's nonwhite population increased by 26 percent, while the white population decreased by 20 percent. In 1960, there were 219,958 people in the capital city, and 42 percent of the city's total residents were African American. Many of the city's African American households, more than 50 percent, earned a little more than $3,000 annually; the proportion of whites in this income bracket was, in contrast, nearly 30 percent.[45]

The problem of public schools was inextricably linked to poverty and went beyond resistance to integration. Of Richmond's nearly 50,000 African Americans who were older than twenty-five, nearly 22,326 (45.6 percent) had less than eight years of formal education; 14,282 had completed grades 8 through 11; and only 10,208 had twelve or more years of education. Although the area had undergone significant suburban expansion (Richmond's suburban population tripled between 1950 and 1970), many of the city's African Americans continued to live in extremely dense urban neighborhoods. The U.S. Census Bureau reported, "A high proportion of tenant-occupancy is usually characteristic of blighted areas. Richmond is no exception. The blighted areas in which clearance programs have been conducted have approximately 805 tenant-occupied dwellings. . . . The older, high density districts (Fan, Church Hill, Jackson Ward, and a portion of South Richmond) began to lose population before 1950 . . . Richmond's present overall density of 5,500 persons per square mile is considerably above that for cities of comparable size." A large number of African Americans "were compelled to endure" this density and poverty as a fact of life.[46]

The RCC's leaders had gotten so caught up with the political implications of the city charter reforms that they failed to question how urban-renewal plans might affect the development of black neighborhoods. Richmond adopted its first Master Plan in 1946, one year before the charter reforms of 1947. The political reforms of 1947 were not just about making local government more efficient: the RCA whittled down the structure of local government because it knew it would be much easier for nine council members to orchestrate urban reforms than thirty-two council members. In terms of urban renewal, Richmond's city council, like the councils of many American cities during the 1940s and 1950s, relied on outside consultants, builders, and engineers. Richmond officials eventually sought out a St. Louis planning consultant. Harland Bartholomew drafted the Master Plan of 1946, which proposed to clear Richmond's slums and alleviate automobile congestion by building a series of expressways straight through the central city. During the 1950s, Richmond spent millions of dollars—the Federal Housing Act of 1949, which provided the financial basis for slum clearance and redevelopment, eventually subsidized a great portion of this amount—trying to alleviate the problems of decaying neighborhoods. Unfortunately, urban-planning firms like the one Bartholomew worked for were often indifferent to the problems of indigenous black communities, and local white leaders rarely advocated on behalf of these neighborhoods.

Decades of systematic withdrawal of whites had taken a toll on Richmond's urban neighborhoods. By the late 1950s, 7,517 homes in these now predominantly black areas were overcrowded, 13,977 without indoor private toilets, 13,221 without private baths, 2,635 without running water, and 20,486 with cold-water access only. Well more than 20,000 of Richmond's homes were substandard, and a sizeable number of those homes were located in black enclaves. Sixty percent of all cases of tuberculosis, a disease that had abated significantly after the introduction of streptomycin in the late 1940s, came from these blighted areas. Of the city's sixty-eight precincts in 1960, fifteen of the poorest were scattered throughout the north side, East End, and south side—all fifteen were overwhelmingly African American and bore the brunt of municipal neglect, deepening poverty, and severe dilapidation. In 1950, the Oakwood–Chimborazo area of Church Hill was 75 percent white; just ten years later the same area was 96 percent African American. Portions of Church Hill and the "Shockoe Valley slums" were two of the city's most infamously blighted communities. The City of Richmond, for instance, failed to install sewage systems in the African American sections of Church Hill until 1953! Many of the African American homes in these areas had been constructed haphazardly on steep hills, and so by the 1950s this collection of shanty-style homes resembled contemporary Brazilian favelas. Robert M. Andrews of the *Richmond Times-Dispatch* wrote, "Indigent families now crowd the shadows of old St. John's Church. The clip-clop of horses drawing family hansoms has given way to the roar of traffic, the din of beer halls and children with streets for playgrounds." These types of problems, African Americans understood, might have been averted had local lenders and officials invested New Deal programs in black communities.[47]

Contrary to "separate but equal," black Americans paid the price for segregationist proclivities. During the 1950s, officials began the process of funneling poorer African Americans from tenements to public housing. Shortly after Washington passed the Federal Housing Act of 1949, which subsidized public housing, the City of Richmond and the Richmond Redevelopment and Housing Authority (RRHA, est. 1940) put in an application for $1.3 million in slum-clearance funds and another $33,000 to survey land for public-housing units. Between 1955 and 1957, the RRHA, a locally administered and nationally funded organization, not only cleared out scores of dilapidated homes but also relocated more than 7,000 of Richmond's most economically vulnerable African Americans, roughly 10 percent of the total black population, to public-housing projects: Jackson Ward's Gilpin Court (1942, named after famed black actor Charles Sydney Gilpin) and the East End's Creighton Court (1952) and Hillside (1953). Over a roughly thirty-five-year period after World War II, city planners used state funds and federal money to finish what private lenders started during the New Deal. These plans intensified local patterns of residential segregation by destroying a significant number of Richmond's black neighborhoods and compressing a greater number of displaced African Americans into public-housing units that were legally segregated by race until 1964. Planners built these projects within five miles of one another and three miles from the city center.[48]

African Americans had mixed views about redevelopment initiatives and public housing; socioeconomic considerations often dictated how people felt about this process. In clearing so-called slums, local authorities not only honored segregation patterns by relocating blacks to segregated public housing but also often razed areas that segregationist leadership had done the bare minimum to maintain in the first place. There was "a general awareness" in black communities of the "slum problem" and officials' desire to raze blighted homes. However, where African Americans stood on the matter of urban renewal often had deeply rooted class implications. Many African Americans, to be sure, were fed up with the city's dilapidated neighborhoods and the lack of infrastructure. Neverett A. Eggleston, owner of the Eggleston Hotel, was torn on the issue. He knew that slum clearance would hurt his business but felt that "these projects . . . discourages [sic] people from owning property." Mrs. Edith Davis maintained that while the housing projects appeared to be viable alternative to Church Hill's slums, she was unsure if she could "cover the rent. I know," she argued, "I can cover it here. My husband is a junkman. Some weeks he does all right, some weeks nothing." Older African Americans, however, were reluctant to leave the Shockoe and Seventeenth Street corridor. Mrs. Ophelia Saunders, a seventy-six-year-old widow, stated, "What do they want to take me to South Richmond for? I don't want to break up this little home that my husband left me. I don't own it, of course, but I rent it." Individuals such as Mrs. Saunders found little recourse against the city's plans to construct a new expressway system.[49]

Black Richmonders again found themselves at the mercy of local policy makers over expressway construction. By the mid-1950s, it had been a contested issue for nearly a decade. On August 1, 1955, the Richmond–Petersburg Turnpike Authority sold $67,500,000 worth of bonds to pay for the construction of a 34.8-mile toll road (currently Interstate 95/64). Before 1955, voters had rejected two referenda to build the turnpike. Between the late 1940s and mid-1950s, those who opposed the construction of the turnpike split into three camps: some called for the plan to bypass the central city; others rejected the proposal altogether; and a number of influential policy makers wanted to run the highway across and over the Shockoe Valley in downtown Richmond. The last group won out—powerbrokers feared that running the turnpike through the suburbs would alienate white allies in the counties. Their plan, designed with the help of a Cincinnati-based planner named Ladislas Segoe, cut directly through Jackson Ward and Navy Hill—the two most heavily populated African Americans areas in Richmond. With little to no representation on state and local governing bodies, African Americans struggled to resist urban redevelopment.[50]

Richmond's leaders used the power vested in Virginia's exclusively white General Assembly to build the turnpike. In the commonwealth, counties and cities were and are fully independent of one another. To this day, Virginia, a Dillon's Rule state, limits counties' and cities' powers by prohibiting them from amending charters without specific approval by the General Assembly. Cities and counties, as independent political bodies, thus have no administrative authority to work with one another outside of rules that have been explicitly mandated by the General Assembly. Although voters in the commonwealth could decide on referenda to amend city charters, the General Assembly had the final say on these amendments. In the case of the turnpike, the nine-member Richmond City Council turned the tables. Councilman J. Randolph Tucker influenced the council to pass a resolution that circumvented voters and went straight to the General Assembly. Tucker called for the creation of an administrative subdivision with political powers, the Richmond–Petersburg Turnpike Authority. The General Assembly and governor not only approved the authority in April 1955 but also granted it eminent domain. By completion in 1958, the turnpike project had demolished nearly 400 predominantly African Americans homes, displaced more than 2,000 families, and cut directly through the heart of Jackson Ward, effectively severing the area's northern half. The turnpike ran over the Shockoe Valley slums, and Navy Hill, a predominantly African American neighborhood adjacent to the east side of Jackson Ward, was almost entirely demolished. In total, the construction of the Richmond–Petersburg Turnpike cost Richmonders "180 acres of city-owned land and 210 acres of privately owned land."[51]

After 1955, the RRHA struggled to meet the housing crises caused by the expressway and slum clearance. In the Randolph area, for instance, city officials had rehabilitated 2,800 homes and removed 400 outside toilets. Yet many areas still lacked the types of infrastructure that most Americans associated with mid-twentieth-century modernity. By 1959, rehabilitation efforts still labored to bring areas such as Church Hill, Carver, and Randolph up to the Health Department's minimum standards. In 1959, the executive director of the RRHA estimated that 25 percent of the residents in Richmond's worst enclaves had "adequate income to obtain private housing." The problem, it contended, was that few "individual homes have been built" to accommodate middle-class demand. The real problem, of course, was that redlining and restrictive covenants often prevented middle-class blacks from moving into white or even integrated neighborhoods. Although private developers had constructed roughly 500 new homes in black neighborhoods by 1959, by the end of the 1950s the city had not only destroyed roughly 4,700 homes in black neighborhoods but also replaced these homes with a mere 1,736 public-housing units (the RRHA built Fairfield, Whitcomb, and Mosby Courts in 1958 and 1962). Middle-class African Americans, because of residential segregation, restrictive covenants, and manufactured housing shortages, often "doubled-up in existing" black neighborhoods or moved into areas that real estate agents designated as transitional. Whites had previously occupied these transitional neighborhoods, particularly on Richmond's north side near Highland Park, before they fled to suburbs.[52]

Turnpike construction and slum clearance hit tenant-occupied African American areas hard. Systematic disinvestment and urban-renewal efforts instigated much of the population decline the Census Bureau reported in 1960, and the RRHA's housing projects often provided little relief for people such as Ophelia Saunders who resided in the tenant-occupied areas, including Church Hill, Navy Hill, and Jackson Ward. The state charged the RRHA with relocating many of these predominantly low-income residents. Planners met these challenges by providing 894 units in Whitcomb Court and Fairfield Court—two of the city's newest public-housing projects—for the displaced. In fact, however, this number was paltry in comparison to the number of people city officials effectively relocated to housing projects in the mid-1950s. By 1959, city officials and the RRHA planned to spend another $3.6 million (two-thirds of which was provided by the federal government) to eliminate forty blocks of slums on Seventeenth Street in the Shockoe Valley slums. The city council authorized the construction of another 874 public-housing units to accommodate those displaced by the clearance.[53]

The social cost of Richmond's urban-renewal programs had profound contemporary and future implications. It took the city roughly four years to build a neighborhood school on the East End for relocated children. During the city's Seventeenth Street redevelopment project, the city finally cleared roughly thirty acres for the new Mosby School. Mosby serviced an astounding 1,500 junior high school students and more than 1,000 elementary school students. Scholars of urban American history argue that the fallout from mid-twentieth-century urban-renewal programs—most notably, high concentrations of black poverty—helped instigate an urban economic crisis that characterized predominantly black cities in the decades to come. The same is true for Richmond. The city's densely populated and disproportionately poor public-housing developments had profound implications for the future of the civil rights movement. These areas set the stage for much of the class conflict that characterized black politics during the 1970s and 1980s, and black officials inherited social and economic problems that segregationists had set in motion. If segregationist leadership tried to reduce these communities to invisibility during the 1950s and 1960s, some of the most vocal criticism of Richmond's political leadership during the 1980s came from these enclaves. More immediately, African Americans learned about the relationship between public opinion and public policy the hard way—without state and local representatives, blacks had no political recourse against these initiatives.[54]

The Crusade mobilized voters to fight against segregationist policies. By the 1960s, Richmond's African Americans were positioned mathematically and demographically to exert tangible electoral power on city hall. They made up roughly 42 percent of the capital city's population, approximately 90,000 residents. According to the State Board of Elections, the number of eligible black voters rose from 12,486 in 1956 to 16,396 in 1961. The *Afro-American* estimated that the Crusade had helped register close to 16,000 voters by 1960. As of April 1, 1960, 15,641 of Richmond's African Americans were registered to vote, a slight rise from the previous year, compared to 51,362 eligible white voters, a number that had dropped by roughly 2,500. Just prior to the first city council election of the 1960s, the Crusade, in conjunction with the NAACP, provided an education and information service on the electoral process six months prior to the election. The *Afro-American* estimated that 13,500 of Richmond's eligible black voters had paid that year's poll taxes, and the Crusade eventually mailed out a series of sample ballots to registered voters. Crusade president George A. Pannell expanded the research committee's efforts. Two months before the election, the research committee disseminated a questionnaire to twenty-two aspiring candidates. Thornton, with the help of VUU historian Dr. Tinsley L. Spraggins and political scientist Franklin J. Gayles, posed eight questions to candidates pertaining directly to racial issues. First, they asked, "How far would you, yourself go in implementing the U.S. Supreme Court's decision in 1954 regarding school desegregation of our public schools"? The research committee knew that the public-school question was the proverbial litmus test for white politicians. They also asked questions about forming a biracial commission to address integration and direct-action protests. Although no record of the candidates' responses to the questionnaire exists, the Crusade intimated that almost all of the twenty-two candidates responded to it. Most candidates argued that they favored an interracial commission if both sides approached racial issues reasonably and judiciously.[55]

In 1960, the Crusade abandoned the practice of single-shot voting in favor of what it called "balance-of-power" politics. Under Richmond's at-large system, voters selected nine council members from a slate of candidates. Although no black candidates ran in the council election of 1960, the Crusade, based on responses to the questionnaire, decided to endorse nine of the least-disagreeable white candidates. They were the candidates whom the Crusade's research committee thought sincerely answered the questionnaire and might be amendable to some of blacks' demands. The objective was to throw blacks' support behind white candidates in an effort to render these candidates indebted to black voters. Three days prior to the election, the Crusade used the *Afro's* front page to define its balance-of-power strategy and what that strategy might mean for the future of Richmond politics: "If 9,000 colored voters all vote for the same 9 men, these 9,000 votes will put these 9 candidates ahead of the 13 others on the ticket. The same 'balance of power' which will assure election of the nine men who get support of 9,000 colored voters can at the same time unseat several councilmen who are definitely against the rights of colored citizens." During the election of 1960, the Crusade also initiated the practice of waiting until the eleventh hour to release its slate. The board of directors and the research committee decided to wait until the Sunday prior to the election to avoid confusion from competitive political organizations. The Crusade also waited until Sunday to release its slate because black ministers, who had long since abandoned old-line RCC strategies, preached the primacy of politics from pulpits.[56]

The balance-of-power strategy paid huge dividends on June 14. Richmond's blacks helped elect seven of the nine candidates, whereas only six of the nine candidates endorsed by the RCA were elected. Richard Wilson of the *Times-Dispatch* claimed, "Beyond any doubt, Negro votes played a decisive part in the election. In 15 of the city's precincts, they voted overwhelmingly for 10 candidates." The Crusade not only endorsed a few of the same candidates that the RCA slated but also recommended these candidates to prove that the winners needed more than an RCA endorsement to win a council seat. The *Afro-American* exclaimed that the blacks "batted .777." Newspapers estimated that roughly 8,000 blacks of a total 27,823 voters voted in those districts: roughly 30 percent of the city's total votes. The election of 1960 was Richmond's second largest in terms of voter turnout in recorded election history. (For election results in 1960, see table 1 in the appendix.) Roughly eight days after the election, the Crusade and Richmond's new mayor, Claude W. Woodward, agreed to establish a biracial organization, the Richmond Citizens Advisory Committee. The city council also appointed an African American, B. A. "Sonny" Cephas, to the Richmond Planning Commission.[57]

By 1962, the Crusade and the *Afro* began to demand that the city council do more to address African Americans' economic needs. The Crusade convened a meeting on April 7, 1962, to formulate a resolu-

tion that would urge city officials to integrate public schools and eliminate discriminatory practices in municipal employment. After thousands
of Richmond's African Americans signed the resolution, Crusade president Pannell, finance chairman Overby, and Brooks personally delivered
their demands to city manager Horace Edwards. The resolution argued
in favor of compulsory school attendance, a separation of local school
boards from the state's Pupil Placement Board, a $1.15 minimum wage,
and four-year council terms (current terms were two years). The research
committee also found that only 26 percent of city employees were African American, and of the total number of black municipal employees 80
percent were menial laborers—chiefly custodians, kitchen workers, truck
drivers, animal control workers, and the like. More ominously, black
employees disproportionately made up the lowest pay-scale bracket. The
Crusade was cautiously optimistic about the resolution—its leaders knew
that resolutions were not laws. Although the city council unanimously
passed the measure, the Crusade was also skeptical of the council's desire
to meet its demands. Yet the fact that African Americans, particularly in
the South, presented whites with a list of economic demands and influenced city council elections was nothing short of revolutionary. J. West-
wood Smithers, who finished ninth of nine candidates and surely would
not have been elected without a Crusade endorsement, introduced the
Fair Employment Ordinance.[58]

The Crusade named the city council election of 1962 the "fair employment" election. Although African American candidates ran and lost, their
balance-of-power strategy again paid dividends. Two African Americans,
Mrs. Ester Smith of Church Hill and Clarence W. Newman (advised by
L. Douglas Wilder), ran for council seats in 1962. Both Smith and Newman were well connected to Richmond's organizing community. Smith,
who called herself a homemaker, was an active member of the NAACP's
membership campaigns and a Roanoke native. Newsome was a graduate of VUU and Howard University's Law School. He was also a Korean
War veteran and the Crusade's former executive secretary. Although both
candidates failed to crack the top nine, 22,300 Richmonders voted in the
election of 1962. Newsome placed eleventh with 7,903 votes, and Smith
received 1,254 votes for twentieth place (of twenty-five candidates). (For
election results in 1962, see table 2 in the appendix.) The research com-

mittee successfully endorsed seven of the nine white candidates elected to council, including Eleanor Parker Sheppard, who became the first female mayor in Richmond's history. The council also appointed Phil J. Bagley Jr. as vice mayor. Sheppard and Bagley turned out to be only temporary allies of the Crusade.[59]

In 1964, the Crusade threw a considerable amount of its energy into Sonny Cephas's bid for a council seat. Election officials estimated that roughly 18,400 African Americans registered to vote in Richmond that year. The Crusade believed that it had the numbers not just to swing the balance of power but also to elect an African American to city council. Cephas had been a resident of Richmond since 1910 and was a VUU graduate. He had also operated a successful real estate agency in the area for twenty-five years. Cephas represented the types of politicized professionals who made up the Crusade's decision makers. He was a member of the Advisory Board of Parks and Recreation and the Richmond Planning Commission and was the former president of the Virginia Association of Real Estate Brokers. In 1962, the Crusade encouraged Cephas's appointment to the Richmond Planning Commission in the wake of the employment resolution and the slum-clearance disaster of the 1950s. Following the resignation of Councilman George W. Sadler in February 1963, the Crusade's research committee and board of directors suggested that Cephas should run for city council. The Crusade endorsed, along with Cephas, eight white candidates: A. Scott Anderson, Phil J. Bagley Jr., Morrill M. Crowe, Robert J. Herberle, Henry R. Miller III, Eleanor P. Sheppard, Robert C. Throckmorton, and James C. Wheat Jr.[60]

During the election of 1964, the Crusade faced its first significant challenge from rival organizations. Early that year, Doug Wilder, Ronald K. Charity, and Neverett A. Eggleston established an alternative to the Crusade, Church Hill's Voters' Voice. The three decided that Charity and Eggleston would also make a run for council seats in 1964. Charity was Arthur Ashe's first tennis coach and a ranked tennis player himself. Eggleston owned and operated Jackson Ward's Eggleston Hotel, which, along with Slaughter's Hotel, was one of only three hotels within Richmond's city limits that permitted black guests. Voters' Voice, along with a loose association of black civic organizations, believed that Richmond's black community needed more diverse political representation. Wilder and company also thought that the Crusade's practice of circulating its endorsements at the proverbial eleventh hour did little to develop candidates over the course of an election. Wilder argued, "The primary purpose of the Crusade is to encourage Negroes to register and vote. [Voters' Voice] is the first organization allowing full voter participation throughout a campaign." In many ways, Wilder's criticism of the Crusade's late endorsements had merit—by waiting to release its slate of endorsements, its research committee excluded potential voters from the process of electing candidates. Just prior to the election in 1964, Voters' Voice fielded its own slate of nine candidates.[61]

Across town, whites had been brewing up their own plans to challenge the Crusade. In 1963, Richmond Forward (RF) supplanted the RCA. Established on November 13, 1963, RF was a nonpartisan, lobbying division made up of roughly forty civic and business groups from the Richmond metropolitan area. Edwin P. Conquest and a battery of West Enders led the organization. Conquest and RF's founders had apparently learned a thing or two since 1948. In a controversial move, RF endorsed Cephas, which nearly cost Cephas the election. A number of black civic organizations, led by the West End Council of Leagues, translated the endorsement to mean that the Crusade had sold out. The Crusade's refusal to endorse Charity and Eggleston made matters worse. When the Crusade endorsed two white candidates over Eggleston and Charity—it likely wanted to remain free of entanglements with Voters' Voice—African Americans were reminded of the RCC's failed interracial alliances of the late 1940s.[62]

The controversy forced the Crusade to appeal to the politics of racial solidarity. The Crusade had established a tradition of mailing out sample ballots shortly before elections. On the eve of the election in 1964, it sent out these sample ballots and added a section that defended its decision to support white candidates. The research committee's leaflet read, "Is there really confusion among our voters or is there an effort to split our vote because in the past, we have been too successful and Negroes are fast becoming a political influence in the City of Richmond? . . . [W]e ask you to read our story on the back of this letter, make up your mind, then go to the polls." As far as the Crusade was concerned, African Americans had the electoral authority to vote public officials in and out of office if they failed to accommodate African Americans' demands. Balance-of-power strategies overshadowed the politics of symbolism. In 1964, that meant supporting white candidates over black ones on occasion.[63]

Cephas's victory was bittersweet. The results of the election demonstrated blacks' overwhelming support for the Crusade. The election broke a record for local turnout: 30,931 people voted. (For election statistics from 1964, see table 3 in the appendix.) The *Afro-American* reported, "Richmond got its first colored councilman in 14 years in the election of B. A. (Sonny) Cephas, Jr." Cephas garnered roughly 16,000 votes and placed second among the top nine. He finished roughly 550 votes ahead of James C. Wheat Jr., who finished third overall. The Crusade split the ticket with RF. Richmonders elected all but one of the Crusade's endorsements. Neither Eggleston nor Charity came close to cracking the top nine. Cephas's election was a watershed moment for racial politics. Nearly a decade before the local election of 1964, Roy Wilkins had observed, "In Virginia the four-year increase [in the number of registered voters], 1952–1956, was only 13,772, with all observers noting that no special restraints were imposed on Negroes who sought to register. In fact, in Virginia the current problem of Negro leaders is not to secure payment of the poll tax, but to get those who have paid their poll tax to go the polls and vote." The Crusade not only capitalized on this momentum in the early 1960s but also met the challenges of massive resistance, machine politics, and moderate race reforms with broad-based voter mobilization. This mobilization had far-reaching implications. Yet African Americans still had real grievances about political and economic discrimination. By the mid-1960s, Virginia's schools were obsolescently segregated (only 312 of roughly 26,000 black students were enrolled in predominantly white schools); African Americans were a sizeable portion of Richmond's most impoverished residents; and city officials had relocated thousands of black residents to densely packed public-housing units. After 1965, the Crusade doubled its efforts.[64]

2

Systematically Done In

Black Electoral Empowerment, Vote Dilution, and the Push for Annexation after the Voting Rights Act

Tyranny over the Mind

In 1966, *Ebony* magazine's politics section featured an article on Richmond's African American vice mayor Winfred Mundle. The city council had recently appointed Mundle to the vice mayoralty. He was one of three African Americans (along with Sonny Cephas and Henry Marsh III), elected to the nine-member council following the passage of the VRA and the abolition of state and local poll taxes in 1966. The article claimed, "In the four months since taking office, Mundle has fully mastered the somewhat ambiguous job of vice mayor, playing the twin roles of administrator and diplomat with a veteran's hand. Under Mayor Morrill M. Crowe, his job has been enlarged over that of his predecessor and Mundle's very presence as a representative of his city has been a morale-booster among Richmond's growing Negro citizenry." On one hand, hope does indeed spring eternal: Marsh, Mundle, and Cephas were part of a much larger complexion revolution in American racial politics. These men rode the tide of voter mobilization into America's city halls. On the other hand, although their elections represented one of the most monumental changes in American political development, African Americans also wanted more than symbolic politic victories; they wanted to undo the legacy of segregationist policies that had wreaked havoc on their communities.[1]

The story of African Americans' struggle for electoral power underscores the underhandedness that often accompanies political reforms. By removing franchise restrictions, the VRA of 1965 redistributed political authority along racial lines. African Americans, who had been systematically excluded from the New Deal, saw the Great Society and the VRA as their own New Deal. White southern leaders, who had grown accustomed to nearly a century of political overrepresentation and one-party rule, met these demands by embarking on campaigns of redisenfranchisement. As African Americans grew impatient with the pace of racial reform and urban unrest swept across America during the late 1960s, these white powerbrokers used the power vested in local and state government to beat back the democratizing forces of the freedom struggle. Richmond's annexation of Chesterfield County shattered the symbolism of the election of Mundle, Cephas, and Marsh to the city council. By 1970, white antipathy to federal voting rights mandates threatened the Crusade's early achievements.[2]

Black voter registration developed sporadically prior to 1965. If the will of African American voters and the audacity of direct-action demonstrators stimulated Washington to action, the Civil Rights Acts of 1957 and 1960 provided the framework for what became the VRA. Southern resistance to black voting was stronger than Washington's defense of the earlier acts. Although these acts were limited in their ability to effectively combat black disenfranchisement, when combined, according to leading scholars of voting rights, they were essential to three developments in black voting rights. First, they "lowered the stakes in federal litigation against local election officials" by requiring that federal action into local voting matters be *civil* rather than criminal. Second, the Civil Rights Act of 1957 created the USCCR, and the Civil Rights Act of 1960 reinforced the DOJ's and USCCR's ability to collect voting data—data that were crucial to federal litigation against disenfranchisement and ultimately to the VRA. And third, both acts required that civil action against state and local election officials be held in federal courts. African Americans prior to 1965 continued to meet firm resistance from southern election officials, and the process of suing local jurisdictions proved to be extremely time consuming. Segregationist federal judges in southern jurisdictions often obstructed litigation before it reached Washington.[3]

The dialectic between black voters and white detractors eventually motivated the White House to action. Just before signing the VRA into law, President Lyndon B. Johnson acknowledged the contested battle over black ballots. He maintained:

> Every device of which human ingenuity is capable has been used to deny this right. The Negro citizen may go to register only to be told that the day is wrong, or the hour is late, or the official in charge is absent. And if he persists, and if he manages to present himself to the registrar, he may be disqualified because he did not spell out his middle name or because he abbreviated a word on the application. And if he manages to fill out an application he is given a test. The registrar is the sole judge of whether he passes this test. He may be asked to recite the entire Constitution, or explain the most complex provisions of State law. And even a college degree cannot be used to prove that he can read and write.

Many of the VRA's draftees had collected data with the USCCR or sued southern voting systems with the DOJ as early as the late 1950s. Led by Attorney General Nicholas Katzenbach, federal policy makers were all too familiar with the recent legacy of disenfranchisement. The suffrage crusades of the late 1950s and early 1960s informed what became the VRA.[4]

On August 6, 1965, President Johnson signed what he called "the goddamndest, toughest, voting rights bill" in U.S. history. In many ways, the VRA was a panic reaction to the persistence of southern disenfranchisement. To this end, Katzenbach, who led the team that drafted the voting rights bill in 1965, originally offered President Johnson three alternatives for enfranchising southern blacks. The first was a constitutional amendment that prohibited reasonable voter qualifications, excluding things such as age and residency requirements. The attorney general then proposed legislation that would establish a new federal agency to supervise federal elections. The last suggestion granted an existing federal agency "the power to assume direct control of registration for voting in both federal and state elections" where the percentages of voting-age African Americans was low. Given the debacle at the Democratic Convention in Atlantic City in 1964 caused by the struggle between the Mississippi Freedom Democratic Party and racist Democrats, the SCLC's efforts in Selma, and Johnson's skepticism of a federal regulatory commission, the president chose a variation of the third alternative. The VRA initially contained permanent provisions (sections 1–3) and temporary provisions that needed to be renewed after five years (sections 4–9). The Eighty-Ninth Congress passed the act with relative ease, 328–88 in the House and 78–20 in the Senate. The vote was attributable to Congress's overwhelming Democratic majority at the time, 68–32 in the Senate and 295–140 in the House.[5]

The VRA was arguably the most robust civil rights act of the twentieth century. Unlike previous acts, it had preventative and punitive elements. It first suspended discriminatory tests and devices as prerequisites for voting in federal elections. More specifically, section 2 disallowed voting qualifications, prerequisites, standards, practices, and procedures such as grandfather clauses and literacy tests. The act also authorized federal examiners to supervise and register voters in areas that were in violation of the law—this provision, section 4, came equipped with a triggering formula. The triggering process was twofold. States and political subdivisions that used voting tests and prerequisites (excluding poll taxes) were not only subject to federal scrutiny but also subject to preclearance if less than half of the adults in a particular jurisdiction had not registered or voted on or after November 1, 1964. The act then covered states and localities that were in violation of sections 2 and 4. The coverage formula in section 4 (which also came equipped with a bailout clause that allowed jurisdictions to appeal coverage in cases of overinclusiveness) applied to all elections—federal, state, and local. Furthermore, the VRA prohibited voting laws and election-based changes in states and subdivisions that fell under the triggering mechanism. Section 5 required preclearance from the DOJ (the DOJ had sixty days to determine whether the changes were discriminatory) or from the district court of the District of Columbia. Preclearance meant that covered electoral jurisdictions were prohibited from making election-based changes without federal permission. Without preclearance, policy makers recognized that the DOJ would have to sue individual jurisdictions, and litigation—particularly in light of the Civil Rights Act of 1957—had proven to be a laborious undertaking. This provision, in fact, was the product of "enforcement-minded lawyers in the Civil Rights Division" of the DOJ who not only had read the data gathered by the USCCR but also had been in the trenches against segregationists after *Brown*. Policy makers designed section 5 to preclude resistance—the CRD's lawyers made sure that southern federal judges could not approve preclearance cases. Section 10 also gave attorneys general the authority to investigate states and localities that used poll taxes as registration prerequisites. The Senate–House conference committee struggled to find an agreement on poll taxes and in lieu of banning the levy gave the attorney general the apparatus to pick up where the Twenty-Fourth Amendment ended. By 1965, only Arkansas, Virginia, Texas, Mississippi, and Alabama continued to use these taxes as a disenfranchising mechanism. Immediately after Johnson signed the VRA, it covered ten states and a sizeable number of counties in North Carolina.[6]

The years 1965 and 1966 were two of the most transformative years in southern politics. Black voters, in rural and urban areas alike, revolutionized southern politics. Two years after the VRA's ratification, blacks had registered to vote in record numbers. By May 1967, the DOJ estimated that 416,000 African Americans had signed up to vote. Blacks' registration immediately rose to more than 50 percent of the voting-age population in every state covered by the act. Mississippi witnessed the biggest change: blacks' registration there rose from 6.7 to 59.8 of the total voting-age population. In the rest of the Deep South, the proportion of registered voting-age African Americans also grew by large amounts: in Alabama, from 19.3 to 51.6 percent; in Georgia, from 27.4 to 52.6 percent; in Florida, from 51.2 to 63.6 percent; in Louisiana, from 31.6 to 58.9 percent; and in South Carolina, from 37.3 to 51.2 percent. In the Upper South, the number of North Carolina's registered voting-age African Americans increased from 46.8 to 51.3, while the number of Virginia's registered voting-age African Americans rose from 38.3 to 55.6 percent. To the west, the number of registered voting-age African Americans increased from 69.5 to 71.7 percent in Tennessee, from 40.4 to 62.8 in Arkansas, and from 53.1 to 61.6 in Texas. Southern African Americans also transitioned from exerting little to no political influence to expectations that massive voter registration might translate into real electoral power. The rise in blacks' registration also led to an upsurge in the number of actual African American voters. The Voter Education Project of the Southern Regional Council reported exceptional black turnout in 1966. In Alabama, the USCCR estimated that 74 percent of Alabama's 250,000 voting-age African Americans participated in the May primary of 1966. In Mississippi in 1966, 50,000 of approximately 170,000 registered black voters voted in the general election. Black turnout also gave rise to an increase in the number of black elected officials. In 1966, the number of black officeholders reached approximately 159 and 200 by 1967. Yet southern African Americans wanted more than symbolic political victories, and with the landslide of registration they had the votes to realize these ends.[7]

African Americans in Richmond celebrated the VRA cautiously. By 1966, they were well familiar with the transition from voter registration drives to governance. These African Americans, in keeping with Bayard Rustin's recent claims in the article "From Protest to Politics," "now sought advances in employment, housing, school integration, police protection, and so forth." The Crusade for Voters and the *Richmond Afro-American* remained central to these objectives. Not only did the *Afro* continue to advocate on behalf of the Crusade and black voters, but the paper's new editor, Raymond Boone, was determined to increase political consciousness. From its headquarters in Baltimore, Maryland, the Afro-American Company sent Boone to Richmond in 1965 to become the paper's editor and boost circulation. Boone, a native of Suffolk, Virginia, had earned a bachelor's degree in journalism from Boston University and a master's degree in political science from Howard University. Upon graduation, he worked for the *Quincy Patriot-Ledger* in Quincy, Massachusetts, outside of Boston, and wrote the *Suffolk News-Herald*'s sports section from 1956 to 1964. In 1964, Baltimore's Afro-American Company, established by John Henry Murphy Jr. in 1922, hired Boone to cover the Johnson administration. After being sent to the *Richmond Afro-American*, Boone immediately renovated the paper. He hired Milton A. Randolph, then president of the Crusade, and Howard H. Carwile to write weekly political commentaries in the opinion section. He also hired Crusade member Preston Yancy—who eventually led the Crusade's merger study commission—to write for the editorial section as well. By 1966, Boone doubled the weekly paper's circulation and steered it toward an even stronger civil rights agenda.[8]

Despite all of these signs of progress, black Richmonders remained guarded about how much political change the VRA might engender. An *Afro* editorial in early 1965 articulated this cautious optimism, arguing, "There will be a bitter end fight by the old Confederates, because the Byrds, the Eastlands, the Talmadges, and the Ellenders and even Sheriff Jim Clarks well know that full and unrestricted suffrage means for them the end of the line. Indeed it spells the death of the so-called 'Southern way of life' . . . . It means equitable representation on school boards, in city councils, on county commissions, in state legislatures in dozens of city, county, and state offices." Although the VRA gave federal officials the authority to investigate the legality of state and local poll taxes, the levies were still legal in local elections. Richmond's African Americans knew that poll taxes were still a major obstacle to broad-based involvement in local politics. Prohibiting poll taxes, "the last major shackle," was essential to changing the culture of city hall. Yet although the VRA failed to eliminate poll taxes, it put the levies in the proverbial crosshairs.[9]

The VRA confounded Virginia's white racial conservatives and moderates. It covered the commonwealth because fewer than 50 percent of Virginia's voting-age population had registered to vote in the presidential election of 1964. Southern officials understood that section 10 could lead to the destruction of poll taxes and Democrats' time-honored one-party system. On one hand, racial moderates, who had grown accustomed to granting and restricting blacks' freedoms, believed that the VRA would have the same impact as *Brown*. The act, they believed, might ignite yet another wave of segregationist recalcitrance. William S. White of the *Richmond Times-Dispatch* claimed, "It is he [the southern moderate], and not the outside reformers who largely have passed this act who must indispensably assist the transformation with patience, tolerance, and fortitude which have marked him for decades as he has sought to advance racial justice without brining anarchy. . . . This central problem is not to help the newly enfranchised Negro not only to register but also to vote with an intelligence and integrity. . . . [N]o one but the white Southern moderate can give to the Negro this highest tutorship for free men." Although White's contentions smacked of the types of paternalism that often characterized mid-twentieth-century race relations in Virginia, his tone also represented moderates' acquiescence to Washington's defense of racial equality. Others not only vowed to resist the VRA but were anxious about what the act meant for the state's Democratic machine.[10]

Racial conservatives made a mockery of the VRA. Democrats such as A. Willis Robertson and Harry Byrd, both of whom were integral to massive resistance and voted against the act, did in fact attempt to reinvigorate the politics of interposition. Byrd argued, "This so-called Voting Rights Bill of 1965 will demonstrate the bias and prejudice under which the bill was conceived and with which it will be enforced. The bill is literally based on discrimination as between the states." These segregationists, as historian Kevin Kruse demonstrates in his study of Atlanta, often claimed that they were fighting *for* rights of their own, not against the rights of others. The VRA, which came equipped with a special scrutiny formula and a direct supervision provision, personified southerners' deepest fears of federal oversight. Men such as Byrd and Robertson immediately charged that the VRA exceeded congressional power and unlawfully encroached on rights reserved to the states. These leaders had allies. One week after Johnson signed the VRA, the headline on the *Richmond Times-Dispatch*'s front page read, "Virginia to Challenge Voting Act in Court." Roughly a week later Virginia's attorney general made public the commonwealth's plans to "move as expeditiously as possible" to file a joint suit with other states against the VRA.[11]

South Carolina fired the first shot against the VRA. Legalistic resistance to the VRA eventually culminated in *South Carolina v. Katzenbach* (1966), argued before the Supreme Court. Officials in South Carolina contended that giving federal examiners the right to investigate abnormalities in local elections was unconstitutional. This portion of the VRA, plaintiffs argued, violated states' rights to implement and control their own elections. The Court disagreed in an eight-to-one vote. Warren and seven other justices held that the Fifteenth Amendment (prohibiting the federal and state governments from denying anyone the right to vote based on race, color, or previous condition of servitude) gave Congress the power to prevent racial discrimination in voting. The VRA, the Court argued, was a constitutional response to racist southern voting patterns that had characterized the region since the adoption of the Fifteenth Amendment. In the meantime, most Virginians remained fixated on developments with poll taxes. Whites, regardless of their position on the race question, understood that African Americans, who made up nearly 50 percent of Richmond's population, had the numbers to exert real pressure on city council elections if Washington forbade the use of poll taxes in local elections.[12]

Harper v. Virginia Board of Elections (1966) was a watershed moment for Virginia politics. The Twenty-Fourth Amendment, ratified by states on January 23, 1964, struck down poll taxes in federal elections, but the levies were still legal in state and local elections. On March 24, 1966, the Supreme Court, following congressional precedent established in section 10 of the VRA, ultimately prohibited the use of poll taxes in state and local elections. Again, Virginia's black women led the charge. In March 1964, attorney Allison W. Brown Jr., Annie E. Harper, and three additional plaintiffs from Fairfax County, Virginia, filed suit against the commonwealth's $1.50 poll tax. Draftees of the VRA knew that poll taxes impinged upon minorities' right to vote, but these policy makers also knew they had to tread lightly on this issue (as did Congress) because the levies kept poor whites and other low-income Americans from voting as well. In 1966, the Court affirmed section 10, contending that the imposition of poll taxes in state elections made voters' income an electoral standard and, as such, violated the Equal Protection Clause of the Fourteenth Amendment. In a six-to-three majority opinion, Justice William O. Douglas held that the right to vote was not necessarily constitutional, but it was fundamental. He argued, "In determining what lines are unconstitutionally discriminatory, we have never been confined to historic notions of equality, any more than we have restricted due process to a fixed catalogue of what was at a given time deemed to be the limits of fundamental rights." Voter qualifications, the Court argued, had no relation to wealth; state levies as prerequisites to voting were thus unconstitutional.[13]

On April 2, 1966, the front page of the *Afro* declared in capital letters, "POLL TAX DEAD! 'IT'S UP TO US NOW,' SAY RIGHTS LEADERS." William Thornton anticipated that the Crusade could double the number of black voters immediately. He also claimed that black voters had to go beyond electing more black officials by getting those black officials to promote better jobs, schools, and housing in Richmond's black communities. Crusade president and *Afro* columnist Milton Randolph planned massive voter registration drives on April 15 and May 1, just two weeks after the

Court's decision on section 10. Randolph, who knew that the levies prohibited most low-income people from voting regardless of race, argued that *Harper* represented a "victory for the common man of both races; it's not necessarily a Negro victory." Henry Marsh III implored African Americans to flood "the city's registration office to take advantage of the lull" before whites emasculated the Court's decision. Marsh's contention that they needed to "take advantage of the lull" reflected the caution that the *Afro* voiced after Johnson signed the VRA into law. "Being joyful," the *Afro* urged, was "not enough." The Crusade met the demand. By the end of 1966, it claimed that its registration drives had increased the number of registered black voters by 65 percent. On the verge of June's election, 29,970 African Americans—of roughly 73,000 total eligible voters in Richmond—were registered to vote in local elections, compared to 18,161 in 1964. In light of *Harper,* Thornton stressed, "we have no more excuses. We intend to take the ball and carry it."[14]

White leaders knew that the *Harper* decision would have grave implications for politics in the Old Dominion. Since the early twentieth century, poll taxes had not merely preserved Virginia's place as an elite white man's commonwealth but were also central to the preservation and maintenance of the state's one-party system. Democratic Virginia congressman William M. Tuck, a former governor and rabid segregationist, claimed that *Harper* was the "worst of several horrendous decisions handed down by the Warren Court in 12 years." Henry Marsh and African Americans were not the only Richmonders who anticipated resistance. The leader of Virginia's Republican Party, Linwood Holton, also predicted backlash. Holton argued, "Mark you, there will be some move within the element which dominates the Virginia Democratic party to re-create barriers to voting. I suspect there will be some move like requiring qualification six months prior to an election." The day after the Court handed down its decision in *Harper, Richmond Times-Dispatch* contributor James E. Davis argued that the abolition of poll taxes would substantially influence state- and local-level politics. Experts anticipated that the Supreme Court's decision would add roughly 10,000 black voters and 5,000 white voters to Richmond's list of eligible voters. Election of more African American city council candidates in 1966, the *Times-Dispatch* believed, seemed "virtually assured."[15]

Harry Byrd Sr. died six months after the *Harper* decision, on October 20, 1966; his machine was all but dead by then, anyway. Massive resistance to public-school integration had revived Byrd's machine only temporarily. By 1958, school closures were, according to scholar James Ryan, "too high a price to pay for most metropolitan whites." Token integration and compliance, which characterized public-school integration until the Court held that freedom of choice was unconstitutional in *Green v. County School Board of New Kent County* (1968), replaced Byrd's calls for massive resistance. Even before the demise of massive resistance, however, younger Democrats from Virginia's growing urban areas, many of them veterans of World War II, had challenged Byrd's tax-and-spend approach to infrastructure building and internal improvements. These Democrats could see around the corner: led by Mills Godwin, antimachine Democrats supported the repeal of poll taxes, called for equitable redistricting of the General Assembly's districts, and favored more enlightened policies on racial segregation. The Court's ruling in *Reynolds v. Sims* (1964) also forced Virginia's General Assembly to redistrict in accordance with the state's growing urban and suburban populations. This redistricting, by reapportioning rural and urban districts in the commonwealth, was the actual death blow for Byrd's machine—particularly as the machine derived representative power from drawing district lines that favored a handful of rural officials. These forces allowed Godwin to win the governorship as an antimachine Democrat in 1966.[16]

African Americans were essential to the Byrd machine's demise. *Harper*, the VRA, and the rise of black voters crushed it. The number of registered black voters in the commonwealth had increased by almost 100,000, from 144,259 before the VRA to 243,000 by early 1967. As African Americans voted in greater numbers, whites had to do more than make token overtures to the black body politic. This trend was strikingly similar to developments in the presidential elections of the early 1960s as African Americans, particularly in the North, began to vote in greater numbers for the Democratic Party. Antiestablishment Democrats actually needed blacks' votes to resist the machine. With the help of black voters, moderate Democrat William Spong defeated A. Willis Robertson in 1966. An overwhelming majority of African Americans also voted for Godwin. Even the fiery James Kilpatrick, who was nearing the end of his stint at the *Richmond News-Leader,* sensed defeat. Roughly five months before the *Harper* decision, Kilpatrick stated, "These shifting blocs and potential coalitions offer an absorbing picture of Southern politics in transition. Chiefly because he stayed with LBJ, Mr. Godwin won not only the Negro vote, but the labor vote as well. If this suggests that Southern Negroes and Liberals automatically will stick with regular Democrats in State elections, the Old Southern Democrats parties . . . face a total reorientation." Kilpatrick actually portended a trend that had profound implications for national and presidential politics well into the twenty-first century—he forecast the reddening of the South! This reorientation bore fruit four years later when Linwood Holton became Virginia's first Republican governor since Reconstruction, but Richmond's policy makers had more immediate plans to stem the tide of electoral reforms.[17]

Old habits do not die easily. Although the VRA changed southern politics, it failed to stamp out disenfranchisement. If the old one-party system of southern politics was patently racist and paternalistic, after 1965 policy makers manufactured discrete ways to perpetuate old racial hierarchies. White powerbrokers in Richmond and the South, who often had done and continued to do just enough to maintain black communities, realized that African Americans wanted more than symbolic politics victories. With the realization of the VRA and the prohibition of poll taxes, African Americans had the material resources to back their demands. Yet they were able to elect only a small number of black officials following the VRA, and they continued to meet resistance during the electoral process. In 1968, the USCCR released yet another data-collection report, *Political Participation.* This progress report, written just as race conflict broke out during the long hot summers after 1965, was 222 pages. More than half of it explained the methods that whites had recently devised to maintain control over local politics: they combined black and white districts, moved polling places to white neighborhoods, switched city council meetings to working hours, changed to at-large elections systems, annexed predominantly white suburbs, and in some cases threatened African American voters and candidates with violence or economic reprisal or both. Politicians often pushed through many of these reforms as color-blind initiatives designed either to promote political continuity or to increase cities' tax bases.[18]

Not to be outdone, Richmond's white council members were in the process of drawing up plans to maintain their control over city hall. Resistance to voting rights in Richmond happened immediately after the ratification of the VRA and the *Harper* decision because African Americans had been exerting pressure on local politics since the early 1960s. As the Byrd machine faded, local powerbrokers scrambled to devise new solutions to maintain their authority over city hall. In 1966, African Americans were outregistering whites in local elections. Between 1964 and 1966, the number of black registrants increased by 65 percent; in the same period, however, the number of registered white voters increased by only 13 percent. According to the Virginia State Board of Elections, approximately 30,000 blacks, representing about 48 percent of Richmond's total population in 1966, were registered to vote, compared to 58,000 whites. In 1964, white registrants outnumbered blacks by roughly 34,000. Although in 1966 white voters still maintained a numerical advantage over African Americans, whites understood that blacks had the numbers to elect officials who might actually do something real about discrimination in municipal employment, urban-renewal efforts, and the state of Richmond schools.[19]

Before African Americans gained a city council majority, whites pushed forward their first ostensibly color-blind mechanism to dilute the power of blacks' votes. Locals anticipated that the Supreme Court might rule against poll taxes in *Harper,* so several months before the Court made its decision, three council members, all affiliated with RF, crafted the city's first scheme to nullify black voters. Councilpersons Henry Miller III, Eleanor Sheppard, and James C. Wheat Jr. recommended a change in the city charter to replace two-year council terms with four-year terms. The trio found allies in Mayor Crowe and council member Robert J. Habenicht. This plan rewarded the highest four vote getters in the upcoming election with four-year terms; the assumption, of course, was that the top four vote-getters would be white candidates. The five candidates who finished behind the four winners were to serve two-year terms. During the next election, the five council seats up for grabs were to be filled for four-year terms by the top vote getters, and the fifth-place candidate would serve a two-year term; and so on in subsequent elections. The city council passed the resolution to amend the city charter by a five-to-four majority on December 13, 1965. Council members Robert Throckmorton, A. Scott Anderson, Phil Bagley Jr., and Sonny Cephas voted against the measure. The General Assembly, however, still had to approve the change to the city charter. The Richmond–Henrico delegation in the House of Delegates refused to introduce the resolution— known as HB224—without a referendum that would allow Richmond's residents to vote on the matter. Once again, white elites demonstrated their disdain for democracy.[20]

The referendum for a popular vote met resistance in the General Assembly from a contingent of well-heeled Richmonders. The resolution's supporters wrote to several legislators asking them to remove the portion of the referendum that required a citywide vote in the upcoming election of 1966. Virginia's elites and their public representatives had grown accustomed to ignoring the people's prerogatives. The General Assembly's Senate deleted the referendum. Senator Fitzgerald Bemiss, whose father was an RF trustee; Senator Edward E. Willey, who also had strong RF support; and Senator George M. Cochran of Staunton led the charge. On March 7, 1966, five members of the House of Delegates requested that the Senate's bill be passed. It turned out that these three senators and five congressmen belonged to the Commonwealth Club of Richmond. Established in 1890 and located in the Fan District on West Franklin Street, the Commonwealth Club had an established history of elitist exclusivity and racial bigotry. The private gentlemen's association refused to admit African Americans either as members or as guests. This club, furthermore, had strong RF support, and 32.6 percent (thirteen) of the General Assembly's senators were members. Yet the voting referendum survived: the House rejected the proposal to remove the referendum from the bill sixty-one to twenty-seven, and Governor Godwin eventually signed the bill allowing Richmond's voters to decide the matter in the upcoming election on June 14. If voters approved the referendum, the election in 1966 would be the last time "all nine City Council members would be elected together."[21]

Proponents of term staggering argued that the measure had nothing to do with race. More specifically, they contended that the staggered plan provided better political continuity by mixing experienced candidates with newcomers. Richmond's daily newspapers, in editorials and news coverage, spent the months prior to the June election drumming up support for the referendum. An editorial in the *Richmond Times-Dispatch* contended, "So it is understandable, though discouraging, that an automatic reflex action of suspicion is the Negro community's response to a governmental improvement proposal which has no racial overtones and which would benefit citizens of all races. . . . The first public discussion of the advantages of the four-year staggered system appeared in the editorial columns of this paper in the mid-1950s." Although Richmonders had discussed staggering elections in the *Times-Dispatch* prior to 1965, these deliberations never gained significant political traction. Moreover, RF specifically told the council members and candidates it supported to be discreet about the staggering plan. An RF memo specifically instructed council members and candidates to cautiously engage African American when the staggering issue came up on the campaign trail or at town hall meetings. The memo read, "When explaining the stagger system give a clear, simple explanation so as to eliminate doubt in the minds of the Negro public that it was designed and approved solely to keep Negro candidates from being elected to City Council." Court documents later revealed that the system had been "designed and approved" for this very reason. Louis Robinson Jr., a member of the East End Retired Men's Club, speaking at an election rally on May 30, 1966, suggested openly that four-year terms might help deny African American communities "proper representation of [*sic*] council." These private conversations and public machinations spoke volumes of whites' true intentions.[22]

Critics of term staggering eventually charged that it might further polarize race relations. An up-and-coming white Democrat in the House of Delegates, J. Sargeant "Sarge" Reynolds, heir to Henrico County's Reynolds Metal Company, was one of the few local elites to publicly condemn the staggering plan for what it was: vote dilution. Reynolds, who had expressed sincere friendship with African American leadership, represented just how far the Old Dominion's Democrats had come since massive resistance. He argued that staggering terms intensified an already apparent "lack of trust between white and Negro leadership" in Richmond. His claim that staggering elections would polarize local race relations fell in line with the position held by the Crusade. The Crusade favored four-year terms, but it, the *Afro*, the NAACP, and several other organizations, including the Richmond Area Democratic Council, were unambiguously opposed to staggering council terms. The Crusade specifically spoke of staggering within the context of vote dilution. In an *Afro* article on April 9, a spokesperson for the organization insinuated that the supposedly color-blind referendum to stagger elections was a ploy to "stunt" blacks' voting power. The organization called a meeting of thirty Richmond African American leaders on April 6, 1966, to discuss attempts to "stunt" black voters. Implicit in the staggering proposal, African Americans contended, was the notion that blacks were incapable of managing city hall. Howard Carwile, one of the few white men to run a weekly editorial column in the *Afro-American,* claimed that staggering terms was tantamount to political conspiracy. *Afro* columnist and NAACP official David E. Longley quit the RF over the referendum, and his desertion represented the transmogrification of interracial political relations. In an article by *Afro* editor Raymond Boone, Longley argued, "I find myself in considerable disagreement with a majority of the persons who have received Richmond Forward's endorsements for re-election or election to City Council. . . . I have joined the Crusade for Voters and [the] NAACP in total opposition to the plan of staggered terms." By the city council election of 1966, blacks no longer believed that the RF was an ally.[23]

The Crusade's research committee put an end to its balance-of-power strategy by refusing to support the least-objectionable white candidates. RF's attempt to stagger terms convinced Crusade leaders that they needed to pay closer attention to white council members and candidates. In fact, during the election of 1964 the Crusade had endorsed some of the candidates who introduced the referendum. In 1966, the research committee endorsed five of a possible sixteen candidates for city council. At that time, independents Henry Marsh and Howard Carwile were longshots. Carwile, a white lawyer who wrote a weekly column in the *Afro,* had lost eighteen consecutive elections. Marsh, a native Richmonder, had proven to be an expert civil rights lawyer but had no political experience to speak of. By 1966, Marsh, like Oliver Hill, had litigated nearly sixty cases involving voting registration, police brutality, employment discrimination, and public-school desegregation. The Crusade also endorsed Cephas and an African American insurance salesman named Winfred Mundle. A graduate of Allen University, Mundle was district manager of the North Carolina Mutual Life Insurance Company, assistant campaign chairman for the Republican Party in Virginia's third congressional district, and a member of the Richmond City Planning Commission. The Crusade refused to endorse three candidates whom it had supported in 1964: Eleanor Sheppard, Morrill Crowe, and James Wheat.[24]

The Crusade got out the vote in June 1966. The city elected all five of the Crusade's endorsements and defeated the referendum on staggering the election of council members. Richmonders broke turnout records by more than 5,000 voters; African Americans represented nearly 40 percent of the total vote—Cephas finished second; Mundle placed fifth; Marsh finished sixth; and Carwile filled the ninth seat on the council. (For the election results in 1966, see tables 4 and 5 in the appendix.) Seven of RF's endorsements were elected, including Cephas and Mundle, but the election of Marsh and Carwile left many Richmonders speechless. One *Richmond News-Leader* editorial argued, "Henry Marsh is not ready to accept the responsibility in such an important capacity. . . . Howard Carwile . . . should not be a member of Council. He has yet to embark upon an important view." The Crusade helped not only to elect three African Americans to council but also to defeat two incumbents: Henry R. Miller III (one of the trio responsible for the staggering referendum) and city council veteran Robert C. Throckmorton. Black voters and their allies also helped crush the referendum to stagger elections: 87 percent of black voters in predominantly black precincts opposed the referendum, whereas only 57 percent of white voters supported it (21,760 people voted against the referendum, and 13,412 voted in favor of it).[25]

By the summer of 1966, the Crusade positioned itself to do battle with RF not merely at the polls but on the city council as well. With the election of three African Americans and Howard Carwile to the council, African Americans attempted to usher in a new era of black governance. Council members elected Morrill Crowe to the mayoralty and made, in a historic maneuver, Winfred Mundle the first African American vice mayor in Richmond's history. A *Times-Dispatch* editorial stated, "Also, as to the Negro voters' influence, it is to be noted that five of the seven candidates backed by the Crusade for Voters won election. The effectiveness of the Crusade in influencing the outcome will be the subject of detailed study of precinct returns."[26] African Americans were unable to elect black candidates without some white support, though, and whites failed to elect officials without support from black voters. In reality, many whites believed that the Crusade's influence on local elections meant that African Americans might not need whites' support in the future.

Building a Better Virginia

Armed with the new civil rights bills, black Americas built upon the momentum of registration drives, direct-action demonstrations, and civil disobedience strategies. After 1965, African Americans and their allied carried the struggle into city halls, courtrooms, and legislative chambers. These men and women occupied a central role in what was, according to historian Leonard Moore, "the greatest accomplishment of the black freedom struggle: the entry of African Americans into the political mainstream." An editorial in the *Afro-American* argued, "Finally we are convinced that if the Commonwealth is willing to move positively and deliberately to bring colored into the decision making process and to use its influence throughout the state to remove barriers that prevent colored upward economic and political mobility, the colored will eagerly do his share in building a better Virginia. Indeed the time could come when concentrations of coloreds will be viewed with no more apprehension than are concentrations of whites." The promise of electoral politics was not specific to Richmond. In 1967, African Americans in Cleveland, Ohio, "kept it cool" for Carl Stokes. Voters made Stokes the first black mayor in that city's history. Chicagoans elected their future black mayor Harold Washington to the Illinois House of Representatives in the same year. In 1966, four African Americans received enough votes in South Carolina's Democratic primary on June 28 to take seats in the state's formerly all-white legislature. In a nine-to-zero decision, the Supreme Court defended Julian Bond's Atlanta-based bid for the Georgia House of Representatives (Bond was one of eight African Americans elected to Georgia's House) in *Bond v. Floyd* (1966). Although future Atlanta mayor Maynard Jackson lost his bid against segregationist incumbent Herman Talmadge for a U.S. Senate seat in 1968, he carried Atlanta, where African Americans made up nearly 45 percent of the population. African Americans in Greensboro, North

Carolina, elected Henry Frye to the state legislature and Elreta Alexander to a district judgeship in early 1968. Blacks also elected African American officials in Virginia. In 1967, Richmond's African Americans helped elect Crusade cofounder William Ferguson Reid to Virginia's House of Delegates. He was the first African American to be elected to Virginia's General Assembly in the twentieth century. Petersburg and Fredericksburg, Virginia, elected African Americans to their city councils in 1966. Unshackled from the chains of poll taxes, an undertaker named Virgil Dimery beat out five white candidates for state senator in 1966 in Williamsburg County, Virginia. The civil rights acts had done their part, it appeared, in bringing an end to legal segregation, and African Americans carried the spirit of the movement into the political arena.[27]

The historic political progress African Americans achieved shortly after 1965 often obscures the ways whites continued to resist black governance, however. Men such as Stokes, Washington, Marsh, and eventually Jackson recognized that decades of institutionalized racism, be it de facto or de jure, had left many of their communities in disarray. African Americans had concrete grievances with urban redevelopment, police brutality, jobs, schools, and the reemergence of vote dilution. As these men and women used their positions as mayors, city council members, judges, and legislators to finally address deepening crises in their communities, they often met firm opposition. White resistance to black governance became a defining characteristic of urban politics in the South for years to come.

Between 1966 and 1968, the Crusade transitioned from balance-of-power politics to the politics of black empowerment and governance. Having registered thousands of voters in the early 1960s, black Richmonders shifted their attention to more aggressive public policies. Marsh and Carwile were two of the most democratizing forces in Richmond politics during the 1960s. Both men demonstrated that they wanted the public to influence public policy. They achieved this goal by directly challenging the continuation of discriminatory policies at city hall. Before 1965, one African American council member posed little threat to policy outcomes on city council. Although Cephas's election represented a monumental development in pre-1965 electoral politics, one councilman alone could do little to affect real change. Council members, policy makers, and civic organizations knew that it took five of nine votes to pass a city budget and six votes to pass special appropriations. African Americans and their allies may have fallen short of a city council majority in 1966, but they had enough representation at city hall to promote interests that white politicians had traditionally ignored.[28]

Although Henry Marsh had no experience in office holding, he had been active in local and national civil rights struggles for nearly a decade. In his early thirties in 1966, Marsh was very similar to Oliver Hill. He graduated with honors from VUU in 1956 with a degree in sociology. During his senior year, he served as president of student government and testified against massive resistance to integration in Virginia's General Assembly. He attended law school at Howard University, where his roommate was another Richmond native and VUU alum, Doug Wilder. Upon graduating from law school in 1959, Marsh dedicated his legal career to becoming the very type of social engineer that Hill and Charles Hamilton Houston had embodied in the late 1940s and 1950s. Marsh became a member of Hill's law firm, and they changed the firm's name to Hill, Tucker, and Marsh in 1965. By 1965, Marsh had already established a reputation as a legal advocate for civil rights. He also took on one of the most powerful institutions in Richmond and the Commonwealth of Virginia: big tobacco. He eventually litigated one of the first cases under Title VII of the Civil Rights Act of 1964, *Quarles v. Philip Morris* (1968). *Quarles* set the legal precedent for criminalizing departmental seniority systems and for requiring equal pay under Title VII. Marsh and S. W. Tucker also argued *Brewer v. School Board of City of Norfolk* (1968), which set the standard for school districts to devise sufficient desegregation plans and free transportation for students. Even before becoming a public servant, Marsh had proven that he was a champion for Richmond's most vulnerable communities. Shortly after his election to the Richmond City Council, he held, "It's a mistake to relax now and to worry about too much power. Only by using power . . . can Negroes force action to improve education, housing, recreation, and job opportunities." From the moment Marsh entered the public sphere, he argued that good government was contingent on residents' participation.[29]

Howard Carwile also fought on the frontlines for racial justice. Known in Richmond for his weekly *Afro* columns and for losing eighteen consecutive bids for public office, Carwile was a fiery Charlotte County,

Virginia, native and graduate of the Southeastern University School of Law in Washington, D.C. From the 1940s to the 1960s, Carwile represented a number of African American clients against the Richmond Police Department (RPD) and Virginia's penal system. By the mid-1960s, most of Richmond's African Americans considered the white trial lawyer a genuine friend of black communities. Even staunch segregationist James Kilpatrick of the *Richmond News-Leaders* admitted that Carwile represented "a kind of special ultra-liberal, lone-wolf, back-handed conservative whose public career had been built entirely upon his passionate opposition to the state." In his first day on the council, Carwile put forth a motion to change council meetings from day to night so that working-class Richmonders might participate effectively in local government. Between 1966 and 1968, Marsh and Carwile invested in the city's residents by championing police accountability, defending residents from the politics of eminent domain, and fighting against annexation.[30]

The problem of police brutality was one of the first major issues that emerged after the election of 1966. Southerners' use of official police power to maintain and enforce Jim Crow dated back to the post-Reconstruction era, the rise of black codes, and the reorganization of the black labor force, and police brutality remained a constant theme throughout the civil rights movement. Over the course of the twentieth century, white America officially reinforced racial apartheid in the North and the South by using police forces to restrict blacks' freedom in both public and private life. Accusations of police brutality echoed throughout the black freedom struggle, particularly when direct-action demonstrators engaged southern officials. As African Americans elected public officials to governing bodies, this issue took center stage. Like many police departments throughout America, the RPD had a checkered reputation with African Americans. On one hand, it had appointed its first black police officers in 1942 and gave them the authority to arrest and detain the city's white residents. On the other hand, the city's white officers often trumped up minor charges on African Americans, used indiscriminate force to arrest and detain black suspects, and held black communities in general contempt. During 1966, Richmond's African Americans took these grievances straight to city hall. Richmond's police records, *Afro* columnists charged, "were replete with genuine cases of police brutality" that had been historically ignored and suppressed by the RPD and the city council. In early 1966, African Americans organized a series of meetings following an incident in which witnesses watched white officers slap a pregnant African American female, drag her across an intersection, and throw her into a squad car. That same year witnesses also reported that a group of three young black men were pulled from their car at gunpoint for no apparent reason and severely beaten by officers in broad daylight. African Americans' testimonies traditionally fell on deaf ears—but not in 1966.[31]

The RPD's critics found a champion in Councilman Carwile, John Brooks, and the NAACP. Carwile made good on his promise to promote transparency on the city council and the interests of Richmond's residents. He put forward a resolution that called for an interracial citizens' review board of the RPD, to be called the Civilian and Police Complaint Review Board. The city council was to appoint five residents for the review board, and the Board of Public Safety was to appoint four police officers. The review board, if approved, would have the authority to review complaints against police, evaluate police complaints against supervisors, employ private investigators, and report findings to the city council. In his attempt to increase political transparency, Carwile suggested that the review board would also report directly to the city council, not to the city manager's administration. As things stood at the time, bureaucracy characterized the process of lodging complaints against the RPD. Residents reported incidents of police misconduct to the city manager and officials in the city manager's office, who then forwarded these complaints *to the RPD* for further investigation. In September 1966, Carwile, Brooks, and E. L. Slade, president of Richmond's NAACP chapter, urged African Americans to attend council meetings to lobby for the resolution to form the Civilian and Police Complaint Review Board. Proponents stressed that the review board would not only mitigate tension between Richmond police and African Americans but also convince African Americans that city hall finally planned to defend black communities from the bureaucracy that had sheltered local law enforcement for decades.[32]

More than one hundred people attended the police review board hearing at city hall. Mayor Morrill Crowe, council members, and Richmond residents listened to three hours of testimony by twenty-one Richmond residents, four local ministers, John Brooks, W. Lester Banks, Curtis Holt of the Creighton Court Civic Group, and a white student from Richmond Professional Institute (now Virginia Commonwealth University). Citizens' testimonies ranged from complaints about being called "boy" to claims of unjustifiable arrests and unprovoked gun pointing. Two local reverends argued that denunciation of the review board was tantamount to a rejection of men who favored a peaceful resolution. As Rev. Reginald Wimbush maintained, "If we turn down this good ordinance, we're opening the door to people who want things done less peaceful. I beg you to give the ordinance a try." Shortly after the testimonies, the city council voted down the resolution seven to two. Marsh and Carwile, in fact, were the only two council members to vote in favor of it. After black councilmen Cephas and Mundle sounded off nays, Brooks and Lester Banks stormed out of council chambers murmuring profanities about both men. It is hard to know whether class considerations or loyalty to the RPD influenced these two council members' votes. Although both men shared business interests with the white establishment, it is more likely that neither Mundle nor Cephas wanted to support Carwile—who in 1966 had few allies at city hall—at the expense of alienating members of the RPD or the council. One thing is certain—the matter of police review had profound implications for both men's prospects in the council election of 1968.[33]

The next phase of expressway construction led to more controversy on the Richmond City Council. In 1966, Virginia's General Assembly created the Richmond Metropolitan Authority (RMA) in order to build an intercounty expressway system that more efficiently connected the City of Richmond to Henrico and Chesterfield Counties. Because of strict regulations governing city–county independence, Richmond, Henrico, and Chesterfield needed the General Assembly's approval to build an intercounty expressway system. It also turned out that five of the RMA's six board members were active RF members. The RMA and the engineering firm Howard, Needles, Tommen, and Bergendoff from Alexandria, Virginia, released their plan to construct a limited-access tollroad system that would lead from the city's suburbs into downtown Richmond. These toll roads were to serve two purposes—generate revenue and ease the commute for suburban workers and shoppers. The 12.8-mile stretch of expressways and parkways, policy makers argued, was to "become the metropolitan area's . . . backbone." Four sections made up the $95 million system: Riverside Parkway would extend 3.1 miles from the Huguenot Bridge to Powhite Parkway; Powhite Parkway would stretch 2.3 miles from Chippenham Parkway to the north abutment of the James River Bridge; the Beltline Expressway would then take over from the James River Bridge and cover 3.6 miles to the interchange with the Richmond Petersburg Turnpike (Interstates 95 and 64); and last, the Downtown Expressway would connect to the Beltline Expressway near the City Stadium neighborhood and run 3.8 miles through the Idlewood Street corridor toward downtown Richmond. The City of Richmond, in conjunction with the State Highway Commission, the Chesterfield Board of Supervisors, and the Henrico Board of Supervisors, proposed to clear $2,050,000 of operating capital and to guarantee another $20,000,000 to help support construction of the downtown segment. The Downtown Expressway, which would effectively sever the Randolph and Oregon Hill neighborhoods from Richmond Professional Institute, drew the most criticism. The Alexandria firm proposed to build this section of the system directly through three communities just west of downtown: Oregon Hill, Randolph, and Byrd Park. The construction had to wait until a public hearing in November 1966.[34]

Marsh and Carwile were the Downtown Expressway's chief critics. If the RMA implemented the current plan, they argued, the expressway system would displace nearly 1,000 residents. Marsh had a large number of constituents in the predominantly African American Randolph area, and Carwile came to the defense of Oregon Hill, a predominantly working-class, white neighborhood. Marsh, Slade, and Thornton urged developers to build the expressway closer to the James River, where there were fewer homes. The RMA, however, was under the authority of the General Assembly. In fact, by state law the Richmond City Council had no authority to build an expressway that extended to Henrico and Chesterfield Counties—Richmond officials could vote to approve only the Downtown Expressway and partially fund its construction. Marsh and Carwile argued that $2 million worth of city loans and the guaranteeing of another $20 million to cover the cost of planning made the construction of the expressway the city residents' business. When the council voted six to three to approve the downtown segment's construction in late 1966 (Carwile,

Cephas, and Marsh voted against the measure), Carwile protested that he and hundreds of protestors would stand in front of the RMA's bulldozers! Marsh, ever the consummate lawyer, attempted to delay construction of the expressway in order to find an alternative route. The city council, under pressure from metropolitan forces that needed the downtown route to connect to the entire system, voted Marsh's measure down five to four in November—this time, Mundle, Cephas, and Carwile voted with Marsh. At the meeting on whether to delay the downtown segment's construction, the Crusade's Milton Randolph articulated, "We are conscious of and fully sympathetic to the alleged progress needed in this community, but we also definitely feel that government has the moral responsibility to be fair and honest with its entire citizenry." Randolph knew that the displaced African Americans would struggle to find alternative housing.[35]

Debates about eminent domain and neighborhood clearance again heightened concerns about the relationship between public opinion and policy outcomes. During the 1950s, African Americans had been essentially powerless against the forces of urban renewal and slum clearance. If the expressway dilemma raised African Americans' anxieties about the city's redevelopment policies, it also piqued their reservations about the relationship between policy implementation and property ownership. Black residents often paid more for substandard housing than whites, and Richmond's long-standing practice of allowing restrictive covenants often made it harder for African Americans to find housing. It was going to be even more difficult to find housing when nearly 1,000 displaced Richmonders were on the market. Although the expressway system was going to displace more white than black families, the displaced African Americans would have an additional problem: their homes in the Randolph area had exceptionally low property values. Ninety-two percent of the owner-occupied homes in Randolph's two census tracts most affected by the downtown route reported values of less than $10,000 in 1960, even though the median home price in Richmond in the same year was roughly $58,000. These two census tracts were also 75 percent and 69 percent African American, respectively. More ominously, 52.6 percent of the people (492) in one of Randolph's census tracts and 39 percent (297) in the other made less than $3,000 annually. African American leaders knew that these people—renters and homeowners alike—would struggle to find alternative housing. "Not a single one of them," Oliver Hill argued, "is going to get a fair market value for their property." At a special city council hearing, Crusade vice president Wilmer Wilson argued, "We were driven out of Navy Hill, out of East Leigh St., and out of the East End for Route 64. We've got no place to go, and we're going to stand up here and fight. . . . [T]his is a Richmond Forward effort to divide and conquer. . . . We're going to meet you gentlemen (RF) again at the ballot box." As African Americans came to understand the harsh nature of the policy process, the link between voting and policy outcomes became decidedly more apparent. Mundle, who was the only African American to vote in favor of the Downtown Expressway plan, contended that Richmond's economic viability was contingent upon building a direct route, free of traffic stops, that connected commuters to the city's center. Although that proposition is debatable, the certainty that Mundle's position depended on the will of the people was not. They would soon remind him of the connection between votes and his voting record. After the expressway affair, black voters realized the imperative to form an autonomous political bloc capable of offering its own planning agenda.[36]

Many of the homes in the Idlewood corridor were reappraised at full value, and the RMA covered homeowners' moving expenses, but poorer individuals generally lost out. Randolph's most vulnerable residents, like the residents displaced earlier by the Richmond–Petersburg Turnpike, were often relocated to public-housing projects. In August 1967, the RRHA approved the construction of 824 public-housing units, 500 of which were located in the Blackwell School area of South Richmond. The city used $15 million of federal grant money to support the relocation of Randolph's residents—the displaced were to be moved to new housing projects in Gilpin Court, Mosby Court, and the Blackwell area. One year later these residents were to bypass 1,500 people on Richmond's public-housing waiting list because there were only 2,885 total public-housing units in the entire city in 1967. The U.S. Department of Housing and Urban Development also set aside $80,000 to finance the Calhoun Community Center in Gilpin Court. City officials contended that these relocation initiatives were commensurate with modernity. Councilman Bagley argued, "This is a gigantic step to replace substandard housing with modern and acceptable living accommodations." Few of Randolph's low-income residents would have considered their neighborhood's quaint bungalows unacceptable living conditions, and even fewer, given the number of people who stood with Carwile at city hall in the spring of 1966, wanted to move. In the spring of 1967, construction crews broke ground on the Downtown Expressway, and it took roughly ten years to complete the entire project. Even Crusade cofounder William Thornton was not immune to the expressway's construction; the downtown section of the expressway system destroyed his childhood home in the Idlewood corridor.[37]

Not long after the expressway debates, city officials and RF revived the possibility of suburb annexation. Richmond's expressway crisis was chockfull of anxiety about class, urban decline, suburban growth, and the flow of revenue sources across county lines. Henrico and Chesterfield Counties, both of which were administratively and financially independent of Richmond, had undergone exceptional population growth between 1950 and 1970. Not only had the city obliterated black neighborhoods and compressed low-income residents into public-housing projects to make way for expressways, but these efforts and the possibility of broad-based public-school integration had also set off a "chain reaction" of white flight to the counties. It just so happened that Henrico and Chesterfield Counties had thousands of acres of available land to accommodate both population growth and business growth.

Figure 2.1

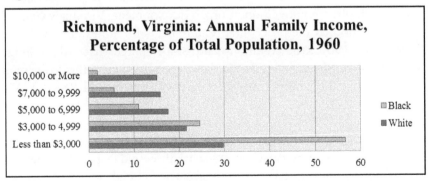

Source: U.S. Bureau of the Census, "Annual Family Income, Richmond, Virginia, 1960," Social Explorer, table, http://www.socialexplorer.com/tables/C1960TractDS/ R11289279 (accessed November 20, 2016).

Table 2.1. Richmond, Henrico County, and Chesterfield County, 1950–1970

Location and Year	Total Population	Total Square Miles	White Population	Nonwhite Population	Percentage of White Population	Percentage of Nonwhite Population
Richmond, 1950	230,310	39.98	157,228	73,082	68	32
Chesterfield County, 1950	40,400	459.56	31,969	8,431	79	21
Henrico County, 1950	57,340	244.60	51,650	5,690	90	10
Richmond, 1960	219,958	39.98	127,627	92, 331	58	42
Chesterfield County, 1960	71,197	459.56	61,762	9,435	87	13
Henrico County, 1960	117,338	244.60	111,269	6,069	95	5
Richmond, 1970	249,621	62.55	143,842	105,779	58	42
Chesterfield County, 1970	78,855	436.99	68,056	8,799	89	11
Henrico County, 1970	154,364	244.60	143,692	10,672	93	7

Sources: Data from U.S. Bureau of the Census, *Census of Population and Housing* (Washington, D.C.: U.S. Bureau of the Census, 1950, 1960, and 1970), and Eleanor P. Sheppard Papers, 1924–1978, M277, Cabell Black Collection, James Branch Cabell Library, Virginia Commonwealth University.

During the mid–twentieth century, the commonwealth's arrangement of city–county separation and the procedural requirements for annexation often impinged upon urban development. Virginia's General Assembly adopted the procedural requirements for annexation in 1904. During the 1960s, the commonwealth still required that a three-judge panel approve annexations. To this day, experts recognize the problem of annexation in the commonwealth. Andrew V. Sorrell and Bruce A. Vlk maintain:

In comparison to other states, Virginia's annexation process is unique with its reliance on a special three-judge panel. Other states, where the stakes are not generally as high for cities and counties because an annexation would not remove a portion of a county's tax base, use a variety of methods, such as special legis-

Table 2.2. Richmond Metropolitan Area Land Use, 1964

Land-Use Type	Henrico County		Chesterfield County		Richmond		Metro Area	
	Net Acres	and % of Developed Land	Net Acres	and % of Developed Land	Net Acres	and % of Developed Land	Net Acres	and % of Developed Land
Residential: Single Family and Duplex	15,755	51	9,379	42	6,794	34	31,928	44
Residential: Multifamily	485	2	92	1	847	4	1,424	2
Manufacturing: Industrial	734	2	986	4	1,304	7	3,024	4
Transportation, Terminals, Communication, Public Utilities, Public and Semipublic Buildings, Wholesale and Contracting	3,238	11	945	4	1,343	7	5,526	7
Retail and Services	895	3	545	2	769	4	2,209	3
Schools	684	2	330	2	613	3	1,627	2
Parks and Recreation	1,957	6	3,159	14	2,062	10	7,178	10
Transport Garages and Parking Lots	6,913	23	7,026	31	6,266	31	20,205	28
Developed Land, subtotal	30,661	100	22,462	100	19,998	100	73,121	100
		% of Total Land		% of Total Land		% of Total Land		% of Total Land
Vacant Land	123,436	80	265,899	92	5,666	22	395,001	84
Total Land Area	154,097	100	288,361	100	25,664	100	486,122	100

Sources: Data from U.S. Bureau of the Census, *Census of Population and Housing* (Washington, D.C.: U.S. Bureau of the Census, 1950); U.S. Bureau of the Census, *Census of Population and Housing* (Washington, D.C.: U.S. Bureau of the Census, 1960); U.S. Bureau of the Census, *Census of Population and Housing* (Washington, D.C.: U.S. Bureau of the Census, 1970); and Eleanor P. Sheppard Papers, 1924–1978, M277, Cabell Black Collection, M306, James Branch Cabell Library, Virginia Commonwealth University, Richmond.

lative act, ordinance, popular determination, judicial process and
administrative agency. Virginia's use of a judiciary-led process can
take on political and legislative roles at times. In the past, most
annexations occurred by a city filing suit in the annexation court
to annex a stretch of land in a neighboring county. . . . In addition, the prevailing city was typically required to compensate the
neighboring county for the annexed land.

Virginia's system of city–county separation and the cumbersome annexation process also hurt Richmond's ability to accommodate urban growth
during the mid–twentieth century. Richmond had not annexed a surrounding area since 1942, when state officials awarded the city a little
more than 17 square miles of Henrico County. The question of a boundary expansion reemerged again in the early 1960s. At that time, the
city's need to annex portions of an adjoining county was strictly financial. Richmond required vacant, developable land to accommodate postwar growth. In 1961, city officials petitioned again to annex portions of
Henrico County, which had roughly 123,000 net acres of vacant land.
After the three-judge panel rejected Henrico County's appeal, the court
awarded Richmond 16.16 square miles (10,340 acres) with a population
of 45,310 and ordered the city to spend $13,490,000 within five years on
capital improvements in the annexed area. City officials, however, turned
down the award in 1965 because the target area lacked the undeveloped
and commercial land necessary for future development.[38]

Richmond and Chesterfield County officials scheduled a pretrial conference for annexation in early 1967. The pretrial established hearings
for an annexation suit on August 5, 1968. In the meantime, Virginia's
General Assembly and Governor Godwin had established a commission
in 1966, led by Dr. T. Marshall Hahn of Virginia Tech, to study the
implications of urban growth in the commonwealth. Known as the Virginia Metropolitan Areas Study Commission, or Hahn Commission, the
fifteen-member committee spent nearly a year examining the impact of
urbanization on local governments and the problems associated with
regional planning and annexations. The Hahn Commission released its
report in 1967 and made a series of proposals about the future of annexations in the commonwealth. It first proposed that the General Assembly

overhaul the state's three-member judicial commission that specialized exclusively in annexation suits. It then suggested that policy makers could streamline the commonwealth's otherwise unwieldy system of judicial annexations by placing special annexation courts in major population centers. Although the "major thrust of the commission dealt largely with the impact of urbanization on local governments" and with the state's role in addressing these circumstances, the focus on annexations represented a growing anxiety among Virginia's white policy makers: African Americans now had or were close to having population advantages in many of the commonwealth's major cities.[39]

The politics of race and urbanization saturated the commission's report. The commission argued, "The steady concentration in the city of colored, the disadvantaged and the low-income groups is a major concern not only to the city but to the entire metropolitan area. If the governments of the Richmond area do not resolve this problem together, the effects will damage not only the Richmond area but the state as a whole." Implicit in this recognition was the notion that mergers were a necessary means to maintain the economic viability of Virginia's urban centers. Councilman Phil Bagley represented whites' anxieties about the closing window of opportunity for a merger should blacks take over the city council in 1968. He contended, "It should be noted that there are at least 250,000 people in Chesterfield and Henrico County, and these (board) actions represent the opinion of a few men whose terms of office expire in several months." Bagley knew that the election of future white council members was contingent upon stemming the tide of black population growth in the city.[40]

The Crusade rallied against the Hahn Commission's report. In 1967, the Crusade, Carwile, and Marsh thought that the commission, though introduced as a color-blind initiative to probe the relationship between state-level regulations and cities' financial sustainability, was nothing more than a data-collection scheme to support annexationist proclivities. Carwile contended in early February that annexation was tantamount to vote dilution and that a Chesterfield merger represented the "last desperate hope of the survival of white supremacy in this metropolitan area." Seven days later he suggested in an *Afro* editorial titled "A Merger Would Dilute Votes" that annexation might undermine roughly ten years of progress. The Crusade believed that city officials' preoccupation with annexation had taken precedent over more pressing issues—namely, the growing problems of poverty and schools. Marsh agreed, maintaining that the acquisition of an adjoining county would do little to alleviate problems such as poverty. Marsh, Carwile, and the Crusade also understood that state regulations made it difficult for Richmond to meet the challenges of growth.[41]

In a revolutionary maneuver, the Crusade threw its support behind annexation on the condition that the city switch from an at-large to a district-based election system. Thornton claimed in June 1966, "I would think we'd not be opposed if different areas could have representation. Maybe there should be 13 districts and 13 members of Council so we'd be always assured of representation." The last portion of Thornton's contention was essential to the Crusade's approach to the annexation question. The notion of "assured" representation drove its creation of the merger study commission in 1966 and guided its approach to the annexation dilemma throughout the 1970s. The Crusade wanted African American council representation in proportion to the number of Richmond's voting-age African Americans. The merger study commission argued: "We contend that any plan to merge or consolidate Richmond and any of its neighboring governments should provide for area representation within the merged or consolidated complex. These areas should have equitable apportionment and geographic integrity. This method of district or ward election of local and also state officials should be employed to help assure that areas of any merged complex be fairly represented and that the people who live in the various areas have the opportunity to participate in the political complex." Should Richmond annex portions of a predominantly white county and keep its at-large election system, African Americans did not have the numbers to win a city council majority or to elect more than a handful of black officials. At a meeting of roughly twenty-five Crusade members on July 18, one member asked, "How would we benefit as a city [from annexation]? I heard that it would dilute the Negro Vote." Thornton answered, "If we get representation on Council, there would be no dilution."[42]

Richmond's city council election of 1968 also coincided with a series of monumental national crises. The assassinations of Martin Luther King

Jr. on April 4, 1968, and Senator Robert Kennedy on June 6, 1968, had a profound influence on the tenor of the election. Both King and Kennedy had emerged as champions of civil rights and defenders of America' poor communities. Their assassinations devastated not just America but also progressives' and civil rights activists' momentum. By 1968, King had long since started the transition from civil rights to human rights, and the SCLC had begun to focus more broadly on economic justice regardless of race. Created in November 1967, King's Poor People's Campaign organized an interracial coalition of activists that was to travel by caravan from Memphis to the nation's capital. The campaign's organizers resolved to bring attention to the national crisis of poverty by building a shantytown in Washington, D.C. Shortly after King's death, SCLC president Ralph Abernathy led nearly 3,000 predominantly African American volunteers from Memphis to a camp near the Washington Monument, which they called "Resurrection City." The campaign made a stop in Richmond on its way to the District of Columbia. While in Richmond, the participants held a series of small demonstrations that rebroadcast their list of demands: adequate jobs, decent minimum-wage standards, guaranteed annual income, adequate housing for the poor. The stop in Richmond, court testimony later revealed, "was well received" by many of the capital city's African Americans. Just prior to the city council election of 1968, the Crusade decided to honor King's memory by carrying the banner of his final initiative, the Poor People's Campaign. It endorsed an interracial slate of five candidates and called it the "Poor People's Ticket." On June 9, 1968, the eve of the city council election, the front page of the *Richmond Times-Dispatch* ran three headlines: "Mass for Kennedy Attended by 2,000"; "Scotland Yard Arrests King Murder Suspect"; and "16 Candidates Vie for 9 Seats Here." Both the *Afro* and the *Times-Dispatch* claimed that this election was the most important contest in Richmond's political history.[43]

Although the annexation question dictated the election, national crises also brought voters out in record numbers. The Crusade capitalized on the racial tumult of that year. For the first time in the 1960s, it chose not to endorse an RF candidate. The Poor People's Ticket also uniformly renounced any form of annexation if it did not contain a ward plan. The Crusade ballot included Howard Carwile and Henry Marsh as well as a white Presbyterian minister named James "Jim" Carpenter. By 1966, Carpenter, a native of Coal City, Illinois, and a graduate of Monmouth College, had been in Richmond for roughly seven years. He was also the senior pastor at the predominantly African American All Souls Presbyterian Church on Richmond's north side. He had also done several years of missionary work in and around what is now the Democratic Republic of the Congo. In explaining his reasons for entering the council race, Carpenter claimed, "It's sometimes much easier to go to the Congo and be a missionary than to serve among American Negroes; many people find it easier to love their brothers who are far away than those who are next door." Carpenter had proven to be an advocate for African Americans over the 1960s and argued for a city–county merger only if planners adopted "a plan of fair representation." The Crusade also endorsed thirty-six-year-old African American Walter T. Kenney. An Armstrong High graduate and East Ender, Kenney was executive vice president of Richmond Postal Clerks Local 199 and an active member of Richmond's chapter of the NAACP. The Crusade also threw support behind its president and *Afro* columnist Milton Randolph, who resigned his presidency upon entering the race. The Poor People's Ticket vowed to place the people's interests over individual and corporate pursuits by emphasizing jobs and adequate housing for the city's poorer residents. Above all, each candidate would support annexation only if the city adopted a district system.[44]

RF intensified its efforts to maintain a council majority. Whites endorsed an interracial slate of candidates who favored annexation without a district system: Phil J. Bagley Jr., Thomas J. Bliley Jr., Morrill M. Crowe, Nathan J. Forb, James C. Wheat Jr., Sonny Cephas, Winfred Mundle, and Nell B. Pusey. Unlike their previous campaigns, however, whites organized precinct-based strategies to counter the Crusade's registration efforts. Teams of RF supporters manned telephones and contacted registered voters in predominantly white precincts. RF's ultimate plan was to maintain a council majority in order to move forward with annexation plans. Just prior to the election, Councilman Wheat argued that if Richmond were not allowed to annex a suburb in the immediate future, the city would be flooded by blacks, who were not only unproductive but incapable of managing city affairs. Mayor Crowe told the *Afro* that annexation "should be aggressively pursued to increase the tax base." Bagley, Crow, and Wheat openly expressed opinions that drove the annexation debates privately: white Richmonders had declared a demographic crisis as a cover for their plans to appropriate nearly 45,000 white suburban residents.[45]

The Crusade failed to sweep RF out of office, though it had enough electoral pull to oust Mundle and Cephas. Voting patterns in 1968 continued to creep toward an even split between white and black voters. In the election of 1968, 44,880 Richmonders voted—8,632 more than in the election of 1966. Of this total, 44 percent (19,821) were African American, and 56 percent (25,059) were white. The number of white voters increased by 4,547 between 1966 and 1968. Voters reelected Carwile and Marsh, and elected Jim Carpenter to his first council term. In predominantly black precincts, Carwile and Carpenter garnered nearly 10,000 more votes than Cephas and Mundle, who also trailed RF candidates in predominantly white precincts by nearly 1,200. Carpenter finished fifth of nine, and Carwile won the election with 25,576 votes. (For the full election results, see tables 6 and 7 in the appendix.) If there were any doubts about Carwile's standing with African Americans, this election put them to rest. The self-proclaimed populist won 89 percent of the black vote. Marsh finished sixth and received 91 percent of African Americans' votes. The election results of 1968 had profound implications for the future of racial politics in Richmond: Marsh was the only African American left on the city council, and Carwile shocked the city by winning the election.[46]

Mundle, and to a lesser extent Cephas, met the same fate as gradualist leaders a decade earlier. In his delineation of African American presidential appointees, N. D. B. Connolly argues that "one generation's progressives are often another generation's obstructionists." If the election of 1968 demonstrated anything, it showed that African Americans wanted representatives, regardless of race, who advocated on their behalf. Cephas and Mundle's failure to crack the top-nine vote getters was proof that African Americans were a collection of moving and at times contradictory constituencies. In 1966, the Crusade hoped that both men would split their allegiances between RF and African American constituents. *Ebony* magazine's article in 1966 had praised Mundle's rise to local political prominence. Mundle was a successful businessman, an influential member of local civic organizations such as the Young Men's Christian Association, and a leader in the Boy Scouts of America. But *Ebony* also recognized that the vice mayor struggled to negotiate the pressure "between the Crusade for Voters and the downtown business establishment." Mundle, for instance, voted to appoint Morrill Crowe mayor in 1966 against the Crusade's wishes, supported staggered elections, and voted in favor of the Downtown Expressway. Both Cephas and Mundle also voted against Carwile's proposal to establish the Civilian and Police Complaint Review Board, after which Brooks, who still held sway over the Crusade and the Richmond black body politic, claimed that both had sold out their race. RF confirmed Brooks's contention by supporting the reelection of both men. The Crusade refused to place Cephas and Mundle on the Poor People's Ticket after they also failed to support the adoption of a district plan should Richmond annex portions of a surrounding county. Ultimately, community advocacy and the politics of civil rights dictated whom black Richmonders voted for in 1968. Although Marsh was the only African American left on the city council, blacks felt assured that at least three council members were allies of their communities' interests. As supporters of the Black Power movement began to challenge the civil rights movement's integrationist tendencies, Richmond's African Americans rejected the practice of supporting black officials simply because they were black. The question, however, was whether the three council members supported by the Crusade could effectively contest six members of the RF team.[47]

The Politics of Dilution

Just five days after President Johnson signed the VRA on August 6, 1965, an urban rebellion erupted in a predominantly African American section of Los Angeles called Watts. Thousands of African Americans had relocated to southern California during World War II in search of wartime employment. By the 1960s, Watts had become synonymous not with African American upward mobility but with the perpetuation of poverty and bigotry. Thirty-four percent of Watt's black males were unemployed in the 1960s. More ominously, "200 of the 205 police officers" in the district police force that patrolled Watts "were white." The rebellion broke out after white police officers arrested an African American male for allegedly driving under the influence. After six days of arson and looting, thirty-four people had lost their lives, and city officials estimated the damage at $45 million. The Watts rebellion drove home the reality that American bigotry was not exclusive to the South. When Richmond's Rev. Wimbush argued that not passing a resolution to form the Civilian and Police Complaint Review Board would open the door to "people who want things done less peaceful," he had Watts and the Black Power movement in mind. Watts also portended a succession of long, hot, violent summers. During the summer of 1967, 163 racial uprisings spread from Newark, New Jersey, to Detroit. One year later tens of thousands of African Americans responded to the assassination of Dr. King, arguably the most peaceful representative to emerge from the freedom struggle, by participating in dozens of uprisings. After King's death, rebellions broke out in cities such as Baltimore, Chicago, and Washington, D.C. The rebellion in Watts in 1965 and then the scores of uprisings after King's death in 1968 signified blacks' growing discontent with the continuation of oppression in America. The poverty in Watts also confirmed that the Great Society's civil rights reforms were not happening fast enough.[48]

Few cities were immune to urban unrest between 1965 and 1968. As whites devised backlash mechanisms to weaken civil and voting rights mandates, many African Americans lost faith in America's capacity to reform itself through politics. Racial turbulence and heightened demands for full equality also piqued whites' nervousness about growing black radicalism. The fear of a black takeover rose not only in cities that witnessed actual racial unrest but also in cities such as Richmond, where African Americans had few ties to black radicalism or interest in popular appeals to the Black Power movement. By the election of 1968, even Richmond's Poor People's Ticket gave rise to suspicions of latent radicalism. William S. White of the *Richmond Times-Dispatch* claimed less than two months after King's assassination, "Sad and slick are the words of plain truth for the poor people's march on Washington—sad . . . because this is an exercise in brazen hucksterism from top to bottom. . . . White politicians who so tirelessly proclaim their own unique compassion for the black race are egging on this thing." White represented the silent majority of white Americans who had grown weary of African Americans' insistence on immediate access to power and of liberal policy makers who indulged these forces of equality from Washington. As African American populations eclipsed white populations throughout America's cities, this weariness turned into defensive action. In Richmond, defensive action found a home in boundary expansion.[49]

At the very moment Richmond's African Americans began to make strides toward black governance, whites began to associate their appeals for representative equality not merely with Black Power movements but with the urban tumult unfolding in America's cities in the late 1960s. The USCCR's report on voting rights in 1968, *Political Participation,* was in many ways a reflection on the dialectic between black political power and white resistance. The commission, with the aforementioned urban unrest in mind, claimed, "A major theme running through the history of Southern politics has been the fear of a Negro take-over of the political and governmental structure. . . . [T]he Negro has exercised a tyranny over the mind of the white south, which has found continuous expression in the politics of the region." Virginia's General Assembly anticipated that African Americans would destroy the statues on Monument Avenue commemorating fallen Confederate officers. State senator and Richmond pharmacist Edward E. Willey (the same Willey who attempted to pass the term-staggering resolution without a popular vote) proposed and passed a bill to protect these monuments should blacks overrun the city and attempt to destroy them. Councilman James Wheat believed that if blacks won the city council election of 1968, Richmond would become "a black ghetto." Even just the concept of Black Power piqued white anxiety. In fact, Richmond's white leadership often associated black political empowerment with black radicalism, despite the fact that the city's African Americans rarely engaged in public protest.[50]

There was a small yet lasting memory of student radicalism in Richmond before 1968. To be sure, Richmond's legacy of polite protest, respectability, and racial moderation informed the black leadership's approach to voting rights. Paternalism and racist civility also played a role in shaping the types of black activism that did and did not emerge in the capital city. Yet black college campuses such as VUU were fertile ground for student activism in the 1960s. Of the hundreds of thousands of black collegians in the early 1960s, 51 percent were enrolled in historically black colleges and universities. Although the types of violence and racial rigidity that helped radicalize Student Nonviolent Coordinating Committee workers and students in the Deep South—who were, in effect, shock troops for direct-action demonstrations—rarely took place in Richmond, students at VUU did organize direct-action strategies. The Richmond 34, a group of thirty-four VUU students, staged a number of demonstrations that eventually led to sit-ins at the lunch counter of Thalhimer's Department Store in February 1960. This student movement, unlike the movements led by younger generations of black Richmonders in the early 1970s, had the full support of the NAACP and men such as Oliver Hill. When the RPD arrested, jailed, and fined the students (to the tune of $20 per violation) for the events at Thalhimer's, it was Hill, local lawyer Clarence Newsome, and the NAACP who came to their legal defense. With the help of the NAACP, these protests continued for weeks. When the thirty-four students struggled to find bodies to sit at counters, members of local branches of the NAACP, including branch presidents, filled in. Two of the Richmond 34, Raymond B. Randolph Jr. and Charles Sherrod, even went on to participate in the Freedom Rides of 1961. Sherrod eventually settled at Shaw University in Raleigh, North Carolina—the very university where Ella Baker recruited black collegians into the Student Nonviolent Coordinating Committee during the early 1960s. At Shaw, Sherrod became one of the committee's founding members and went on to coordinate dozens of student-led movements across the South. Yet after these sit-ins Richmond did not witness another highly publicized, student-led outburst until 1970, when a young, Yale-educated attorney, Jeroyd Greene Jr. (who later changed his name to Sa'ad El-Amin), emerged as the city's most vocal critic of the white establishment and of older generations of middle-class black leadership (see chapter 3).[51]

African Americans—in Richmond and in the nation—struggled over the contested definitions of Black Power. "Black Power" emerged as an expression in the mid- to late 1960s and represented a host of things—from self-determination and cultural pride to self-defense, black nationalism, and separatism. In many ways, Richmond's African American leadership, who were the inheritors of gradualism, moderate race relations, and a strong NAACP presence, championed a regionally specific brand of black political empowerment rather than black nationalism or separatism. Until the early 1970s, Black Power in Richmond found continuous expression as a fundamentally political endeavor—black leadership expressed the ideals of self-determination and community empowerment through the competitive interaction of political interest groups. In terms of encouraging political self-determination, the Crusade and black leadership, for better or worse, held fast to the belief that black governance would engender greater community control. In this sense, they were not merely consummate pluralists; they believed that participatory democracy was essential to community empowerment. Richmond's black ministers also cautioned African Americans regarding the more *radical* elements within Black Power. When Carwile and demonstrators protested the construction of the Downtown Expressway in the spring of 1966, the minister of Riverview Baptist Church, E. E. Smith, made a point to distance the demonstrations from radicalism. Smith not only told the group to stay away from Black Power tactics but also argued, "We don't need black power as much as we need . . . spiritual power." Milton Randolph summed up these circumstances in 1966: "The colored race must form alliances and coalitions with liberal, progressive whites. Since he is [*sic*] a clear minority constituting only 10.5 percent of the total population, sheer arithmetic is against the success of any isolated program of action. There is no possibility of any black takeover of power. They, therefore, must have allies and friends. In pragmatic terms, Black Power, or domination, is a dangerous myth and self-defeating illusion." Men like Randolph and Smith continued to steer a course toward moderation despite the fact that Smith's church was almost demolished by the Downtown Expressway. To this day, Riverview Baptist sits just feet from the expressway's barrier fence.[52]

Richmond's final push to annex portions of Chesterfield County arose more immediately as a panic response to the election of 1968 and the racial unrest that overcame America during the late 1960s. Whites' attempts to nullify and dilute black political power were, however, more sophisticated and legalistic by the late 1960s. Although whites maintained a majority on the Richmond City Council after the election of 1968, they were disturbed by a number of trends. The Crusade failed to secure a council majority that year, but people began to associate the

Poor People's Ticket with a rise of black extremism. African Americans were also close to becoming nearly half of Richmond's total electorate, which led whites to believe that blacks might have enough votes in 1970 to elect a city council majority. It was mathematically possible that African Americans could outvote their white counterparts by 1970 if the number of black residents continued to increase and black voter turnout rose between 1968 and 1970. Howard Carwile, for example, won the election of 1968 with 89 percent of the black vote. Aside from Marsh, the Crusade, and the *Afro*, Carwile had been the white power structure's chief critic. In fact, the council members supported by RF tried to neutralize Carwile by refusing to appoint him to committees. His position as a defender of vulnerable communities, both white and black, was evident after he won the election. Moreover, both Carpenter and Carwile's elections "supported the analysis that the Negro voter was now more concerned about activism than color." This last point was particularly disturbing for RF because it had failed to forge interracial alliances in the run-up to the election, and Carwile's victory signified the fact that African Americans had embraced the politics of community control as much as race.[53]

If white leaders feared black radicalism, the fact that Richmond was becoming a majority-black city heightened their anxieties. During the 1960s alone, the black population of America's major cities increased nationally by an average of 35 percent, whereas white populations in those cities dropped by an average of 9 percent. Richmond was not only becoming more African American but also losing significant tax revenue to the surrounding counties as whites left the city. In September 1966, the *Richmond News-Leader* claimed, "For Richmond's purpose in boundary expansion is to keep the municipal body healthy, and without the youthful, productive families which traditionally settle in suburban areas, the city cannot keep pace with the demands of modern urbanization." Ironically, as historian Matthew Lassiter demonstrates, "the city's historical pattern of residential segregation, problematic urban renewal schemes, and other development policies had set this [process] in motion." These coded conversations about inner-city poverty and suburban productivity dictated public dialogue about annexation.[54]

Long-term demographic trends also gave rise to the push for annex-

ation. The Richmond metropolitan region's total square area, including
Chesterfield and Henrico Counties, was 744.14 square miles in 1960. Of
that total area, Richmond made up 39.98 square miles; Henrico County
comprised 244.6 square miles; and Chesterfield was the largest portion,
at 459.56 square miles. Richmond, in accordance with federal law, had
long since prohibited de jure residential segregation, yet blockbusting
and restrictive covenants remained common practices in 1968. Of Richmond's total sixty-two precincts in 1960, twenty-three were more than
80 percent white; eighteen were more than 80 percent African American; five were 99 percent white; two were 100 percent white; one was
100 percent African American; and two were 99 percent African American. In 1960, Richmond had a total population of 219,958. By 1968,
the city's population had decreased by nearly 3,500 to 216,451. The
U.S. Census Bureau estimated that in 1968 there were 108,398 whites
and 108,053 African Americans in the capital city. More ominously, it
reported that nearly 29 percent of Richmonders lived at or beneath the
poverty line. Conversely, Henrico and Chesterfield underwent significant
population growth. Between 1950 and 1970, the population of Henrico County increased by roughly 96,000 people, and 90 percent of the
county's inhabitants were white. During the same period, Chesterfield
grew by approximately 38,000 people and was 89 percent white. Not
only did Henrico and Chesterfield Counties increase in population, but
population growth in these suburbs began to drain Richmond's revenue
sources. For instance, the average value of the multifamily dwelling unit
in Richmond was $4,288 in 1970 compared to $11,972 in what became
the annexed area.[55]

Faced with the prospect of becoming a majority-black city, white
leadership decided to expedite the annexation of Chesterfield County in
1968. The actual plans for an annexation had been in the works for some
time. After an initial meeting with Mayor Crowe in 1965, Irvin Horner,
chairman of the Chesterfield County Board of Supervisors, met council
member Jim Wheat at the latter's country home in Farmville, Virginia. In
a sworn affidavit, Horner recalled:

This meeting was the first time [I] learned of the volume of people
that the city wanted, 44,000 people. This was the City's first and

Table 2.3. Comparison of Annexed Area Sought for Richmond in Court and Compromise Area Offered by Chesterfield County

	Annexed Area Sought	Annexed Area Agreed Upon
Area (in square miles)	50	23
Total Population	72,941	43,780
Nonwhite Population	3,300	3,000
Number of School-Age Children	20,329	11,921
School Capacity (total 19,716)	9,105	
Total Assessables	$202,517,000	$103,148,000

Source: Data from Richmond Annexation Files, 1942–1976, M183, Cabell Black Collection, M306, James Branch Cabell Library, Virginia Commonwealth University, Richmond.

Prime condition. No mention was made of amount of territory, tax base, or any other considerations by the City. The 44,000 figure was firmly established at the beginning. . . . I knew the county had to save its water plant and utilities, and there based on our absolute need to save these facilities. . . . Every attempt I made to have the City discuss geographical limits was ignored and Mr. Wheat and the others continued to limit the conversation purely to the amount. . . . The City demanded 44,000 people.

After the General Assembly rejected the Hahn Commission's suggestion to overhaul the state's annexation process, local elites began to secretively iron out a boundary agreement that the commonwealth's three-judge annexation panel might approve. Richmond mayor Phil Bagley and Chesterfield County chairman Irvin G. Horner led this process. The City of Richmond initially sought to annex a little more than 50 square miles and 72,000 people—roughly 65 percent of Chesterfield County's total population. Chesterfield officials rejected this proposal on May 3, 1969, offering instead a line that would give the city 38,000 residents. Richmond officials, however, "could not agree on less than 48,000 people."[56]

In May 1969, Bagley and Horner agreed on a plan that would award Richmond roughly 23 square miles (14,842 acres) and 44,000 people. The Horner–Bagley line, should the annexation panel approve of the settlement, was to run across southwestern portions of Richmond—starting at Walmsley Boulevard, the line would wind its way around Fall Creek to Chippenham Parkway and after a series of twists and turns end up at the James River along the original annexation line that officials had proposed in 1961. The compromise also included financial considerations. Richmond agreed to pay the Chesterfield County School Board costs, proposed a five-year capital improvement program, absolved Chesterfield's outstanding sewage- and water-facility debt (all $24,190,000 of it), and paid for a host of other transitional costs. Horner later argued that Chesterfield's growing sewage and water problem, which was completely independent of the City of Richmond and the James River, had been one of the motivating factors in the annexation compromise. The city promised also to build five new schools in the annexed area. The deal ultimately, and this would prove critical years later, lacked substantial undeveloped industrial, commercial, and residential space—the original justification for a city–county merger in the first place. Of the entire 23 square miles proposed in the annexation suit, only 27 percent lay vacant.[57]

In May 1969, the Richmond City Council (in a vote of six to three) and the Chesterfield County Board of Supervisors approved the Horner–Bagley compromise. Richmond filed its final suit against Chesterfield County on January 2, 1969, and the three-judge annexation panel rushed a decision on July 1, 1969. Marsh, Carpenter, and Carwile were virtually frozen out of Horner and Bagley's negotiations. In a decree entered on July 12, the state annexation panel, led by Judge Earl L. Abbott, adopted verbatim the compromise settlement ironed out by Horner and Bagley. Richmond's annexation of Chesterfield was to take effect at midnight on December 31, 1969. The final settlement, which cost Richmond an initial $27 million, included only half of the land the city originally sought and fewer residents from Chesterfield County than city officials wanted. On January 1, 1970, the City of Richmond incorporated roughly 44,000 new citizens. Of those 44,000 new residents, only 1,557 were African American. The annexed area's residents, experts later concluded, contributed $337.47 per capita per year in local revenue to Richmond and sustained $239.15 per capita in expenditures. The median family income of the annexed area was $12,400, whereas that of Richmond's stood at $7,692. In the fiscal year before annexation, Richmond brought in

$19,648,975 in real estate tax; in the fiscal year 1970–1971, one year fol-
lowing annexation, the city collected $30,424,500. All told, annexation
was going to reduce Richmond's black population from 52 to 42 percent
of the total population. The proportion of voting-age African Americans
would drop from 45 percent to 37 percent.[58]

African Americans were not the only people in the Richmond metropolitan area to oppose annexation; many Chesterfield County residents
and a handful of companies openly fought the city–county merger. Antiannexation movements in Chesterfield also affirmed that race alone was
not the sole barometer of the metropolitan area's political culture. White
residents in what became the annexed area rarely openly expressed their
opposition to a merger in terms of race and instead often communicated
their desire to remain independent of Richmond in terms of upward
mobility and economic freedom. Between 1966 and 1969, the DuPont
Corporation, located in Chesterfield County, intervened to stop the
annexation of its property; the Bon Air Transit Company, which feared
a merger with Richmond's transit system, advanced a claim for losses it
anticipated; and roughly 12,000 county residents and eleven civic organizations filed a host of intervening petitions against a possible merger.
The substance of residents' petitions was that there should be no annexation of any kind. By the end of 1969, the Chesterfield County Council of
Civic Associations had exhausted all of the potential appellate remedies
for a possible merger: state-level officials stonewalled all of their appeals.
By December 8, 1969, the deadline to appeal Richmond's annexation
case with the commonwealth's court of appeals, the Civic Associations'
attorney, L. Paul Bryne, refused to file another appeal. Bryne and Chesterfield residents, who had lost their most recent appeal on November 24,
realized that the commonwealth's court system was going forward with
the annexation proceedings regardless of their protests. White residents
of the annexed area soon realized that they, too, were not immune to the
ways political leaders ignored public opinion.[59]

The annexation of Chesterfield County became a referendum on
class, education, and race in the Richmond area. As many of Virginia's
cities trended toward becoming majority–minority, the commonwealth's
suburban residents often expressed their antipathy to annexations in terms
of schools and economic independence. One resident from Chesterfield

exemplified the class-based and financial considerations that motivated anti-annexationist proclivities in the county, claiming, "For the first time in my life I feel nothing but contempt for those who are attempting to destroy all that I have worked so hard for. The elite can pay the price, I cannot. Perhaps the Horner–Bagley agreement was God-sent to arouse the people. There is no doubt that Richmond needs help but I cannot solve the problems. . . . The 44,000 people who have been sold down the river are the answer." The possibility of merging with Richmond Public Schools (RPS) often eclipsed financial concerns. Although antipathy to court-ordered busing became more evident during the deannexation campaigns of the early 1970s, annexed residents were often careful not to express their hatred of RPS in overtly racist language. Before the 1970s, white Richmonders of means avoided integration by simply relocating to the area's immediate and predominantly white counties. Token integration, white flight, and, in time, deannexation litigation came to characterize passive resistance to school integration in the suburbs. Those who stayed in the city often put their children in the dozens of private schools that sprang up as a response to *Brown* during the 1950s and 1960s. By the late 1960s, RPS was approximately 60 percent African American. Those white children who remained in the public-school system often attended predominantly white schools, especially elementary schools, in predominantly white neighborhoods. In many ways, these strategies supplanted the massive resistance campaigns of the late 1950s. By 1970, the racial homogeneity that characterized RPS was as much a product of residential segregation as of massive resistance. Yet, under the proposed annexation plan, the annexed area's eleven schools were to see no real change in their racial composition. There were approximately 200 African American students in Chesterfield County's schools. That number remained virtually the same after Richmond annexed portions of the Chesterfield. Horner and Bagley had crafted a line that specifically avoided large pockets of African Americans. But they had not crafted a line that avoided white resistance to financial, educational, or residential integration. Although Chesterfield County residents lost the immediate battle over annexation, the war over boundary expansions became a defining characteristic of suburban politics in Virginia after 1970.[60]

The VRA may have revolutionized representative democracy in America, but it also heightened opposition to the possibility of black governance. Richmond's black politicians, their liberal white allies, and the Crusade spent most of the late 1960s fighting against police brutality, urban-renewal projects, and the construction of an expressway system. White officials associated these demands with urban unrest and black extremism. As African Americans began to elect more than a handful of black officials, whites disguised mechanisms of vote dilution as color-blind urban reforms. Yet just as Richmond annexed Chesterfield County, the Supreme Court, Congress, and the DOJ resolved to combat the forces of bigotry. Washington's defense of voting rights mandates had far-reaching consequences for local politics and representative democracy in America.

3

From Intent to Effect

The Long Struggle for Voting Rights Litigation during the 1970s

Strange Bedfellows

On Monday, June 30, 1969, Virginia judge Earl L. Abbott ruled that Richmond was entitled to twenty-three square miles and 44,000 people in Chesterfield County. *Richmond News-Leader* reporter Bill Sauder observed that as Abbott read the court's opinion, for the first time during the annexation trial he seemed noticeably nervous while sipping from a glass of water. Abbott's anxiousness likely signified growing concern about the legality of boundary expansions. In their rush to incorporate more than 40,000 white residents, city officials had failed to acknowledge the Supreme Court's decision in *Allen v. Virginia State Board of Elections* (1969) four months prior to Abbott's verdict. *Allen* extended the federal government and citizens' capacity to seek preclearance when electoral procedures impinged on minorities' rights to cast votes that mattered as much after the procedure as before. "The voting rights bill," President Johnson had argued four years earlier, "will be the latest . . . in a long series of victories. . . . We seek . . . equality as a fact and equality as a result." Over the next eight years, voting rights advocates and their allies in Washington used the VRA and the *Allen* decision to defend the very "equality of results" standard that President Johnson evoked during his celebrated commencement speech at Howard University. Johnson's results standard *eventually* gave rise to proportional racial representation on governing bodies across America—but not before annexation deepened racial friction in Richmond. Judge Abbott was not the only person

111

in Richmond uneasy about the nature of annexation. Richmond's merger with Chesterfield County stalled the Crusade's momentum, and the latter knew that the annexed area's roughly 22,000 voters could tip the balance of power in RF's favor. The wheels of justice do indeed grind slowly. It took nearly seven years to resolve the annexation question.[1]

By 1970, the upsurge in black voters often hid the persistence of bigotry in American politics. On one hand, the VRA did its job. By suspending structural barriers to the franchise such as literacy tests, grandfather and understanding clauses, and so on, the act immediately increased black registration. Section 5, which anticipated the likelihood of white resistance, even prohibited changes to electoral laws until the U.S. attorney general or the U.S. District Court for the District of Columbia approved the changes. If the DOJ or the federal court rejected changes to electoral laws or voting procedures, local officials then had to prove that these laws were not discriminatory. Yet in 1968 John A. Hannah, chairman of the USCCR, wrote to the president in the preamble to his report: "Many new barriers to full and equal political participation have arisen, including measures and practices diluting the votes of Negroes, preventing Negroes from becoming candidates, discriminating against Negro registrants and poll watchers, and discriminating against Negroes in the appointment of election officials. Intimidation and economic dependence in many areas of the south continue to prevent Negroes from exercising their franchise or running for office fully and freely. . . . Neither the Democratic nor the Republican national party organization has taken adequate steps to deal with this problem." The persistence of "the same old discriminatory practices and the development of new ones" threatened the VRA, and so eliminating disenfranchisement in the South proved difficult. As local officials continued the fight against black ballots, federal officials initially struggled to work through the process of preclearance. Southerners were responsible for submitting vote-related changes to Washington but submitted only 255 changes for preclearance between 1966 and 1970 (after *Allen*, between 1971 and 1975, southern jurisdictions submitted 5,337 changes).[2]

Ambiguity over the VRA's application complicated the struggle against white opposition to it. For a brief period between 1965 and 1969, southern officials thought that certain provisions in the VRA had no bearing on laws that did not directly disenfranchise voters. In fact, Richmond officials had little reason to believe that the federal government would apply the preclearance clause of section 5 to Chesterfield County's annexation. Richmond was not alone. The persistence of southern racism ensured that the lawyers of the DOJ's CRD had full dockets. These lawyers were responsible not just for supervising voting rights complications but also for overseeing school segregation matters, instances of employment discrimination, and segregation in public accommodations. The CRD's forty lawyers spent much of the late 1960s understaffed and overworked. Because of limited manpower, the DOJ and the CRD also concentrated most of their efforts in areas commonly associated with venomous southern bigotry—namely, Alabama, Louisiana, and Mississippi. Southern officials often argued that changes in electoral procedures such as annexations denied no one the right to vote and therefore did not violate the VRA. Procedures such as annexations, they held, kept cities financially solvent. Although vote dilution had been around long before the VRA, these ostensibly color-blind urban reforms, for a brief moment in time, overwhelmed federal officials. The DOJ brought only one suit against voting-related changes before the USCCR released its report on the state of voting by blacks in 1968. Richmond did not submit the annexation of Chesterfield County to the DOJ, a decision the proponents of annexation eventually regretted.[3]

Annexation all but ensured that some cities in the South with sizeable black populations would eclipse the commonwealth's capital in terms of racial electoral achievements. Like Richmond, both Charlotte, North Carolina, and Atlanta, Georgia, promoted economic progress by on the surface embracing the principles and practice of racial moderation. Atlanta, which called itself the "city too busy to hate" in the early 1960s, and Charlotte, whose leaders championed a Sunbelt-specific brand of racial restraint called the "Charlotte Way," spent the better portion of the early 1970s building, albeit anxiously, interracial political coalitions. Atlanta, whose white population declined by 60,000 and black population increased by 70,000 during the 1960s, was a black-majority city by 1970. The city's suburban and urban populations, however, successfully resisted officials' attempts to annex Fulton County during the 1970s. Although whites still held a slight voting-age majority, the election of

1973 broke the tradition of segregationist political history, when Atlanta's city council was evenly divided between nine black and nine white members, and Maynard Jackson became the city's first black mayor.[4]

Charlotte also broke new political ground by the early 1970s. It initially succeeded in precluding a city–county annexation of the outer-ring suburbs in 1971. White suburban homeowners and civil rights attorneys successfully responded to boundary expansion with a series of legal challenges, and voters eventually defeated the initiative. More importantly, in 1974 Charlotte's city council appointed an African American named Harvey Gantt to complete the term of Fred Alexander, the city's lone black councilman. Gantt, who was eventually elected to the mayoralty in 1983, *immediately* worked to make Charlotte's electoral system reflect the city's racial population. In 1970, African Americans made up slightly more than 30 percent (nearly 73,000) of Charlotte's population (241,215). Gantt successfully lobbied to have some council members elected from districts (seven members) and others at-large (four members). Although Charlotte's white council members opposed Gantt's proposal, the *Charlotte Observer* (unlike the *Richmond Times-Dispatch* and *Richmond News-Leader*) supported the district plan as a way to redirect some political power to the region's urban areas. An interracial coalition eventually passed Gantt's referendum in 1977, the same year Richmond elected its first BMC. Over the duration of the 1970s, however, the prospect of black governance brought Richmond politics to a standstill.[5]

On the eve of the Richmond City Council election of 1970, black professionals continued to dominate the Crusade's decision-making process. Its board of directors elected Dr. M. Philmore Howlette president in 1970. Howlette, a local optometrist and graduate of VUU, served as president until 1972. Crusade chairman Dr. William Thornton, House of Delegates member William Ferguson Reid, and John Brooks were still largely influential in shaping the Crusade's voter registration efforts and electoral directives. Preston Yancy also helped formulate the Crusade's political strategies during Richmond's annexation proceedings. Ethel Overby was still its chair of finance, a position she held until 1975. Although women held leadership positions within the Crusade, they were not permanent fixtures on its executive committee until the late 1960s. They often dominated the Crusade's rank and file during the 1960s, and they used their numbers to move up the organization's ranks in the years after the U.S. Congress passed the VRA. By 1970, Lola Hamilton remained the Crusade's chief secretary, and its executive committee appointed Edwina Clay Hall vice president. Three years later Hall became the Crusade's first female president. A native Richmonder, member of the NAACP, and registered voter since the age of twenty-one, Hall was a graduate of VUU. She had been a teacher in the RPS system since 1929 and after retiring in the late 1960s went on to teach courses at VUU. The Crusade's research committee continued to investigate, recommend, and slate candidates just prior to elections. The organization's original structure also remained largely intact by the early 1970s—it still maintained precinct captains, and these captains continued to instruct local registration efforts and everyday voters. The Crusade also remained independent of party politics. Most of its efforts immediately after 1969, however, were directed toward meeting the challenges of annexation and the impending city council election of 1970.[6]

After annexation, the Crusade struggled to regenerate the electoral momentum it had established during the 1960s. Crusade leadership ran a tight ship (so tight, in fact, that critics often charged that it was too insular). A small handful of officers and executives still directed it. If the Crusade's administrative structure helped it weather the storm of competing interests from within the black community, annexation, which reduced the proportion of voting-age African Americans among the total number of voters in Richmond by nearly 10 percent, forced its leadership to reevaluate the politics of black empowerment. Not only had Richmond's African American population increased by nearly 20 percent over the 1960s, but the VRA and the abolition of poll taxes had also led to a significant increase in eligible African American voters. By 1970, the Crusade struggled to formulate a strategy that might result in a favorable BMC. By the election of 1970, it had become glaringly apparent that annexation had the effect its proponents intended: it not only tempered the Crusade's electoral momentum but also turned back the clock on appeals to black political empowerment and the politics of poor people's campaigns. The only way to beat RF, it appeared, was to reintroduce the balance-of-power strategies utilized in the early to mid-1960s.[7]

On the eve of the election of 1970, the Crusade tried to form a working alliance with a core group of political elites from the annexed area. It briefly entertained the notion that an agreement with annexed residents might give both groups sufficient votes to drive RF off of the city council. More specifically, it tried to join forces with the Chesterfield County Council of Civic Associations—the very organization that attempted yet failed to stop annexation in the waning months of 1969. Crusade leadership ultimately wanted to capitalize on these residents' anger with RF for the latter's part in the merger. Crusade cofounder William Reid argued, "Just because they are mostly white Chesterfield people coming in, we forget they might even be political allies. Many of these people are angry with Richmond Forward themselves. We should make overtures and see if they won't submit some independent candidates we might both support. . . . We can counteract any dilution by intensifying our efforts." On Friday, January 23, 1970, William Thornton met with three leaders of the former Chesterfield County: Robert T. Fitzgerald, Roger C. Griffin, and Ronald P. Livingston. These men represented an organization known as the Team of Progress (TOP), which had recently formed from the Chesterfield Council of Civic Associations and whose members were also apprehensive about joining forces with RF. In due course, however, it became apparent that a different set of concerns drove the leaders of the annexed area.[8]

TOP and the Crusade's fleeting attempt at an interracial coalition went nowhere. By the early 1970s, overtures to interracial political cooperation (which seemed to work in the early 1960s) were often met with deep skepticism. Blacks' appeals to political empowerment and whites' persistence on maintaining control of city hall had effectively polarized local politics by 1970. Three days after their meeting with the Crusade, TOP leaders presented residents of the newly annexed area with a set of four options: Should TOP enter a formal alliance with RF, align with the Crusade, join the Richmond Area Taxpayers Association, or remain independent? Residents chose the first option. Thornton and Crusade directors were also reluctant to enter into a coalition with members of the recently annexed area. They recognized that entering into relationship with white leadership from the former county might jeopardize their standing with African American voters.

If leaders in the annexed area could not beat RF, they resolved to join them. Before the election of 1970, TOP members met with RF, and the two groups merged to prevent the Crusade from electing a city council majority. During a February 10 meeting at the Jefferson Hotel, RF members—including Henry Valentine II, William V. Daniel, Councilman Thomas Bliley (Bliley not only became mayor but was also later a member of the U.S. House of Representatives until 2001), and Councilman Nathan Forb—met with a TOP contingent led by Roger Tuttle and Aubrey Thompson. These men understood that members of the annexed area could potentially swing the balance of political power toward RF —annexation added roughly 22,000 voting-age whites to Richmond's ranks. At the meeting, both sides agreed that their failure to form an alliance might split whites' votes and lead to a Crusade council majority in the upcoming election. Valentine, court testimony later revealed, contended that the alliance might preclude Richmond from becoming "an all black city." His reference implied that a BMC would give rise to even more white flight. TOP members also voted, eight to four, to merge with RF. They then agreed that both groups would from that point forward use the name "Team of Progress" in lieu of "Richmond Forward." Tuttle claimed, "We have formed a brand new political organization of young business and professional men." The group also secretly guaranteed that at least one of the original TOP members in attendance would be elected to city council in the upcoming election. Even with the addition of Chesterfield County, whites still feared that the Crusade might assume control of city hall.[9]

The politics of annexation and public-school integration guaranteed that the election of 1970 would be a bitterly contested affair. TOP endorsed white candidates exclusively, throwing its support behind William V. Daniel, Nathan Forb, Wayland W. Rennie, Aubrey H. Thompson, and Henry L. Valentine II. TOP also resolved to use the issue of public-school integration to get out the white vote. More specifically, the organization campaigned in opposition to establishing neighborhood schools based on a "grade-pairing plan." To get Richmond to comply with *Brown*, the U.S. Department of Health, Education, and Welfare and the Richmond School Board introduced a plan on May 11, 1969, to pair white and black schools in the same attendance zones. By 1968, white flight, residential segregation, and the proliferation of private schools had taken their toll on the RPS system, which by the end of the 1960s was almost entirely African American. It was also glaringly apparent that Richmond's earlier "freedom of choice" plan had led to token integration at best. White students and their parents rarely chose to attend black schools, and black parents and students were understandably reluctant to send their children to predominantly white schools. Even after the commonwealth disbanded the reputed Pupil Placement Board in 1968, parents were disinclined to cross the proverbial color line.

By 1970, the annexed area's schools were nearly 95 percent white. The paring plan arranged to integrate schools in adjacent attendance zones, yet the initiative would work only if black and white schools were

Table 3.1. Richmond Public Schools, East End: School Years 1969–1970 and 1970–1971

School	Grades	White/Black [Students], 1969–1970	White/Black [Students], 1970–1971 [Projected Numbers]
Armstrong High	9–12	0/1,749	73/1,637
Kennedy High	9–12	0/1,579	225/1,641
East End	8–9	0/834	52/728
Mosby	K–9	2/2,376	7/2,436
Bacon	K–6	1/681	3/866
Bellevue	K–6	0/399	3/306
Bowler	K–6	0/528	0/646
Chimborazo	K–7	1/811	3/855
Webster Davis	4–6	0/412	139/293
Fulton	K–3	377/25	151/264
Fairmont	K–6	0/870	0/925
Fairfield	K–7	0/732	0/839
Mason	K–7	0/807	0/1,061
Whitcomb	K–6	0/864	10/871
Woodville	K–7	0/802	0/954

Source: Table published in *Richmond Times-Dispatch*, May 13, 1970, B3; some changes made to the column headings.

Table 3.2. Richmond Public Schools, South Side: School Years 1969–1970 and 1970–1971

School	Grades	White/Black [Students], 1969–1970	White/Black [Students], 1970–1971 [Projected Numbers]
George Wythe High	9–12	1,415/324	1,470/580
Blackwell	K–8	0/1,055	no data
Franklin	N/A	0/720	no data
Patrick Henry	Primary	591/46	761/557 (accommodated school closure)
Ruffin Road Annex	K–6	593/78	592/111
Westover Hills	K–6	539/3	459/179

Source: Table from *Richmond Times-Dispatch,* May 13, 1970, B3; some changes made to the column headings.

in close proximity to one another. The annexed area was far enough removed from Richmond's most heavily populated black enclaves that the plan would in reality lead to very little integration at all. The process of pairing—or clustering—schools to serve a single geographical zone was going to have the greatest effect on the Henrico County side of Richmond's eastern border. Under the proposed plan, the annexed area's schools were to be made up of roughly 200 African Americans—the same number of black students before annexation. Campaigning against the pairing plan, which had yet to be approved by U.S. District Court judge Bob Merhige, was a ploy between the RF and TOP to inspire annexed residents to go to the polls. TOP knew that drumming up opposition to the plan would help turn out white voters.[10]

The addition of 22,000 white voters forced the Crusade to soften its appeals to black political empowerment. The organization supported an interracial slate of nine independent candidates in the election of 1970. Following the abolition of state poll taxes in 1966, the Crusade had abandoned its celebrated balance-of-power strategy—the practice of racking up political debts by endorsing the least-objectionable white politicians. By 1970, however, the addition of approximately 22,000 mostly white suburban voters to the city forced the Crusade's research

Table 3.3. Richmond Public Schools, West End and North Side: School
Years 1969–1970 and 1970–1971

School	Grades	White/Black [Students], 1969–1970	White/Black [Students], 1970–1971 [Projected Numbers]
Thomas Jefferson High	10–12	1,601/161	1,054/405
Maggie Walker High	10–12	0/1,407	129/1,287
John Marshall High	7–12	442/947	458/1,192
Chandler	7–8	123/875	175/683
Hill	7–9	837/81	591/226
Graves	7–9	0/983	76/929
Binford	7–9	181/479	303/533
Randolph	N/A	0/429	CLOSED
Westhampton	K–8	665/104	494/123
Highland Park	K–6	296/1,029	644/765
Norrell	K–6	0/1,093	45/965
Stuart	K–6	0/617	0/669
Scott	N/A	0/254	no data
Ginter Park-Brook Hill Annex	N/A	607/265	no data
Mary Munford	K–6	689/25	633/133
Lee	K–6	549/57	472/117
Fox	K–2	572/62	533/578
West End	3–6	0/672	no data
Maymont	N/A	0/403	no data
Clark Springs	3–7	4/557	no data
Baker	K–6	1/980	76/878
Carver	K–6	0/780	0/807

Source: Table from *Richmond Times-Dispatch,* May 13, 1970, B3; some changes made to the column headings.

committee to reinstitute the very strategy that black mobilization and federal mandates had rendered obsolete. In an appeal to members of the recently annexed area, the Crusade's research committee endorsed three candidates from what had been Chesterfield County: Robert E. Shiro, Oates McCullen, and TOP member Ronald Livingstone. In the city, the Crusade endorsed independent incumbents Henry Marsh, Jim

Table 3.4. Richmond Public Schools, Annexed Area, 1969–1970 and 1970–1971

Schools	Grades	White/Black [Students], 1969–1970	White/Black [Students], 1970–1971 [Projected Numbers]
Huguenot	10–12	1,344/10	1,344/10
Elkhardt	7–9	762/25	762/25
Thompson	7–9	1,360/26	1,360/26
Broad Rock	K–6	491/12	491/12
J. B. Fisher	K–6	709/0	709/0
J. L. Francis	K–6	502/13	502/13
Greene	K–6	649/59	649/59
Redd	K–6	541/0	541/0
Reid	K–6	1,056/21	1,056/21
Southampton	K–6	747/40	747/40

Source: Table from *Richmond Times-Dispatch,* May 13, 1970, B3; some changes made to the column headings.

Carpenter, and Howard Carwile as well as two African Americans and one white candidate from Richmond: Walter Kenney, Curtis L. Holt Sr., and Andrew M. Lewis. The Crusade met the challenges of annexation by reversing its appeals to black empowerment, slating six white candidates out of nine.[11]

Annexation gutted the growing promise of a Crusade council majority. Richmond's African Americans were able to elect only three Crusade endorsements. These candidates, however, finished first, second, and third. Carwile won the competition again with 29,031 votes; Marsh, the only African American elected to the council, finished second with 26,012 votes; and Carpenter followed Marsh with 25,502 votes. TOP endorsements occupied the remaining seats: Bliley, Forb, Daniel, Valentine (president of RF), Wayland Rennie, and Thompson. Curtis Holt and Walter Kenney, two other African Americans endorsed by the Crusade, were soundly defeated: Kenney garnered 17,592 votes, and Holt finished seventeenth with 13,009 votes. None of the Crusade's white endorsements garnered more than 16,500 votes.[12] (For the election results in 1970, see tables 8 and 9 in the appendix.)

The election of 1970 had profound implications for racial representation on the Richmond City Council. Although the council appointed
Marsh to the vice mayoralty, the appointment seemed like an empty ges-
ture—especially given the electoral momentum that African Americans
had established prior to the annexation. Of the city's nine council members, five lived in West End (Bliley, Daniel, Forb, Carwile, and Valentine).
Rennie and Carpenter lived on Richmond's north side, and Thompson
came from the annexed area of Chesterfield County. Henry Marsh lived
in the predominantly African American East End. In 1968, three of the
Crusade's nine endorsements had won council seats. Crusaders did not
lose ground in 1970, but they failed to gain ground—despite Richmond's
growing African American population. Annexation gutted the possibility
of electing four black candidates, let alone a council majority. Richmond's
African Americans made up 42 percent of the city's population in 1970,
yet Marsh was the only representative on the city council that lived in—
or near—a predominantly African American neighborhood. Marsh, one
of annexation's biggest critics, lamented, "I don't feel very happy. . . .
[T]he lineup is still 6–3. . . . [T]he city of Richmond lost in this election."[13]

The Richmond City Council of 1970 did not represent the type of
racial progress blacks had in mind in 1965, nor did the state of Richmond's black neighborhoods. For many African Americans, life after passage of the civil rights acts looked eerily reminiscent of life before their
passage. If the election of 1970 affirmed people's fear of local government, so too did the demographic data. At $13,073, the median fam-
ily income in the annexed area was roughly $3,100 higher per year than
the family income of residents in the city, $9,973. In the year following
annexation, Richmond's real estate tax revenue increased by $10.8 mil-
lion. Although annexation increased the local tax revenues (taxable revenue accounted for 71 percent of all local tax sources) by about 21 percent,
nearly 25 percent of black families in Richmond were still beneath the
poverty line. The median income of families at the poverty line stood at
$2,240. The poverty threshold for an urban family of four in 1970 was
$3,743. Ten years before annexation, nearly half of Richmond's blacks
had less than eight years of education. By 1970, city schools in Richmond
proper were nearly 66 percent African American, and yet an alarming
number of black adolescents failed to finish high school. There was also a

palpable fear that white council members, after the pairing-plan scheme, might devise yet another mechanism to circumvent the Supreme Court's ruling in *Green v. County School Board* (1968) to more effectively integrate public schools. After the election of 1970, the Crusade had every reason to contest annexation and the state of Richmond's black communities. The most vocal challenges, however, came not from the Crusade (which remained fixated on a district system) but from public-housing residents and younger African Americans.[14]

Generational fissures in the black body politic grew more apparent after annexation. By the early 1970s, younger generations of black Richmonders had grown weary of the pace of racial progress. The American civil rights movement, Sidney Milkis argues, was "a fissiparous mixture of interest-oriented organizations that sought traditional rights long denied African Americans and militants intent on recasting the very framework of political life." Jeroyd Greene Jr. squarely represented the latter and signified that the fight for racial justice in Richmond went beyond the Crusade. This new generation of younger African Americans directly challenged black leadership and blamed both black and white leaders for the poverty that continued to envelop many of Richmond's black communities. Greene, a Long Island, New York, native, was a Yale-educated attorney who had permanently relocated to Richmond in the late 1960s upon marrying an Ashland, Virginia, native. Although Greene defended Willie Dell in his *Afro* editorials in the early 1980s, became president of the Crusade in the late 1980s, and was eventually elected to Richmond's city council in 1998, he first emerged in the city as its most outspoken critic of local leadership. It was Greene who argued after the annexation of Chesterfield County that Richmond's government was not "responsive to the body politic" because the city charter's at-large election system "forces blacks and poor out."[15]

If Curtis Holt Sr. came to represent the ways the Crusade struggled to negotiate class considerations, Greene typified a growing generational divide among black leadership. This generation of young activists, unlike the students who staged sit-ins at Thalhimer's in 1960, did not have— nor did they care for—the support of older black leadership. They, like their white counterparts, rejected their parents' mores. By 1970, there were more than half a million African American black collegians in the

United States, of which 34 percent attended black colleges (in contrast to the early 1960s, when roughly 51 percent were enrolled in predominantly black institutions). A significant number of these black collegians were radicalized by their experiences with racism on recently integrated college campuses, and both the freedom struggle and the emergence of the Black Power movement influenced their intellectual development. Greene's generation staged a "sociocultural" revolution against the black establishment that emerged in the late 1960s. They were the youth who embraced the belief that black culture was intrinsically beautiful and valuable, listened to the sounds of psychedelic soul, and screamed, "Say it loud, I'm black and I'm proud." Greene, who was in his late twenties during the late 1960s and eventually changed his name to "Sa'ad El-Amin" in the 1970s, grew into one of Richmond's most outspoken proponents of black nationalism. For a brief spell in the mid-1970s, he was the general counsel and business manager for Louis Farrakhan's Nation of Islam.[16]

Ten years after the Richmond 34 sat in at downtown lunch counters, Greene and black collegians organized their own demonstration against the continuation of racism in Richmond. On November 2, 1970, nearly five hundred mostly African American high school and college students descended on the steps of Virginia's state capital in honor of Black Solidarity Day. Inspired by Douglas Turner Ward's play *The Day of Absence* (1965), young African Americans had organized the first Black Solidarity Day in 1969. Richmond's participation in this event was not without controversy. Between the rally at the state capital and a "black caucus" at Monroe Park near Virginia Commonwealth University later that evening, people looted several stores—three on Broad Street, five on West Cary Street, and one on West Main. Although authorities failed to link the looters to the rally's attendees, whites associated Black Solidarity Day with rising radicalism. Greene, who was one of the demonstration's keynote speakers, obliged. At the solidarity rally, he specifically called for increased black unity and a "program for action" to fight against racism. Roughly three months later, while Greene gave a Black History Week speech at George Wythe High School, white students walked out of the auditorium after he specifically referred to them as "devils" and "honkies." It was Greene who contended that white leadership camouflaged "polite racism" with "cordiality and saccharine dialogue." Greene's charge, by the way, was an indictment not just of white leadership but also of African American leaders who worked within the framework of white control. For Greene, Virginia's legacy of white paternalism was as prevalent in 1970 as it had been during the era of gradualist leadership.[17]

Curtis Holt had been involved in the fight for voting and civil rights for nearly a decade: he, like Greene, had also grown weary of the Crusade's leadership. Holt was born in Rocky Mount, North Carolina, in 1920. His mother relocated to Richmond with Holt and seven of his siblings in 1934. After falling down an elevator shaft while working at VUU, Holt began to receive long-term disability compensation and was a tenant of the Creighton Court housing project beginning in 1960. Like many public-housing residents, he struggled to take care of his two sons, Walter and Curtis Jr., and two daughters, Valerie and Constance. Yet he established a reputation as a social activist, and was integral to Richmond's struggle against segregation and black economic vulnerability. Holt was a member of the Crusade, assisted its early voter registration drives by organizing fellow public-housing tenants, served on Richmond's Human Relations Commission, led the Creighton Court Civic Association, and was an executive board member of the NAACP's Richmond branch. The self-proclaimed grassroots organizer had also established a reputation for directly confronting institutionalized racism in Richmond. Holt testified against police brutality during Carwile's attempt to establish a citizens' police review board in 1966. Just prior to the election in 1970, he was arrested for coming to the aid of a twelve-year-old African American whom RPD officers had allegedly brutalized. A local court threw out Holt's case out after he swore to argue his claims in front of "the highest court." After years of pressing for improvements to living conditions in public housing, Holt also sued the RRHA. A federal judge not only ruled in Holt's favor but also contended that the RRHA had unlawfully tried to evict Holt as retaliation for his participation in protests and civic meetings. Henry Marsh, *Afro-American* columnist David Longley, and NAACP chapter president E. L. Slade underwrote Holt's suit. For more than a decade, Holt, like Marsh, demonstrated that he understood how to challenge discrimination by working within the democratic system.[18]

Curtis Holt and public-housing residents spent the better portion of the 1960s fighting against intensifying income inequality in Richmond. These groups initially worked hand in hand with the Crusade because they believed that black elected officials would confront the deepening marginalization and invisibility affecting their communities. They lost faith in the Crusade after annexation, however. Holt, who emerged as a spokesman for Richmond's working class, had been complaining about the compression of black people into the city's segregated public-housing developments for years. As early as 1966, the living conditions in these developments, many of which were less than ten years old and struggled with funding issues, had deteriorated rapidly. By 1969, the RRHA had 1,300 people on the waiting list for housing, an occupancy turnover of 24 percent annually, and an average family occupancy of roughly four and a half years. Two years later, only one of the 447 families in Whitcomb Court was white; that number was the same for Fairfield Court; and only two of the 450 families in Mosby Court were white. All of the 635 families in Gilpin Court and 504 families in Holt's Creighton Court were African American. Hillside Court, which had been specifically designated for whites, was still 70 percent white by 1971. Public-housing activists argued that these developments were "located in formerly Negro areas to preserve a pattern of segregation in the city." These residents called for more effective rent control (RRHA had initiated a $10 rent hike in 1969) and a police presence that was more sympathetic to the communities' needs (the latter issue came up repeatedly during debates over the citizens' review board). The Creighton Court Civic Association even wrote to Philip G. Sadler, the federal director for the Public Housing Authority, about segregated public housing in August 1966. Although Sadler stated that the federal government would help local authorities find "suitable sites" for future developments, the density of poverty (one-third of public-housing residents were completely sustained by welfare aid) was still a major dilemma in public housing in 1970. Curtis Holt was one of the first community organizers to remind the black body politic that class mattered—and he would not be the last. By the 1980s, the strongest criticism of the black political leadership came out of these very public-housing developments.[19]

The Crusade's preoccupation with implementing a district system eventually cost it a valuable ally. Although the Crusade endorsed Holt's candidacy during the city council election in 1970, black leaders believed that Holt lacked the intellectual capacity for public office holding. Holt later revealed that he had received several phone calls from influential African Americans asking him to withdraw from the election in 1970. It is likely that the Crusade endorsed Holt's candidacy because of his long-standing commitment to registering voters in Richmond's most economically vulnerable communities. Deannexation was another matter. The Crusade's leaders refused to support deannexation litigation because they wanted a ward system that might guarantee seats on the city council. They recognized that boundary expansion had in fact bolstered Richmond's tax base. The Crusade's merger study committee was also aware of the Supreme Court's recent decisions concerning annexations and at-large elections. After the Court ruled in *Perkins v. Matthews* (1971) that at-large elections coupled with annexations diluted minority voting strength, the Crusade believed that the implementation of a district-based system in Richmond was imminent, and so Holt's preoccupation with deannexation compromised the Crusade's preference for majority–minority districts. Holt later recalled, "They [Crusade leaders] gave me the runaround. . . . You know, they're all so busy. . . . Some didn't even return my calls."[20] He eventually found a sympathetic ear.

In February 1971, Holt, with the help of an unlikely ally, challenged the legality of annexation in federal court. Shortly after the election, he charged that annexation diluted blacks' voting strength and prohibited a BMC. He also insisted that the dilution of black voting strength prohibited him from winning a seat on the council, despite the fact that he failed to crack the top-sixteen vote getters. A young white lawyer named W. H. C. "Cabell" Venable, out of a sense of legal conscientiousness and with a nose for viable cases, agreed. Venable, a native of the Richmond area, was no political and social justice crusader. Just prior to taking on Holt's case, he had been retained by a local branch of the Ku Klux Klan to defend a group of Richmonders incriminated under the commonwealth's truancy laws. These people, it turned out, had pulled their children out of schools that were on the verge of integrated busing. Venable believed that Holt had a legitimate grievance, and the two filed a class-action suit in Richmond's U.S. District Court on February 24, 1971. Venable argued that the incorporation of Chesterfield County diluted black votes and subsequently violated section 1 of the Fifteenth Amendment. The two also contended that annexation violated Holt's due-process rights in terms of section 1 of the Fourteenth Amendment. The suit sought to declare the annexation void, to nullify the election of 1970, to declare the present council unconstitutionally convened, and to enjoin the city from exercising political authority over the annexed area.[21] Holt and Venable confirmed judge Abbott's deepest fear. Few knew it at the time, but they eventually brought local elections to a standstill.

A critical mass of white residents from the annexed area soon joined Holt in his effort to deannex Chesterfield County. Annexed residents originally couched their resistance to annexation in terms of tax revenue— a concern assuaged by the generous terms of the consolidation's financial considerations. As noted earlier, to clinch the annexation deal Richmond agreed to pay Chesterfield's County School Board costs, proposed a five-year capital-improvement program, absolved Chesterfield's outstanding sewage and water facility debt (totaling more than $24 million), and paid for a host of other transitional costs. When a district court ordered Richmond to speed up public-school integration, the annexed-area residents' real intentions became clear. Fearing that annexation meant desegregation of public schools, these residents organized strategies to support Holt's lawsuit. Holt was a godsend to the annexed residents of Chesterfield County—they knew that they could more effectively challenge annexation in the courts if the plaintiff were an African American.[22]

Metropolitan busing and annexation made strange bedfellows of people who had little in common. On April 5, 1971, District Court judge Bob Merhige invalidated Richmond's attempts at a "pairing plan." Merhige contended that Richmond needed a plan that ensured that the ratio of black-to-white students in each school reflected the proportion of blacks and whites in metropolitan Richmond. He also extended busing to students across county lines. Merhige's ultimate objective was to consolidate a metropolitan school system that would service more than 100,000 students; he required a new desegregation plan that sponsored pupil placement, faculty reassignments, and free citywide transportation. It was this ruling that ultimately inspired whites to support Holt's suit. Merhige also paid the price for the ruling, spending more than two years under the protection of federal marshals when he received persistent death threats, and protestors regularly demonstrated outside of his home in Henrico County. In an article published in the *Washington and Lee Law Review* twenty years later, Merhige reflected: "The Ku Klux Klan paraded around my home every Sunday for months. Another hostile group would from time to time organize what they referred to in signs as 'Merhige funeral dirges.' On these days a hearse, with a long row of cars behind, would circle the court-house, sometimes for hours at a time. In the interim, my dog was shot, my guest house was burned to the ground, and calls for my impeachment emanated not only from what might be described as 'ordinary citizens,' but from state legislators, at least one United States Senator, and one congress-man." While Merhige found allies in J. Sargeant Reynolds and Governor Linwood Holton (who helped integrate schools by sending his four chil-dren to black-majority city schools), less-radical whites met the challenge of integration and annexation by forging a working alliance with Holt.[23]

The prospect of court-ordered public-school integration gave rise to what the Chesterfield County Board of Supervisors called a "people's revolt." If affected residents could repatriate the annexed area, returning it back to Chesterfield County, they believed that they could keep pub-lic schools mostly white. On May 3, 1971, the South Richmond Council of Civic Associations and the Broad Rock Council of Civic Associations, led by Arthur R. Cloey Jr., called a meeting at Huguenot High School. Huguenot was located just west of the Willow Oakes Country Club on the city's south side. Observers estimated that approximately 800 to 1,000 residents of the annexed area were in attendance. The featured speaker was none other than Cabell Venable. Shortly after the meeting, annexed-area residents agreed to pay for Holt's litigation as it made its way through U.S. District Court in Richmond. Annexation ironically brought together suburban whites fearful of racial integration and an African American resident of public housing. Such was the strange fruit borne of decades of racial exclusion, the mobilization of black voters, and the reinforcement of these trends by the Voting Rights Act.[24]

Meeting the Demands of Dilution

Curtis Holt personified a quiet trend in the post-1965 fight for civil rights: African Americans utilized the federal government and courts to defend their right to vote. As they did so, the civil rights movement went beyond the progression from protest to politics. After 1965, the movement in many ways returned to the NAACP's focus on legal activism. In other ways, Holt's decision to seek recourse with the federal government against annexation was a referendum on the nature of post-1965 voting rights. Federal officials convinced African Americans and minorities, especially after 1969, that Washington was dedicated to the process of defending equality as a right and a result. The Great Society had implications beyond the War on Poverty. Holt and Richmond were part of a broader policy-making revolution that redefined the size and scope of the VRA to do battle with the continuation of vote dilution. Great Society policy makers initially advanced regulations, embodied in the Civil Rights Act of 1964 and the Voting Rights Act of 1965, which emphasized unrestricted institutional access. As southern whites impinged upon racial minorities' abilities to reap the benefits of inclusion, Washington got serious. In terms of politics, Earl Warren's Court first struck down malapportioned legislatures and local governing bodies during the early 1960s. As racial minorities flooded Washington with antidilution litigation, the Court, Congress, and the DOJ carried the spirit of voting rights reform well into the 1970s.[25]

In *Allen v. Virginia State Board of Elections* (1969), the Supreme Court obliged African Americans' pleas to address vote dilution. It dived into the affairs of political cartography when it began regulating state and local voting systems in the early 1960s, and continued this trend in 1969. *Allen* consisted of four appeals: three from Mississippi and one from Virginia. In Virginia and Mississippi, whites used various mechanisms to dilute black votes. In all four cases, local officials had refused to submit voting-related changes to the DOJ after 1965. Litigants, however, contended that changes to the structure of elections were subject to preapproval under section 5 of the VRA. Prior to *Allen*, the Preclearance Clause in section 5 covered registration procedures exclusively, and *Allen* itself represented the first time the Court questioned whether preclearance regulations should reach beyond equal-access statutes. Should section 5, federal justices pondered, include electoral policies that made it more difficult for voters to elect preferred candidates? In a seven-to-two decision in *Allen*, the Court contended that procedures such as the qualification of candidates, the switch from elective to appointive offices, and conversion to at-large elections from single-member district elections fell under section 5. More broadly, Chief Justice Warren held that section 5 applied to election laws even if the laws had no direct connection to voter registration or casting ballots—in fact, this section was a direct attack on procedures such as annexations. Following the Court's decision in *Allen,* the DOJ sent out letters to covered states that they intended to enforce the VRA's preclearance clause, and compliance with section 5 rose dramatically. Between 1966 and 1970, southern jurisdictions sent the DOJ 255 submissions for preclearance; between 1971 and 1975, there were, according to experts, 5,337 submissions for preclearance.[26]

In *Allen,* the Court extended the federal government's ability to intervene in state and local politics under the authority of section 5 of the VRA. Chief Justice Warren extended section 5 to cover the rights of minority populations with what amounted to recognition of their entitlement to be proportionally represented in the results of an election. In *Reynolds v. Sims* (1964), Warren argued: "The right to vote can be affected by a dilution of voting power as well as by an absolute prohibition of casting a ballot . . . Voters who are members of a racial minority might well be in the majority in one district, but a decided minority in the county as a whole. This type of change could therefore nullify their ability to elect the candidate of their choice just as would prohibiting some of them from voting." Warren began to apply the logic used in *Reynolds* to *Allen.* The Court also ruled that section 5 authorized that private litigants could bring suits in their local district courts—people, not merely the DOJ, had the ability to request judicial preclearance in cases where it appeared that blacks' electoral strength had been diluted. The ruling in *Allen* eventually had profound implications in Richmond because it focused squarely on changes to election-based systems. By the early 1970s, Congress followed the Court's lead.[27]

The reapportionment revolution would have been impossible had Congress failed to extend the VRA. During the Ninety-First Congress, federal legislators extended the act for another five years. Lawmakers had initially designed the VRA as a five-year temporary provision to solve the South's restrictions on black registration and voting. Their extension of the VRA for another five years was an implicit endorsement of the Court's *Allen* decision. The USCCR report *Political Participation* in 1968, it turned out, had also motivated many members of the House and the Senate to defend the VRA—particularly because a sizable portion of the report focused on white backlash to the VRA. The report convinced a generous number of federal officials that the VRA needed to be renewed with the Court's *Allen* decision in mind. Yet nothing, according to leading voting rights scholars, motivated the preservation of the VRA more than President Richard Nixon's attempt to shore up southern support and solidify his Southern Strategy by attacking the VRA.

By 1970, the Nixon administration and southern legislators attempted to undermine critical elements of the VRA—most notably sections 4 and 5—in what became a drawn-out crusade against these two provisions. They contended that the VRA's triggering formula in section 4 and preclearance in section 5 should apply to all political jurisdictions in the United States or be struck from the act. Southerners agreed—during the Ninety-First Congress, southern representatives attempted to "deregionalize" the VRA by having it apply to all fifty states, not merely to political jurisdictions below the Mason–Dixon line. However, a bipartisan coalition led by Senate minority leader Hugh Scott (R–Pa.) not only approved a five-year extension of the VRA in its original form but also added a provision sponsored by Senate majority leader Mike Mansfield (D–Mont.) to enfranchise eighteen-year-olds. Given growing disapproval of military endeavors in Southeast Asia, the enfranchisement of eighteen-year-olds tipped the scales. The House voted to accept the Senate bill by 224–183. On June 22, 1970, Nixon, despite opposing constitutionally impermissible statutory enfranchisement and an amendment to the Constitution that allowed eighteen-year-olds to vote, signed the extended Voting Rights Act for five more years.[28]

Having lost the battle over the VRA's renewal, Attorney General John Mitchell attempted to reorganize the CRD, another decision that had unintended implications for Richmond. The Nixon administration continued the fight against the VRA's section 4 during the summer of 1970. After creating the CRD in the Civil Rights Act of 1957, policy makers had organized it into sections that covered specific geographic regions. These sections were responsible for handling the full panoply of civil rights matters in their respective jurisdictions; in fact, the southern region was the one that the report *Political Participation* said suffered from limited manpower because the number of attorneys covering the region had been reduced from forty to twenty-seven in November 1967. John Mitchell reorganized these attorneys into issue-specific branches that had a nationwide focus. The departmental reorganization, for instance, created branches that focused entirely on monitoring school integration or employment discrimination or voting rights violations. Much to the chagrin of southerners, the newly established Voting Rights Section almost exclusively covered the South. In fact, the section brought together a group of lawyers—many of them liberals left from the Johnson administration—that were specifically dedicated to enforcing section 5. After *Allen,* communication between the CRD and local jurisdictions increased dramatically. Within a year of the creation of the Voting Rights Section, the number of preclearance submissions rose by nearly four hundred. The lawyers in this section, including the CRD's assistant attorney general, David Norman, were instrumental in crafting what became Richmond's district system. Suffragists also found unlikely allies in Warren Burger's Court.[29]

When Chief Justice Earl Warren stepped down in the summer of 1969, Nixon looked to Warren Burger to reverse the jurisprudential permissiveness that had characterized Warren's tenure. Burger's appointment to the chief justiceship in the summer of 1969 and the subsequent appointments of Harry Blackmun in 1970, Lewis Powell in 1972, and William Rehnquist in 1972 were supposed to represent an integral phase in the realization of the Nixon–Phillips Southern Strategy (which Nixon devised by Kevin Phillips, a political strategist). Nixon intended to win over conservative voters by attacking the previous Court's latitudinarian approach to civil and social justice, and Burger claimed that he had every intention to overrule cases like *Reynolds.* Nixon believed that Burger would advance a type of constitutional jurisprudence predicated on restraint (i.e., "judicial conservatism"), which was exemplified by loyalty to the Framers' original understanding of the Constitution. Yet no counterrevolution to the Warren Court's "reapportionment revolution" ever transpired during the 1970s. In fact, the Burger Court further affirmed the previous Court's penchant for permissiveness, transforming the franchise into a concrete measure of power that could not be diluted through majoritarian manipulation. And it is difficult to separate the Court's record on minority rights from the broader context of race relations in the 1970s. Race riots in the late 1960s and black radicalism in part influenced the Burger Court's minority voting rights record of the early 1970s. The Court defended and strengthened race-conscious voting rights because resistance to these principles might be characterized as undemocratic. It is impossible to understand Richmond's relationship to antidilution litigation without examining how the Burger Court became a force for race-conscious voting rights.[30]

Arguably, no case had more of a lasting impact on the Burger Court's civil rights legacy and the future possibility of voting rights litigation than *Griggs v. Duke Power Company* (1971). The Burger Court established an equality-of-results standard and utilized a disparate-impact analysis in *Griggs*. In *Griggs*, fourteen African Americans claimed that North Carolina's Duke Power Company relegated blacks to lower-paying labor jobs before Title VII of the Civil Rights Act of 1964 went into effect. The company's intradepartmental transfer policy required a high school diploma and a minimum score on two aptitude exams. Plaintiffs claimed that even though the policy did not discriminate explicitly on racial grounds, it did so implicitly because African Americans had been systematically denied equal access to high school degrees and the quality of the education that they had obtained was demonstrably inferior to that of whites. Both of these factors, in turn, had undesirable effects on their employment under Duke Power's personnel policies.[31]

In March 1971, the Court found (eight to zero, with Justice William Brennan Jr. abstaining) that no relationship existed between the company's criteria for advancement and job performance. These policies, though racially neutral, disparately impacted African Americans and reinforced disproportionate white representation in higher-paying positions. Even more importantly, the Court believed that the South's separate and unequal public schools made workplace competition inherently unfair. The poor quality of segregated schools for blacks in North Carolina all but ensured, as far as the Court was concerned, that whites were better positioned to benefit from Duke Power Company's policies. This specific belief had tapped into the Warren Court's logic in *Brown*.

The Court had held then that segregated schools negatively *affected* the intellectual and social development of black school children and that these *effects*, accordingly, deprived minority children of the equal-protection laws guaranteed by the Fourteenth Amendment. Burger contended in *Griggs* that Title VII forbade overt discrimination and practices that were "fair in form, but discriminatory in operation." *Griggs* signified the Burger Court's evolution from an equal-treatment standard to an equal-results standard of case law. Prior to *Griggs*, plaintiffs needed to show discriminatory intent in things such as hiring practices; following *Griggs*, plaintiffs needed to demonstrate the inequitable effects in hiring or promotional practices.[32]

The Court eventually applied the "disparate impacts" test to voting rights cases in *Perkins v. Matthews* (1971). In 1969, a group of appellants from Canton, Mississippi, represented by Armand Derfner (who later represented the Crusade in *City of Richmond v. United States* [1975]), sought to enjoin local elections after city officials made changes to elections rules without preclearance from the DOJ. Canton, which the VRA covered, moved polling places out of black neighborhoods, annexed an adjacent area with hundreds of whites, and switched from a ward-based system to at-large elections in 1969. Although a district judge temporarily restrained Canton's city council election in 1969, a three-judge appeals court not only dissolved the injunction but also held that none of Canton's changes had "a discriminatory purpose or effect." The Supreme Court disagreed.[33]

The Court voted eight to one in favor of the plaintiff in *Perkins* and held that the three-judge court should have submitted the changes for preclearance. It also contended that each of the changes fell within the purview of section 5 and held that boundary expansion diluted the weight of voters who had the franchise prior to Canton's annexation. Last, the Court argued that changes from ward to at-large elections (in Canton's case for alderman) fell under the authority of section 5. In a finding that eventually influenced local elections in Richmond, it held that annexations coupled with at-large election schemes in purpose and effect could enhance the ability of municipal majorities to maintain power over city elections by diluting minorities' votes. If whites, for instance, made themselves majorities by expanding municipal boundaries into predominantly white suburbs, black candidates were at a sizeable disadvantage if they were made to campaign throughout an entire city at large instead of representing specific districts. If whites had population advantages in local elections, then the top vote getters or a majority of the top vote getters were likely to represent the majority. With a 52 percent majority, Richmond's whites had the power in an at-large election system theoretically to prohibit African Americans from obtaining a council majority. *Perkins* expanded both the size and scope of section 5 delineated previously in *Allen* and the concept of vote dilution. After the VRA's ratification, white southerners realized that they could not keep most African Americans from the polls. As whites in places such as Canton, Mississippi, and Richmond, Virginia, crafted policies that minimized or neutralized the power of black votes, the Court recognized that the concept of "one person, one vote" needed to be applied more thoroughly at the local level. In cases such as *Perkins,* the Court met the challenges of boundary expansions and at-large elections by widening the definition of vote dilution to cover what it eventually referred to as a "totality of circumstances." The Court recognized that southern whites often used multiple mechanisms simultaneously to cancel out blacks' votes.[34]

By the early 1970s, it was clear that federal officials were committed to making sure that the Second Reconstruction reversed the outcome of the first. The Second Reconstruction initially succeeded, Morgan Kousser contends, "in fostering political equality for minorities because, until recently, judicial decisions have been more favorable, partisan division over civil rights policy much less pronounced, and congressional lineups much more stable than those of the First Reconstruction." African Americans also quickly realized that voting for its own sake meant little if ballots did not bring material results. Richmond had just as many black council members in 1964 as it had in 1970. Men such as Curtis Holt alleged that the right to vote mattered little unless minorities could parlay the franchise into effective office holding. Holt realized that it would take more than a scattering of black officials to change the nature of policy making. The Crusade eventually got the memo. On Monday, October 16, 1972, the Crusade held a meeting at Slaughter's Hotel about the nature of Holt's suit. Vice Mayor Marsh "told the Crusade members that the move to intervene is needed so that the Crusade will have a voice in the suit that city officials have begun in the District Court of the District of Columbia." If the Crusade were going to get the district system it wanted, now was the time to act.[35]

"The Court Can Unscramble an Egg"

After the Court mandated that boundary expansion violated section 5 of the VRA if it was exercised to dilute black voting strength, black Americans realized that Washington meant business. As Henry Marsh put it, "It can be done. The Court can unscramble an egg. . . . I'm not saying it [deannexation] ought to be done. If black people decide to let those (annexed) citizens stay in the city, we ought to get some concessions in addition to participating in drawing the lines for districts for councilmanic [sic] elections because the annexation does dilute the black vote." To unscramble the annexation egg, the Court and Richmonders had to reach conclusions on three fundamental questions that the Holt cases raised: Was annexation racially motivated? To what degree did boundary expansion dilute black voting strength in at-large elections? And if annexation did dilute black votes, what measures should lawmakers take to counterbalance the harmful effects of boundary expansion? These questions put federal and local authorities, Holt's litigation team, and the City of Richmond on a complex legal course that began with the suspension of local elections and culminated in the election of a BMC.[36]

In 1971, Richmond officials nervously clung to the hope that *Perkins* would not apply to the Chesterfield annexation, especially since officials annexed portions of the county prior to the Supreme Court's ruling. The city's attorney, Conrad B. Mattox Jr., held, "My initial understanding of the ruling leads me to believe that it would not deal retroactively with the city's annexation of . . . Chesterfield County. I do not believe that the award will be overturned." Despite his claims, Mattox wrote U.S. attorney general John Mitchell concerning the legality of Richmond's recent boundary expansion in light of the *Perkins* decision. Mattox heard back from chief of the CRD, Assistant Attorney General David Norman. Norman had actually helped Nicholas Katzenbach write the VRA, and his response left little doubt about the DOJ's position:

As you know, the Supreme Court recently held . . . that [c]hanging boundary lines by annexations . . . constitutes the change of a "standard, practice, or procedure with the respect to voting" within the meaning of Section 5. . . . The Attorney General is obliged under Section 5 to be concerned with the voting changes produced by an annexation. . . . In the circumstances of Richmond, where representatives are elected at large, substantially increasing the number of eligible white votes inevitably tends to dilute the voting strength of blacks voters. Accordingly, the Attorney General must interpose an objection to the voting change, which results from the annexation. You may, of course, wish to consider means of accomplishing annexation, which would avoid producing an impermissible adverse racial impact on voting, including such techniques as single-member districts.

Beyond turning the tables on the use of the term *interposition* in a states' rights context, Norman's initial response to Mattox set a pattern that underlined deliberations through the 1970s. First, the assistant attorney general held fast to the Court's recent rulings on vote dilution. As far as the DOJ was concerned, boundary expansion along with at-large elections diluted black votes. Next, he suggested that reversing annexation was not the DOJ's major objective as long as Richmond fashioned single-member districts, a position that paralleled exactly the Crusade's stance on the matter.[37]

Norman's response to Mattox reflected the CRD's defense of the Supreme Court's emerging preference for single-member districts. In 1971, the Court made it clear that plaintiffs could make cases against at-large systems if those systems diminished the power derived from voting. The Court (six to three) devised in *Connor v. Johnson* (1971) a solution to vote dilution. In *Connor*, African Americans in Hinds County, Mississippi, challenged disproportionately inequitable variations in multimember (at-large) districts. The plaintiffs submitted four plans that called for Hinds County to change its electoral scheme to single-member district systems. These Hinds County applicants ultimately wanted the attorney general to postpone elections under the authority of section 5 and eventually approve the new plan. The case was eventually appealed to the

Supreme Court, where the justices established that single-member districts were preferable to at-large elections and could be used as remedies for local apportionment plans. The Court ordered that Hinds County implement these districts by June 14, 1971.[38]

Norman and the Supreme Court fell directly in line with the Crusade and voting rights advocates' growing desire for single-member districts. The DOJ's suggestion that Richmond introduce majority–minority districts emboldened the Crusade. During the late 1960s, the organization's merger study commission, headed by Preston Yancy, was the only group in Richmond to call for majority–minority districts. The Crusade supported annexation as long as the city switched from its at-large system to a district-based system. Not long after Norman's response to Mattox, in the summer of 1971, Crusade leadership again advocated that Richmond replace its at-large city council election system with nine single-member districts. Councilmen Marsh and Carpenter refused to endorse anything less than the Crusade's call for a nine-ward plan. Marsh argued several months prior, "If someone would have told me a month ago that we would be taking the side of Attorney General Mitchell in Washington against Attorney General Miller in Richmond I wouldn't have believed it. I would have thought I was dreaming." When Marsh later traveled to Washington in the summer of 1971 to meet with Norman, he went in full support of the Crusade's plan. Norman's report confirmed much of black Richmond's long-standing contention (Holt notwithstanding) that keeping Chesterfield County was a viable option as long as policy makers implemented a voting system that guaranteed city council seats for blacks.[39]

The idea that whites might have to change the city's at-large election rules did not bode well for the future of white-majority city councils. But whites were also relieved that Norman did not call for complete deannexation. Norman's claim that annexations accompanied by at-large elections diluted black votes made whites anxious, and they understood that the DOJ intended to defend blacks' political prerogatives. They initially (and presciently, it turned out) argued that wards instigated parochial politics and patronage. Many white officials were keenly aware of Richmond's extremely inefficient thirty-two-member, bicameral ward system that dated back to the Charter Reform movements of the late

1940s. City Manager Alan F. Kiepeper and Councilman Henry Valentine asserted that ward politics went "hand in hand with political corruption." The Crusade had answered this question years earlier, though: "There is no cause and effect relationship between district representation and corrupt politics. All of Virginia's large counties have district representation. There is no evidence that there is any more corruption in Arlington and Henrico than there is in Norfolk or Richmond. The causes of political corruption are almost always related to patronage." Richmond's white officials started to contemplate new election models that might satisfy federal authorities without giving blacks political control over city hall. They also, however, needed to devise a plan that would pass Virginia's General Assembly. Under the assistant attorney general's suggestion, the city could maintain its current boundaries only by amending the city charter, which required the approval of the state legislature. After Norman's initial letter, Henry Marsh insisted that city officials (including Councilpersons Carwile, Carpenter, and Thompson as well as Mayor Bliley) and administrators travel to Washington to meet with Norman. Although no record exists of the conversation held then, city officials left the meeting with one firm understanding—the DOJ would let annexation stand only if Richmond adopted a fair district-based system. Immediately upon their return to Richmond, councilmen began preparing a plan that called for five wards and four at-large council seats.[40]

Holt, however, was driven by a different set of concerns. Just as city officials pieced together an acceptable compromise, Holt's deannexation coalition filed its first suit against the City of Richmond. In September 1971, Judge Merhige heard Holt's first suit and concluded that racism motivated Richmond's annexation of Chesterfield County. On September 29, 1971, Merhige unofficially presented his findings after five days of testimony. Influenced largely by Mayor Bagley's openly racist comments about not letting blacks take over city hall, Merhige found that Richmond's annexation in 1970 was racially motivated and orchestrated largely for the purpose of diluting blacks' voting strength. He specifically stated, "The impairment of voting rights which is rooted in racial considerations is unconstitutional." The judge also told Richmond officials that the proposed five-to-four plan would do little to ensure black council seats. However, Merhige, to the surprise of Holt, Venable, and

Chesterfield County, did not mandate deannexation. He suggested that Richmond hold a special council election in September 1972 based on a seven-to-two plan: an at-large election of seven candidates from the city and a district-based election of two candidates from Chesterfield County. City Attorney Mattox traveled to Washington after Merhige's unofficial decision in September but found little sanctuary. In a letter addressed to Mattox, Assistant Attorney General David Norman wrote:

> We have reviewed and considered the additional information you furnished, as well as the comments and views expressed by yourself and Mr. Lewis F. Powell, Jr., who submitted the memorandum in support for the resubmitted change, and the recent findings announced by Judge Merhige. . . . While we found this additional material both relevant and useful, we find no basis for withdrawing our objection. Although you point out the intervening decision of the Supreme Court in *Whitcomb v. Chavis* . . . in our view, the annexation of a large, almost exclusively white area does have a discriminatory racial effect on voting in the context of an emerging black majority electorate. . . . [I]t is therefore objectionable under Section 5 of the Voting Rights Act.

The attorney general's office not only refused to deviate from its previous course of action but also rejected a city proposal for five wards and four at-large districts.[41]

In late 1971 and early 1972, Holt changed litigation strategies, which led to the suspension of council elections. In *Holt v. City of Richmond* (1972), Holt's attorney, Cabell Venable, initially argued that the addition of large numbers of whites violated section 1 of the Fifteenth Amendment and the Due Process Clause of the Fourteenth Amendment. Venable's second suit tapped into the CRD's recent interpretations of statutory law. *Holt II* maintained that Richmond had not acquired the proper authorization for annexation, thus violating the terms of VRA section 5. When combined with at-large elections, Richmond's new boundaries made it impossible for Holt to win a council seat. Holt sought to return the twenty-three square miles to Chesterfield County by proving that annexation had racial motivations. The initial suit, however, did not request that elections be suspended. Holt and Venable now intended to have city council elections suspended until the Court ruled on the discriminatory nature of annexations that accompanied boundary expansions. On April 27, 1972, seven of nine Supreme Court justices voted to indefinitely postpone Richmond's May 2 city council election on the grounds that the city had violated section 5 by not seeking preclearance for annexation. The Court, along with the DOJ, also agreed that the use of at-large elections made it even harder for Richmond's blacks to elect preferred candidates.[42]

Following the suspension of city council elections, Richmond appealed to the DOJ a third time. Mattox, petitioning the new U.S. attorney general, Richard Kleindienst, wrote, "It is the City's view that the Holt case should be considered as it has become final [the Court's denial to hear *Holt I* on the grounds that Richmond did not violate the Equal Protection Clause of the Fourteenth Amendment as articulated in *Whitcomb v. Chavis* (1971)]. . . . [W]e respectfully urge you to reconsider the City's request for approval of the election of councilmen at-large as has been the practice since 1948." As was customary, Richmond had to wait for a response from the attorney general. With pressure mounting from *Holt II,* Richmond began to contemplate filing its own suit in defense of annexation. City officials presumed that if they could attain a declaratory judgment stating that annexation was not racially motivated, Richmond could irretrievably put an end to the possibility of deannexation and the Crusade's plan for a strictly ward-based system.[43]

In the meantime, the Supreme Court reaffirmed in a Petersburg, Virginia, case its growing preference for mandating single-member districts. The City of Petersburg—like Richmond—had annexed a surrounding territory, and the DOJ continually rebuffed its appeals for clearance. Petersburg, again like Richmond, also sought a declaratory judgment from Washington that annexation did not deny or abbreviate black electoral strength. In *City of Petersburg v. United States* (1973), the Court found that "the annexation of parts of Dinwiddie and Prince George Counties . . . dilutes the weight, strength and power of the votes of the black voters in the City, with a concomitant effect upon their political influence." After the Supreme Court's decision, a lower court ruled that it would approve Petersburg's annexation only if the city devised a seven-ward plan that returned the electoral clout that blacks had prior to the annexation. Charles S. Rhyne, Richmond's attorney, believed that the Court's decision did not bode well for the capital city. He claimed, "I speak for myself without having consulted Richmond counsel, but as a lawyer, I must tell you that in reading it [the *Petersburg* decision] I can't see any great major differences." Rhyne knew that *Petersburg* affirmed the recent precedent.[44]

Around the same time as the *Petersburg* decision, the Burger Court widened the definition of vote dilution to cover what was eventually referred to as a "totality of circumstances." Southern whites, as demonstrated in Petersburg, often used multiple mechanisms simultaneously to cancel out blacks' votes, so the Supreme Court initially struggled to find a simple standard for vote dilution. In *White v. Regester* (1973), the Court overturned multimember districting plans in Dallas and San Antonio because they discriminated against Latinos and African Americans. More specifically, the Court found whites used a "presence of factors" (e.g., language barriers, majority vote, and numbered post requirements) that made it less likely for minority groups to elect legislators of their choice in at-large elections. Richard Valelly argues, "The Court held that an accumulation of indirect evidence . . . sufficed to show discriminatory intent. This became known as the Court's 'totality of circumstances' test." In *Zimmer v. McKeithen* in 1973, the Fifth Circuit Court of Appeals eased its probative requirements and recorded four *primary* and four *enhancing* factors that demonstrated if electoral changes were driven by racial intent or diluted minorities' votes. The four *primary* factors included demonstrating a lack of access to the slating process, unresponsive legislators to the needs of minorities, state policies that maintained at-large systems, and a historical legacy of discrimination that precluded minority participation in the political process. The *enhancing* factors were at-large election districts, majority-vote requirements, a lack of residency districts, and anti-single-shot voting provisions. The Richmond case included most of the primary factors, and federal courts used the *Zimmer* factors over the course of the 1970s to assess vote-dilution claims. Following Petersburg's implementation of the suggested majority–minority system, the DOJ approved the annexation there. In light of *Petersburg, White,* and *Zimmer,* Richmond officials began to realize that adopting a ward-based election system that properly reflected the number of blacks in Richmond was the only way to solve the annexation predicament.[45]

By the spring of 1973, the suspension of city council elections began to take its toll on the inner workings of local government. Richmonders had grown increasingly disgruntled over the suspension. By 1973, three members of the city council had resigned: Jim Carpenter to pursue missionary work in Ecuador, Howard Carwile to run for a seat in Virginia's General Assembly, and William Daniel, who was a successful banker, because he was tired of the racial animosity in Richmond politics. Although most business at city hall went on as usual, the Court's enjoinment meant that city officials were prohibited from organizing a special election to replace these councilmen. The city council had to fill vacant seats by appointing new members. Julius Johnson and Raymond Royall—both TOP endorsements—filled two of the vacant seats. Henry Marsh suggested the third appointee, Willie J. Dell. The first African American city councilwoman in Richmond's history, Dell was a professor of social work at Virginia Commonwealth University, a member of Richmond's Commission on Human Relations, and an active participant in the Crusade. She had planned to run for a council seat before the Supreme Court suspended local elections. In 1973, local officials also began to work together as provisional allies to solve the problem of Richmond's electoral system. An interracial contingent of council members and local officials, led by Henry Marsh, began working on electoral plans that the DOJ might approve. On August 25, 1973, the DOJ approved a nine-ward plan that consisted of four wards with a majority black voting-age population and five wards with a majority white voting-age population. The Court denied the DOJ's endorsement, however, because it had not yet made a decision in Holt's deannexation suit. By late 1974, the city moved to offset *Holt II* by filing its own suit in defense of annexation, *City of Richmond v. United States*.[46]

By the mid-1970s, Holt, Venable, and annexed residents continued the push for complete deannexation. The contention between pro- and antiannexationists reached a critical point after three judges appointed U.S. magistrate Lawrence S. Margolis as a friend of the court to hear Richmond's case and make recommendations to the U.S. District Court for the District of Columbia. Margolis filed his opinion on the city's suit on January 28, 1974. He found that annexation was racially motivated and recommended that the city deannex Chesterfield County. Margolis's decision dismayed the Crusade and the Richmond City Council. The *Times-Dispatch* continued to champion the politics of states' rights and contended that Margolis's proposal illustrated "the offensive restrictions that have been imposed upon self-government in Virginia and, indeed, in most of the South." The Crusade continued its support for majority–minority system. It argued, "Even if blacks voters stood a chance of gaining significant political power from de-annexation, [deannexation] would give them precious little because of the [economic] difficulties facing the city within its old borders. . . . Both expansion and a political voice . . . are necessary. Richmond public schools would instantly be transformed from a black majority system to a virtually all-black system with staggering implications for the course of desegregation efforts in which Richmond blacks have been involved in for more than a decade." White leadership and the Crusade disagreed with Margolis's suggestion to deannex because the city's bonded debt, should Richmond be forced to return Chesterfield, would have been close to the legal debt ceiling. The annexed area contained 23 to 25 percent of the city's total taxable values. Chesterfield residents and Holt/Venable viewed Margolis's decision— though not law—as a comparative victory. At a meeting of nearly one hundred Chesterfield residents, C. G. Loomer, a spokesman for Chesterfield County Council of Civic Associations, received the loudest applause of the evening when he mentioned, "My children are going to go back to neighborhood schools." Loomer's statement could easily be translated to mean that his kids were going to return to white schools.[47]

By late 1974, Richmond's lawsuit inched closer to the Supreme Court. On May 29, 1974, the U.S. District Court for the District of Columbia found that annexation was a direct result of the Crusade's success in the city council election of 1968 and a panic reaction caused by the fear of a black political coup in 1970. Although the city failed to delay *Holt II,* it appealed to the U.S. Supreme Court to overturn the District of Columbia District Court. On December 16, 1974, the Supreme Court announced its decision to consider Richmond's suit. On April 23, 1975, the Court heard twenty-minute arguments from Venable, the Crusade's representative Armand Derfner, the DOJ, and attorney Charles S. Rhyne, representing Richmond. Venable continued Holt's quest for deannexation. During oral arguments, he contended, "We have a basic assumption that an award of the deannexation in this case would result in the end of annexation for cities and that simply isn't the case. An award of deannexation in this particular case would uphold a dignity of the Voting Rights Act in 1965 and would serve notice that you can't go out to 'keep the niggers from taking over a municipal government' and serve that purpose well." Derfner and the Crusade proposed that a ward-based system could offset vote dilution. Derfner argued, "The question is how that diluting effect is to be overcome and I think what the Petersburg case said and the way the District Court here read the Petersburg case is that at least where you have no discriminatory purpose, you can—you can meet your burden as to effect by making a good faith showing that you have minimized the dilutive effect to the extent possible, or to the extent reasonable." The City of Richmond's attorney, Charles Rhyne, agreed with the Crusade. He argued, "An election under the nine ward plan . . . is the only fair election where the black citizens of Richmond will have full representation and participation in the political process because they are guaranteed four seats."[48]

Two months later the Court handed down its decision in *Richmond*. In a five-to-three vote (Justice Louis F. Powell abstained), it held "that an annexation reducing the relative political strength of the minority race in the enlarged city as compared with what it was before the annexation is not a statutory violation as long as the post-annexation electoral system fairly recognizes the minority's political potential." During testimony in *Holt I* and *II*, RF representatives, including councilman and future vice mayor Henry Valentine, acknowledged that white officials had annexed Chesterfield County to preclude a BMC. The Court further argued: "Richmond's focus in the negotiations was upon the number of new white voters it could obtain by annexation; it expressed no interest in economic or geographic considerations such as tax revenues, vacant land, utilities, or schools. The record is replete with statements by Richmond officials which prove beyond question that the predominant (if not sole) motive and desire of the negotiators of the 1969 settlement was to acquire 44,000 additional white citizens for Richmond in order to avert a transfer of political control to what was fast-becoming a black-population majority." All eight justices agreed that Richmond's annexation was racially motivated. In the end, however, they allowed Richmond to keep Chesterfield County because they believed that repatriating portions of the suburb might do irreparable fiscal harm to the city. In the short term, deannexation would cost the City of Richmond an immense amount of time and financial resources. Had the Court ruled in favor of deannexation, state regulations mandated that both Richmond and Chesterfield County would assume liquidated damages from terminating contracts with private and official service providers. At the time the Court ruled on annexation, Richmond had an uncommitted debt margin of $6 million, and deannexation would have resulted in the city exceeding this margin by $18 million. Richmond had also hired roughly 509 people to accommodate the merger and provide services to the annexed area, including 163 new employees in the Department of Public Safety alone. Had the Court ruled in favor of deannexation, all 509 people would have lost their jobs with the city.[49]

The Court then returned the city's suit to the District of Columbia District Court where the questions of implementing single-member districts had emerged. After a series of hearings that spanned nearly one year, the district court ended the city's suit, ruling that "under the circumstances as required by the mandate of the Supreme Court, it is hereby declared that the plaintiff [Richmond] has complied with the Voting Rights Act of 1965 with respect to the annexation of 1970 in the context of the ward plan for council-manic elections." The district court allowed Richmond to implement four presumably white and black districts and a swing district—which contained a voting-age population that was 59 percent white and 41 percent African American.[50]

Given the Court's decision in *Richmond,* Holt and Venable gave up their fight. Venable argued, "I consider we won three-fourths to ninety percent. . . . We set out to prove that the annexation was racially motivated, that it had a racial effect and that a meaningful remedy was needed." The Crusade convinced Holt that even without deannexation it was probable—given the city's nearly 50 percent black population—that blacks could mathematically elect a council majority and a mayor with four or possibly five black districts. Blacks not only had overwhelming majorities in the Third, Sixth, and Seventh Districts but were also the majority in the Eighth District. Holt got the message. He eventually chose not to appeal *Holt II* to the Supreme Court. Following his decision to suspend the appeal, the Supreme Court lifted its five-year injunction of city council elections. The *Afro* claimed, "Under the new district system . . . we will have the opportunity to . . . change the complexion of City Hall." After nearly a decade of arguing for a district system, the Crusade sat poised to make history.[51]

On Wednesday, March 2, 1977, the *Richmond Afro-American's* front-page headline read, "Power to the People." Richmonders elected the first BMC in the city's history according to a district system that Henry Marsh had helped design: Willie J. Dell, H. W. "Chuck" Richardson, Walter T. Kenney, Henry L. Marsh, and Claudette McDaniel. (For election results in 1977, see table 10 in the appendix.) An African American candidate ran in every district except the district that covered the West End. The city council went on to appoint Marsh to the mayoralty; he thus became the first African American mayor in Richmond's history. Conspicuously absent from the list of victors, however, was Curtis Holt. Running in Marsh's district, he finished last with 687 votes. The Crusade did not endorse his candidacy. Although Holt was never elected to public office, he continued to remain active in Richmond politics throughout the 1980s.[52]

Districts revolutionized city hall. On the ten-year anniversary of the VRA, the USCCR released a new report on the state of voting in America, *The Voting Rights Act: Ten Years After.* The commission recognized that Virginia had closed the gap between voting-age whites and blacks more effectively than any other state in the former Confederacy. It also claimed that lawsuits were one of the most important weapons in the VRA's enforcement arsenal. With the exception of Chuck Richardson, who won by a mere twelve votes, all members of the BMC in 1977 soundly defeated their closest opponents. The BMC contained one social work professor (Dell), an occupational therapist (McDaniel), a union representative in the U.S. Postal Service (Kenney), and a twenty-eight-year-old Vietnam veteran, Richardson, who was in the process of completing a bachelor's degree in urban planning from Virginia Commonwealth University. Richardson's sister was also the wife of Atlanta mayor Maynard Jackson. The Vietnam veteran also had ties to Gordon Blaine Hancock, the former VUU professor, who had regularly hired a teenage Richardson to do odd jobs around his house. Among those who lost bids for reelection were the president of a Main Street brokerage firm, a retired oil company executive, the president of one of Richmond's prominent realty firms, the owner of a successful automobile dealership, a building materials company executive, and the president of a major funeral home—all were TOP members or had been endorsed by TOP. Annexation, in an odd twist of fate, brought about the very racial equality in electoral politics that white powerbrokers sought to preclude in 1969. The fallout from annexation, however, continued to influence Virginia's politics in the decades to come.[53]

In their anxious pursuit to maintain white control over city hall, white officials in Richmond detonated a groundswell of antiannexationist tendencies. Richmond's merger with Chesterfield County had consequences for the future of annexation law in Virginia and the commonwealth's constitution. Washington's civil rights acts nullified many of the discriminatory practices mandated by the commonwealth's constitution of 1901–1902. In 1971, the Commission on Constitutional Revision, convened in 1969, recommended that Governor Godwin and the General Assembly rewrite the constitution in accordance with federal civil rights law. Virginia's policy makers not only amended the discriminatory voting procedures and guidelines in Article 2 but also sustained the "separate and distinct" philosophy for cities and counties in Article 7. If antiannexationists found their first ally in Curtis Holt, antiurbanism eventually crept into the General Assembly. By the early 1970s, unparalleled white flight from Virginia's cities eventually gave rise to greater county and suburban representation in state government. The commonwealth's lawmakers responded to the flood of annexation suits during the 1960s by imposing a moratorium on new annexations for cities with populations larger than 125,000. After a series of studies on Virginia's city–county relationships (the Stuart Commission from 1971 to 1977 and the Michie Commission from 1977 to 1979), the General Assembly passed HB603 in 1979. The bill significantly altered all future annexation proceedings in the commonwealth. After 1980, lawmakers mandated that Virginia's counties had the right to request immunity from all future annexations. Chesterfield, Henrico, Prince William, Roanoke, and York Counties immediately filed for this immunity. These counties, from 1980 forward, nullified all future annexations. A significant number of Virginia's major metropolitan areas remain landlocked to this day.[54]

In the end, not only had Richmond failed to procure the vacant land the city needed for growth and expansion, but the public officials' rush to dilute the power of the city's black voters also left Richmond blocked in by its surrounding counties. To this day, Richmond has no authority to annex any portion of its adjoining counties, and it has been difficult for lawmakers to amend the mandate of 1979 because suburban and rural voters—who became increasingly conservative during the 1970s—still hold sway over Virginia's General Assembly. The members of the BMC were in many ways the benefactors of this backlash, but they found, in due time, that segregationists' lack of political vision would impinge upon the city council's ability to meet the needs of municipal governance.[55]

4

"The Dream Is Lost"

Henry Marsh and Black Governance in an Era of White Political Resistance

On Friday, August 20, 1982, members of the Crusade and a handful of Richmond's most prominent African American political figures assembled for a private retreat at the Roslyn Conference Center in Henrico County, Virginia. Shortly after Ellen D. Pearson called the meeting to order, the state director of the NAACP, Jack Gravely, interjected, "What the hell is going on in Richmond? What is the Crusade doing"? Gravely would not have asked that question in 1977. Had he, not a member in attendance would have struggled to answer the question. Even fewer would have scrambled to defend the Crusade's legacy. Yet in 1982 the Crusade called the closed session to address a crisis of black political leadership. It appeared that African American city council newcomer, Dr. Roy West, had clandestinely negotiated with white members of the city council to appoint himself mayor. West's appointment to the mayoralty was the biggest threat the Crusade had faced since the annexation of Chesterfield County—and few people saw West coming. Roslyn became a referendum on the future of the black body politic. The city's district system may have ensured a five-to-four BMC, but it did little to safeguard the character of candidates. Majority–minority districts did even less to shield black communities from intensifying economic vulnerability or impede the persistence of white obstructionism. Shortly after the election of the BMC, Atlanta mayor Maynard Jackson commented, "The politics of Richmond are now controlled by Afro-Americans, [but its] economics [are] still controlled by white Americans. It is a question now of whether there will be a standoff or a standing up together." Richmond had answered Jackson's query by the early 1980s. In the years following 1977, African Americans came to realize that it would take more than majority–minority districts to bring about broad-based racial equality. Sa'ad El-Amin (formerly Jeroyd Greene), a political consultant to the Crusade, had Roy West and the state of Richmond's black communities in mind when he lamented at Roslyn, "The dream is lost."[1]

The rise of black governance eventually proved to be one of the civil rights movement's most enduring legacies. The election of the BMC in 1977 represented nearly a decade of unprecedented African American political empowerment. African American voters elected hundreds of local and county-level officials, namely in cities with black-majority populations or cities that were on the verge of becoming majority black. By April 1974, the total number of black elected officials in the seven states covered by the VRA reached 963: including one member of the U.S. Congress, 36 state legislators, 429 county officials, and 497 municipal officials. Not only had the spirit of electoral politics led to a cascade of rising black expectations in the South, but the belief that African American involvement in local electoral politics would lead to greater community control also characterized politics beyond the region. African Americans during the 1970s and 1980s elected more than half of the country's black mayors in cities where blacks were not the majority. Carl Stokes of Cleveland, Ohio, and Richard Hatcher of Gary, Indiana, led the way when they were elected in 1968. A number of black mayors followed Stokes and Hatcher's lead—Kenneth Gibson in Newark, New Jersey, in 1970; Tom Bradley in Los Angeles in 1973; and Coleman Young in Detroit in 1974. Many of these northern (and western) mayors were elected to office by forging interracial coalitions with white Democrats and liberals. Some of them garnered a considerable amount of white votes by de-emphasizing race and racially polarized language. In many ways, these mayors' electoral strategies became a blueprint for black governance in Richmond after 1977, and they portended the conflict that precipitated the meeting at the Roslyn Conference Center.[2]

The federal government also played a critical role in the process of black political empowerment and governance during the 1970s. Black governance in that decade was the result of a calculated alliance between African Americans and Washington that dated back to the 1930s and culminated in the civil rights acts—African Americans, like whites during the New Deal, cast their lot with the liberal state. For a brief moment in twentieth-century history, it appeared that the Great Society would raise the standard of living for African Americans, much like the New Deal had for white ethnic communities. In fact, the American civil rights movement, the consummate era of possibility, seemed to be followed by an era of real material changes. The reapportionment lawsuits of the 1970s had eliminated racially discriminatory multimember district systems in a majority of southern states. Majority–minority district systems gave rise to an unprecedented number of black legislators and in many ways instigated a durable shift toward a racial democracy. Governing bodies that finally reflected the diversity of the American experience characterized this racial democracy. It also appeared that federal officials were committed to defending the legacy of the Voting Rights Act. Although voting and electoral politics continued to be contested matters during and after the 1970s, African Americans had allies in Washington. Jurisdictions covered by the VRA, for instance, submitted 30,332 potential changes to voting practices and procedures under section 5 between 1975 and 1980. In response to these potential changes—in many of these cases, policy makers made electoral changes with no discriminatory intent—the DOJ issued more than 700 rejections. Of the changes that federal officials rejected, however, the vast majority pertained to minority-vote dilution. Annexations accounted for 30.5 percent of the rejected changes, the highest percentage among dilution tactics recorded by the USCCR. By the early 1990s, federal officials made hundreds of American cities and state-level jurisdictions switch from at-large to single-member district systems. These districts, it turned out, had ominous implications for urban America.[3]

Richmond's majority–minority district system was also the product of demographic and structural developments. For the first time in Richmond's history, black council members—three of them with virtually no previous experience as public officials—numerically outnumbered white city council members. There were, however, worrying consequences to this symbolic political victory. Predominantly minority districts and precincts were the product of the undemocratic face of Jim Crow. Richmond's BMC was not just the culmination of black voter mobilization and the district system. In the mid–twentieth century, the capital city also witnessed an increase in the number of nonwhite residents, an out-migration of whites to surrounding counties, and the fixity of municipal boundaries. The furtherance of residential segregation and the compression of poorer African Americans into a handful of densely populated, racially homogeneous precincts worsened white flight and the situation of fixed city–county boundaries. In the late 1970s, African Americans made up approximately 48 percent of Richmond's total population (nearly 70 percent of that number were of voting age) and occupied five council seats. These council seats were in many ways contingent upon larger troublesome demographic trends. Of Richmond's seventy census tracts in 1970 (the district system was derived from the 1970 census), twenty-seven were more than 90 percent white, and nineteen were more than 90 percent African American. Put another way, well more than half of Richmond precincts were almost entirely racially homogenous. Many of Richmond's racially mixed neighborhoods were only temporarily integrated as blacks moved in and whites moved away. A few of these areas existed on what was once Richmond's periphery, so that after whites moved away during the postwar period, these areas became the equivalent of African Americans' suburbs. In fact, the black middle-class area of Highland Park on Richmond's north side, known for its historic Queen Anne homes, was one such neighborhood. The census tracts in Highland Park that eventually voted for Roy West in 1982 were overwhelmingly African American. Two tracts, numbers 106 and 108, with the highest median annual household income, $14,197 and $15,720, respectively, were more than 90 percent black. Census tract 105, which was roughly 87 percent African American, had a median household income of $17,379. In 1980, Richmond's average median household income was $13,606, and the Commonwealth of Virginia's was $17,475. These Highland Park census tracts were eventually instrumental in changing the nature of black governance in Richmond.[4]

Richmond's neighborhoods were divided as much by class as by race. In 1970, the U.S. Census Bureau reported that only 8.3 percent of Richmond's whites lived below the poverty line. That number was nearly triple for African Americans, with 25.2 percent living below the poverty line. The vast majority of Richmond's most economically vulnerable residents resided in densely clustered public-housing complexes on the city's East End and south side—particularly in the districts of Henry Marsh, Claudette McDaniel, and Walter Kenney. Walter Kenney's district was home to the Gilpin Court housing projects. In Gilpin Court's precinct, census tract 301, 67.6 percent of the people lived below the poverty line. In Henry Marsh's East End district, census tracts 204, 201, and 202 were home to Mosby, Fairfield, and Whitcomb Courts, respectively. These tracts were also decidedly poor and overwhelmingly black. Census tract 204 was 99 percent African American, and 31 percent of its inhabitants fell below the poverty line; census tract 202 was also more than 99 percent African American, with 41.9 percent of the tract's residents below the poverty line; and, last, census tract 201 was 97.3 percent African American, with nearly 45 percent its residents below the poverty line. In 1970, 33.6 percent of African Americans across the United States lived below the poverty level. In fiscal year 1977–1978, the City of Richmond averaged roughly 6,800 households and 20,400 individuals on the Food Stamp Program—roughly 11 percent of the city's total population. African Americans elected the BMC in 1977 to address issues of this nature.[5]

All five members of Richmond's BMC had campaigned on a civil rights agenda. African Americans' success in electoral politics during the 1970s led to mounting expectations throughout America's black communities. The same was true in Richmond. These candidates had very openly addressed the desire to bring material resources to black communities, ultimately to make good on the symbolism of their elections. During his campaign, Henry Marsh expressed Richmond's need to "launch an attack on poverty" and argued not only that economic vulnerability was a major cause of Richmond's social problems but also that city officials needed "to get away from having a little department in the city fighting poverty." These candidates' principle goals were to "attack poverty," achieve "greater racial understanding," forge stronger commitments to "excellence in education," establish "greater community involvement in municipal affairs," and, finally, extend a "hand of friendship and cooperation to the business community." Each one also campaigned on solving unemployment (especially for African American youth), defending communities from crime and police brutality, and addressing the problem of increasingly segregated city schools. Their election to city council was evidence that people believed them. The *Richmond Afro-American* contended on March 5, 1977: "When the new Council takes office next Tuesday, March 8, it will not only have a new look—but undoubtedly will have a new philosophy. All the winning black candidates ran on a power-to-the-people philosophy. . . . Therefore philosophically, it is expected that there will be a shift to people-oriented programs with less emphasis on programs designed to largely benefit the business community." Five days after the council's election, the Afro-American Corporation's chief editor, Raymond Boone, suggested that because African American candidates ran and were subsequently elected on civil rights platforms, the community expected a movement toward empowerment programs that would emphasize social welfare and affirmative action.[6]

Of the five-member BMC, commonly referred to as "the Team," incumbents Willie Dell and Henry Marsh came equipped with civil rights legacies. These two, decidedly more so than Walter Kenney, Chuck Richardson, or Claudette McDaniel, had been integral to Richmond's fight for political, social, and economic justice. Marsh had been an early and passionate supporter of Jimmy Carter in 1976. Not long after being appointed mayor, he turned down an appointment to a federal judgeship by the Carter administration. Unlike other African American mayors such as Marion Barry, who often marched in "blue jeans and dashikis," Marsh had earned a reputation as a soft-spoken legal and political strategist. In 1979, Tim Smith, who directed Jimmy Carter's Virginia reelection campaign, stated, "[Marsh is] clearly a politician who is perceived as having influence with a national black constituency." Shortly after the election and his appointment as mayor, Marsh emerged as the Team's unofficial leader. If Marsh was the BMC's tactician, Willie Dell was the fire.[7]

Dell, who was the first African American councilwoman in Richmond's history, had been on the city council since 1973. During the enjoinment, when no city council elections could be held by order of the Supreme Court, council members had appointed Dell to replace Jim Carpenter. Dell, whose husband was the pastor of the East End's Woodville Presbyterian Church, did not emerge on the political scene out of thin air. She had earned a bachelor's degree from St. Augustine College, a historically black college, in Raleigh, North Carolina (now St. Augustine University) and had gone on to earn a master's degree from Virginia Commonwealth University in 1960. Dell was a caseworker for the Richmond Department of Public Welfare between 1956 and 1961. By 1969, she headed that department's maternal and infant care project. In the same year, she left public service to work as an assistant professor in the Virginia Commonwealth Graduate School of Social Work. When she decided to run for city council in 1972 (just prior to the enjoinment), Dell had the full support of Henry Marsh, Curtis Holt, the Creighton Court Civic Association, Edwina Hall, and the Crusade. Marsh put Dell's name forward to replace Carpenter, and the Crusade argued years later that both black and white leaders made an agreement to appoint Dell to the city council. The Crusade, which "did not want the white establishment to anoint its own black leadership," put pressure on the city council to appoint her. She came to epitomize what sociologist Belinda Corbett later called a "bridge leader"—her supporters realized that she had a knack for negotiating the space between communities and official leadership.[8]

Gendered expectations about female leadership also shaped Willie Dell's political career. Historian Laurie B. Green argues that African American women, not just men, during the civil rights movement invested "in their own roles as protectors . . . against racial violence and other hardships." Marsh and the Crusade put Dell's name forward in 1973 precisely because of her dedication to the fight against poverty. Dell not only diversified the Social Work School's curriculum by emphasizing economic vulnerability in black communities but also taught courses such as "Authenticity Techniques and the Black Experience." If Sonny Cephas and Winfred Mundle had struggled to accommodate the politics of black empowerment in the 1960s, Dell was one of the first black councilpersons to emphasize racial politics. For instance, Dell and Marsh instigated the redevelopment of Jackson Ward during the mid-1970s (discussed later in this chapter). They eventually funneled thousands of dollars in block grant funds from the U.S. Department of Housing and Urban Development to Jackson Ward and the George Mason area of Church Hill. It was also Dell, like Curtis Holt before her, who sought more community control in Richmond public housing by trying (although failing) to appoint a female public-housing resident to the RRHA's board. Dell also resisted assumptions about how black female public officials were supposed to dress and behave. As common as African-style clothing and Afros were to black style in the 1970s, it was extremely rare to see black leaders and public officials in Richmond dress in this fashion. Although respectability politics had long since fizzled out by the 1970s, members of Richmond's black establishment, especially women, continued to dress conventionally. Dell, however, dressed in the then popular image of cultural nationalism. She was the first member of Woodville Presbyterian Church to openly wear an Afro. Many whites and middle-class blacks often considered Dell too outspoken, but she came to embody Black Power's artistic renaissance in dress and spirit. Dell often wore a dashiki, a loose-fitting West African tunic decorated with colorful patterns, and unapologetically spoke in what experts would later call "Ebonics." Although she later came to believe that politicized African Americans detested her for these very reasons, she was one of the Crusade's most relevant members in the late 1970s.[9]

The Crusade was still an electoral force during the late 1970s. By 1977, this 1,200-member political action group continued to exercise considerable influence over local electoral politics. In 1977, the organization elected Norvell Robinson, a banquet manager for the downtown Holiday Inn, as its president. The *Richmond Afro-American,* whose circulation ranged from 10,000 to 15,000 in the late 1970s, continued to be the organization's chief ally and outlet. During the late 1970s, the Crusade had come to terms not merely with its success in helping implement a ward system and the election of a BMC but also with the fact that many of its 1,200 members were younger and more progressive than the professionals who had dominated the organization since 1956. These new members had come of age during the civil rights movement. The spirit of civil rights reforms, not Jim Crow, motivated these younger members to join the Crusade. Robinson argued, "The professionals had the time and the expertise to get things done." For nearly twenty years, some of Richmond's most influential African Americans had directed the Crusade, including Henry Marsh, Ethel Overby, podiatrist William S. Thornton, optometrist M. Philmore Howlett, Lola Hamilton, physician Frank Royal, John Brooks, physician William Ferguson Reid, Union Mutual Savings and Loan president Garfield F. Childs, and lawyer L. Douglas Wilder. By 1977, the Crusade's membership included an even wider-cross section of the city's black communities. Robinson argued further: "We have what we call young Turks, fire and brimstone preachers. And the teachers, we have them, they're young. They want us to abandon the practical politics of yesterday. They want to be sure that if there are blacks running, they will get Crusade support. They don't feel whites have ever really done anything to help the black community, the lower elements of the black community." By the late 1970s, even Sa'ad El-Amin, a chief critic of the black political establishment in the late 1960s, was active in the Crusade, and by the early 1980s he was a chief political consultant to the Crusade. The diversification of the Crusade challenged the organization during the mid-1980s, but on the heels of the election in 1977 these cleavages were not yet apparent. What did seem apparent, however, was the fact that although African Americans had a numerical advantage at city hall and majority–minority districts had shifted the balance of power toward Richmond's African American voters, the capital city's economic powerbrokers were still exclusively white. Indeed, Robinson recognized this problem when he told Shelley Rolfe of the *Richmond Times-Dispatch* that black Americans needed to establish dialogue with "Richmond's white financial establishment" and "search for an end to almost total black dependency on it."[10]

African Americans' political victories at the local level belied a more menacing reality: whites were still the gatekeepers to Richmond's business community. After the election of 1977, two competing strains came to dominate Richmond politics—African Americans, who held the balance of political power yet had little economic muscle, and whites, who maintained a monopoly over the city's business sector. The symbolism of blacks' transition from protest to politics often obscured a harsh truth. Decades of institutional bigotry meant that African Americans' wealth and influence paled in comparison to that of their white counterparts. In time, black politicians, black voters, and black political organizations came to view winning control over city halls as a vital bargaining chip. The Crusade and the BMC, which were previously skeptical of Richmond's private sector because it was dominated by racist white elites, believed that elected office gave minority communities the leverage they needed to negotiate with local powerbrokers. Wealthy white powerbrokers also had strong ties to the council minority and were often among the richest men not just in Richmond but also in Virginia. Although some of these powerbrokers had been elected to city council, most of them were not elected officials. They were most often appointed to the boards of civic agencies and held sway over the informal business relationships between city hall and Richmond's powerful business sector.[11]

Tension between politicized African Americans and well-heeled white elites became a defining characteristic of municipal politics in Richmond after 1977. In an article titled "Richmond's Silent Decision Makers," published in February 1978, Bill Miller of the *Richmond Times-Dispatch* was one of the few reporters from Richmond's daily newspapers to acknowledge this dichotomy. He argued, "Within the black community, leaders tend to be less financially endowed than their white counterparts, but they are generally professional or self-employed business leaders, just as is true for the white establishment. The black community leaders also tend to be major figures in organizations such as the city's major black political force, the Crusade for Voters." Miller was right—African Americans' political power derived almost exclusively from their associations with civic organizations. Yet, Miller pointed out, membership in Richmond's white elite establishment carried "a requisite of successful business community membership. . . . The city's power structure tends to be oriented toward its business and financial community and the leaders of the establishment can be found generally in the executive offices of the major businesses, corporations, and law firms." The white establishment occupied not just the same business-oriented groups but also the same social and political circles. These elites, Miller demonstrated, tended "to share moneyed lifestyles that accompany business success. Homes are located in the fashionable sections. Children are enrolled in private schools. The men are members of *the* downtown clubs." Members of Richmond's moneyed establishment most often lived in the exclusively white West End. Of the twenty-one men whom the *Dispatch* associated with Richmond's moneyed establishment, all but four lived in the West End, and more than half were Richmond natives.[12]

Even after African Americans assumed control of the city council, a decidedly paternalistic culture continued to characterize municipal politics. "Naturally," argued Robert Martin, the Richmond Chamber of Commerce vice president, "there was going to be some question in whites' minds about the relationship between black council members and Richmond's business community." One month following the BMC's election, council member Wayland Rennie argued in the *Richmond Times-Dispatch* that if Marsh and the BMC were not careful, they "could start the second major wave of white flight from the city." Councilman Henry Valentine, a West Ender and president of a Richmond brokerage firm whose old family home had been converted into a museum of history and art, echoed Rennie's incredulity. It was Valentine who openly expressed to McDaniel, the daughter of a chauffeur and a housewife, that blacks were incapable of running the city. As African Americans pushed for full equality over the mid–twentieth century, Richmond's white elites often struggled to maintain the long-standing practice of restricting and granting freedoms on their own terms. Informal social and business relationships often crept into local politics. These informal arrangements, urban historians and political scientists argue, assume special priority in local government—particularly because political tradition, constitutional law, and private autonomy limit the formal workings of municipal governance. The representatives of white elites had dominated not merely city council but also the relationships between the city council and local economic life: "Like every other city, Richmond has a group of people who are influential with those who make major decisions—an establishment. In some cities, the establishment members are the conspicuous kingmakers who can deliver voters and are regularly in the headlines. But in Richmond, the power structure is made up of a more subtle network of business-oriented leaders," explained Miller.[13]

Many, but not all, of these white powerbrokers—led by former councilman James C. Wheat Jr., businessman Thomas C. Boushall, and attorney Andrew J. Brent—were extremely reluctant to share power with African Americans. For instance, it was Brent, a lawyer with one of Richmond's most established legal firms, who helped lead the way on the construction of Richmond's Downtown Expressway and headed up the RMA in the late 1970s. Brent, Boushall, and Wheat were also active in the establishment of RF, TOP, and Richmond's downtown-redevelopment plans—what became known as Project One. They were also closely affiliated with some of Richmond's most influential and wealthy businessmen in the commonwealth, including pharmaceutical entrepreneur

E. Claiborne Robins of A. H. Robins Company (of Robitussin fame), department store owner William C. Thalhimer Jr., and Phillip Morris vice president B. A. Soyers. These local business elites had grown accustomed to working with close white associates at city hall. Mayor Marsh argued, "I am not privy to many of the situations where leaders of the white community meet. A lot of this is done in socializing and a lot of socializing is done where blacks are not present." Marsh could have easily argued that a great deal of this socializing and decision making took place in spaces where blacks were not just "not present" but in truth not welcome.[14]

Unlike the economy of a number of black cities in the Rust Belt with sizeable African American populations, Richmond's economy was in relatively decent shape during the 1970s. African Americans did not inherit a dying city, but Richmond's local economy underwent a dramatic transition from manufacturing to service, semiprofessional, and professional employment. The commonwealth's capital, just five hundred miles from nearly 50 percent of the entire U.S. population, trailed only Atlanta among southern cities that headquartered national and international firms.

During the late 1970s, Richmond had a double-A bond rating and was the leading producer of cigarettes and tobacco products. The Reynolds Corporation (formerly the Reynolds Metal Company) led America in synthetic fibers production, and the commonwealth's capital headquartered the Fifth District Federal Reserve Bank. Because Richmond was the capital, there were approximately 30,000 state jobs in and around the greater Richmond area during the late 1970s and 1980s. Most of its government jobs required not only semiprofessional and professional skills but also a high school diploma. In time, this movement toward specialized employment and professionalism proved to be Richmond's equivalent to Rust Belt deindustrialization.[15]

The trend toward professionalization and specialized employment did not bode well for many of the city's African Americans. Few manufacturing-based cities were exempt from the economic malaise of the 1970s. As economic stagnation and inflation slowed American manufacturing and middle-class black people entered the professional labor force, many working-class African Americans fell back into poverty. Just as Richmonders elected the BMC to city hall, the city began to lose the types of

Table 4.1. Employment Losses and Gains in Richmond, 1973–1976

Industry	Number of Jobs Lost (Total 8,031)	Number of Jobs Gained (Total 7,975)
Furniture	236	
Stone, Clay, and Glass	276	
Primary Metal	270	
Fabricated Metal Production	120	
Electrical Machinery	335	
Misc. Manufacturing	152	
Food	619	
Apparel	501	
Paper	515	
Printing	546	
Rubber, Plastics	100	
Mining	30	
Contract Construction	1,506	
Transportation and Public Utilities	1,418	
Wholesale and Retail	580	
Finance, Insurance, and Real Estate	257	
Local Government	570	
Federal and State Government		3,717
Service		2,870
Tobacco		1,049
Miscellaneous		339

Source: Data from *Richmond Times-Dispatch*, July 30, 1978, B2.

jobs that kept most African Americans above the poverty line—unskilled and semiskilled labor. At the same time, however, the metropolitan area gained jobs that required clerical, semiprofessional, and professional skill sets. In fact, the number of manufacturing establishments in Richmond proper fell from 418 in 1967 to 376 in 1976—nine major manufacturing plants closed between 1970 and 1976. Between 1954 and 1973, Richmond, like many American cities, witnessed the rise of the suburbanization of retail shopping. The city's share of regional retail sales within the metropolitan area also fell from 89 percent to 57 percent, and the number of retail establishments fell by 665. Tobacco production remained the cornerstone of Richmond's manufacturing base. Those African Americans who did not work in tobacco production or other manufacturing jobs— outside of a handful of growing technocratic elites—often found it difficult to deal with the professionalization of Richmond's workforce and the suburbanization of retail and service jobs. African Americans who struggled in public school did not transition to professional employment.[16]

Even as early as the 1970s, census data demonstrated that an alarming number of African Americans not only failed to graduate from high school but were also unskilled and semiskilled workers. For instance, the U.S. Census Bureau recorded that there were 140,401 white and black Richmonders twenty-five years of age and older. Of that total number, 36.4 percent of the African Americans older than twenty-five (51,105) had an elementary education or slightly higher; 20.3 percent (28,461) had finished high school or had attended some high school; and 3.8 percent (5,285, roughly 15 percent lower than whites) had attended or graduated from college. Of Richmond's sixteen- to twenty-one-year-old African Americans, 24.7 percent had either dropped out of high school or were not enrolled in 1970. The remainder of African Americans had finished middle school and attended some high school. Clerical work (21 percent), professional work (roughly 15 percent), manufacturing (12.3 percent), and service work (14 percent) made up the largest percentage of Richmond's occupations in 1970. Over the course of the late 1970s and throughout the 1980s, many of these jobs moved into outlying counties. Between 1972 and 1977, the amount of taxable income from businesses in downtown Richmond decreased by 3 percent, from 14 percent to 11 percent—a sizeable portion of that revenue stayed in the Richmond metropolitan area but moved beyond county lines. The suburbanization of work was often made worse by the fact that the Greater Richmond Transit Company, which was initially wholly owned by the City of Richmond, only sporadically serviced suburban counties (another casualty of the city–county independence).[17]

Marsh and the four other black council members spent their first year in office running a campaign of reassurance. African American political leaders needed to convince business groups and private lobbies that blacks could keep the city above water. To do this, they needed to work with the very business elites who were skeptical of blacks' ability to run city hall. On the eve of the special election in 1977, most Richmonders believed Marsh was a "force for good." Marsh argued: "Our interdependence is obvious. We recognize the vital role that business must play if our city is to realize its potential. If we are to obtain resources to satisfy our human needs, we must expand our economic base and create the jobs needed by our citizens for dignity." The new majority did not institute any policy changes that appeared to be too radical. If whites had any fears about a black agenda, such an agenda failed to materialize during the first year. Mayor Marsh and Vice Mayor Valentine spent the majority of their first year in office trying to solidify plans to revitalize downtown. The plan was to build a $12 million convention and exhibition center to attract nearly $30 million worth of surrounding private investments. The so-called Project One development plan became a point of deep contention.[18]

On the Horns of a Dilemma

If majority–minority districts allowed African Americans to obtain some (though not nearly enough) political power in Richmond, whites officials and elites continued to resist blacks' claims to full citizenship. Unable to cap the wellspring of African Americans' electoral victories with vote-dilution techniques, whites attempted to delegitimize black elected officials in the court of public opinion. Resistance to black governance and suspicions about African American mayors and predominantly black city councils, unfortunately, was not specific to Richmond. Political scientist and urban planner J. Phillip Thompson argues, "Business and middle-class allies often had unrealistic expectations that black mayors could maintain racial peace despite popular racial hostility." In many cases, these detractors knew that African Americans lacked the types of economic ties that were essential to maintaining cities' viability. In *The Voting Rights Act: Ten Years After*, a study of voting rights in 1975, the USCCR recognized that America's legacy of economic subordination—namely of African Americans, Mexican Americans, Puerto Ricans, and Native Americans—often impinged upon minority officials' abilities to govern. The commission reported, "Underlying many issues of the abuses reported here is the economic dependence of minorities." The polarization of politics along racial divisions occurred in a handful of cities that elected black mayors and BMCs or that contained black-majority electorates or both.[19]

As African American officials challenged their positions as political cue takers, they struggled to negotiate the tension among rising black expectations, the maintenance of racial harmony, and outright racial hostility. The highest-profile instances of this trend were black mayors. In Cleveland, for instance, whites—particularly a white city councilman named James Stanton—used the media to shell Carl Stokes after black nationalists engaged in a gun battle with law enforcement in the Glenville Community on July 23, 1968. Stanton and a number of white politicians associated Stokes with the very radicalism that he tried to restrain. Whites challenged mayor Richard Arrington Jr.'s legitimacy in Birmingham after he endorsed a uniformly black ticket for five city council vacancies. Atlanta's whites erupted when Maynard Jackson—in response to blacks' cries for police accountability—attempted to fire an overtly racist white police chief. Even Los Angeles mayor Tom Bradley was not exempt from the association between black governance and black nationalism. During Bradley's campaign for mayor, his Democratic opponent, Sam Yorty, contended that his election would bring about a radical takeover of city government. Richmond's political elites—like white political leaders across the United States—were convinced that governance by blacks was synonymous with governance for blacks exclusively. The Richmond BMC, like black mayors and councilpersons in many of America's black-majority cities, had to consistently defend against charges that they were race leaders rather than city managers. Resistance of this nature characterized the first terms of most black mayors; detractors often manufactured crises that intensified whites' skepticism of black political leadership. In Richmond, this hostility did not emerge until after the regularly scheduled city council election in 1978. In fact, Richmond's daily newspapers and the white council minority appeared to have conceded defeat because they believed that they could return a white-majority council in 1978.[20]

Racial tension at city hall reemerged during the election of 1978. The City of Richmond followed up the special election of 1977 with a regularly scheduled council contest in 1978. In the early months of 1978, TOP maneuvered to regain a city council majority, while the Cru-

Brook Road in Richmond's Jackson Ward area (now Abner Clay Park), August 1955. Photograph by Edith Shelton. From the Edith Shelton Collection, Valentine Museum.

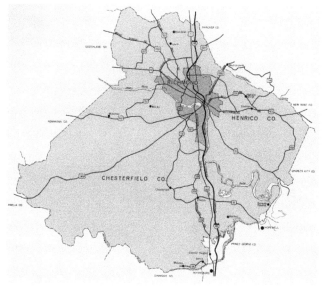

Map of the City of Richmond just prior to annexation of parts of Chesterfield County, ca. 1969. From the Eleanor Sheppard Papers, Cabell Black Collection, M306, Special Collections and Archives, James Branch Cabell Library, Virginia Commonwealth University, Richmond.

Map of the City of Richmond, with the annexed portion of Chesterfield County. From the *Richmond News-Leader*, September 18, 1969. Courtesy of the City of Richmond.

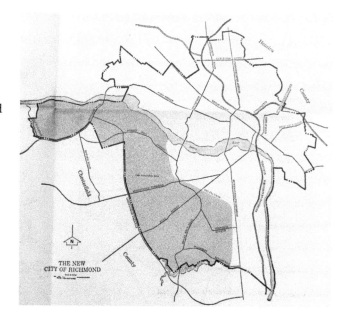

Gordon Blaine Hancock, date unknown. From Archives and Special Collections, Virginia Union University, Richmond.

PHIL J. BAGLEY
Elected to Council 1952 — Served 14 years as Councilman, 4 years as Vice-Mayor and 2 years as Council representative on City Planning Commission. Former Chairman, Council Agencies Committee and member of Tax Study Commission. Patron of ordinance creating Bi-racial Committee; Council Member Trafficways Committee.

B. ADDISON CEPHAS, JR.

Owner B. A. Cephas Real Estate. Elected to City Council 1964. Member, Library Board and Council Agencies Committee. Former member, City Planning Commission. Past-President, Virginia Real Estate Brokers Assn. and Richmond Real Estate Assn.

MORRILL M. CROWE
Vice-President, William P. Poythress & Company, Inc. Elected to City Council 1964. Currently serving as Mayor. Past-Chairman, Richmond section, Virginia Manufacturers Assn. Past-President, Kiwanis Club. Past-President, Richmond area unit American Cancer Society.

ROBERT J. HABENICHT

Attorney, Director of Trade Relations, A. H. Robins Co. Elected to City Council 1964, presently serving as Vice-Mayor. Member, Coliseum, Stadium and Arena Committees. Chairman, Council Agencies Committee and Regional Planning Commission. Past-President, Boy's Club of Richmond.

ROBERT T. MARSH, JR.

Honorary Board Chairman, First and Merchants National Bank. Member, Richmond Citizen's Advisory Comm. on Community Development; Board member, Va. Public School Authority and James River Assn. Served on Boards of Va. Union Univ., and Richmond Memorial Hospital.

HENRY R. MILLER, III

Secretary, First Federal Savings and Loan Association. Elected to City Council 1964. Member, Stadium, Legislative and Supplemental Retirement Study Committees. Past-President Richmond Jaycees. Past National Chairman, "Honesty Today and Tomorrow". Active in Kiwanis, Navy League, Boy Scouts, Big Brothers, Inc., and Richmond Area Unit, American Cancer Society.

WINFRED MUNDLE

Manager, Richmond District North Carolina Mutual Life Ins. Co. City Planning Commission. Member, Advisory Board of Recreation and Parks. Chairman, Board of Management, Leigh Street Y.M.C.A. Member boards: Robert E. Lee Council, Boy Scouts; Metropolitan Y.M.C.A.; Richmond Area Community Council; and Urban League.

ELEANOR P. SHEPPARD

Elected to City Council 1954. First woman Mayor — 1962. Member, City Planning Commission. Serves on the Council Agencies and Legislative Committees of Council. Member, Governor's Commission on Status of Women and VALC Committee on Grants-in-aid to Localities. Member, Boards of Senior Center, Richmond Area Council Mental Health.

JAMES C. WHEAT, JR.

President, J. C. Wheat & Company. Elected to City Council 1964. Chairman, Legislative and RPI Council Committees. Member, Council Committee on Trafficways and Ports. Past-President, Richmond Society of Financial Analysts. A Director, Eye Hospital. Chairman of the Board and Past-President, Boys' Club.

Richmond Forward's endorsements in the Richmond City Council election of 1966 (just prior to the "term staggering" incident), on the back of an RF campaign flyer. From the Eleanor Sheppard Papers, 1924–1978, M277, Cabell Black Collection, M306, James Branch Cabell Library, Virginia Commonwealth University, Richmond.

Howard Carwile (*right*), date unknown. From the Howard Carwile Collection, M294, James Branch Cabell Library, Virginia Commonwealth University, Richmond.

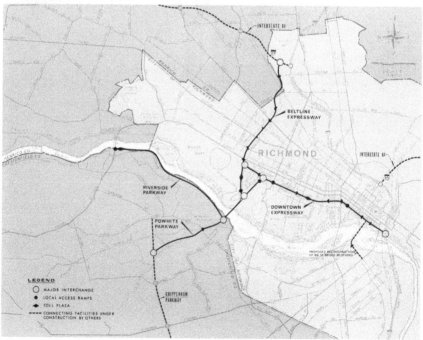

Map showing Beltline Expressway, Powhite Parkway, Riverside Parkway, and Downtown Expressway, Richmond, ca. 1966. From the Eleanor Sheppard Papers, 1924–1978, M277, Cabell Black Collection, M306, James Branch Cabell Library, Virginia Commonwealth University, Richmond.

Howard Carwile (*white man, third from the left*) and Curtis Holt Sr. (*center at the back*) at a city hall protest, ca. late 1960s. From the Howard Carwile Papers, M294, James Branch Cabell Library, Virginia Commonwealth University, Richmond.

Richmond Crusade for Voters sample ballot for the city council election of 1970. From the Howard Carwile Papers, M294, James Branch Cabell Library, Virginia Commonwealth University, Richmond.

Curtis Holt Sr. campaign flyer during the city council election of 1970. From the Howard Carwile Papers, M294, James Branch Cabell Library, Virginia Commonwealth University, Richmond.

VOTE JUNE 9TH.

Leadership!

Success in Local Community Leads to Progress for Our Country, Our World

Mr. Curtis Holt, President Creighton Court Civic Assoc. Leads Group Aboard Char- tered Bus for Baseball Game at Parker Field.

STRIKE YOUR BALLOT FOR HOLT!

ELECT CURTIS HOLT, SR.,.........

TO RICHMOND CITY COUNCIL !!!

◆◆◆◆◆◆◆◆◆◆◆◆◆◆◆◆◆◆◆◆◆◆◆◆◆◆◆◆◆

Yes, CURTIS HOLT, SR, THE POOR PEOPLES COORDINATOR,... A MAN WHO WILL TELL IT LIKE IT IS, A MAN WHO HAS DEDICATED HIS LIFE TO HELPING THE POOR PEOPLE, HERE, THERE, AND EVERYWHERE.........

.... CURTIS HOLT, SR. FAVORS LOWER TAXES, CURTIS HOLT, SR. FAVORS PAY RAISES FOR OUR CITY EMPLOYEES.

CURTIS HOLT, SR. FAVORS MORE HELP FOR SICK, MORE FOOD FOR THE HUNGRY, MORE MONEY FOR THE NEEDY, BUT ABOVE ALL

CURTIS HOLT, SR, NEEDS YOUR VOTE....

◆◆◆◆◆◆◆◆◆◆◆◆◆◆◆◆◆◆◆◆◆◆◆◆◆◆◆◆◆◆◆

CURTIS HOLT, SR. FIRST PERSON TO ORGANIZE A CIVIC GROUP IN THE RRHA PROJECT
CURTIS HOLT, SR. A MEMBER OF THE BOARD OF HUMAN RELATIONS COMMISSION.
CURTIS HOLT, SR. SENIOR WARDEN OF THE EAST END LODGE #233.
CURTIS HOLT, SR. PRESIDENT OF CREIGHTON COURT CIVIC ASSOCIATION.
CURTIS HOLT, SR. EXECUTIVE BOARD MEMBER OF N.A.A.C.P. (NAACP).
CURTIS HOLT, SR. EXECUTIVE BOARD MEMBER OF THE CRUSADE FOR VOTERS.
CURTIS HOLT, SR. BOARD MEMBER OF THE RCAP ADVISORY BOARD.
CURTIS HOLT, SR. MEMBER OF THE 4th. BAPTIST CHURCH AND CHAPLAIN OF SUNDAY SCHOOL AND USHER BOARD.
CURTIS HOLT, SR. MARRIED TO THE FORMER MAE BURTON OF CHESTERFIELD (2) SONS, WALTER AND CURTIS, JR. (2) DAUGHTERS, VALERIE AND CONSTANCE, COMPRISES THE HOLT FAMILY.

A new city council took office on July 1, 1978: (*from left*) William I. Golding, Walter T. Kenney, Willie J. Dell (barely visible behind Golding's upraised hand), Wayland W. Rennie, Claudette B. McDaniel, Henry W. Richardson, Henry L. Marsh III, Aubrey H. Thompson, and George S. Kemp Jr. From "Marsh Retiring after 22 Years in Virginia Senate," *Richmond Times-Dispatch,* July 1, 2014. Courtesy of the *Richmond Times-Dispatch.*

Henry Marsh embraces Willie Dell following their respective victories in the city council election of 1978. Photograph by Rich Crawford. From the *Richmond Times-Dispatch* Collection, Valentine Museum, Richmond.

Richmond City Council Districts, 1982

Richmond City Council districts according to the Marsh
Plan following the council election of 1980. Courtesy of
the City of Richmond.

sade endorsed all five black council members. In Richmond's second district-based election, the council's racial composition was "very much an underlying—if not the only—issue" of the election. Chuck Richardson's Fifth District, which had the most diverse racial population of the nine wards (61 percent African American), and Claudette McDaniel's Eighth District (63 percent African American) proved to be most pivotal. Willie Dell and Walter Kenney ran unopposed: blacks made up 88 percent of the voters in Kenney's Sixth District, and Willie Dell's Third District was 86 percent black. Curtis Holt Sr., not yet convinced that he was unelectable, challenged Henry Marsh in the Seventh District. Marsh's district was 89 percent African American, but the mayor also held sway over most of the Seventh District's voters. Challenges to Wayland Rennie of the Second District, George Stevenson Kemp of the First District, Aubrey Thompson of the Fourth District, and Raymond Royall of the Ninth District came from white opposition.[21]

TOP believed that it could win a council majority by outspending the Crusade. It had reorganized after 1977, briefly changed its name to "Teams for Progress," and planned to preclude another Crusade victory by hiring consultants from Washington. It also spent roughly $33,000 (roughly $108,000 in 2015 dollars) on the election. It eventually concentrated on the Eighth District and its only nonincumbent hopeful, G. Richard Wainwright. Of the $33,000 in campaign donations, the Teams for Progress spent $21,600 in McDaniel's district, including $4,400 that went directly to Wainwright. Wainwright not only outspent McDaniel but also spoke openly about the need to return a white-majority council. In the Fifth District, the rumor mill alleged that Teams for Progress had encouraged Richardson's challenger, an African American named William R. "Randy" Johnson, to run. The Crusade believed that Johnson ran simply to split the vote so that a third candidate, a white man named F. Wilson Craigie Jr., might win. Richardson, who had won in 1977 by just twelve votes, was particularly vulnerable. The Crusade campaigned heavily in the Fifth District and eventually brought Richardson's brother-in-law, Atlanta mayor Maynard Jackson, to speak on the incumbent's behalf. Jackson may have saved Richardson's then nascent political career. Fewer than 30,000 of more than 98,312 total registered voters showed for the May 2 election. Dell and Kenney ran unopposed, and Marsh beat Curtis Holt 2,011 to 422. Richardson beat his nearest competitor by nearly 1,500 votes, and McDaniel won by roughly 1,000 votes. (For the full election results, see table 11 in the appendix.) The election of 1978 was less of a mandate on the Crusade's ascendancy over the black electorate than it was a referendum on the power of majority–minority districts. In fact, whites outvoted African Americans—particularly in predominantly white districts. Teams for Progress candidates, all told, garnered roughly 12,600 votes, whereas the Crusade's candidates received approximately 10,300 votes. Given the nature of majority–minority district systems, the ratio of black-to-white voters at large was of little consequence to the election's results. In time, however, low black voter turnout eventually proved vital to future backlash against the district system.[22]

Just as things cooled down from the election, however, the BMC, seeking to make up for lost time, fired Richmond's white city manager, William J. "Bill" Leidinger. The council–manager model in Richmond's city charter delegated that managers had control over administrative affairs, economic directives, the city budget, and the day-to-day financial undertaking of running the city. If Richmond's mayors were the symbolic, titular leaders of the city, city managers were the chief operating officers. In many ways, Marsh's and the BMC's ability to redirect resources to their districts was contingent upon the city manager's will. Council members had appointed Leidinger as assistant city manager in 1971 and had promoted him to city manager in 1972. The Chicago native had become integral to developments in Richmond's expressway system, which was still under construction in the 1970s, and to city hall's attempts to revitalize the downtown business section. During the mid-1970s, Leidinger, the city council, and Richmond's Downtown Development Commission spearheaded the city's revitalization plans for downtown, published as *A Strategy for Action in Downtown Richmond, 1976–2000.* This plan revitalized the downtown riverfront area and Broad Street corridor near downtown. Kanawha Square, a plaza that overlooked the James River area of downtown and the historic Kanawha Canal, was also completed. Over the course of the 1970s, Leidinger's career as city manager was inextricably linked to downtown redevelopment. Despite his accomplishments, the BMC felt that Leidinger was unresponsive to its demands.[23]

During the first week of August 1978, the BMC followed through on the threat to remove Leidinger. After three hours of heated debate and bitter exchanges between white and black council members, the city council voted along strict racial lines, five to four, to ask for Leidinger's resignation. An article in the *Washington Post* in June 1979 stated not only that Leidinger and the council majority clashed but that Marsh exerted "more influence over Richmond's government" with Leidinger gone. Indeed, Henry Marsh wanted to be more than a ribbon-cutting mayor: he aspired to take on managerial responsibilities. He knew that the city manager position, as the charter mandated, was the most powerful administrative position at city hall. Yet Leidinger's removal was evidence that members of the BMC also wanted more control over the city's financial and administrative apparatus. Within the council–manager model, it was difficult to control the flow of service deliverables without the city manager's support. If the BMC were going to make good on the symbolism of its members' elections by addressing "the plight of Richmond's decaying neighborhoods, its impoverished residents, and its pockets of high unemployment," it needed to replace Leidinger with its own man.[24]

Leidinger's dismissal stunned Richmond and flattened the BMC's momentum. Leidinger told the *Richmond Times-Dispatch* that his career and the City of Richmond were "on the horns of a dilemma." Even *Afro* contributor Preston Yancy initially appealed to fairness over the city manager's removal:

> But Mr. Leidinger deserves fair treatment. If he is to be fired, it should be on the basis of issues and it should be open and above board. . . . If, in fact, the reports are true about his situation, Mayor Henry L. Marsh and Councilman Walter Kenney have demonstrated gross inconsistency and deceptiveness and all the black councilmembers have shown a bush league, crude approach to the political process. . . . For the Council members to praise Mr. Leidinger . . . then turn around and fire him simply because they want their own man is incredible.

In fact, Marsh had only briefly discussed his plans with Leidinger, and he refused to broach the issue with the council minority. Members of the majority council also took a "no comment" approach to questions by local media. Leidinger's removal gave Marsh's detractors the ammunition they needed to scrutinize the BMC's decision-making capabilities. "The Leidinger Affair," one Richmonder contended in the *Times-Dispatch* editorial section, "has been brewing since federal government interference forced a ward system of government on Richmond, thereby racially dividing the white voting majority four ways and the black voting minority five ways." Councilman Richardson, nearly forty years later, recalled that some of the "richest white men in Richmond" raked Marsh over the proverbial coals for firing Leidinger. Even county officials, who were reluctant to speak openly about city affairs because they were in the process of working with Richmond to expand the Interstate 95 beltway, rapped Marsh over the matter. The chairman of the Henrico County Board of Supervisors, George W. Jinkins Jr., believed that incident had "racial overtones" and might influence city–county relations.[25]

Blacks came to view Leidinger's firing as a natural prerogative of power, whereas whites believed that it represented the raw exercise of power. The council minority—with the exception of Wayland Rennie's replacement, Muriel Smith—and the editorial sections of the daily newspapers believed that Leidinger's firing was tantamount not merely to reverse racism but also to minority rule. *Times-Dispatch* readers were quick to point out that whites had actually outvoted blacks in the election of 1978 and that had it not been for the district system, whites would have regained a majority on council. That contention is debatable, but the Crusade members' assertion that the election of 1978 was their "greatest political victory" belied the data—the organization registered more black voters in the late 1960s than the total number of voters who cast ballots in 1978. "If the fate of William Leidinger were to be left up to the popular vote," one editorial claimed, "then the matter would cease to be an issue. When there was an at-large system of municipal government in Richmond, the voting, tax-paying majority was in control. Under the ward system it is just the opposite." By the fall of 1978, the council minority and white power structure came to associate Leidinger's firing with the emergence of a black agenda. Council members Kemp, Thompson, and recent appointee Carolyn Wake (who replaced William Golding Sr.) agreed that the black council members had fired Leidinger simply because he was white. Even Cabell Venable, Curtis Holt's lawyer during the deannexation suits, claimed that

Marsh privately referred to Leidinger as a "honky." Although the truth of Venable's contention is questionable, the white establishment's belief that Marsh fired Leidinger unfairly is not. Henry Valentine put the matter in its proper historical context: "They have done to us exactly what they said we used to do to them."[26]

The BMC answered the question of who ran Richmond when it declined to annul Leidinger's dismissal and hired an African American city manager. If blacks were initially apprehensive about Leidinger's removal, community support swelled after a thirty-seven-year-old African American was hired to replace him. After reviewing eighty-four potential candidates to replace Leidinger, Marsh and city clerk E. A. Duffy swore Manuel Deese into office on January 23, 1979. Deese, a native of Toomsboro, Georgia, and a graduate of Morgan State University and American University (where he earned a master's degree in public administration), had been Richmond's assistant of operations for four years under Leidinger. Prior to that, he had also worked in Alexandria, Virginia, as assistant city manager. Deese, who described himself as a "fiscal conservative," was in many ways different from Leidinger in race and temperament only. In the wake of Leidinger's removal and Deese's appointment, council minority members threatened—for the first time—to bring downtown revitalization to a standstill.[27]

Leidinger's firing definitely complicated downtown revitalization. By the late 1970s, many black-led cities suffered from structural and demographic constraints such as deep population, income, and employment losses. The commonwealth's moratorium on new annexations in cities with populations larger than 125,000 and county–city independence meant that Richmond, like many American cities in the 1970s and 1980s, needed to lure investors into the central city area to stimulate the local economy. Mayors such as Henry Marsh (and later Roy West) of Richmond; Kenneth Gibson of Newark, New Jersey; Richard Hatcher of Gary, Indiana; and Coleman Young of Detroit had to counterbalance civil rights agendas with economic pragmatism, and they came to believe that building malls, shopping centers, conventions centers, stadiums, and skyscrapers was synonymous with economic growth. These endeavors in high-profile politics, policy makers believed, would reverse the course of urban retrenchment by stimulating tax bases. Despite criticism from downtown business owners, most African Americans—who sought to solidify stronger relationships with business elites—fully supported efforts to develop downtown Richmond.[28]

The BMC's support of Project One, for instance, represented black officials' commitment to revitalization and redevelopment. Marsh, Deese, and the BMC often approached fiscal matters much like their white counterparts. City hall hoped that Project One, a mixed-use development project originally introduced in the 1950s and revamped by the *Strategy for Action* plan, would revitalize Richmond's retail and business core. The objective was, in Leidinger's estimation, to "eliminate . . . blight in the downtown area," secure nearly 3,000 jobs, and assure millions of dollars for the city's property and tax base. As it stood, the area slotted for redevelopment accounted for only $89,000 in property taxes annually; the new revitalization effort would bring in a minimum of $450,000. Planners estimated that the project would eventually occupy a six-block area bound by the Richmond Coliseum (another controversial undertaking) and Broad Street on two ends and by Fourth and Seventh Streets on the other two. The first phase of the $15 million project included a new convention center, a 375-room hotel, a fifteen-story office building, 800 parking spaces, 30,000 feet of retail space, and an atrium-plaza. Project One's second phase, slated to cost another $36.9 million, would eventually add another 600 parking spaces, a second fifteen-story building, and expansions to the hotel and retail sections proposed in phase one.[29]

In the wake of the Leidinger affair, white council members used Project One as a bargaining chip. Contention over these plans arose when members of the black majority recommended a hotel be built and operated by the Marriot Company, whereas whites favored a hotel from the Hilton Corporation. The bickering between black and white council factions stooped to new lows over the issue of hotel construction. The black council members insisted that building the hotel north of Broad Street would influence economic development in Jackson Ward. The white council members, however, were certain that no respectable individual would patronize a hotel built on "the wrong side of Broad." Conflict intensified when the BMC passed an ordinance to protect the Marriot Company's bid by requiring private developers to pay a fee based on their potential impact on Project One. When whites and the Hilton Corporation objected, the BMC—in another five-to-four vote—denied two parcels of undeveloped land to Hilton. Again, the white council members threatened not merely to pull development out of the city but also to stall downtown construction if blacks refused to reverse the decision. It took nearly two years and a Hilton lawsuit, which culminated in a $5 million dollar settlement in favor of the Hilton Corporation, to resolve the issue. Reflecting on the Leidinger and Project One incidents, Councilman Wayland Rennie stated, "It boiled down to a white vs. black issue and it was resolved on that basis. I was disappointed . . . I still haven't gotten over that." To this day, two hotels sit directly across from one another on the 500 block of Broad Street, one a Hilton on the Monument Avenue side and the other a Marriot on the Jackson Ward side. Both hotels are a living testimony to Richmond's contested racial history and the conflict between council factions.[30]

By the end of 1978, distrust of the BMC had given way to open hostility. The contention between black and white council members grew so bad that *Richmond Times-Dispatch* reporter Bill Miller referred to city politics as "an embattled ship" that "survived the shells of 1978." The white establishment considered the Leidinger incident, Deese's appointment, and Project One evidence of a growing black agenda. They found an ally in the *Richmond News-Leader*, whose editorial pages began to routinely lambaste the BMC. These editorials were also often laced with racial overtones, referring to the BMC as "a bunch of clowns in a Chinese fire-drill" and, on one occasion, as the "monkey-see, monkey-do leaders of a banana republic." Richmond's dailies began to refer to Marsh as "Boss Henry," "Empire Builder, " and "Controversy Man"—critics charging that Marsh used the council majority to pervert the council–manager model and emphasizing the mayor's merely ceremonial authority. The daily editorials argued that Marsh "flagrantly disregarded the intent of the City Charter" and that "the majority members of Council have united to give Mayor Marsh far more power than he is supposed to exercise." In 1978, Norvell Robinson actually took time out of the Crusade's annual banquet, a celebratory occasion, to address this barrage of criticism. He argued, "As painful as it may be, I feel impelled to touch upon one force in Richmond that has been everything except fair . . . the Richmond newspapers[,] which has [*sic*] been cited on many occasions for their unabated editorial attacks and one-sided reporting of our leadership."[31]

The issue of redistricting further polarized race relations at city hall. The problem of redistricting proved to be one of the inherent disadvantages of Washington's solution to vote dilution. Local and federal officials conducted a trial census of Richmond, Henrico County, and Chesterfield County during the first week of April 1978. Although the Census Bureau placed administrative restrictions on the use of data obtained from this trial census, it released some of its findings to city officials and local media. In the fall of 1978, the *Times-Dispatch* published some of those early results. Between 1970 and 1978, the capital city lost 11.6 percent of its residents, while Chesterfield County's population rose by 64 percent (from 77,045 in 1970 to 126,124). Henrico County showed an increase in population of 12.3 percent. The mock census also showed that African Americans had a slight population advantage over whites, outnumbering whites 109,130 to 108,983. The city's white population had also decreased from 143,854 in 1970. Experts and city officials knew that white flight had continued apace and that many of Richmond's districts showed no trace of diversification. These districts were also severely malapportioned. Richmond's initial district system contained roughly 27,700 people. Marsh believed that the data legally required new boundaries, and he immediately made plans to draw new districts.[32]

The disparities in Richmond's districts led to even wider differences between white and black council members. The dilemma, council minority members held, was that Marsh and the BMC sat on the rest of the census data for a year, until August 1979. They also believed that drawing new boundaries before the results of the 1980 census placed a "burden on the people" that violated the city charter. Minority council members felt as if they had been frozen out of the process. In reality, Marsh not only believed that federal law trumped the city charter but also approached the trial census like a lawyer rather than like a mayor. He thought that the city was obligated to redistrict when it was aware of malapportioned wards and argued further that both state and federal law called for "one man, one vote." Councilperson Carolyn Wake, who represented the annexed portion of Chesterfield County, was Marsh's harshest critic on the redistricting matter. She was convinced that Marsh had planned to draw new

Table 4.2. Estimates of Richmond District Demographics after Trial Census, 1978

District	Council Member	Location	Population	Percentage African American	Percentage White
District 1	George Kemp	Northwest End	23,708	4	96
District 2	Wayland Rennie	north side	23,441	21	79
District 3	Willie Dell	northeast side	27,438	86	14
District 4	Aubrey Thompson	West End	27,564	8	92
District 5	Chuck Richardson	The Fan— Central City	18,401	61	39
District 6	Walter Kenney	Jackson Ward— Central City	24,060	88	12
District 7	Henry Marsh III	East End	19,644	89	11
District 8	Claudette McDaniel	south side	27,564	63	37
District 9	Carolyn Wake	Former Chesterfield County— Southwest	28,180	17	83

Source: Data from *Richmond Times-Dispatch*, August 22, 1979, A1.

district boundaries months before releasing the census findings to the public. Wake also argued at a city council meeting in the fall of 1979, "I feel very strongly a decision [months ago] was made to redistrict this city. I can go out and get counsel that can be just as convincing that we don't need to redistrict." Wake's comments epitomized the deep skepticism between black and white council members. Not to be outdone, the *Richmond News-Leader* embarked on a nearly two-month tirade against the mayor, whose mayoralty it labeled "Marshgate." It was during this period that the *Leader* charged the mayor with misrepresenting the council–manager model of city government. All parties to the dispute—the *Leader,* the BMC, and the white minority—knew what was on the line: if officials reapportioned the city's district system, it was possible that certain districts could dictate local elections for the next decade.[33]

Conflict over the trial census eventually landed city hall in court. If whites believed Marsh's firing of Leidinger signaled an emerging black agenda, African Americans' demographic advantages and Marsh's willingness to maximize them provided the wherewithal to realize that agenda. Council members also correctly contended that plans to devise new district boundaries violated section 24.1–40.3 (B) of the city charter. This section mandated new districts once every ten years and thus prohibited redistricting until the summer of 1981. In October 1979, three white council members and a Richmond resident from the Ninth District, Meade C. Folts, filed a suit to counter Marsh's plans to redistrict. Folts argued that state law required redistricting *only* after the decennial census. The circuit court judge, Frank Wright, agreed. He concluded in December 1979 that Richmond had no constitutional duty or obligation to draw new district boundaries until June 1, 1981. Wright's decision immediately tabled the issue in the short run. Marsh, however, struggled to rehabilitate his reputation.[34]

The seriousness of anti-Marsh sentiment cannot be understated. Hatred for the mayor reached fever pitch during the late 1970s. After Leidinger and the trial census incidents, Marsh found himself in a precarious position. After receiving death threats months before the fall of 1979, Marsh requested plainclothes protection. He and his staff also had to contend with regular bomb threats, and they often chose not to appear in public for safety reasons. In a poll conducted in 1981, only 47 percent of white Richmonders gave Marsh satisfactory or good ratings. One-third of the whites polled put Marsh in the "poor" category. In August 1979, Marsh used the daily newspapers to make a broad appeal for cooperation. The BMC and the mayor released a statement asserting, "We call upon the three councilmembers (Aubrey H. Thompson, G. S. Kemp, and Carolyn Wake) involved and the Richmond Newspapers to lower their voices and to end this campaign of accusation and suspicion." Marsh and the four black council members also implored "the Teams for Progress–supported members of council of the city of Richmond to lower their rhetoric and terminate their campaign of wild accusations in order that Council of the City of Richmond may devote itself full time and wholeheartedly to its duties as members of council and in providing effective leadership to and for the city of Richmond." In reality, some African Americans and the *Afro* had anticipated the blowback against Marsh and the BMC. Preston Yancy had warned in his appeal to be fair with Leidinger that firing Leidinger might have severe implications for black governance. History proved Yancy correct. By the end of the 1970s, relations between black and white leaders eroded, and the trial-census controversy seemed to ensure that redistricting after the census in 1980 would be even more contentious.[35]

The election of 1980 again split voters along racial lines. The *Times-Dispatch* believed it would be difficult to change the five-to-four BMC, but TOP (which dropped the name "Teams for Progress" in 1980 in favor of its original name) again poured considerable resources into the city's most diverse districts. By the spring of 1980, the most heated battles occurred between Bill Leidinger and Muriel Smith in the Second District and between Claudette McDaniel and Andrew J. "Drew" Gillespie in the Eighth District. TOP very openly argued that it aspired to return a white-majority council to city hall. Leidinger maintained that he was not seeking office to exact revenge on Marsh, a contention that later developments proved to be untrue. On the south side, Marsh called the Eighth District campaign one of the dirtiest he had seen in years. In April 1980, a *Richmond Times-Dispatch* editorial entitled "The Last Chance" typified whites' frustration not merely with redistricting but also with the composition of the city council:

> Councilmembers who are elected next month will be responsible for redistricting Richmond on the basis of 1980 census results, and the district lines they will draw will influence—if not actually determine—the philosophy and quality of the city's government for a decade. Richmond will face a bleak future if it is condemned to continue to endure the kind of government that Mayor Marsh and the Council clique that controls have provided for the past few years, for it has been a government characterized by racism, by arrogant use of power and by contempt for the views and money of Richmond's taxpayers. . . . The city's future rests with voters in the First, Second, Fourth, Eight, and Ninth Districts who will have the chance to vote for candidates dedicated to the principles of fair and responsible government.

Of the five BMC members, opponents challenged only McDaniel and Kenney. Kenney's opponent, Frederick C. Williams, was a twenty-nine-year-old VUU student whom most experts recognized as posing little threat to the incumbent.[36]

The Second and Eighth Districts were the key battleground districts. During her brief stint on city council, Muriel Smith, a former missionary, had actually defended the BMC against white criticism. Although the Richmond Black Police Officers Association, the Richmond Regional Labor Council, and the Richmond Education Association endorsed her campaign, she faced an uphill battle against Leidinger. Smith eventually proved ill equipped to handle the former city manager's anti-Marsh momentum. On the other side of town, TOP knew that it needed only one district to overturn the BMC. Although African Americans constituted roughly 63 percent of McDaniel's district, that district, located on Richmond's south side, had a diverse collection of blue-collar and middle- to upper-middle-class whites. McDaniel actually faced a viable challenger in Phillip Morris engineer Drew Gillespie. Gillespie campaigned not only on bringing an end to racism at city hall but also on ending residency requirements for city employees (critics charged that this proposal would further expedite white flight). Black leaders and the Crusade again claimed that TOP attempted to split blacks' votes by putting forward an African American, Frank J. Wilkins Sr., who campaigned on bringing an end to racial polarization on the council but drew heavy criticism from the black electorate for suspicions of being financed by wealthy whites.[37]

The white establishment, led by TOP, campaigned on restoring normalcy to city hall. TOP rallied behind what the *Times-Dispatch* called "the Best Five" and threw much of its support behind Drew Gillespie. Gillespie ran the longest and best-funded campaign of the nine districts, and TOP donated $9,000 to his campaign alone (roughly $25,000 in today's money). *Richmond Times-Dispatch* editorialists argued: "Without doubt, the council-manic election to be held next Tuesday will be one of the most important in Richmond's history. The City Council members elected will be responsible for redrawing the city's ward lines on the basis of the 1980 census results and those lines will have a profound influence on the quality and philosophy of Richmond's municipal government for a decade. It is imperative that voters choose a majority—five members— that would be dedicated to the city as a whole and that would be committed to the principles of responsible and efficient government." Despite whites' efforts, African Americans won another majority on the council. The Crusade and McDaniel generated enough support to eke out a victory against Gillespie. Both Henry Marsh and Dale Wiley, former president of TOP, argued that the *Richmond News-Leader* editorial attacks on McDaniel and Marsh had galvanized black voters in the Eighth District. Voters reelected the city's black incumbents, and McDaniel beat Gillespie 3,183 votes to 2,913. Kenney walloped his closest contender 1,890 votes to 146. Thompson and Kemp soundly defeated their opponents, and Carolyn Wake beat out William Golding and Tyrone Gaines. Smith's inability to fend off Leidinger proved pivotal in the coming years as the former city manager emerged as the council minority's leader.[38] (For the election results in 1980, see table 12 in the appendix.)

Council factionalism often obscured just how much the BMC accomplished in its first three years. Under Marsh, the percentage of capital budget allocations directed at neighborhoods increased from 48 percent to 57 percent after 1977. Marsh traveled to the nation's capital about twice a month and directly lobbied federal agencies for money "for housing, jobs, and other programs." In 1979, he secured a $4 million Department of Housing and Urban Development grant with the help of his associate, Secretary Patricia Harris, to renovate the aging Jefferson Hotel in downtown Richmond. Marsh and the BMC also made good on their promises to address blight. He pumped millions of federal block grant dollars into rebuilding Jackson Ward during the 1970s. In 1970, Jackson Ward—which residents referred to as "Central Richmond"—had roughly 2,800 residents, and nearly 100 percent of them were African American. Most of the area's residents (84 percent) earned less than $8,000 annually, and of those 2,800 residents 35 percent were older than fifty-five, and approximately 82 percent were older than forty-four. In 1975, 201 of 606 families in Jackson Ward received Social Security benefits, and 139 received public assistance. By the end of the 1970s, absentee landlords (only 20 percent of Jackson Ward's residents owned homes), poverty, and shoddy building inspections had left the neighborhood in shambles. City officials recognized that the viability of the convention center and downtown revitalization was contingent upon addressing years of institutional and physical neglect in Jackson Ward. In 1976, civic groups and the city council began to transform the area with the help of federal Community

Development Block Grant funds. Dell, Marsh, Leidinger, and Jackson Ward residents not only blocked out 261 structures for restoration but also filed to have the area recognized on the National Register of Historic Places. The RRHA provided low-income loans of $35,000 and $18,000 to eligible residents in 1976, and two years later the area was awarded national Historic Landmark Status.[39]

Despite these improvements, when it came to people's perceptions of local politics and politicians, media mattered. After the minicensus incident, whites' apprehensions about a federally mandated ward system deepened. As fewer African Americans voted and blacks maintained a solid five-to-four council majority, whites organized new ways to return a white-majority council. Over the duration of the early 1980s, they took these grievances to Washington and found newfangled ways to end African Americans' majority at city hall. Although the *Richmond News-Leader*'s and *Richmond Times-Dispatch*'s criticisms of Marsh electrified black voters in the Eighth District during the 1980 election, the white establishment's criticism of black leadership in general had the opposite effect two years later.

"Setting Aside Negative Differences"

The year 1980 proved to be the high-water mark of the Crusade's electoral strategies. Shelley Rolfe of the *Times-Dispatch* wrote, "Telling of an election night visit to a Church Hill precinct where a Crusade-based candidate outdistanced a rival by something like 1,000 to 48, Del. Franklin P. Hall, D–Richmond, recalled that he told a Crusade poll worker, 'Not even [Chicago's late] Mayor [Richard] Daley could get this kind of support. And she told me, "Just wait until I find out who the 48 are."' That is discipline." As African Americans continued to rack up victories in Richmond's city council elections, their white counterparts came to view majority–minority districts as inherently undemocratic. After the city council election of 1980, whites openly criticized districts as an affirmative-action remedy and grew increasingly disillusioned by the strategic political alliance between African Americans and Washington. The struggle over local political power reached fever pitch after the U.S. Census Bureau released its report for 1980. Redistricting, the *Times-Dispatch* held, became "perhaps the most important development in Richmond since the court decision in 1976 that imposed single-member districts on the city made a black majority politically possible." By the early 1980s, disgruntlement over federal voting rights mandates gave rise to another populist revolt in Richmond. This revolt not only rivaled resistance to public-school integration in its intensity but was also strictly political. It just so happened that redistricting in Richmond coincided with the renewal of the VRA in 1980. Resistance to the BMC and the city's district system became a bellwether for anti-VRA sentiment. Richmond's officials settled redistricting along strict racial lines, and the debate over drawing district boundaries further heightened animosity between white and black council members.[40]

The U.S. Census Bureau released its report for 1980 in March 1981, and the data again demonstrated that Richmond's districts were significantly malapportioned. Between 1970 and 1980, the City of Richmond's total population declined by more than 30,000: from 249,332 to 219,214. From 1950 to 1980, the capital city lost residents at a rate of 3,000 persons per year. Richmond's white population dropped from 143,857 to 104,743, whereas the number of African American residents rose from 104,766 to 112,357. Blacks made up a majority of the city's population at slightly more than 51 percent. According to the census, African Americans narrowly outnumbered whites by 7,600 people (down moderately from 10,000 in 1978). Under a legal nine-member district system, Richmond's nine districts needed an equal number of people in each district, near 24,350 based on the total population. Of the nine districts, the Fourth, Eighth, and Ninth were the most severely malapportioned: Carolyn Wake's Ninth District had 28,529 residents; McDaniel's Eighth District and Aubrey Thompson's Fourth District were nearly dead even at 27,972 and 27,974. If the VRA now required newly drawn districts "to demonstrate sensitivity to minority voter areas" with a history of political discrimination, the decennial need to redistrict was not without conflict.[41]

The need to reapportion Richmond's districts led to another wave of council factionalism. Both the BMC, led by Marsh, and the council minority, led by Leidinger, understood that any districting scheme in 1981 would dictate the tempo of local elections until the next census in

Table 4.3. Population and Family Income of Richmond, Henrico County, and Chesterfield County, 1980

Location	Richmond		Henrico County		Chesterfield County	
Total Population	219,214		180,735		141,372	
White	104,743	47.8%	151,187	83.7%	125,841	89.0%
Black	112,357	51.3%	27,096	15.0%	13,910	9.8%
Median Annual Family Income	$16,820		$22,685		$25,753	
Average Annual Family Income	$20,881		$25,617		$27,763	

Source: Data from U.S. Bureau of the Census, *Census of Population and Housing* (Washington, D.C.: U.S. Bureau of the Census, 1980).

1990. To this end, both Marsh's plan and Leidinger's plan twisted and contorted district lines in a manner that favored their respective factions. Marsh, under the instruction of Washington, D.C., districting lawyer Armand Derfner, proposed Ordinance 81-118, referred to as the "Marsh Plan" or "Citizen Marsh." Leidinger and Drew Gillespie, with the support of the white minority, drew up Ordinance 81-119, commonly referred to as the "Fair Play Act." The contention began in Richardson's Fifth District (or District E under Marsh's plan) and spread to the remaining eight. Richardson's district was the least populated (17,580 residents) and most diverse of all the districts, so both whites and blacks seized opportunities to swing it in their favor. They also recognized that McDaniel's district was, by Richmond's standards, relatively diverse and particularly vulnerable. Historical patterns of residential segregation meant that Kenney and Marsh's districts, both of which were removed from pockets of white residents, were the safest. The Third, Fifth, and Eighth Districts contained just enough racial integration to change the balance of power.[42]

The Marsh Plan for redistricting pivoted on the racial composition of Chuck Richardson's district. It designed boundary lines from Richardson's district outward in a counterclockwise manner. Federal law mandated that districts needed to contain a roughly equal number of inhabitants—that number was 24,357 based on the census of Richmond. According to the Marsh Plan, the numbers went as followed: District A, 25,086; District B, 24,867; District C, 24,279; District D, 24,405;

District E, 23,772; District F, 23,632; District G, 24,604; District H, 24,505; and District I, 24,604. Architects of the Marsh Plan attempted to pack Richardson's district with more blacks, which they achieved by extending the district's boundary past Belvedere Street into the central-western (Highland Park) portions of Kenney's district. Marsh, Derfner, and City Registrar May Alan Lynch, designed the district to give African Americans a 17,000 to 7,163 advantage over whites. Marsh's plan compensated Kenney by extending into the northeastern (north side) portion of Willie Dell's district. The plan also extended Dell's district into a predominantly white portion of Leidinger's district. This section of Leidinger's district contained an upper-middle-class white neighborhood, just to the west of Chamberlayne Avenue, known as Imperial Plaza. At the time, Marsh seemed to believe that redrawing Dell's district was a benign maneuver, particularly because blacks maintained a sizeable numerical advantage in District C. On the other side of town, south of the James River, Marsh also planned to remove Gillespie's precinct out of McDaniel's district (District H in the Marsh Plan) by creating District D. This district extended from the southwestern portion of the former Chesterfield County to the southern border of what had been the mostly white section of McDaniel's district. Marsh's plan also created a District A out of portions of Aubrey Thompson's district and Steve Kemp's district. In an age-old gerrymandering maneuver, the plan placed two opposition incumbents in the same district.[43]

The Fair Play Act was as committed to restoring a white-majority council as Marsh's plan was to maintaining the BMC. Leidinger designed Fair Play—also referred to as "Patrons Liedinger, Thompson, Wake, and Kemp"—to shrink the gap in districts where blacks had a marginal numerical advantage in registered voters. Although Fair Play manipulated fewer boundaries, it apportioned the districts in a manner that produced four-to-four parity and one swing ward. Leidinger, Drew Gillespie, and the council minority proposed to extend Richardson's ward across the James River—a natural boundary—into a decidedly white section of the city called Woodland Heights; this predominantly white collection of precincts voted in favor of Andrew Gillespie in 1980. Leidinger found powerful allies. Along with the council's white-minority members, a number of highly influential local business elites publicly supported Fair Play, including Thomas P. Bryan Jr., vice president of the local department store Miller & Rhoads; J. Harwood Cochrane, chairman of Overtine Transportation Company; Virginius Dabney, retired *Times-Dispatch* editor; Howard B. Cone, vice president of Universal Leaf Tobacco; and Charles E. Moore, vice president of United Virginia Bank. Leidinger's ultimate objective was to "crack," or dehomogenize, certain portions of Richardson's Fifth District. Moving Richardson's boundary across the James River and into the predominantly white Woodland Heights area evened the ratio of blacks (13,500) to whites (11,085). Leidinger also proposed to move portions of McDaniel's district past Terminal Avenue into a predominantly white portion of what was once Chesterfield County. The Fair Play Act thus apportioned its districts as such: first, 23,880; second, 24,106; third, 24,181; fourth, 24,245; fifth, 24,595; sixth, 24,405; seventh, 24,075; eighth, 24,452; and ninth, 25,275. Even the *Times-Dispatch* argued that although the minority's plan contained fewer changes than Marsh's proposal, its objective was to give the minority a chance at regaining control of city council. Claudette McDaniel was more blunt. "They're trying to screw Chuck [Richardson]," she argued.[44]

Redistricting in Richmond was bitterly contested, and it reached a boiling point during the council's public hearings on June 23 and 24, 1981. Richmond's black leadership stood uniformly behind the Marsh Plan. Just prior to the meetings, Marsh tried to put the fight over redistricting in its proper historical context. He ran a two-page editorial in the *Richmond News-Leader* urging readers to remember Richmond's disreputable legacy of disenfranchisement. On the evening of June 23, Oliver Hill, who was now head of Richmond's chapter of the NAACP, Crusade member Willie Williams III, and Crusade president Norvell Robinson argued that African Americans needed to do everything in their power to maintain a council majority for as long as possible. Hill's position spoke volumes about the possibility of returning to a white-majority council:

> The real issue as I see it and as it is perceived by a large body of citizenry . . . is whether or not the minority bloc on council, the Richmond power structure, and white citizens generally . . . have reached the level of maturity where they are able to accept the fact that blacks have a right to exercise the symbols of power and

to cooperate in the development of a state of affairs where skin color will no longer be a factor in the election, selection or evaluation of the performance of persons performing public service. . . . For centuries the city of Richmond was governed with very little, if any, regard for the sensibilities of its black citizens. While in more recent years some constructive efforts have been made . . . the local response is still unending resistance.

Hill's reference to the legacy of institutionalized racism and the persistence of white resistance also spoke volumes about African Americans' commitment to majority–minority districts. Williams, Hill, and Robinson were keenly aware of the ways whites had used federal and state resources to stunt the development of black neighborhoods and businesses in the mid–twentieth century. In this way, many African Americans, given the resilience of white resistance, feared deeper marginalization should whites recapture a council majority. Politics ensured that African Americans, who had little economic power but made up more than half of Richmond's population, could exercise some power. To the surprise of few, Willie Dell spoke most frankly about the relationship between white skepticism and black governance: "White folks have problems being niggers. That is, not niggers in terms of race but in terms of position. There are persons in this town who—[even] if we could part the James, if we could instantly make the economic picture in Richmond more favorable, if we could solve all the crime problems—would still question black leadership." Districts were not only a way to rectify the political discrimination that characterized black life in Richmond for most of the twentieth century but also a defense against the continuation of racist trends in Richmond's political and economic culture.[45]

Whites made no apologies about their desire to reclaim a council majority or their disdain for majority–minority districts. If wards were in part implemented to offset blacks' population and political disadvantages in at-large systems, why, whites wondered, were districts still relevant if blacks made up more than half of the city's population? The *Richmond News-Leader* and *Richmond Times-Dispatch* continually argued that wards encouraged political provincialism. Although the dailies refused to acknowledge the city's history of disenfranchisement, their critiques of the district system in some ways had merit. Majority–minority districts all but ensured that council members were loyal not merely to particular racial constituencies but also, in essence, to portions of the city. On June 28, just before the city council was scheduled to vote on the districting plans, Councilman Steve Kemp continued to leverage whites' ties to the private sector. He argued that if blacks continued to use districts to centralize political power and perpetuate Hill's type of rhetoric, white flight would continue apace, and their businesses would follow closely behind. Kemp, a long-standing partner of Paine Webber, Inc., and former president of CFA (Chartered Financial Analyst) Virginia, argued that Hill's statements were "disgusting" given the fact that Richmond's corporate community had recently saved and continued to sponsor many of Richmond's black institutions. Kemp was not just referring to the legacy of benefaction in Richmond but also specifically indicating a recent donation to the tune of $600,000 to bail out VUU from a possible loss of accreditation.[46]

Just as local officials began to vote on a redistricting plan, the council minority embarked on yet another campaign of obstructionism. The DOJ, as was commensurate with VRA section 5, reviewed and approved the Marsh Plan on August 29, 1981. In its approval of the plan, the DOJ also admonished the Fair Plan Act. The assistant attorney general of the CRD, William Bradford Reynolds, argued that Leidinger's plan "would . . . result[] in significant retrogression in the opportunities of black voters" in Chuck Richardson's district, so it turned out that McDaniel's assessment was right all along. Marsh's plan, Reynolds held, "did not appear to have been drawn with an invidious purpose. . . . [T]he net effect . . . is a maintenance of the status quo." It was this new status quo that whites had a problem with. Just prior to the council's and the DOJ's approval of the Marsh Plan, members of the council minority resolved to withhold the two-thirds majority of votes necessary to release city bonds for capital improvements in 1982. Although Leidinger argued that he influenced the minority's vote against the budget because he disliked the majority's last-minute decision to add $1.9 million for Main Street capital improvements, black leaders were convinced that the maneuver was retribution for Marsh's redistricting plan. The minority members stressed that if the BMC accepted Leidinger's "four–four and one" plan, they would vote to release capital funds for city improvements in 1982. Marsh explicitly referred to the minority's threats as "white-mail." Although the minority's threats over bond authorization proved idle after the BMC passed the Marsh Plan, disgruntlement about voting rights continued.[47]

The BMC's attempt to fashion safer districts and use those districts to consolidate political power fanned the flames of white Richmonders' interpositionist and anti-Washington proclivities. The issue of redistricting gave rise to yet another people's revolt—this revolt, however, was not about public-school integration but about court-ordered majority–minority districts. White Richmonders were at the vanguard of anti-VRA movements, and their resistance to majority–minority districts became a defining characteristic of conservative politics in the early 1980s. Just prior to the summer of 1981, as the redistricting debate began to gain steam, whites put the VRA in the proverbial crosshairs—the act was currently in the process of being renewed by Congress. On May 20, 1981, Marsh and state senator Doug Wilder spoke in front of Congress about the urgent need for voting rights mandates. They argued that Richmond's history of recent vote dilution confirmed the need for an extension of the VRA, including the extension of sections 5 and 2. On the same day, Virginia's Third District congressman and former Richmond mayor Thomas Bliley (R) went before the same House Judiciary Subcommittee to argue against the act's extension and the creation of what experts call "the Senate factors." Bliley, in fact, attempted not just to strike down the bill but, in Congressman Barney Frank's (D–Mass.) words, to "gut the bill fairly effectively" by attacking section 2. More specifically, Bliley lobbied against the creation of stronger criteria—the "Senate factors"—for the courts to consider when assessing the "totality of circumstances" test. In total, nine of Virginia's ten congressmen voted against the VRA's extension in 1981. These congressmen, with the help of Councilman Kemp, found likeminded allies in Richmond.[48]

Resistance to majority–minority districts and the VRA eventually trickled down to Richmond—whites attempted to deny preclearance of the Marsh Plan on the grounds that *they* were the population minority. Immediately following submission of the Marsh Plan to the DOJ, the minority council encouraged whites in the Fifth District to bombard Attorney General William Bradford Reynolds and Assistant Attorney

General James P. Turner with letters urging the federal government to deny preclearance on grounds of reverse discrimination. At the height of the redistricting controversy, the *Richmond Times-Dispatch* editorial page ran several columns about the unconstitutionality of majority–minority districts and section 5. These editorials were not just about local politics but were part of the broader national debate about the VRA's extension. The paper cited a Republican think tank's examination of the post-1965 developments in voting rights. It placed a portion of this study on its editorial page: "'The right to vote does not mean the right to be elected. Democracy is based on the rights of individuals, not groups. The logical conclusion concerning proportional representation in regards to the Voting Rights Act would be to establish a quota system concerning the election of minorities to office. Any quota system for elected officials will destroy a democratic government.'" Councilman Kemp applied further pressure. He eventually sent out a series of letters to influential whites in Richmond's Fifth District urging them to contest the Marsh Plan with the DOJ. Kemp also sent out a memorandum that instructed white citizens on how to write letters to the DOJ. He argued that as the employers of major companies, whites needed to "solicit vigorously officers and employees who may have the same concerns." Kemp's letter also implied that white business owners should motivate their white employees to petition the attorney general about the nature of the Marsh Plan.[49]

Kemp's constituency argued that the Marsh Plan denied and abridged whites' right to vote on account of race. At the time, African Americans composed 50 percent of Richmond's population but were in the process of submitting a ward-based system that guaranteed them 55 percent of the city council's seats. In 1980, one editorial argued, "In my opinion, the ward system should be changed so that the white vote will not be diluted, and then we will have a fair election by all the people for council members." In August 1981, a group of white citizens traveled to Washington to demonstrate how the Marsh Plan discriminated against white voters. Although no record exists of the conversation, the council minority's effort in this instance was the first time in the sixteen-year history of the VRA that a group of white citizens made such an argument. Whites found little sanctuary in Washington, however. The Marsh Plan, according to the DOJ, apportioned Richmond's districts in accordance with federal law, and the attorney general explicitly argued that the VRA and single-member district systems were meant to protect minority voting rights. The *Afro* found it quite ironic that Richmond's whites, whose annexation had facilitated the ward system in the first place, were now arguing that districts diluted white votes. Although no one knew it at the time, Kemp's revolt did not bode well for the BMC. The city's white voters were as determined as ever to return a white-majority council. They eventually overcame their aversion to the district system by tapping African Americans' discontent with Henry Marsh.[50]

The conflict over district boundaries eventually culminated in a precinct-level assault against Willie Dell. Marsh, it turned out, believed that Dell's district was one of the least politically vulnerable of the five black districts. As such, his plan deposited a large bloc of highly organized white voters into the district from the northernmost part of the city—Leidinger's district. These whites came into Dell's district armed with a deep disdain for the mayor. After the DOJ approved the Marsh Plan, Dell's district contained not only a contingent of anti-Marsh whites but about 20 percent more white voters in general. On the eve of the election in 1982, it appeared that Dell still had enough black voters to stem the tide of resistance from the Imperial Plaza contingent. These white voters alone did not have the electoral muscle to defeat the incumbent should a majority of the district's blacks vote for Dell. But in a strange twist of fate some black voters communicated their contempt for Marsh by organizing strategies with the district's recently incorporated white voters.[51]

Dr. Roy West, a Richmond native, announced his candidacy in early February 1982. By 1982, West had been affiliated with Richmond's public-education system for thirty-two years in various capacities, as a teacher, administrator, and ultimately a principal at Albert H. Hill Middle School. West attended Maggie Walker High School and earned a bachelor's of science degree from VUU. Upon graduating, he earned a master's degree in education from New York University and a doctorate in education from George Washington University. During his work with Richmond's public schools, West had also taught as an adjunct professor at VUU. Although few knew it at the time, it was West's appointment as the principle of Hill Middle School that eventually gave rise to his political career and his mayoralty. Superintendent Richard C. Hunter, who was Richmond's first African American school superintendent, was indirectly responsible for that rise. In an attempt to rectify underenrollment in RPS during the early 1980s, Hunter consolidated the city's high schools. "Plan G," as it became known, met the challenges of declining high school enrollment by grouping all of the city's high schools into three complexes. West, who publicly opposed Hunter's plan, eventually became a casualty of the consolidation. School board officials demoted West in 1980 from his position as principle of John Marshall High School and moved him to Hill Middle School. During his opposition to Hunter's plans, West became somewhat of a cause célèbre. His criticism of the plan and RPS were in keeping with people's skepticism of local government and the public-school system. In 1982, West decided to parlay his populist approval into political office. Fifty-two years old in 1982, he had virtually no experience in official politics and had never been heavily committed to Richmond's political struggle for civil rights.[52]

West's campaign slogan, "A New Direction for Richmond," eventually became a referendum on his approach to politics. West quickly distanced himself from the BMC, set out to prove that he was not the Crusade's candidate, and established that he planned to run a campaign of reassurance. He also stressed that he was philosophically independent of the black body politic and that he would also help bring an end to race-based power struggles. His campaign pamphlet emphasized interracial unity for the sake of "setting aside the negative differences that plagued City Council and for council to be truly representative as it establishes policy and passes ordinances in the best interests of the *entire* city." African Americans were immediately concerned that West might actually pose a threat to Dell's incumbency. Kenney was extremely frank about what West represented; "it is ironic," the councilman argued, "that we have a black running a negative campaign against the black majority. Yet, I hear nothing negative about those who have tried to stop the accomplishments of the majority." West capitalized on the racial division at city hall by blaming Marsh rather than the white council minority for the conflict. Dell, who had not faced a formidable political opponent in nearly a decade and was a staunch defender of Mayor Marsh, proved ill equipped to defend herself against West's assault.[53]

Willie Dell ran as a candidate of continuity but became a victim of the district system. It is impossible to talk about her political career without mentioning how gendered expectations influenced the development of that career. By 1982, Dell had fallen out of favor with some black residents of her district in the Highland Park area. These Highland Park voters argued that she was generally inaccessible. A sizeable number of those voters also believed that the incumbent, who had become a poor folks' champion, had it in for the middle-class residents of the Highland Park area. According to these voters, Dell did not carry herself in a manner that was commensurate with a black female public representative—she was "too black," they believed. These were the very people who had rejected Curtis Holt and openly criticized Dell for sporting an Afro, wearing African regalia, and speaking in so-called black English. Reports later confirmed that a number of these African Americans very quietly worked to undermine Dell's campaign. Many of the Crusade's long-standing members and allies had backed away from Dell's campaign behind the scenes. The grapevine had it that Senator Wilder, who lived in Dell's district, had actually encouraged Roy West to run in 1982, a suggestion that Wilder vehemently disputed in court.[54]

Although Dell resisted gendered and class-based attacks on her character, voters believed that ousting her was the safest way to undermine Henry Marsh's control over the mayoralty. Dell argued that ministers' wives should "maintain their own identity": "I'm not going to be what other people want me to be. I go barefoot if I'm in the mood." Dell had spent much of her career before politics working with economically vulnerable communities, and she remained committed to these issues throughout her career. She very openly held that her adversaries had little interest in understanding the way she carried herself in public and approached politics. She knew, for instance, that middle-class African Americans were critical of her strong southern accent and Afro. They may have further resented that she refused to concede to the pressures placed on her. Over the course of the 1970s, however, the number of middle-class African Americans grew in the Highland Park area, and these middle-class voters were not as committed to the fight against poverty as Dell continued to be. Dell's greatest problem with the Imperial Plaza and Highland Park coalition may have been that charges of unresponsiveness in reality meant that she failed to secure business relationships for a class of people uniquely positioned to take advantage of having blacks on the city council.[55]

The face-off in District C represented a contest between two distinct approaches to local government—the desire to build the way to a better Richmond through entrepreneurship and the commitment to raising poorer blacks' standard of living. Some black leaders believed that in trying to secure safer seats, the BMC obstructed African Americans' abilities to get in on the redevelopment plans taking place throughout Richmond. These black voters associated Dell and BMC members with the Project One debacle and nearly five years of council factionalism. The conflict between Dell and West was not unique to Richmond—it epitomized a struggle in black politics that emerged in general in the early 1980s. Technocratic politicians, who represented a growing black middle class, began to directly challenge the first wave of civil rights–era politicians. The contest between Roy West and Willie Dell was, in essence, a battle between those who promoted race-based, affirmative-action initiatives (West) and those who championed targeted programs for vulnerable African American communities (Dell). Dell had argued nearly a decade earlier, "I'm . . . working at the grassroots level about the importance of people priorities and their problems over bricks and mortar." As Sister Helen Legeay of the Catholic Diocese of Richmond stated during Dell's council appointment in 1973, Dell had "insight into the welfare system and social aspects of urban life" that diversified the city council's interests. She refused to compromise over her commitment to social issues—even at the expense of losing the middle-class vote. In an April debate against Dell, West argued that "the issues . . . of non-responsiveness to the needs of the district, on the district level, and on the citywide level, the perennial conflict on City Council," had become synonymous with Dell's tenure on the city council. West's appeals to good government and responsiveness were another way of articulating that he could solidify coalitions with whites. The white council minority's threats to sever connections between Richmond's private and public sector also led groups of middle-class African Americans to believe that the BMC cared more about exercising power for its own sake than about interracial coalition building. Dell held that "what other folks promise you, I can and have delivered and I will continue." The people in Imperial Plaza and Highland Park disagreed.[56]

The contest in District C in 1982 took its toll on both Dell's campaign and her political career. Dell, who had been appointed to the council during the enjoinment, actually had minimal experience organizing campaigns. Even her campaign manager, Sandra Mitchell, admitted that the campaign struggled to organize strategies against West in the early stages. It also suffered because Dell refused to distance herself from Marsh. West continually put forward the idea that he was a "free thinker," and, given his run-ins with RPS administration, voters seemed to believe him. Marsh's critics argued that the mayor spent more time campaigning in Dell's district than in his own. On May 5, 1982, election day, Peter Bacque of the *Richmond Times-Dispatch* wrote, "It was a fine day in Richmond, a fine day for an election, a fine day for anything, for everything. Grass-roots politics, the politics of friends and sidewalks, of rights and in-betweens, politics bloomed in the city's streets." The *Dispatch* knew what West represented. He defeated Dell by 497 votes, 3,858 to 3,361, and in five out of nine precincts. In the three white precincts west of Chamberlayne Avenue, West picked up 2,202 votes: 91 percent of the vote in Precincts 307, 308, and 309 and 30 percent of the vote for the entire district. He also garnered 34 percent of the African American vote. He won Precincts 301 and 302, which were made up largely of middle- and upper-class blacks. West also grabbed a decent chunk of Dell's votes in precincts that vocalized overwhelming support for the incumbent. The rest of Richmond's incumbents decisively overwhelmed their opponents, and Andrew Gillespie, a chief architect of Fair Play, joined them on the council. (For full election results in 1982, see table 13 in the appendix.)[57]

Richmond's majority–minority district system may have secured African Americans seats on the city council, but it also had unintended consequences. Black mayors and councilpersons had little time to celebrate their historic victories. They quickly realized that political power alone was not enough—their white counterparts were still the gatekeepers to local political economies. Whites also carried on the politics of obstructionism and anti-VRA sentiment well into (and beyond) the 1980s. Factors beyond the realm of politics also tempered the symbolism of black governance. At the very moment black Americans assumed control over the symbols of local political power, their communities began to suffer from deepening economic vulnerability. Marsh, McDaniel, Richardson, and Kenney rode out this storm, but Dell refused to succumb to gendered expectations about female elected officials, and her devotion to poverty and principle cost her a council seat in 1982. Roy West fancied himself a solution to racial conflict at city hall—voters agreed. The conflict between Roy West and Willie Dell typified a much larger problem within the Crusade—they represented two distinct approaches to local government. In the coming years, the Crusade failed to reconcile these differences.

5

"All He Gave Me Was a Foot"

Black Technocrats, Richmond's Urban Woes, and the Crisis of the Crusade for Voters

"I Voted for Me"

On July 1, 1982, Richmond's city clerk, E. A. Duffy, swore in what looked like another black-majority city council—five African Americans and four white council members. On its face, it appeared that African Americans voted for yet another black city council majority—the fourth in four elections since the capital city implemented a majority–minority district system. In accordance with the city charter, following the opening ceremony, council members began the process of voting for mayor. Again, the votes split evenly along racial lines. Henry Marsh, Claudette McDaniel, Chuck Richardson, and Walter Kenney, to the surprise of few, voted to reelect Marsh. In an unexpected maneuver, however, the council minority did not cast votes for Bill Leidinger (the unofficial leader of the council minority), Steve Kemp, Carolyn Wake, or Andrew Gillespie. Leidinger and the remaining members of the council minority voted for the newest African American councilman, Roy West. *Richmond Times-Dispatch* staff writer, Tom Campbell, wrote that after a dramatic and elongated pause, West, who was the last to vote, broke with the council's African Americans. West quietly spoke his name into the microphone. The chamber, Campbell observed, broke into deafening applause. West later commented on this outcome, "I voted for me. I wanted to broaden the base of black political leadership. I wanted to eliminate factions on council." Although few knew it at the time, West's vote for himself represented the BMC's Waterloo.[1]

Roy West's campaign in 1982 capitalized on nearly four years of racial polarization, and his mayoralty eventually exposed deep-rooted weaknesses within the Crusade. If West's election to city council was a vote of no confidence for Willie Dell, his selection to the mayoralty became a referendum on the white council minority's aversion to Henry Marsh. During their election-night victory party at the Flamingo Restaurant and Lounge, Crusade members seemed concerned about whether West would side with the council minority. West quickly put the Crusade's uneasiness to rest, but not in the way it had hoped. On the day of his appointment, he broke another four–four deadlock by supporting the choice of another council rookie to the vice mayoralty, Drew Gillespie, over five-year council veteran Chuck Richardson. West's vote for Gillespie was the first in a series of decisions that fractured the BMC's voting bloc. By 1986, it had become glaringly apparent that West did what whites had been unable to do since 1977: he single-handedly shifted the balance of power on the city council, outwitted the Crusade, and crippled Henry Marsh's domination over city hall.[2]

West's decisions—the first of many to align squarely with white members of city council—gave way to a new era of governance in the commonwealth's capital. After decades of direct disenfranchisement and black voter mobilization, Richmond's district system finally allowed African Americans to elect preferred candidates. Majority–minority wards may have protected African American voters from vote dilution, but they did little to protect black people from the quality of black representation. After years of high-profile bickering and obstructionism, council minority members and organizations such as TOP realized that they could not out-Crusade the Crusade. In the two city council elections following 1977, whites' private political lobbies had tried and failed to defeat black candidates. They pumped vast sums of money into ostensibly vulnerable districts, mobilized white voters in swing wards, and used local media to generate support for the return of white control. The white establishment also came to realize that Washington, even into the early 1980s, was still committed to defending African American voters under the Voting Rights Act of 1965. The tide turned in 1982. The voters of District C, Kemp, Wake, Leidinger, and Gillespie found an African American who agreed with their aversion to the BMC. In terms of the Crusade, West represented something far more ominous: his mayoralty symbolized that blacks' responses to the common experience of racism were more varied in 1980 than they had been during the 1960s and 1970s. West had his own ideas about how to solve the communities' problems—namely, a commitment to black entrepreneurship and a tough-on-crime stance. Although he was belabored by the *Richmond Afro-American* and Richmond's black political establishment, he also had his own vision of racial politics—one predicated on interracial cooperation. This vision was not entirely attributable to Roy West; over the course of the 1980s, a new generation of black political leadership emerged from the shadows of the civil rights movement. These middle-class black mayors and politicians met the challenges facing America's cities and the rise of Ronald Reagan not by embracing the politics of race but by dampening appeals to racial favoritism. West in many ways symbolized the beginning of the end of African Americans' fleeting alliance with Washington and the rise of a new technocratic black elite.[3]

Local and national media took immediate notice of West's election. Both the *Richmond Times-Dispatch* and the *Richmond News-Leader* endorsed West's campaign in 1982. Historically, an endorsement by both local dailies had usually guaranteed a black candidate's defeat; the Crusade often used such endorsements to generate support for its candidates. Even prior to West's election, the *Times-Dispatch* recognized that West's appeals to racial cooperation and black respectability might bring about a "renaissance" in racial politics. *Jet* magazine, which referred to Marsh as the "the state's most publicized political civil rights champion," had strong opinions about West's mayoralty. It charged that state senator L. Douglas Wilder (who eventually became both Virginia's and America's first black governor in 1990) and Marsh were involved in a contest of political one-upmanship that had far-reaching implications for racial politics in Richmond. Wilder, *Jet* contended, had encouraged West to run—not against Dell per se, but against Marsh. Some African Americans were of the persuasion that West could iron out better relationships with Richmond's business elites. Although Wilder later refuted *Jet*'s claim in a court of law, Richmond's leaders seemed to know that Marsh and Wilder's friendship had deteriorated by the early 1980s. West's emergence on the local political scene also had national implications.[4]

Roy West, whether he knew it or not, represented a changing of the guard in municipal black politics. His election to the Richmond City Council and appointment to the mayoralty demonstrated that Richmond was not immune to national political trends and economic developments. By the early 1980s, a new generation of technocratic black politicians came to power in local and state politics. Public officials such as West were not only elected with the help of middle-class black and white voters but also often used these votes to beat out the first generation of post-VRA black officials. If the first wave of black elected officials rode the tide of civil rights reform into public office, the second wave crashed into the first. These politicians gained local favor by tempering appeals to racial partiality and targeted social welfare programs. In many ways, West predated black mayors such as Bill Campbell of Atlanta, Dennis Archer of Detroit, and Mike White of Cleveland. On the one hand, these men and women were elected by a groundswell of emerging black middle-class voters and their white allies. On the other hand, they were forced to accommodate not just structural economic forces beyond the control of local politics but also the millions of black Americans whom the civil rights movement had left behind. These politicians had to contend with decaying school systems, deepening poverty, white flight, and unprecedented levels of violent crime. Rather than fight against the stream of growing antipathy to blacks' appeals to civil rights and social welfare, mayors such as West in the early 1980s swam with the current. They downplayed race in favor of promoting efficient government, and their appeals to interracial respectability were often undergirded by an imperative need to lure businesses and investors back into their cities. Cities from Detroit to Atlanta were awash with social and economic problems by the 1980s—many of these problems were rooted firmly in the economic, social, and urban policies of the mid–twentieth century. West's "deracialized" campaign strategies eventually tested the Crusade's mettle. His rise to the mayoralty also demonstrated that local politics in Richmond was not immune to political developments in Washington under President Ronald Reagan's first administration.[5]

The momentum of civil rights reform was in jeopardy under the Reagan administration's New Federalism. As many of America's cities struggled to respond to white flight and mounting poverty, federal officials changed Washington's approach to urban funding. Although increasing interest in developing public–private partnerships at the state and local levels gained particular energy under President Reagan, these initiatives were not entirely Republican in origin. As funding for the War on Poverty dried up alongside the American economy during the 1970s, the Nixon and Ford administrations, Congress, and the U.S. Department of Housing and Urban Development began to fund Community Development Block Grant programs. These grants, which allocated funds to localities for various forms of social welfare and infrastructural development, attempted to return regulatory authority back to the states by granting them more autonomy over community development. Jimmy Carter further advanced these types of policies, which eventually "floundered on the shoals of stagflation," by putting forward community job-training initiatives such as the Comprehensive Education and Training Act (CETA), an act signed by Nixon in 1973. As white evangelical Christians, middle-class property owners, and neoconservative intellectual leaders revolted against what they believed were the twin big-government evils of social liberalism and high taxes, however, the Reagan administration reduced appropriations for these types of programs. Under New Federalism, an attempt to reverse nearly fifty years of liberal domestic policy by making state and local governments more dependent on market mechanisms, the Reagan administration and Congress transferred decision making to localities by "disassembling the constellation of grants to city and states governments." This process was characterized not only by cuts in federal programs that financed a minimum level of income in housing, food, medical care, education, and job training but also by cuts to federal subsidies to state and local government programs that were not related to poverty—that is, infrastructure-building programs, neighborhood rehabilitation funds, and various federal grant programs.[6]

In August 1981, the Reagan administration's domestic-spending cuts sent shockwaves through cities such as Richmond. The so-called Reagan rollbacks, which forty-eight Democratic U.S. congresspersons supported, cut federal income taxes by 25 percent over a three-year period and furthered the process of returning regulatory authority to the states and reducing appropriations for liberal federal programs. The CETA program eventually lost all of its funding. The history of how CETA succumbed to local abuse, conservative opposition, and national economic forces is well documented. Although contemporary Americans associate CETA with social welfare programs gone horribly wrong, these programs actually meant something to local people who were on the frontlines of a war against intensifying urban poverty. In 1980, CETA provided work for 300,000 people, but in March 1981, for instance, the Virginia Employment Commission, which administered CETA, estimated that 1,200 Virginians would lose their jobs. Nationally, African Americans constituted slightly more than 93 percent of total CETA participants in 1981. Cutbacks in programs like CETA decimated job training for Richmond's low-income African Americans, the long-term unemployed, and black teenagers. Federal aid to Richmond dropped from $4 million in 1981 to $2.8 million in 1982.[7]

In Richmond, where the unemployment rate for black teenagers between the ages of sixteen and nineteen was 31 percent in 1982, local officials and activists expressed growing concern about cuts in social programs—even if these programs had failed to work as policy makers had intended. In March 1981, Pat Hickey of the Bainbridge Community Center—which serviced a south side housing project that the city had created to combat the housing crisis brought on by the Downtown Expressway—and Alma Barlow of the Anti-Hunger Coalition went to Washington to protest CETA cuts. Barlow and Hickey packed 140 Richmonders into three buses, two cars, and a van. Before leaving for Washington, Hickey argued: "The budget shouldn't be balanced at the expense of our senior citizens, our children, and our disabled people. . . . We have no quarrels with fixing the economy. As a matter of fact, we're the prime victims of it. The middle class may go without luxuries, like a vacation or a third car. But we're out of necessities." Hickey's appeals for a poverty platform fell on deaf ears. By 1982, Reagan cut social programs by $35 billion and job-training and service programs related to what remained of the War on Poverty by another $7 billion. New Federalism also created more oversight and red tape for those federal programs that remained on the books. Over time, recipients of Community Development Block Grants were required to hold a specified number of public hearings, advertised in specified ways, to qualify for federal funds. Before Reagan took office, the published requirements for community-development programs had grown from 56 pages in 1975 to 202 pages by 1980. Reagan argued that the federal government intruded excessively into state and local operations through the liberal welfare state, and he promised less money for less regulation.[8]

The notion of getting government off people's backs resonated profoundly in both federal and state governments. On the one hand, the federal government continued to protect blacks' ability to elect preferred candidates in black-majority districts. On the other hand, the Reagan administration either ignored or crafted policies that were openly antithetical to the demographic and economic forces plaguing most majority-black cities. The federal government's new philosophy of making local governments more dependent on the private sector and market mechanisms reinforced the notion that African Americans' special relationship with the federal government had come and gone. Although the federal government continued to defend blacks' rights to cast votes, its economic policies did little to address the disintegration of black communities. State senator Doug Wilder observed that as 1983 came to a close, local and state public servants were growing more racially defiant and less sensitive to minorities' needs than they had been a mere ten years earlier.[9]

Even Virginia's General Assembly, which had only recently shaken off the last vestiges of Harry Byrd's Democratic machine, got swept up in antiurbanism. Between 1970 and 1988, thirteen African Americans served in the 140-member General Assembly. That number did not exceed five until 1984, after the commonwealth adopted single-member districts in 1983. Although African Americans constituted roughly 19 percent of Virginia's total population in 1980, their representatives came from cities with heavier concentrations of black residents. Not only had these cities become blacker and in many cases poorer as whites and middle-class folks—including some blacks—fled to the suburbs, but this mass migration occurred simultaneously with the reddening of America's suburban enclaves. In the commonwealth, this reddening process—that is, the move toward conservative politics—found continuous expression in the General Assembly, particularly in terms of antiurban, antiannexation legislation. By the 1980s, disproportionate numbers of Virginia's legislators were from rural and suburban areas that were, like the commonwealth's cities, predominately racially homogenous. Just as Virginia's single-member district system gave rise to a greater number of black politicians from urban areas, it also certainly solidified white representation from suburban and rural areas. These areas had become extremely defensive about protecting their autonomy by the 1980s. In 1987, for instance, the General Assembly placed yet another "temporary" moratorium on annexations. The law extended a requirement established in 1980 that granted cities immunity from annexations that had populations greater than 50,000 or a density of 140 persons per square mile and 20,000 residents or both. These policies, because of city–county independence, often impinged upon Richmond's ability to meet metropolitan challenges. Antiannexation legislation also spoke volumes about what county residents thought of Virginia's cities. In a manner similar to passive resistance to public-school integration, legislators and supporters couched antiannexation language in individual rights rather than in racial terms. One *Richmond Times-Dispatch* exposé on local crime and poverty in June 1986 epitomized county independence. A former Church Hill resident who had relocated to Henrico County in 1965 argued, "We thought if we were going to invest, we would move to a place where our investment would be protected." These federal and state initiatives, regardless of language, had racial implications.[10]

The legacy of American racism and local bigotry bore strange fruit in the 1980s. Reagan's approach to federalism and state-level policies often flew in the face of the data. By the early 1980s, local leaders, politicians, and civil rights organizations came to terms with a stark reality: changes beyond the spectrum of local politics had undermined many of the prospects of civil rights activism. Between 1979 and 1984, six of ten jobs added to the U.S. labor market paid $7,000 per year or less. African Americans, who were often less skilled and educated, occupied many of these lower-paying, service-industry jobs, and the gap between whites' and blacks' median income widened in the 1980s. By 1981, for instance, the median income of black families, $13,266, was only 56.4 percent of white families' median income, $23,517. Although both black and white family incomes shifted upward between 1960 and 1980, "black families['] [income] did so at a slower pace." Black women were in particularly vulnerable economic shape; even black women who had completed a year or more of graduate work earned less, $13,757, than their white counterparts, $16,782. The ranks of the black middle class grew at the same time as countless African American women struggled with poverty. In Richmond, the census report for 1980 showed that African Americans' average family income, $15,358, was higher than the national average for black Americans but more than $10,000 less than white families' average income, $26,000. In 1980, the median income in Richmond's wealthiest and whitest census tract on the West End (98.2 percent white, in fact) was $53,993. Meanwhile, on the other side of town in one of Richmond's black middle-class enclaves within the Highland Park area, the median income was $17,379. The income disparity between middle-class African Americans and white West Enders confirmed just how much economic power white Richmonders still held. It also demonstrated, in the words of a *Times-Dispatch* reporter, that Richmond was "increasingly a city of the wealthiest whites and poorest blacks." Middle-class African Americans knew this as well—not only did new divisions emerge between Richmond black professionals and the working poor, but these middle-class African Americans also struggled to keep pace with their white counterparts.[11]

Richmond was more segregated in the 1980s than it had been in the 1960s, and many of the city's predominantly black census tracts had become severely impoverished. Thirty-eight of Richmond's sixty-nine total census tracts were predominantly and in some cases almost exclusively racially homogenous: fourteen tracts were more than 90 percent white, and twenty-four were more than 90 percent African American. According to the 1980 census, eight census tracts were more than 95 percent white, and sixteen were more than 95 percent African American. The most exclusively white census tracts were on the city's West End, whereas the East End, central portions of the city, and the Jackson Ward area contained the heaviest concentrations of African Americans. Gilpin Court near Jackson Ward, for instance, was home to 2,300 people, and the number of units totaled 783 in 1986. Of the total number of residents in Gilpin Court, 800 were children, and about half of the households lived on less than $5,000 annually. During the first year of Ronald Reagan's presidency, forty of Richmond's census tracts were more than 75 percent black. Only one census tract in the East End was less than 50 percent African American.[12]

The deepest pockets of segregation were in the poorest census tracts.

These neighborhoods were the outcome of urban planners' ambitions in the 1950s and 1960s. They also relied most heavily on the very assistance that Washington officials now resolved to cut. Between 1970 and 1980, the fraction of people in Richmond living below the poverty level increased by nearly 45 percent to one-fifth of the city's total population. During that same period, the figure for Richmonders living below 75 percent of the poverty level exploded by 60 percent to one-seventh of the city's total population. The average monthly caseload for persons on food stamps in Richmond during fiscal year 1979–1980 was 27,032. That number rose consistently over the 1980s, and by fiscal year 1985–1986 the number of people per month on food stamp assistance was 34,000. During the same year, the unemployment rate for blacks, 4.5 percent, was nearly twice as high as the rate for whites. In 1982, 31 percent of black youth between the ages of sixteen and nineteen were unemployed—a barometer of future problems. Although per capita income in the city's four poorest black neighborhoods grew by 57 percent, in the metropolitan area—including Chesterfield and Henrico Counties—it grew by 125 percent. However, the combined three census tracts on Richmond's West End, the city's wealthiest area located north of the James River, included only thirty-six African Americans in 1980. The average white individual in Richmond earned $9,613 annually. This figure was higher than for whites in the surrounding counties and more than double the amount earned by the average African American, $4,700.[13]

Areas such as Church Hill, the East End, and the south side bore the brunt of this economic dispossession. Between 1960 and 1980, for instance, Church Hill lost nearly 60 percent of its population. Many of the area's African Americans, in what the *Times-Dispatch* called "black flight," met the challenges of heightened poverty and the continuation of restrictive covenants by relocating to the north side (West's district), where they occupied homes that whites had abandoned in their rush to the counties. The north side had roughly 1,000 African Americans in 1960. By 1980, there were more than 10,000 predominantly middle-class African Americans on the north side—the highest concentration of middle-class blacks in Richmond. Meanwhile, for the poor African Americans whom housing officials had compressed into denser enclaves and public-housing units, the continuing poverty seemed inescapable. In some of Richmond's most predominantly black census tracts—namely, the Fulton, Union Hill, Bainbridge, and Fairmont areas—the poverty was ubiquitous. These impoverished census tracts were also home to Fairfield, Mosby, Whitcomb, and Creighton Courts. The *Times-Dispatch* reported that Richmond's poorest black neighborhoods, representing 6,600 people, had an average per capita annual income of $1,990 in 1980. Of those 6,660 residents, only 830 (12.5 percent) were white, and fewer than 1,650 (25 percent) had graduated from high school. Not only was the median age in these neighborhoods less than twenty-one years old, but 18 percent of these area's residents were not working or actively looking for employment. Nearly two-thirds of the residents in the Bainbridge area lived on less than the poverty level—$7,412 for a family of four annually when the Census Bureau released the 1980 report. More dangerously, these very areas had a murder rate four times higher than Richmond proper and fourteen times high than the national average. By the mid-1980s, Richmond was no place to be poor and black. In response to the violent crime that plagued Richmond in the mid-1980s,

Table 5.1. Richmond's Poorest Census Tracts, 1983–1985 (Averages Based on Rates per 100,000 People)

Tract	Population	Per Capita Annual Income	Percentage African American	Number of Murders
201	2,575	$3,901	98.9	104
202	5,249	$3,086	99.6	95
204	5,642	$3,297	96.7	94
206	1,996	$3,972	97.5	67
207	1,746	$3,842	99.3	210
301	3,578	$1,720	98.2	149
302	2,021	$3,900	95.7	214
303	976	$2,743	25.6	102
306	919	$3,819	64.9	36
403	2,422	$3,656	30.3	28
601	2,241	$2,274	87.8	45
City Average	219,214	$7,073	51.3	35

Source: Data from *Richmond Times-Dispatch,* June 15, 1986, A8, citing information from the U.S. Census Bureau and the Richmond Police Department.

a local Richmonder, Preddy Ray, summed up the sense of despair that characterized many of these neighborhoods: "Civil Rights really hasn't changed the fundamentals. . . . Murder is the result of helplessness and hopelessness."[14]

Richmonders and their dailies were not the only ones in America to take notice of the growing problem of poverty and federal cutbacks. The Urban Institute released a report, *Testing the Social Safety Net*, in 1986 after examining four cities between 1981 and 1983—Detroit, Boston, Richmond, and San Diego. The report, one of the first to study how local officials responded to cuts in federal programs, "concluded that Richmond and Virginia had done less than any of the other three areas in making up for federal reductions in aid to the elderly, children, and chronically mentally handicapped." It demonstrated that Richmond and the commonwealth's General Assembly had actually aggravated the condition of poverty by failing to combat the New Federalism. Martha R. Burt, one of the report's authors, stated, "All other states made some effort to compensate for some of the federal cuts." Virginia and Richmond did nothing, the author contended; "even though Detroit, Michigan, had a higher unemployment rate and more strained local revenues" it did more than Richmond. The report demonstrated that the Virginia Adult Services Division caseload for in-home services dropped from 343 recipients per month in 1981 to a mere 60 in 1982, and its budget fell from $615,000 to $162,000. Services for children by Richmond's Department of Public Welfare suffered a similar fate—only 1.5 percent of Richmond's impoverished children remained directly involved with child protective services. Richmond's city manager, Manuel Deese, reported in the budget for fiscal year 1981–1982, for instance, that there was virtually no federal "funding for the Youth Services Commission [or] Commission for the Elderly and the Handicapped Commission." By 1982, Richmond's Social Services Bureau cut 73 positions, and budget constraints forced Deese to cut 419 jobs between 1981 and 1982, with 219 of those positions for full-time employees.[15]

Richmond Public Schools struggled to meet the challenges of rising poverty. A court-ordered mandate for crosstown busing in 1971 and the election of the BMC all but ensured that white flight continued apace well into the 1980s. More than 39,000 whites voted with their feet and

left Richmond between 1970 and 1980 alone. By retreating to the suburbs, whites in northern and southern cities alike continued to raise their
standard of living and to resist integration. Richmond's public-school
population, like that of scores of American cities, often reflected overall
residential patterns. In 1976, one year before the implementation of the
district system, Richard C. Hunter became the city's first African American school superintendent. Hunter inherited what can only be described
as a school system on the edge of a crisis. This crisis was not about a lack of
funding, contrary to the criticism of Deese for not pouring more money
into RPS: between 1981 and 1986, Richmond allocated an average of
28 percent of its total expenditures on public education. The proportion
of funds Richmond distributed to schools far eclipsed other municipal
expenses. The problem was bigger than money. Richmond's acute residential segregation, the growing problem of poverty, people's reluctance
to send children to integrated schools, and the Supreme Court's decision to outlaw cross-county busing in *Milliken v. Bradley* (1974) intensified the quality of local education. On the thirtieth anniversary of the
Supreme Court's *Brown v. Board* decision, Richmond's public schools
were 84.6 percent African American. And a sizeable majority of these
African American children were poor. If people needed evidence that the
common experience of racism was not as common in the early 1980s,
they had only look at the ways middle-class blacks, too, exercised educational alternatives instead of sending their children to Richmond's public
schools. Between 1968 and 1980, for instance, the number of black students in Henrico County schools increased from 8 to 20 percent. By the
late 1970s, RPS high schools with a capacity for 2,000 had fewer than
600 enrolled students. Between 1970 and 1980, total enrollment in RPS
dropped from 47,988 to 30,349, and officials closed fifteen schools. In
1982, Richmond had one of the highest dropout rates in Virginia and a
truancy dilemma. The *Richmond Times-Dispatch* estimated that 1,000
school-age children were out of school on any given day.[16]

The spread of black poverty and Reagan's urban policy befuddled
many black leaders. They were almost immediately skeptical of Reagan's
federal policies. The Crusade for Voters wasted no time expressing its
dislike for the former governor of California, denouncing Reagan during his campaign against President Carter. In November 1980, the Cru-

sade sent out a mailing that blasted Reagan and warned voters that the Republican candidate "would eliminate the Departments of Education and Health and Human Services" as well as other programs designed to help America's vulnerable communities. The Congressional Black Caucus echoed the Crusade's concerns: "In no time in memory has an administration shown less appreciation for the problems affecting minorities and the poor. For 28 million black Americans, the President's slogan 'America is back' had little meaning. . . . [T]he condition of blacks continues to stagnate and deteriorate. . . . There's little reason to expect this administration to be less vitriolic in unraveling civil rights protections of 1964." Many of Richmond's African American politicians were not only concerned about the future of civil rights policies but also unaccustomed to dealing with federal administrations that disregarded socioeconomic conditions in black communities. Politicians and activists who remembered how segregationists stripped black communities of the building blocks necessary for upward mobility found it difficult to reconcile the state of black communities with a federal administration that seemed to blame poverty on the impoverished.[17]

Public officials took the fight against Reagan's rollbacks straight to Washington. In February 11, 1982, Senator Edward Kennedy and the Committee on Labor and Human Relations invited Marsh to address a Senate hearing on the impact of unemployment disparities between black and white communities as well as between black and white youth. Marsh had grown to prominence as a civil rights litigator, but he had also worked diligently to secure the very types of federally funded capital improvements that were in jeopardy under Reagan. During his tenure as mayor, he had increased the percentage of capital budget allocations for Richmond neighborhoods from 48 percent to 75 percent. In Washington, he argued that Reagan cutbacks "would only serve to perpetuate disparities between black and white unemployment rates in . . . Richmond." Manny Deese soon joined the fight. After reading Deese's article "New Federalism Brings New Pressures to Central Cities and Black Managers," published in *Public Management* magazine, the National Governors Association invited the Richmond city manager to a convention in Afton, Oklahoma, in 1982. As the first African American to address the Governors Association and the only city manager to speak at the gathering in August 1982, Deese contemplated local governments under Reagan's New Federalism. He argued that as Washington rolled back federal aid, cities were more dependent than ever on the private sector and states' abilities to meet local demands. He further stressed:

> The most painful area of cutbacks has been in human services. The harshest impact is naturally being felt in our older central cities where minorities and economically disadvantaged are clustered. . . . Reagan's policies are grounded in state–suburban coalitions instead of state–city partnership. . . . [C]ity administrators have to manage more with less and cities often receive notification of program cutbacks too late to cushion ourselves for the consequences. . . . Central cities are left to become dumping grounds for suburban jurisdictions, a place to leave their problems, and so the city is bled for even more services.

Deese, who was keenly aware of state regulations in Virginia that limited county–city relationships, recognized that Richmond was becoming the dependent variable in the local metropolitan equation. He argued in the *Richmond Afro-American*, "Reagan's policies are grounded in state-suburban coalitions instead of the state-city partnerships it should be." Under Reagan's system, Washington not only favored suburbs, they often left cities more dependent on market mechanisms.[18]

When the BMC entered city hall in 1977, Richmond was still thriving economically, but that was not the case in the early 1980s. In 1980, Richmond was home to 233,559 jobs (full-time and part-time combined). After 1980, however, the capital city witnessed a steady decline in employment, which dipped by 6 percent in the 1980s and by 12 percent in the 1990s. Unfortunately for Richmond, most of these jobs moved from the city to the metropolitan area. The suburbanization of jobs quickly followed the suburbanization of Richmonders. By the mid-1980s, Richmond had evolved into what experts call a "hollow prize." Urban African American officials often confronted difficulties that constrained them from distributing important economic and political benefits to their constituents—in Virginia, these circumstances were often exacerbated by home rules that made it difficult for cities and counties to interact without the General Assembly's specific approval. Dwindling tax bases often meant that politicians had to rely on white-controlled state legislatures, the federal government, and what remained of the local private sector. Richmond's local tax revenues decreased steadily from $125 million in 1978 to approximately $110 million in 1981. Deese saw that federal cutbacks to local programs were already evident in the early 1980s. He argued:

> The city had more money than ever before. . . . The city finds, like everyone else, that a dollar no longer buys what it used to. . . . In the president's attempt to develop an economic recovery plan for this country, he has proposed a budget that was characterized by one magazine as cut, slash and chop. The plan submitted by the president to congress on March 10, 1981, proposed 1981–82 budget reductions totaling more than 40 billion dollars. It is anticipated that the budget cuts proposed at the federal level will have a tremendous impact on the way we conduct our business as a government in the future.

Roughly four years later, in 1986, Deese's successor, interim city manager A. Howard Todd, wrote in the annual city budget report: "We are witnessing a fundamental change in intergovernmental relationships. Responsibilities are being shifted from federal and state governments to localities, but unfortunately without a corresponding shift in revenues. It appears that Congress is completely unable to make the tough decisions necessary to solve the national deficit problem." By 1982, Richmond may have appeared to have more money in actual dollars than in the 1970s, but with inflation the value of those dollars meant less.[19]

These national and regional structural forces made Roy West's first months in office all the more confounding. Although West had claimed that he would work toward interracial cooperation on the city council, he did so at blacks' expense. Just weeks after the election, Mayor West and the white council members maneuvered to undo many of the previous majority's policies and appointments. West, Kemp, Wake, Gillespie, and Leidinger first hired a white lawyer who had a history of differences with Richmond's black community to replace a black lawyer in the city's legal defense against the Hilton Corporation (left over from the Project One controversy). They also attempted to gain more control over the affairs of the school board, even though none of their children attended RPS. They resolved to amend the city charter to have more control over the council's school board appointments and financial matters. The amendment stipulated that the council could allocate funds in line items to the school board in lieu of the lump sum that city managers distributed annually. Critics of this plan—black and white alike—found it ironic that the very council members who had criticized Marsh for assuming managerial responsibilities now sought to amend the city charter to give the council more authority. Had the amendment passed and West gotten his way, Richmond would have been the only major city in the United States to contemplate such allocations, and the school board would have been further subjected to political pressures.[20]

African Americans had deep reservations about West's agenda. He not only voted against Marsh's appointments but, along with the white council members, led by Leidinger and Gillespie, also voted Marsh and Richardson off of vital committees, such as Richmond's Housing Committee. On the issue of naming various committee members and city hall positions, West voted with the white council members seventeen of seventeen times before July 1982—less than two months into his first mayoral term. Blacks and liberal whites also accused West and white council members of attempting to pack the school board with members agreeable to West's maturing coalition. West also made it known that he intended to appoint likeminded school board members. His public criticism of RPS superintendent Richard Hunter, who had demoted West years earlier during the Plan G controversy, eventually culminated in Hunter's resignation in the summer of 1984. The City of Richmond eventually filed a legal motion that prohibited the mayor, who was still a middle school principle at the time, from voting on school board appointments because of the apparent conflict of interest. In December 1984, Virginia's supreme court ruled unanimously that West would not be allowed to vote on school board appointments.[21]

The Crusade struggled to cope with West and the type of pluralism he represented. In its early years, the Crusade leadership had been made up of "professional men and educators at Virginia Union who were," according to *Richmond Times-Dispatch* reporter Shelley Rolfe, "largely immune to white economic pressures." The Crusade, stated former council member and local businessman Henry Valentine, "can't be bought. It would be demeaning to try to buy it." The Crusade entered the 1980s still largely intact—professionals still dominated the decision-making process, and the organization remained staunchly independent of white patronage. During the Jim Crow era and the early years of the district system, the organization had capitalized on the momentum it had built during the early 1960s. It also emerged largely intact from the annexation dilemma. West's mayoralty became an immediate point of frustration for the Crusade's leadership. The Crusade had endorsed Willie Dell, and West's first months in office reminded it of just how important Dell had been as a member of the BMC. During the mid-1980s, the Crusade struggled to circle the wagons in response to West's voting record, a record that often flew in the face of persisting institutionalized bigotry in Richmond. It was, indeed, the Crusade that had argued throughout the 1960s that its strictly political approach to civil rights activism would level the political playing field. It had also firmly believed that a district system and black governance, rather than deannexation, would help the city's African Americans realize the dream of greater economic equality. By the early 1980s, people became increasingly unconvinced of the Crusade's strictly political strategies.[22]

It was West's first months in office that motivated Crusade leadership and president Ellen Pearson to assemble the closed retreat at the Roslyn Conference Center in Henrico, Virginia, on August 20, 1982. The retreat at Roslyn was a self-audit. The organization wanted the city's leaders to iron out their grievances privately. To this end, they invited black city council members—including West—along with Willie Dell, Doug Wilder, Jack Gravely (director of the state branch of the NAACP), and a host of other political leaders. At that time, few outside of the meeting knew what happened at Roslyn. The Crusade historian's report later revealed intense conflict not merely between West and Willie Dell but among other members of the Crusade's leadership. Wilder, the report demonstrated, refused to acknowledge Dell when asked why he and other members of Richmond's black leadership had refused to endorse her candidacy against West in 1982. Dell's critics continued to believe that she was unreliable and held Highland Park voters in contempt. Marsh and West were also unable to resolve their differences over the manner in which West became mayor. And West failed to convince retreat attendees that he had blacks' interests in mind. Black leaders knew that West had never been a part of the civil rights movement, and there was an inherent skepticism about his commitment to equality. Gravely argued that West's recent voting in accord with the members of the council minority was evidence not just of the mayor's political proclivities but also of the Crusade's growing weakness. Two things seemed certain: Roy West's feud with Henry Marsh challenged the Crusade's ascendancy over political matters in the black community, and some black leaders were no longer committed to the unity the Crusade coveted. These private apprehensions eventually came to light.[23]

West also received the wrong type of national attention. In July 1982, the *New York Times* took note of his rise to power in an article entitled "Black Backed by Whites Is Richmond Mayor." On the issue of racial polarization in local politics, West told the *Times,* "I think blacks may be rather disappointed because they've had what they perceived as the leader. Now the whites feel a ray of hope in that they now will be brought into the governmental process." One year later Wilder filed suit against *Jet* magazine and forced it to retract its story that he had encouraged West to run. In 1983, the *Wall Street Journal* reported that West was the only one of America's 224 black mayors to work primarily from a white power base. By the end of 1982, West may have ended the stalemate between the BMC and the white minority by voting exclusively with the latter, but he seemed to do so at the expense of intra-racial conflict. In fact, he often solidified relationships with white council members by alienating African Americans—he fired black officials and voted black officials off vital city committees. Marsh lamented in 1982, "I extended my hand and all he gave me was a foot."[24]

African Americans remained divided on West's leadership for most of his first term as mayor. On one side, many of them believed his actions proved he was oblivious to the crises taking place in Richmond's black communities. Howard Wilkinson of the Richmond Commission on Human Relations spoke directly to West during a public information session, arguing, "Black people are disturbed about this. What I'm saying is there's a little thing called racism going on in this city and you're not aware of it." Two weeks prior to Wilkinson's contention, the Baptist Ministers Conference of Richmond and Vicinity, a predominantly African American organization, publicly denounced West. Richmond's black leadership excluded the mayor from a luncheon with Atlanta mayor Andrew Young in August 1983. Yet some African Americans not only took a "time will tell" approach to West's mayoralty but also recognized that the diversity of political opinion was an inherent development of broad-based political inclusion. An *Afro* editorialist argued, "The few elected officials, or leaders in the civil rights struggle were commonly accepted as the spokesmen for the community. Now we have reached the stage in our political evolution where there are enough black elected officials that they might not agree, and some black folks feel as though they have arrived to the point that they no longer need to support the continued struggle for civil rights." Richmond's black electorate and the Crusade were coming to terms with a fact of political participation and pluralism: West represented the very type of political and economic diversity that the Crusade had promoted for decades.[25]

By the winter of 1983, West's ability to help secure construction contracts and downtown real estate deals for minority-owned businesses turned the tide in public opinion about him. Between 1977 and 1982, less than one percent of Richmond's $124 million contract awards went to smaller, minority-owned firms. In February 1983, however, Deese and the City of Richmond awarded a black-owned Atlanta firm, AMC Contractors Inc., a $3 million contract for mechanical construction on the Richmond Marriot Hotel. To that point, AMC's contract was the largest ever awarded by the city to a minority-owned firm. The prospect of setting aside economic opportunities for African Americans emerged from a private–public project called "Richmond Renaissance," created in 1982 by Marsh, Kemp, and T. Justin Moore of Virginia Electric and Power Company (discussed later). Policy makers and local business owners eventually resolved to set aside retail space for African Americans after the completion of a new downtown market at Sixth and Grace Streets—in 1984, the U.S. Department of Housing and Urban Development awarded the city a $4.2 million Urban Development Action Grant to finish what eventually became the Sixth Street Market. More specifically, Manny Deese planned to set aside 15 percent of the 110 retail stores in the downtown mall for minorities. These plans also came to life during the construction of the Project One Marriot Hotel job. West, Deese, and Reginald Harris, chair of the mayor's Minority Business Advisory Board, eventually put forward the Minority Business Utilization Plan of 1983. The plan specified that 30 percent of Richmond's construction-contract money had to be set aside for minority firms and that these firms were to sign contracts directly with the city or through third-party minority contractors.[26]

Shortly after West's proposal, Councilmen Richardson and Marsh and City Attorney William Hefty drew up and proposed an ordinance that further executed West's proposal. If smaller minority firms did not have the manpower to handle particular jobs, the city reserved the right to waive the requirement. In terms of the city's purchasing of goods and services, officials resolved to disburse 20 percent of the total expenditures to minority-owned businesses. Surprisingly, the city council passed the ordinance by a six-to-two vote in the spring of 1983. Even Leidinger voted with African American council members, despite grumblings from white contractors about maintaining the fairness of local bidding. According to public-purchasing officials, construction contracts awarded to black firms rose from roughly 3 percent in 1983 to nearly 40 percent for fiscal year 1986–1987. Minority business owners were also to take charge of revitalization efforts in the Second Street area of the historic Jackson Ward District as well as of the construction of a massive downtown parking deck. During fiscal year 1984–1985 alone, African American firms secured 40 percent of Richmond's contracts, totaling just less than $10 million. Some of these contractors were also leading members of the Crusade who just happened to live in West's district. All told, however, West's ability to secure minority contracts neutralized many of his detractors, especially among the middle-class black leadership. When U.S. district judge Robert Merhige ruled that setting aside construction projects financed by the city was constitutional in December 1984, it appeared that the West had won a major victory for black business owners.[27]

West represented a growing rift between black politicians and black politics. Public support for him grew over the course of 1983; that support, however, had class-based implications. The mayor's appeals for racial reconciliation tested the Crusade's mettle, but he eventually secured service deliverables that nullified a number of his critics. In fact, many of West's supporters were the very African Americans who stood to gain from his entrepreneurial approach to government: the middle-class voters who had recently left areas such as Church Hill for Highland Park and who were suspicious of Dell's ability to secure the types of concessions that would continue to raise their economic status. Yet West's most ardent detractors held out hope that Willie Dell, who announced in August 1983 that she would run for city council again, might mean a return to the so-called faithful five. *Afro* editorialist Sa'ad El-Amin pondered whether black folks wanted to return to black governance or acquiesce to piecemeal economic concessions for a handful of strategically positioned, well-heeled African Americans. West's contention that Richmond's economic well-being hinged upon harmony at city hall had produced material results. Yet his belief that there was a "thin line between black pride and black racism" drove a wedge through the heart of the black body politic.[28]

A Search for the Soul of Richmond's Black Electorate

Although civil rights organizations often disagreed over organizational strategies, African Americans, for a brief moment in the mid–twentieth century, closed ranks over the issue of racial injustice. Politics moderated the movement, however. By the early 1980s, the transformation from protest to politics challenged civil rights advocates' approach to the freedom struggle. The practical limitations of governance and the politics of structural forces often made it extremely difficult for black mayors and elected officials to improve urban conditions. African Americans and their public officials continued to share common grievances about employment discrimination, residential segregation, inadequate public schools, rising crime, and unemployment during the 1980s. Scholars, however, recognize that menacing economic forces and the rising black middle class often meant that the shared experience of racism was not as common for African Americans in the 1980s as it was for African Americans prior to and during the civil rights movement. Although some African American leaders, who had hitched their wagons to the Great Society, held fast to the notion that government could make people's lives more meaningful, others believed that the optimism of the civil rights movement needed to give way to the politics of economic pragmatism. Richmond's city council election in 1984 was a showdown between these systems of belief. As one voter, Luann Bell, characterized the division, "If Roy A. West and his supporters constitute 'Negroes' and not the 'real black folks,' then let's hope we have more Negroes in Richmond than black folks. Mayor West has helped City Council put the past behind us and move Richmond forward as a progressive and vital Southern city, where not only Negroes and white, but also 'black folks' will have more opportunities for better jobs and higher income."[29]

In many ways, Henry Marsh pioneered the pro-growth approach to municipal governance that West later took credit for. At the same time that Marsh circled the wagons around the issue of black governance, he also forged interracial business coalitions with white council members and their allies. Marsh and later West met the challenges of federal retraction by organizing strategies with local business elites. Despite the conflict on the Richmond City Council in the early 1980s, Marsh recognized the imperative need to stem the tide of problematic demographic trends such as white flight, deepening poverty, and city–county independence. At the same time that whites tried to destroy Henry Marsh's reputation in the court of public opinion and business elites threatened to bring vital redevelopment plans to a standstill, downtown revitalization continued apace during the early 1980s. In this way, Marsh was similar to many of his counterparts in other cities, such as Atlanta, Detroit, Philadelphia, and beyond. Marsh and men such as Andrew Young, Wilson Goode, and Maynard Jackson may have come to power within the spirit of civil rights reform, but they also understood the sharp limitations on both local government's authority and the resources at black communities' disposal.

Ironically, Marsh paved the road that made Roy West Richmond's black middle-class champion. After speaking at Ted Kennedy's Labor and Human Relations public hearing, Marsh, Kemp, Clarence Townes (one of Richmond's most successful black businessmen), and T. Justin Moore used $2.4 million—half from a federal Community Development Block Grant and the rest from local business contributions—to create a nonprofit corporation named Richmond Renaissance in 1982. Local business leaders such as Clarence Townes, who had been integral to the Crusade's early development, had long argued that Richmond needed a comprehensive community-development organization. To this end, Marsh created Richmond Renaissance to promote public–private economic development. The objective was to use local business elites' private–public connections to lobby the General Assembly on the city's behalf. The city council eventually appointed an interracial board of thirty-one members and established an economic-development coordinating committee made up of various officials. The council then gave these officials and the city manager the authority to orchestrate future programs—namely, Project One, the construction on the downtown Sixth Street Market, and various other developments.[30]

The Sixth Street Market was not just the brainchild of Henry Marsh. The $23 million market was one of Richmond Renaissance's first large-scale endeavors, and it became a referendum on how local officials thought about growth in struggling cities. One year after the election of 1984, Marsh, Moore, Deese, and others believed that they could give downtown Richmond a much-needed facelift by getting nationally acclaimed developer James Rouse to build a "festival marketplace." Rouse, president of Enterprise Development Company, was in the process of redeveloping Baltimore's inner harbor and had created the Faneuil Hall Marketplace in Boston. He eventually made plans to build a "glass-enclosed promenade of stores, shops, and open areas" that would anchor downtown Richmond's retail core. These types of plans took place in cities throughout America, and many of these cities used the same developers and designers to lure suburban and wealthy urban whites back into the central city. The Renaissance predicted that "the project would attract as many as 2 million to 4 million additional people to the downtown area each year," generate upward of $1.5 million in new revenue for the city, provide nearly 1,000 new jobs, and set aside 15 percent of the total stores for black retailers. These endeavors in high-profile construction projects—the Richmond Coliseum, completed in 1971 and located on what was once Navy Hill, was another $24 million testament to this silver-bullet approach—and the politics of retail sales had a profound influence on local politics. However, unlike Baltimore's inner harbor and Atlanta's underground, which were thriving ten years later, the Sixth Street Market failed by the early 1990s. Its proximity to Jackson Ward and the construction of shopping centers in the surrounding counties led to the market's almost immediate demise. In 1991, the Urban Land Institute in Washington recommended demolishing part of the mall to make space for a park. To this day, the market stands vacant. Although few Richmonders predicted the pace of the downtown market's decline, these revitalization projects and the realization of minority set-asides were monumental developments in the mid-1980s.[31]

The city council contest of 1984 turned out to be a battle between two distinct approaches to black governance and service delivery. The election was really about the crises facing the growing number of poorer people in urban America and ways to combat urban decline. Of all U.S. families in 1983, 40.6 percent lived in suburbs, 26 percent lived in central cities, and 33.4 percent resided outside of metropolitan areas. By the mid-1980s, as the federal government began to focus on the nearly 40 percent of Americans who lived outside of central cities, politicians such as West and Marsh believed that the money earned from luring businesses back into downtown areas and securing contracts for black business would trickle down to the 26 percent of urban Americans. In some ways, Virginia's local politicians had little choice in the matter. City–county independence all but ensured that the commonwealth's cities were on their own, and the Reagan rollbacks drove this point home. Dell, in contrast, believed that the only way to address Richmond's problems was to regain a BMC. The election of 1984 turned out to be, in the word of *Afro* columnist Sa'ad El-Amin, "a search for the soul" of Richmond's black electorate.[32]

The second contest between Willie Dell and Roy West was as contentious as the first, and the Third District dominated most of the media's attention (after redistricting in the early 1980s, the city went back to labeling districts by numbers instead of by letters). In 1982, West had beat Dell seven to one, ten to one, and twenty to one, respectively, in the district's mostly white precincts, 307, 308, and 309. West had garnered 57 percent of his total vote count in these predominantly white precincts. Dell, in contrast, had carried four of the district's mostly black precincts, 303, 304, 305, and 306. Yet the proportions of the vote she received in these precincts were roughly two to one, four to one, three to one, and three to one, respectively. In the two years since Dell's defeat, West's ability to secure contracts and cut ribbons in front of new buildings had actually won over powerful allies. The question, however, came down to the districts Dell carried in 1982 and whether a Crusade endorsement could inspire higher black turnout. Between 1982 and 1983, many black leaders had transformed into staunch West supporters, including a number of influential members of the Crusade for Voters. When John L. Howlette, chairman of the Crusade's research committee, announced the organization's endorsement of Willie Dell in April 1984, the grapevine had it that the vote was far from unanimous. West's supporters maintained that the mayor deserved praise for restoring harmony to local politics and generating good-faith diplomacy between white and black council members. Although West's position as a diplomat and the level of harmony in the council were debatable, Dell found it hard to argue against his ability to secure economic concessions for a handful of powerful African Americans. West, whose slogan was "Make a Good City Better," went into the election believing that his campaign had significant support from people who had voted for Dell in 1982.[33]

Dell's campaign, titled "Let's Get It Back," was again an appeal to nostalgia and black political empowerment. She attempted to close ranks around the issue of anti-West sentiment. Richmond's black clergy, the *Afro,* and the Crusade tried to capitalize on the divisiveness West had created, especially prior to securing minority set-asides. Dell's devotees drove home their belief that West was a "Main Street" pawn and a sellout to his race. His checkered voting record, some blacks believed, was evidence of Uncle Tomming. These were the African Americans who considered West not only to be a traitor but also to be single-handedly responsible for changing the direction of local politics. To them, West's alignment with white council members symbolized a return of the types of gradualism that the Crusade had rendered immaterial in the 1950s. Council factionalism, they thought, called for stronger black unity, not racial reconciliation. The battle between Dell and West was about more than a city council seat. West's biggest critics argued that the mayor had actually taken credit for policies that Marsh, Richmond Renaissance, and Dell had initiated in the previous council term. In some ways, they were right. Dell and Marsh had initiated downtown revitalization and the push toward minority contracts. Unfortunately, the public's perception of

Marsh, especially his insistence on shouldering managerial responsibilities and dedication to black political unity, often made it difficult to see just how much he had actually accomplished. Marsh argued, "I think the critical issue is which path Richmonders will choose to follow in local political leadership. Will policy decisions continue to be made by whites as they were before 1977 or will blacks make the policy decisions for the city? I think that is the overriding issue of this . . . election. I decided to run again to assure that the people of Richmond will have a choice between two philosophies."[34]

The election of 1984 came down to the difference between black politicians and the politics of black empowerment. Deep-rooted class issues resonated throughout the election. Unity, Dell held, was the African American community's most precious resource. Most people knew that the winner of the Third District would help determine the next mayor. Black ministers, who were among West's most vocal critics, urged voters to vote for a return of the "faithful five." As Crusade precinct captains, block administrators, and the Crusade's rank and file, many of these church leaders penetrated into the city's black enclaves beyond class divisions. Speaking on behalf of the Baptist Ministers Conference, Reverend Miles Jones argued that the battle against West was "theological, racial, political, municipal, and otherwise." Over the course of his first term as mayor, many African Americans leaders firmly believed that West was antipoor. As the number of poor African Americans grew, being antipoor, for many of West's detractors, was tantamount to being antiblack. Dell's supporters were hardline civil rights–era voters. Many of them had not only been active in the Crusade for decades but also believed that West had given into the politics of white paternalism. West, Dell argued, was a "television star who spent money in middle- and upper-income neighborhoods and only picked up trash for television stations in the poor areas." If El-Amin and Holt demonstrated that the black middle class and Richmond's urban poor had diverged in the late 1960s, the contest between Dell and West in the early 1980s drove home the two groups' contentions. By 1980, middle-class black voters in Highland Park seemed exhausted by very thing that made Dell appealing during 1970s. Her pleas for racial unity and her defense of vulnerable communities were anachronisms by 1984—at least in the Third District.[35]

West stuck to his guns by reenergizing the Highland Park and Imperial Plaza constituencies that got him elected in the first place. The mayor's campaign emphasized compromise, deemphasized race, championed economic progress, and held fast to the process of political cooperation—the machinery, in West's estimation, of good government. West also evoked the politics of black improvement without alienating his white supporters. He did this by convincing voters that black economic growth and the city's growth were not mutually exclusive. For instance, he repeatedly insisted that he took pride in being black, but blackness had little to do with making "rational" political decisions. This idea of "rational" political decision making was loaded with gender implications. It was also a dog whistle to whites who had grown weary of Dell's appeals to black unity. Throughout her career, Dell refused to succumb to black middle-class assumptions about female respectability—they considered her too outspoken and histrionic for public office. If the district system eventually did Dell in, so too did the proverbial double standard. She was often criticized for behavior that people celebrated in male leaders. Moreover, her critics believed that her frankness about racial solidarity was bad for black business. The ways Dell communicated, what West called that "kind of thinking," "frightens away potential investors and mars economic development." "Keep in mind," the mayor stated, "that cities that have been progressive have been so because the races have gotten along. We must have a balanced approach. Investors have told me in the past that they weren't going to come here to invest money with that kind of anti-cooperative spirit." Many of the Third District's African Americans were of both status and standing—including Doug Wilder, who ran a very similar campaign in 1989. Wilder played down the issue of race, which allowed him to become the first black governor in the history of the United States. By de-emphasizing race, West also paved the way for African Americans who were eager to forge business relationships with the white establishment.[36]

West countered Dell's appeal to Black Power with his own brand of black pride. He was definitely proud to be African American and proud of black progress, but he was also eager to take advantage of those gains to achieve economic parity. That inevitably meant both playing down black exclusiveness and joining the pluralist landscape that had long excluded

African Americans. He acknowledged that African Americans were now in a position to negotiate and form coalitions with whites if doing so promoted the greater good of Richmond. For instance, West received decidedly more campaign contributions than his opponent and any other candidate in the city. His campaign contributors were also politically and ideologically diverse. The *Richmond Times-Dispatch, Richmond News-Leader,* and the Richmond Lodge of the Fraternal Order of Police endorsed him. West raised roughly $42,000 with the help of black conservative groups such as the John Mercer Langston Fund. White conservatives such as J. Smith Ferebee (an ardent supporter of the Byrd organization) also contributed to West's campaign. In fact, West raised $32,300 more than Dell. The ward system may have leveled the playing field for potential African American public officials, but it quickly proved a blessing to an incumbent who could deliver the goods for his constituents.[37]

On the East End, the contest between Alma Barlow and Henry Marsh had severe implications for the problem of black poverty. Alma Marie Barlow was the founder of the Richmond Tenants' Association (est. 1977), a member of Richmond's Anti-Hunger Coalition, and a Democratic Party official who, like Holt, rose to local prominence as an outspoken advocate for public-housing residents and poor folks. Barlow had worked for most of her adult life at the John Marshall Hotel and later in the Office of the Secretary of the Commonwealth. By the 1980s, she emerged not only as the new Curtis Holt Sr. but also, in some ways, as Richmond's incarnation of Fannie Lou Hamer, the reputed civil rights activist from Sunflower County, Mississippi, who had grown famous for her speech at the Democratic National Convention in 1964. After 1977, Barlow proved, without status or station, that she could hold her own with the best and brightest of Richmond's leadership. It was Barlow, in fact, who led the charge against CETA cuts and the pilgrimage to Washington in protest of federal cutbacks. She had also become chief advocate for one of Richmond's most vulnerable demographics—poor black women. A report by the Richmond Urban Institute, published in 1985 and based on data from the 1980 census, showed that 77 percent of Richmond's poor were women and children and that a majority of those impoverished women and children were African American. One year before the election of 1984, for instance, 1,269 of Richmond's girls between the ages of twelve and nineteen, in a total population of 3,300, were pregnant. Barlow was one of the few Richmonders to publicly come to these girls' defense: "Welfare—once you get into that program, it's like a handicap. It's tough get out of it. It's just seems a poor mother just doesn't get credit for being a human being."[38] Barlow's campaign, in many ways, was a reclamation of poor people's humanity.

In terms of women and the black freedom struggle in Richmond, Barlow's campaign against Marsh represented both continuity and profound change. Her presence in the election was on the one hand proof that women were still essential to the fight against racism in Richmond and on the other hand evidence that women, especially those who had dedicated their lives to social vulnerability, were emerging as the chief critics of black political leadership. Barlow did not run against Marsh in 1984 because she believed she could win: she ran against the former mayor to bring attention to the deepening problem of East End poverty. Over the course of 1980s, the East End had become notorious for its housing projects, high crime, and densely concentrated pockets of black poverty. These housing projects were the very ones that had sprung up in Richmond in the mid–twentieth century as white officials rushed to alleviate automobile congestion and blight. Myriad problems characterized these housing projects by the 1980s. By 1985, 7 percent of Richmond's residents lived in public housing, and most of the city's African Americans, because of residential segregation, lived in or in proximity to these units. Over time, some people in the East End began to associate Marsh with the public-housing problem. Barlow stated, "I am a civil rights activist and I have supported my opponent in the past. He is a civil rights attorney, so why should I run against him? Because he has not represented the district." Barlow, who had become a thorn in Henry Marsh's side over the issues of dilapidated homes and the public-housing crises, consistently held that Marsh, whose district was home to some of Richmond's poorest black communities, had been more concerned with downtown redevelopment and citywide matters than with the growing problem of public housing. It was Barlow who emphasized that downtown-redevelopment plans and organizations such as Richmond Renaissance had done very little in the way of mitigating the city's poverty problem. "I am a civil rights activist running against a civil rights attorney. I shouldn't have to do that because we are supposed to be of one accord, working to improve the living conditions of the less fortunate people in the city." Barlow organized her campaign to remind elected officials that they had done very little to stem the tide of growing poverty in Richmond. She was Richmond's reminder that high-profile politics and affirmative-action construction contracts seemed to benefit only a small handful of well-connected African Americans.[39]

On May 4, 1984, Richmonders reelected nine incumbent council members, and West defeated Dell more soundly than he had in the election of 1982. (For election results in 1984, see table 14 in the appendix.) In this election, 1,567 more people voted than in 1982, but that did little to help Dell's cause. Of the 8,786 total votes in the Third District's ten precincts (including absentee ballots), West garnered 4,907 votes to Dell's 3,879. West garnered nine of ten white votes, while six of ten black voters favored Dell. West also soundly defeated Dell in the largely white, middle-class Precincts 307, 308, and 309. He picked up more votes in 1984, whereas Dell lost 55 votes. In the district's most economically and racially diverse precincts, West got enough votes either to edge Dell out or to stay in overall contention. Most importantly, he neutralized his opponent even in the predominantly black precincts, such as 303, 304, and 305, pulling in 266 more votes from these precincts in this election. Newspapers argued that the results reaffirmed Richmond's commitment to effectively cooperative government. Dell insisted, "We ran against all that money and still didn't come out too bad."[40]

Dell's loss took the wind out of the Crusade's sails. In 1982, West won because voters associated Dell with Marsh's "Team," political factionalism, and obstructionism. For many Third District voters, Dell's plea to "get it back" was little more than a call for black solidarity for black solidarity's sake. The contest between Dell and West was really a battle between Henry Marsh and Roy West. Even Claudette McDaniel recognized that the election in this district had more to do with Henry Marsh than with the two candidates. McDaniel, whom the council eventually appointed to the vice mayoralty, argued, "I think the whole campaign was a tragedy. It was not a campaign between Willie Dell and Roy West. It was a campaign for and against someone who was not representative in the district." Dell's suggestion that West was a sellout actually galvanized black middle-class voters and affirmed their belief that the former council member did not have a platform. Beyond referring to West as Leidinger's pawn and an Uncle Tom, she did little to win over voters outside of pre-cincts that were going to vote for her regardless. She did even less to con-vince Imperial Plaza and Highland Park voters that she could solidify the types of concessions Roy West obtained. Money also played a deciding factor in Dell's defeat. West received nearly $42,000 (almost $95,000 in today's money) in campaign contributions and spent upward of $35,000 to defeat Dell. In contrast, Dell received only $9,915 in support. West outspent every candidate in the city council election in 1984, and the *Richmond Times-Dispatch* speculated that West's campaign contributions were the most ever collected for a city council election in Richmond. The contest in the Third District was, according to the *Dispatch,* "one of the hottest battles for a council seat in recent history."[41]

If the divisions in black leadership were not evident to Richmonders during the Roslyn conference, they were in the wake of this election. Sev-eral months after the election, local NAACP administrator Jack Gravely dropped a bombshell in the local newspapers: he had refused to con-duct an NAACP-sponsored voter registration drive in the Third District. Gravely charged that the registration drive was in fact an attempt to shore up votes for Willie Dell. He not only resigned from his position in protest but also claimed that the NAACP had overwhelmingly supported Henry Marsh at the expense of growing divisions among its members: "Put all of that in a pot and cook it and see what the hell you get. I refused to do it. . . . That's why I respect Willie Dell because she told us it [the registration drive] might help her, but would destroy the NAACP. It's a new day and I'm not saying put the old-timers out to pasture. But they should look toward the sunset while training a new cadre of young leaders." Despite what was once a powerful endorsement, even the Crusade had only tep-idly supported Dell's campaign. A number of the Crusade's influential officers privately supported West, and members of its research committee were openly reluctant to throw the organization's weight behind Dell's bid. These were the African Americans who believed that city council looked better under West than under Marsh. A return to the "Team" meant a return to council factionalism. Implicit in this argument, however, was the belief that Marsh, Dell, and the other members of BMC had been exclusively responsible for the obstructionism that characterized city hall between 1978 and 1982. Even the Crusade's Norvell Robinson, who often vacillated on the West question, commented after the election, "West has done an excellent job bringing white and black communities together." When city council elected West mayor for another term and appointed Claudette McDaniel vice mayor, it appeared that West's strategy had paid huge dividends.[42]

"The Crusade Is a Nonentity"

In the summer of 1986, *Richmond Times-Dispatch* reporter Eric Sundquist ran a two-page, multicolumn piece entitled "Violence Rules in Group Rest of U.S. Left Behind." By 1985, Richmond's murder rate was second only to that of Detroit. Sundquist seemed to recognize something Willie Dell intimated in her attempt to regain a council seat: there was an inextricable link between poverty and growing crime in Richmond. "Richmond's own murderous little Third World," Sundquist charged, "is burgeoning." Social activists such as Alma Barlow claimed that city officials' obsession with racial reconciliation and economic pragmatism had taken precedence over the city's poor communities. The rise of the black middle class and the disestablishment of de jure segregation in the wake of the civil rights movement often overshadowed the types of problems Sundquist tried to highlight in 1986. Richmond was not alone. The crime in Richmond during the mid-1980s came to characterize most of the "secondhand" central cities that blacks inherited from whites when whites fled to the suburbs. Urban America in general, Sundquist should have argued, had "its own murderous little Third World," and it was made up of poor nonwhite people whose lives were still demonstrably inferior to the majority of Americans. Alma Barlow and Willie Dell had spent years trying to articulate the problem Sundquist highlighted in the summer of 1986. Their middle-class brethren often dismissed Barlow and Dell not simply because they were women but because they had different priorities. Years of systematic disinvestment, the rise of low-paying service-sector jobs, de facto residential segregation, poor educational facilities, and federal rollbacks had helped ensure that many of America's poor communities stayed poor. Many African Americans, in Richmond and beyond, one historian demonstrated, "had lost faith in the responsiveness of American institutions, the possibility of redressing grievances through the normal channels of American society."[43]

The council contest between Dell and West spoke volumes about the strength of middle-class voters in the Third District and the problems facing Richmond. Richmonders—both black and white—were convinced that West's victory over Dell and conflict within the NAACP was evidence of the Crusade's growing insignificance. Marsh's, Kenney's, and Richardson's landslide reelections in 1984 confirmed that the Crusade still had some strong support. In time, however, the district system was integral to the Crusade's growing insignificance. Before 1977, the Crusade's political authority had been contingent upon meeting the demands of Richmond's at-large voting system. Within this system during the 1960s, thousands of African American voters had united to defend themselves from the common enemy of widespread bigotry. During the Jim Crow era and the election moratorium, Crusade leadership had hammered out their differences privately. After 1982, however, the situation changed dramatically. The days when the Crusade's rank and file rented trucks with bullhorns and shamed people to get out the vote were over. Some of Richmond's neighborhoods were so dangerous by the mid-1980s that violence alone had neutralized those get-out-the-vote strategies. By 1986, the Crusade found out that quantitative voting rights strategies in an at-large system were easier to negotiate than the qualitative implications of a diversifying black electorate. Within Richmond's district-based system, the Crusade proved ill equipped to manage who voted and how. As African Americans challenged one another in various districts, a Crusade endorsement did not carry the weight that it had in the 1960s and 1970s. The Crusade's inability or reluctance or a combination of both to defeat West convinced many African Americans that the organization no longer had the unity that once made it strong. As even one Crusade officer, Mary Cox, put it in November 1983, "I think everybody has reached the Peter Principle or has been bought off. . . . [T]he Crusade is a nonentity. . . . It's clearly a class thing in Virginia. They are interested in being doctors and lawyers, and not interested in others."[44]

Prior to and after the election of 1984, even the Crusade began, for

the first time in its nearly thirty-year history, to contemplate its own inef-
fectiveness. By 1983, this self-criticism began to take place in public view.
In September 1983, Crusade president Ellen Pearson contended, "We're
not serving the people. . . . [W]e need to operate in the 21st century,
not in 1956." Crusade officials suggested that they needed paid officials,
more money from membership dues, younger members, and better communication with the community to remain viable. At town hall meetings
throughout 1984 and 1985, members accused the organization of being
dominated by a handful of old-guard male leaders, especially William
Thornton. The organization's leadership, critics argued, clung steadfastly
to old strategies and ideas that were no longer relevant to the politics of
Richmond's district-based system. They were even less relevant to Richmond's poverty problem. Critics also alleged that Crusade membership
had dwindled significantly because long-standing members relied on civil
rights strategies and ideas that did not apply to politics in the 1980s.
Sa'ad El-Amin, whose column in the *Richmond Afro-American* rarely
held back on criticism of black leadership, argued that the local leadership
was "locked in a time warp." Younger members argued that the group's
research committee often endorsed candidates who campaigned as Black
Power politicians but served as defenders of business interests and property rights. Complicating matters, the Federal Elections Committee temporarily suspended the group for failing to register as a political action
committee. Federal officials ordered the Crusade to reorganize, change
the form of its constitution, and pay a series of fines for voting rights violations during Democrat Richard J. Davis's race for the U.S. Senate. The
very pluralism the Crusade promoted now undermined its ability to control black voters.[45]

It is difficult to tell the story of local black governance during the
1980s without acknowledging how class concerns often took precedent over racial unity. Although these problems were not specific to
Richmond, by 1984 Crusade members were torn between supporting
Marsh, the prototypical civil rights legal activist, or West, who embodied the politics of racial reconciliation. West's victory in 1984 and the
Crusade's deprecating self-reflections brought out the critics. Toward the
end of 1984, nearly every weekly edition of the *Afro* ran a column either
directly or tangentially referring to the dearth of black leadership. Afri-

can Americans correctly insisted that the Crusade's middle-class proclivities were incompatible with the crises of the mid-1980s. As local black leaders such as Marsh continued to argue that they were fighting for a higher cause (i.e., black equality, the welfare of oppressed people, etc.), they drew greater criticism from the very people they professed to defend. Many of these less-affluent community activists began to challenge the notion that Richmond's African American middle class could lead the way out of second-class citizenship. How, detractors such as Alma Barlow wondered, could Richmond's Crusade for Voters remain relevant to less-prosperous African Americans if it continued to mete out administrative roles to individuals of West's social rank? By 1984–1985, African Americans of less means no longer bought into the Crusade's notion that politics alone could uplift Richmond's African American communities. Was Richmond's voting rights movement meant to benefit the black middle class exclusively? they asked. Poverty and crime spoke volumes about whether the Crusade's strictly political strategies and the movement from protest to politics had been the best way to go about improving blacks' lives. To be sure, forces outside the Crusade's power had made poverty a fact of life for many of the city's blacks. But as the preeminent black organization in Richmond, the Crusade drew the heavy fire.

The crisis of black political leadership in the mid-1980s was exacerbated by a lack of immediate solutions to Richmond's growing crime problem. The issues Alma Barlow raised during her campaign against Henry Marsh began to consume the city by 1984. In November 1985, a headline in the *Richmond Afro-American* read, "How Can We Fight Crime?" Over the course of the early 1980s, the city's housing projects began to look like the tenements of the 1950s. Most of these public housing developments were not merely dilapidated and impoverished but awash in violent crime. Between 1983 and 1984, Richmond's murder rate increased by 22 percent, and crime in the city's poorest enclaves was fourteen times higher than the national average. Seventy-six homicides occurred there in 1984, making Richmond the murder capital of the state, with the third-highest per capita murder rate in the nation. According to Richmond's September crime analysis report of 1984, murder, rape, and auto theft had sharply increased since 1983. Near the end of 1985, so-called black-on-black murders (which are often crimes of proximity rather than racial crimes), many inspired by the recent hike in drug (especially cocaine) and handgun trafficking, reached an all-time high. In 1984, Richmond trailed only Gary, Indiana, and Detroit in murder rate per capita. By 1985, Richmond had surpassed Gary and now had the nation's second-highest murder rate per capita, 41.9 per 100,000 residents. The commonwealth's capital trailed only Detroit, which recorded 51.9 murders per 100,000 residents. Although only 25 percent of the city's murders in 1984 had taken place in its housing projects, many of the remaining murders were in close proximity to public housing. According to RPD police captain Randolph R. Carlisle, "There are a lot of people coming into the community who don't live there, who are not residents of record—boyfriends, others who come in and know that the density of the projects provides fertile field for their criminal activities. They also know they have a large number of people who are susceptible to their influence and young people who buy drugs." El-Amin referred to Richmond's rising crime as "coldblooded, indifferent," and lacking in "remorse or conscience." The RPD was at a loss. Major V. Stuart Cook stated, "I don't know why we're number two [in the nation]. I do know that police alone can't solve the problem. When the crime commission finally releases their report, it will be obvious . . . that law enforcement can't be held responsible for the ills of society."[46]

By the mid-1980s, public officials and everyday people began to organize strategies to combat Richmond's problem of violent crime. If Richmond's African Americans mobilized in the 1960s to vote, black communities in the 1980s mobilized citizens to fight crime. In 1984, citizens of the East End and Church Hill areas charged that Richmond and its public servants were not doing enough to protect African American citizens against crime. By 1985, residents in these neighborhoods began to form their own citizens' leagues to publicize and dramatize local crime. On August 24, 1985, 5,000 protestors and politicians participated in a six-mile walk against crime. Although local activist Alma Barlow criticized Marsh and the city council for failing to establish a police precinct in the Church Hill area and to address the ubiquity of dilapidation in the Seventh District, Marsh and Kenney did actually organize policy strategies to meet the crisis, introducing a resolution in late August 1985 to establish a fifteen-member citizens' crime commission to address the issue.[47]

On September 9, 1985, the city council approved and established Marsh and Kenney's Citizens' Crime Commission (CCC)—the third time both men had tried to get such a commission through council. Council members, however, approved the commission only after Marsh and Kenney added an amendment that gave West the authority to appoint a chairperson. The council stipulated that nine of the commission's members would be appointed by their respective district's council member and represent their districts, and the remaining five were to be appointed by the entire council. West eventually expanded the commission by two members to include a representative of public-housing tenants (Barlow) and a representative of RPS (one more slot was added later). West's expansion of the CCC, however, came with strings. West and Gillespie insisted that the city appoint a local businessman, Jack H. Ferguson, president of Virginia Electric and Power Company, to lead the CCC. They got their way—the council eventually gave Ferguson the nod. The commission held several public discussions at local elementary schools and eventually resolved to split into four groups. The first group was to analyze national and local data; the second group was to survey 1,111 residents and eighty-three businesses to measure public sentiment; the third group set out to evaluate other cities' responses to crime; and the last group was to study crime-prevention methods used by law enforcement around the country. Deese had also helped the city create a new narcotics division in 1984. The city spent roughly $500,000 on the new department and hired fifteen additional police and staff.[48]

In February 1986, after five months of research, the CCC released a draft of its 105-page report to the city council. The report emphasized prevention of major crime as well as stiffer penalties. Of its eighty-two recommendations, an entire eighteen-page chapter and twenty-one recommendations were dedicated to reducing the number of murders. Fifty-four percent of Richmond's murders, the CCC found, were preceded by assaults. In these cases, victims had called the RPD at least five times. Seventeen of Richmond's ninety-six murders in 1985 occurred during domestic disputes. As such, the CCC's report focused most of its recommendations not on poverty but rather on more effective proactive policing. Of the recommendations aimed at reducing the city's murder rate, the committee put forward seven suggestions:

- Make arrest the normal and expected police response to domestic violence.
- Seek persecution of misdemeanor assaults in domestic conflict and mandatory counseling and therapy.
- Post in police facilities the photographs of and other info about the city's ten-worst offenders in every precinct.
- Seek legislation to allow juries to consider an offender's record, adult and juvenile.
- Immediately jail chronic offenders.
- Recommend legislation that would allow ordinances imposing mandatory one-year-minimum sentences for gun violations.
- Establish strict rules for permits to carry weapons.[49]

West had his own ideas. His solutions to Richmond's growing crime problem favored punishment over prevention. The idea that white folks were solely responsible for America's war on drugs and the "tough on crime" approach to public safety in this era is one of the biggest misconceptions about American law enforcement during the 1980s. Black Americans whose neighborhoods were under siege often promoted the idea that law officials needed to be tougher on crime. Some black Americans helped generate momentum not just for the war on drugs but also for policy makers' "tough on crime" approach to policing. In fact, because of tireless housing discrimination and residential segregation, "middle-class black were not, by and large, able to distance themselves from the poor as their white counterparts did." In time, both poor and middle-class blacks were integral to the ways law enforcement policed black communities in the 1980s and beyond. By the mid-1980s, West advocated for longer sentences without parole, fewer plea bargains, and, to the community's dismay, more liberal use of the death penalty. He also volunteered to personally appear at state executions. West's contentions about capital punishment flew in the face of African Americans' age-old abhorrence of capital punishment: "Forty years ago, this [view] was because of overt racism," West stated. "The racism has subsided. The system is more covert, more subtle in 1985. Black crime is ignored. Black criminals take advantage of society because they know society will do nothing to them. This is ironic, the zenith of man's inhumanity to man. . . . I realize there also are economic arguments to explain black-on-black crime. But to blame society for killing my brother is not an excuse . . . murder is murder. There has to be a death penalty." The mayor's ambivalent views on institutionalized racism and his Old Testament approach to combatting violent crime drew heavy criticism from some of the city's black leaders. His approach to crime and punishment also affirmed the notion among many blacks that he did not understand institutionalized racism. Many African Americans knew full well that segregationist leadership had replaced lynching with capital punishment during the Jim Crow era. When West authorized the RPD to train police officers in public relations and to assign additional patrolmen, referred to as "new ambassadors," to meet and greet shoppers at the Sixth Street Marketplace, critics erupted. West's "property rights over poor people" approach to policing confirmed Barlow's contention that the city had left poor folks behind. An emerging employment dilemma at city hall further affirmed many people's skepticism of local government.[50]

In the fall of 1984, an employment-discrimination scandal rocked city hall. Dubbed "Sewergate" by the *Richmond News-Leader*, the probe uncovered long-standing racial and sexual discrimination in Richmond's municipal employment. That summer, Richmond's Human Relations Commission and the Virginia NAACP prompted City Manager Manny Deese to appoint a blue-ribbon committee to investigate charges of rampant discrimination in the city's Public Works Department. The problems, according to early allegations, were both long-standing and managerial in nature. African American women complained of being sexually harassed by white supervisors; blacks were rarely promoted; and white supervisors often used racially charged language when speaking with black coworkers. The discrimination, investigators found, was particularly egregious in three Public Works divisions—sewer maintenance, street maintenance, and refuse collection. In mid-September, the committee, headed by Dr. Chong Pak of Virginia Commonwealth University, found institutional racial discrimination in work assignments, promotions, sick and annual leave, training, overtime, and discipline. Deese eventually transferred twelve problematic employees who, according to the *Richmond Times-Dispatch*, had grown accustomed to an "old-boys system." Deese's decision to transfer rather than fire the twelve employees drew heavy fire from the plaintiffs and African Americans in general. His investigation (of his own department, no less) had found discrimination, and a local court agreed.[51]

El-Amin, a Yale-educated attorney as well as a contributor to the *Afro*, eventually brought a suit against the city on behalf of fifteen employees of Richmond Public Works Department who claimed that African Americans employed in the department suffered in promotions, overtime, leave, work assignments, training, and, principally, wages. In November 1985, U.S. district judge Richard L. Williams sided with the fifteen employees. Judge Williams found that although the City of Richmond had made significant efforts to end Jim Crow in municipal employment, these efforts somehow bypassed the sewer-maintenance division, which remained deeply segregated. He ruled that the plaintiffs, represented by El-Amin, were victims of long-standing racist policies. El-Amin, despite the court's ruling, eventually accepted an out-of-court settlement for $80,000. Dr. Edward H. Peeples Jr., the outgoing chairman of the Richmond Commission on Human Relations, argued, "Even with a black mayor, a black city manager, a black majority on City Council, and an affirmative action program, the city administration has yet to clean up its own back yard and move away from the segregated ways of the 1950s." Deese, who had long contemplated leaving public service, resigned following the scandal. His resignation, effective December 31, 1985, ended a seven-year stint as city manager, an eleven-year tenure with Richmond's city government, and twenty-two years of working in local government. Although Deese ostensibly left the city government to become senior vice president of a Richmond-based computer company and Richmonders had anticipated his departure for the private sector, the Public Works Department scandal clearly expedited his resignation.[52]

The scandal also humiliated black elected officials. One of the first things on the African American mayor's agenda, after reining in the RPD, was to increase the number of African Americans working for municipal government. The fact that a racial employment discrimination scandal happened in a majority-black city with a majority-black city council was not lost on Richmonders or city hall. On the heels of losing a serious racial discrimination suit, West, McDaniel, and white council members proposed and passed an ordinance that established a new city entity—the Employee Services and Assistance Department. The city council charged the department with handling discrimination claims by city employees under the city manager's direct supervision. In the end, black Richmonders questioned how a black city manager, a black mayor and vice mayor, and a BMC could allow institutional discrimination to take place right under their noses. More ominously, after nearly thirty years on the political scene, the once powerful Crusade for Voters did not respond to these charges. The irony of the Sewergate incident was that roughly twenty years earlier the Crusade had leveraged blacks' votes to get the city council to pass a fair-employment resolution designed to stamp out institutionalized discrimination at city hall.[53]

In May 1986, Shelley Rolfe, one of the few white staff writers on the *Richmond Times-Dispatch* to handle racial issues evenhandedly, published the article "The Crusade's Blunted Lance." The Crusade, Rolfe argued, not only had "managed to go from riches to rags" but also was on "a losing streak that not too long ago would have been unthinkable." Just six years earlier, Rolfe had written a column entitled "Power of Crusade Has Earned It Respect." The latter article had highlighted the Crusade's recent achievements in bringing about majority–minority districts and a BMC. It quoted both black and white leadership on the Crusade's ascendancy over Richmond politics. "Not even Mayor Daley," another white Richmonder argued, "could get this kind of support." Even Henry Valentine argued that, in terms of Crusade's political power, "you couldn't be that effective in the white community if you used a shotgun." Rolfe's second article on the Crusade outlined what many blacks already knew: the Crusade suffered from a series of self-inflicted wounds. Roy West, Rolfe argued further, "was a symbol of the Crusade's frustration." In 1986, West was reelected with 60 percent of his district's black vote—a significant rise from 30 percent in 1982 and 40 percent in 1984. By 1985, the Crusade had even lost the support of its most fervent ally, the *Richmond Afro-American*. The employment-discrimination scandal, Deese's resignation, and West's reelection were a reflection on the Crusade's increasing frailty. The organization struggled to accommodate the growing diversity of civic-minded African Americans. The reality of an employment-discrimination scandal in a city with a black city manager and a BMC would have seemed unthinkable to the Crusade in the early 1960s—the very organization that had lobbied Richmond's all-white city council to pass an antidiscrimination resolution in municipal employment in 1961.[54]

In mid-1981, *Richmond Times-Dispatch* writer Bill Miller had quoted a recent report by John Hope Franklin and social psychologist Kenneth Clark, "A Policy Framework for Racial Justice," that argued, "Black elected officials, in particular, must be sensitive to the new dimensions of the racial problems of the eighties and to the growing problem of alienation between the black underclass and those blacks who have made it." By the mid-1980s, Richmond's most economically vulnerable African Americans would have had trouble even getting a job at city hall. It turned out that the Crusade, an organization established by professional black elites yet registered a diversity of black voters, had also failed to meet the challenges of structural forces that few people could have foreseen during the Jim Crow era. In time, the very broad-based political inclusion the organization had lobbied for had given rise to a brand of political pluralism that it struggled to negotiate. Rolfe quoted one anonymous source with "Main Street connections" in his article on the Crusade for Voters in 1986. "The man," Rolfe wrote, "said he had a vision for a new bloc built on Main Street and the John Mercer Langston Fund, a group of young blacks attuned to West. It would endorse candidates, black and white, unself-consciously."[55]

Conclusion

The struggle for civil rights persisted well beyond 1977. Even Roy West's fortunes turned during the late 1980s. In 1989, the Supreme Court finally ruled against Richmond's Minority Business Utilization Plan of 1983. A construction firm from Ohio, J. A. Croson, eventually forced the courts to reassess the provision that reserved a percentage of city construction contracts for minority businesses. Croson contested the plan after city officials refused to award the firm a contract to revamp the plumbing system in the Richmond City Jail even though Croson was the only bidder for the job. The Ohio firm requested that the city waive the set-aside requirement because the available minority subcontractors were either unqualified to handle the job or unable to quote prices. Although a Virginia court sided with the city, Croson appealed. The appeal, sponsored by the Associated General Contractors of America, eventually made it to the Supreme Court. In January 1989, the Court held in *Richmond v. J. A. Croson Co.* (1989), a six-to-three decision, that minority set-asides were unconstitutional. More specifically, it argued that past racial discrimination did not justify racial quotas in awarding public contracts to minorities. Justice Sandra O'Connor held that Richmond's Utilization Plan did not serve a compelling governmental interest that justified, under the Equal Protection Clause, the use of racial classification. However, O'Connor failed to recognize Richmond's history of pervasive and systemic discrimination. In time the Court's ruling opened the floodgates across "America toward white challenges of all affirmative action contracting programs." Richmond's 30 percent set-asides, in the Court's opinion, not only were unfair but also discriminated against whites. *Croson*, like Richmonders' criticisms of majority–minority districts in the early 1980s, was the bellwether of mounting claims of reverse discrimination.[1]

Croson proved to be yet another example that special treatment of African Americans in Washington was in deep jeopardy. From Chief Justice William Rehnquist forward, the majority of Supreme Court members seemed "unable to distinguish between legally-required segregation

239

in the service of white supremacy and race-conscious policies designed to offset the pernicious legacies of state-sponsored inequality." The former, the Rehnquist Court seemed to believe, had no bearing on constitutional legitimacy. The types of compensatory legal philosophies that made race central to American politics, economics, and culture (e.g., *Griggs v. Duke Power Company* [1971], *Allen v. Virginia State Board of Elections* [1969], and, yes, *Brown v. Board of Education* [1954]) had given way to either race-neutral legal decisions or legal decisions that completely ignored the historical oppression against African Americans as a group or both. Decisions such as *Croson* did even less to acknowledge the resistance to African American equality that lasted well into the late twentieth century. O'Connor's decision, in fact, flew in the face of the Court's decision in *City of Richmond v. United States* (1975). Warren Burger's Court, using the totality-of-circumstances test, had recognized that in mandating majority–minority districts, the Court had to take into account Richmond's history of institutional bigotry because bigotry continued to shape life in Richmond well beyond 1965. That view was no longer held in 1989.[2]

By 1989, the tide had turned on civil and voting rights laws. In arguing that Richmond had not shown convincing evidence to justify a racial classification for minority contracts, O'Connor contended in *Croson* that the "history of racial classifications in this county suggests that blind judicial deference to legislative or executive pronouncements of necessity has no place in equal protection analysis." Race consciousness in employment and later in voting rights was clearly in danger. In fact, in *Shaw v. Reno* (1993), which tightened the legal parameters for showing discriminatory intent in cases of vote dilution, required policy makers to put forward more convincing arguments for drawing minority–majority districts and insinuated that North Carolina's whites might be harmed by increasing the number of black representatives. Rehnquist's Court continued the process of scrapping the framework against minority vote dilution that the Burger Court had established in the 1970s. The Richmonders who argued that majority–minority districts discriminated against whites as a minority group finally had allies in Washington. The legal permissiveness that was central to the Great Society, the preservation of the civil rights bills, and the movements toward great black equality were coming to a close.[3]

The fight for African American equality in Richmond, Virginia, rose and fell with Supreme Court decisions. To be sure, African Americans in Richmond and throughout the United States had exercised political will long before the Court began to protect black voters against disenfranchisement. Richmond's black middle-class professionals were not passive actors in this process. In fact, Richmonders were integral to the very court cases that constituted the omnibus *Brown v. Board of Education* decision in 1954 and the reapportionment revolution of the 1970s. In this way, Richmond has been more integral to the struggle for civil rights than the historical record often demonstrates. The Crusade spent nearly a decade, with the help of the NAACP, fighting to register voters before Washington even realized the VRA. Not only had these efforts to register millions of voters allowed the USCCR to collect voting data, but these data also became essential to the ways policy makers drafted the VRA. Blacks' political will eventually ushered in an unprecedented era of racial politics in the United States. The long-awaited arrival of racial politics, however, also motivated resistance. Whites did everything in their power to protect the privileges that decades of political overrepresentation engendered. These privileges had costs, and, unfortunately, African Americans paid a heavy price. The Crusade for Voters may have used majority–minority districts to give the Richmond City Council a much-needed makeover, but the economic vulnerability that segregation brought about proved much harder to eradicate.

It is hard to divorce contemporary Richmond from the politics of the mid- to late twentieth century. In some ways, Richmond's hyper-racial history continues to inform the ways contemporaries meet modern challenges. Many of the city's problems with public housing and public schools are a direct result of the urban-redevelopment programs, suburbanization, and retrenchment of the mid–twentieth century. City–county independence also continues to inhibit Richmond's growth, particularly in terms of public transportation, access to employment, and the flow of taxable revenues. Yet Richmond has undergone a recent rebirth. "Over the last several decades," it "has experienced a cultural and reform-based renaissance that has the potential, already somewhat realized, to transform the city's deficits into municipal assets."[4]

The Crusade left a lasting impression on politics in the commonwealth's capital. Both the district system and the Crusade for Voters exist to this day. The Crusade still convenes meetings on the third Tuesday of each month at Second Baptist Church on 1400 Idlewood Avenue. African Americans have consistently served on the city council since 1977, the year they achieved a BMC for the first time. The overwhelming majority of Richmond's mayors have been African American since federal officials mandated the district system—including Walter Kenney, Leonidas Young II, Larry Chavis, Rudy McCollum, L. Douglas Wilder, and Dwight C. Jones. Members of the BMC, like the Crusade, also weathered the storm of the 1980s. Henry Marsh left the city council in 1991 and served in the state Senate until 2014, when he retired at the age of eighty. Walter Kenney served on the council throughout the 1980s and 1990s and was appointed to the mayoralty in 1990 and 1992. Claudette McDaniel, who was Richmond's first female vice mayor, served seven terms on the Richmond City Council from 1977 to 1990. City officials forced Chuck Richardson to resign his council seat in 1995 after he was arrested for heroin distribution (an addiction he had picked up during his tour in the Vietnam War). Richardson had served consecutive terms on the council from 1977 to 1995, and to this day he is beloved by many of the people in the Fifth District. Although Willie Dell was never again elected to political office, she continued fighting for vulnerable communities. She served on the Richmond Community Senior Center Board and spent the decades after 1984 doing mission work in Haiti. Roy West served as mayor until 1988 and sat on the city council until 1994. In recent years, he has been more critical of Richmond's legacy of racism. He has also openly professed respect for Henry Marsh. Sa'ad El-Amin, who was elected to the city council in 1998, met a similar fate as Richardson, albeit under different circumstances: officials forced him to resign after he was convicted of tax fraud. Doug Wilder, the former Virginia governor, became Richmond's seventy-eighth mayor in 2004 (his term started in January 2005). Just prior to his election, Wilder and Thomas Bliley, Richmond's last white mayor before the district system in 1977, put forward a bill to directly elect mayors at-large (up to that point, the city council had appointed a member of the council to the mayoralty). The bill made it through the legislature and found tremendous citywide support in 2003. Wilder then used that system to beat the incumbent mayor, Rudy McCollum, with nearly 82 percent of the popular vote.[5]

The renaissance now taking place in downtown Richmond is a testament to local people's resilience. During the 1980s, Richmond Renaissance, an interracial public–private lobbying organization, began a campaign to revitalize the city's core. Two of Renaissance's key figures were none other than Henry Marsh and George Stevenson Kemp. The two men were essential to the formation of Richmond Renaissance, and many of their early initiatives—for instance, Project One—paved the way for the very downtown reinvestment that persists to this day, despite some failures. To be sure, decades of disinvestment in the central city had depressed property values and heightened vacancy rates, but these low values and high vacancy rates gave rise to unprecedented reinvestment. Richmond's population in 2010 stood at 210,309—the highest it has been since 1986. As of 2015, this population growth outpaced growth in the counties. Downtown Richmond, which was a veritable ghost town during the 1980s and 1990s, has witnessed an outburst of retail, business, and educational growth. For instance, it now has the highest concentration of new restaurants in the city—in 2010, there were nearly one hundred restaurants in the downtown area that employed nearly 1,600 people. Virginia Commonwealth University, whose Monroe Park campus and medical facility are located downtown, has also played a vital and controversial part in downtown redevelopment. Yet, although examples of Richmond's revitalization abound, much of this growth has done very little to address the types of economic and educational vulnerability that has characterized Richmond for decades.[6]

Richmond's recent revitalization has been bittersweet. Poverty, residential segregation, and underperforming public schools have been an unfortunate yet constant feature of African American life in Richmond. For all of Richmond's recent growth and the "kudos" given to "a nationally recognized dining scene," the city has yet to overcome what should be intolerable anachronisms: glaring inequalities in education and wealth. The compression of African Americans into smaller neighborhoods and public-housing developments in the 1960s and the 1970s led to many of the social and economic problems that continue to characterize the city. In 2012, the official U.S. poverty rate stood at 15 percent. Between 2006 and 2010, 30 percent of Richmond's African Americans, roughly 25 percent of the city's residents, fell on or below the poverty line. In 2011, Richmond's mayor, Dwight C. Jones, developed a far-reaching plan to finally and officially address this economic dilemma. Richmond's Anti-Poverty Commission, which has since been transformed into the Office of Community Wealth Building, found that 51 percent of the city's impoverished population (nearly 25,000 people) reside in six census tracts. Some of these tracts are home to the very public-housing units that urban developers constructed during the renewal campaigns of the mid–twentieth century.[7]

Modernity did not come to Richmond without cost. Richmond's contemporary social problems have implications not just in New Deal housing policies but also in the slum-clearance and urban-renewal campaigns of the mid–twentieth century. Richmond's housing developments continue to be points of profound disillusionment. The East End, for instance, is still home to some of the most deeply impoverished enclaves in the Commonwealth of Virginia—the capital city's poverty rate was nearly 15 percent higher than the poverty rate throughout the state between 2006 and 2010. In 1969, 24 percent of Richmond's children lived in poverty; that number was an astonishing 39 percent after the Great Recession of 2008–2009. Most of these children reside in Creighton, Mosby, and Fairfield Courts. The city's "extraordinarily high levels of [child] poverty" also affect the state of Richmond Public Schools. African Americans made up roughly 50 percent of Richmond's population in 2010 yet composed 80 percent of the RPS total student population. An overwhelming majority of the African Americans who attend these city public schools fall at or beneath the poverty line. In 2013, 77 percent of RPS students received free or reduced lunch, and the high school graduation rate stood at roughly 76 percent. Dillon's rule and the moratorium on annexations—made worse by tax-exempt government properties and public housing—has had a profound influence on the flow of local revenue streams to schools. RPS continues to struggle with budget shortfalls and capital needs. Many of Richmond's school buildings are in a state of severe dilapidation, and these problems often motivate many residents to keep their children out of the system.[8]

Cities are never blank slates. Slavery may have made Richmond, but our fascination with the peculiar institution often overshadows just how destructive the grind of twentieth-century urban history was to black Americans' upwardly mobile aspirations. Reconciliation is next to impossible without recognition. In recent years, one of Richmond's greatest accomplishments has been city hall's recognition of not just poverty but of contemporary poverty's relationship to the city's not so distant past. Unless these matters take a turn for the better, it seems likely that the histories of the American civil rights movement and of the backlash against that movement will be written much like the histories of Reconstruction. On the one hand, this story of the Richmond Crusade for Voters and Richmond's quest for political equality is a triumph narrative. It highlights a group of black leaders who recognized the culture of local bigotry and disenfranchisement and used it to their collective advantage. On the other hand, we know now that the struggle for black equality persisted long after Washington's realization of the civil rights acts. White backlash to black governance and structural forces beyond the realm of politics threatened the very tenuous hold black Americans had on symbols of local power. Richmond, Virginia, has embraced elements of racial progressivism—the racial makeup of the city council is testament to progress. Yet cultural diversity and economic equality have not kept pace with the demographic diversification of American politics. Given the current fight against economic dispossession and educational shortfalls, it is clear that the struggle continues.

Appendix

City Council Election Data: City of Richmond, Virginia, 1960–1984

Table 1. Richmond City Council Election of 1960

Rank in Election Standings	Candidate	Endorsement(s)	Race	Number of Votes Received	Percentage of Vote
1	Eleanor P. Sheppard	RCA & Crusade	White	14,879	53.1
2	Claude W. Woodward	RCA & Crusade	White	14,096	50.7
3	George Sadler	RCA & Crusade	White	13,435	48.2
4	R. Hugh Rudd	RCA & Crusade	White	12,611	45.4
5	Ben R. Johns	RCA & Crusade	White	11,389	40.9
6	E. Elwood Ford	RCA & Crusade	White	10,988	39.5
7	Robert C. Thorckmorton	Independent	White	10,707	38.5
8	F. Henry Barber	Independent	White	10,674	38.3
9	J. Westwood Smithers	RCA & Crusade	White	10,574	38.0

Source: Data from Richmond Annexation Files, 1942–1976, M183, Cabell Black Collection, M306, James Branch Cabell Library, Virginia Commonwealth University, Richmond.

Table 2. Richmond City Council Election of 1962

Rank in Election Standings	Candidate	Endorsement(s)	Race	Number of Votes Received	Percentage of Vote
1	Robert J. Heberle	Crusade	White	11,348	50.9
2	Eleanor P. Sheppard	RCA & Crusade	White	11,184	50.0
3	Claude C. Woodward	RCA & Crusade	White	10,353	46.4
4	Robert C. Throckmorton	Independent	White	10,201	45.8
5	Phil J. Bagley Jr.	RCA	White	9,772	43.8
6	J. Westwood Smithers	RCA & Crusade	White	9,493	42.5
7	E. Elwood Ford	Independent & Crusade	White	9,295	41.6
8	Ruth J. Herrink	Crusade	White	9,200	41.3
9	George William Sadler	RCA & Crusade	White	8,960	40.3

Source: Data from Richmond Annexation Files, 1942–1976, M183, Cabell Black Collection, M306, James Branch Cabell Library, Virginia Commonwealth University, Richmond.

Table 3. Richmond City Council Election of 1964

Rank in Election Standings	Candidate	Endorsement(s)	Race	Number of Votes Received	Percentage of Vote
1	Eleanor P. Sheppard	RF & Crusade	White	18,042	58.3
2	B. A. "Sonny" Cephas	RF & Crusade	Black	16,512	53.4
3	James C. Wheat Jr.	RF & Crusade	White	15,965	51.6
4	A. Scott Anderson	Independent	White	15,135	48.9
5	Henry J. Miller III	RF & Crusade	White	13,886	44.9
6	Morrill C. Crowe	RF & Crusade	White	13,846	44.8
7	Phil J. Bagley Jr.	Independent	White	13,333	43.1
8	Robert C. Throckmorton	Independent	White	12,860	41.6
9	Robert J. Habenicht	RF & Crusade	White	12,780	41.4

Source: Data from Richmond Annexation Files, 1942–1976, M183, Cabell Black Collection, M306, James Branch Cabell Library, Virginia Commonwealth University, Richmond.

Table 4. Richmond City Council Election of 1966

Rank in Election Standings	Candidate	Endorsement(s)	Race	Number of Votes Received	Percentage of Vote
1	Phil J. Bagley Jr.	RF & Crusade	White	23,997	66.2
2	B. A. "Sonny" Cephas	RF & Crusade	Black	22,957	63.3
3	Eleanor P. Sheppard	RF	White	19,763	54.5
4	Morrill M. Crowe	RF	White	19,102	52.7
5	Winfred Mundle	RF & Crusade	Black	18,286	50.4
6	Henry Marsh III	Crusade	Black	17,812	49.1
7	Jim Wheat	RF	White	17,803	49.1
8	Robert Habenicht	RF	White	17,066	47.1
9	Howard Carwile	Crusade	White	16,356	45.1

Source: Data from *Richmond Times-Dispatch,* June 6, 1966, 1, 2.

Table 5. Winner in Black-Majority Precincts, Richmond City Council Election of 1966

Rank in Black-Majority Precincts	Candidate	Race	Number of Votes Received	Percentage of Vote
1	Henry Marsh III	Black	11,270	83.4
2	B. A. "Sonny" Cephas	Black	10,432	77.2
3	Winfred Mundle	Black	9,329	69.0
4	Howard Carwile	White	8,454	62.5
5	Phil J. Bagley Jr.	White	7,316	54.1
6	Eleanor P. Sheppard	White	5,691	42.1
7	Morrill M. Crowe	White	4,485	33.2
8	Jim Wheat	White	3,581	26.4
9	Robert Habenicht	White	3,088	22.8

Note: The data provided here are for Precincts 1, 3, 4, 5, 6, 7, 8 9, 18, 19, 24, 46, 47, 55, 62, 63, 64, 65, 66, and 67.
Source: Data from *Richmond Times-Dispatch,* June 6, 1966, 1, 2.

Table 6. Richmond City Council Election of 1968

Rank in Election Standings	Candidate	Endorsement(s)	Race	Number of Votes Received	Percentage of Vote
1	Howard Carwile	Crusade	White	25,361	56.6
2	Phil J. Bagley Jr.	RF	White	24,604	54.9
3	Thomas Bliley	RF	White	23,552	52.6
4	Morrill M. Crowe	RF	White	22,631	50.5
5	Jim Carpenter	Crusade	White	22,091	49.3
6	Henry Marsh III	Crusade	Black	22,014	49.2
7	Nathan Forb	RF	White	21,960	49.0
8	Jim Wheat	RF	White	21,437	47.9
9	Nell Pusey	RF	White	20,556	45.9

Source: Data from *City of Richmond v. United States,* 422 U.S. 358 (1975), Plaintiff's Exhibit 5(b), at 104.

Table 7. Top Vote Getters in Black-Majority Precincts, Richmond City Council Election of 1968

Top Nine Vote Getters in Predominantly Black Districts	Candidate	Race	Number of Votes Received	Percentage of Vote
1	Henry Marsh III	Black	13,363	91.0
2	Howard Carwile	White	13,061	88.9
3	Jim Carpenter	White	12,010	85.0
4	Walter Kenney	Black	10,759	73.3
5	Milton Randolph	Black	9,660	65.8
6	B. A. "Sonny" Cephas	Black	3,433	23.4
7	Winfred Mundle	Black	2,922	19.9
8	Phil J. Bagley Jr.	White	2,388	16.3
9	Morrill M. Crowe	White	2,284	15.5

Note: The data provided here are for Precincts 1, 4, 5, 6, 7, 8, 9, 18, 19, 24, 46, 47, 55, 62, 63, 64, 65, 66, and 67.
Source: Data from *City of Richmond v. United States,* 422 U.S. 358 (1975), Plaintiff's Exhibit 5(b), at 104.

Table 8. Richmond City Council Election of 1970

Rank in Election Standings	Candidate	Endorsement(s)	Race	Number of Votes Received	Percentage of Vote
1	Howard Carwile	Crusade	White	29,031	56.3
2	Henry Marsh III	Crusade	Black	26,012	50.5
3	Jim Carpenter	Crusade	White	25,502	49.5
4	Thomas Bliley	TOP	White	24,928	48.3
5	Nathan Forb	TOP	White	21,781	42.3
6	William V. Daniel	TOP	White	21,429	41.6
7	Henry Valentine	TOP	White	20,977	40.8
8	Wayland W. Rennie	TOP	White	19,767	38.4
9	Aubrey H. Thompson	TOP	White	19,431	37.7
Important Also-Rans					
12	Walter Kenney	Crusade	Black	17,592	34.2
17	Curtis Holt Sr.	Crusade	Black	13,009	25.3

Source: Data from *Richmond Times-Dispatch,* May 14, 1970, 39.

Table 9. Richmond City Council Election of 1970—Old City Results

Rank in Election Standings	Candidate	Endorsement	Race	Number of Votes Received	Percentage of Vote
1	Howard Carwile	Crusade	White	24,132	57.1
2	Henry Marsh III	Crusade	Black	22,738	54.0
3	Jim Carpenter	Crusade	White	21,712	51.4
4	Thomas Bliley	TOP	White	20,084	47.5
5	Nathan Forb	TOP	White	17,597	41.7
6	William V. Daniel	TOP	White	17,158	40.6
7	Henry Valentine	TOP	White	16,855	39.9
8	Walter Kenney	Crusade	Black	16,261	38.5
9	Wayland W. Rennie	TOP	White	16,128	38.2
15	Curtis Holt Sr.	Crusade	Black	12,400	29.4

Note: The data provided here are for the top vote getters in the City of Richmond, not including the recently annexed portion of Chesterfield County
Source: Data from *Richmond Times-Dispatch,* May 14, 1970, 39.

Table 10. Top Three Vote Getters per District and Number of Votes, Richmond City Council Election of 1977

District	Winner and Total Votes Received	Runner-Up and Total Votes Received	Third Place and Total Votes Received
District 1	Henry L. Valentine: 4,906	Nathan Forb: 1,737	E. Hatcher Crenshaw: 1,176
District 2	Wayland W. Rennie: 3,793	John N. Ambrose: 476	Louis A. Michaux: 355
District 3	Willie J. Dell: 4,030	Melvin D. Law: 893	Patrick W. Brown: 141
District 4	Aubrey H. Thompson: 3,383	Andrew W. Wood: 1,123	Edward P. Godsey: 916
District 5	Chuck Richardson: 1,120	William R. Johnson: 1,108	Frank W. Gilbert: 932
District 6	Walter T. Kenney: 1,431	Othel B. Sparks: 910	James H. Elam: 258
District 7	Henry Marsh III: 1,737	Charles E. Walker: 920	Curtis Holt Sr.: 687
District 8	Claudette McDaniel: 2,135	George W. Rowe: 1,534	John M. Clark: 225
District 9	Raymond Royall: 1,246	William I. Golding: 836	James F. Sumpter: 520

Source: Data from *Richmond Times-Dispatch,* March 2, 1977, 1.

Table 11. Richmond City Council Election of 1978, District Results

District	Winner and Total Votes Received	Runner-Up and Total Votes Received
District 1	George S. Kemp: 4,312	Dimitrios Soulios: 914
District 2	Wayland W. Rennie: 2,611	John N. Ambrose: 948
District 3	Willie J. Dell: unopposed	
District 4	Aubrey H. Thompson: 2,984	Perley A. Covey: 1,041
District 5	Chuck Richardson: 2,508	F. Willson Craigie: 1,027
District 6	Walter T. Kenney: unopposed	
District 7	Henry Marsh III: 2,011	Curtis Holt Sr.: 422
District 8	Claudette McDaniel: 2,617	G. Richard Wainwright: 1,710
District 9	William I. Golding: 1,148	Raymond Royall: 1,006

Source: Data from *Richmond Times-Dispatch,* May 3, 1978, A6.

Table 12. Richmond City Council Election of 1980, District Results

District	Winner and Total Votes Received	Runner-Up and Total Votes Received
District 1	George S. Kemp: 5,840	Dimitrios Soulios: 620
District 2	William J. Leidinger: 4,721	Muriel H. Smith: 1,643
District 3	Willie J. Dell: unopposed	
District 4	Aubrey H. Thompson: 5,937	Wilbert H. Patron: 566
District 5	Chuck Richardson: unopposed	
District 6	Walter T. Kenney 1,890	Frederick C. Williams, III: 146
District 7	Henry Marsh III: unopposed	
District 8	Claudette McDaniel: 3,183	Andrew J. Gillespie: 2,913
District 9	Carolyn Wake: 2,513	William I. Golding: 1,180

Source: Data from *Richmond Times-Dispatch,* May 7, 1980, 1.

Table 13. Richmond City Council Election of 1982, District Results

District	Winner and Total Votes Received	Runner-Up and Total Votes Received
District A	George S. Kemp: 5,840	Roger C. Griffin: 818
District B	William J. Leidinger: 4,113	Virginia H. Ritchie: 2,794
District C	Roy West: 3,858	Willie J. Dell: 3,361
District D	Andrew J. Gillespie: 4,302	Cleveland Lamison: 720
District E	Chuck Richardson: 2,852	Julia B. Morton: 593
District F	Walter T. Kenney: unopposed	
District G	Henry Marsh III: 3,504	Sheila Jones-Warrick: 391
District H	Claudette McDaniel: 2,519	Mary Newkirk: 777
District I	Carolyn Wake: 1,666	William I. Golding: 892

Source: Data from *Richmond Times-Dispatch,* May 5, 1982, 1.

Table 14. Richmond City Council Election of 1984, District Results

District	Winner and Total Votes Received	Runner-up and Total Votes Received
District 1	Geline Williams: 4,531	Robert Shiro: 3,092
District 2	William J. Leidinger: unopposed	
District 3	Roy West: 4,907	Willie Dell: 3,879
District 4	Andrew Gillespie: unopposed	
District 5	Chuck Richardson: 2,996	Collie Burton: 824
District 6	Walter Kenney: 2,591	Wilbert Daniels: 1,289
District 7	Henry Marsh III: 3,279	Alma Barlow: 627
District 8	Claudette McDaniel: unopposed	
District 9	Carolyn Wake: 2,218	Stanley Baker: 946

Source: Data from *Richmond Times-Dispatch,* May 2, 1984, 1.

Acknowledgments

This project began in Charlottesville, Virginia, developed during my time in Los Angeles, lay dormant in Buffalo, New York, and came to fruition where it belonged, in Richmond, Virginia. In fact, I wrote most of this book in Richmond's stadium neighborhood due west of Carytown— one block from the constant drone of the Downtown Expressway. This undertaking more broadly originated from a question I once asked Julian Bond during my first semester of graduate school. Mr. Bond, a group of professors, and a handful of graduate students came together in the fall of 2014 to contemplate Laughlin McDonald's book *A Voting Rights Odyssey*. That evening Bond spoke about the book and his experiences as a member of the Georgia Senate and also facilitated a subsequent discussion. I eventually asked, "Was the civil rights movement a failure?" I am almost certain that Mr. Bond thought it was a terrible question. In fact, I know now that it was an awful question. I had just asked a major figure in the freedom struggle if his life's work was for naught. At that time, I lacked the chops as a historian (and I am not sure if I have the chops now) to convey the point I was *really* trying to make.

On that fall evening, it was hard to reconcile my experiences as a child of the 1980s with the triumph narrative of the American civil rights movement. Until very recently, historians and Americans portrayed the freedom struggle as the high-water mark of American equality. I was born in 1975 to Norma and Kevin Hayter in Des Moines, Iowa. My father worked in heavy agricultural industry, and a major health insurance provider employed my mother. My father's family came to Iowa through Missouri and Kansas, while my mother's maternal family came from Virginia to work the coal mines in an all-black mining town, Buxton, Iowa. Both sides made out OK. We were a solid middle-class family, and I grew up in a predominantly African American neighborhood—one of the city's two sizeable black enclaves that straddle the Des Moines River. With age, I came to understand that I was, for the most part, the richest kid on a poor block. I did not know it then, but the farm crisis, urban retrenchment, deindustrialization, rising gun violence, poverty, and drugs during the 1980s devastated what little stability my neighborhood provided its residents. These crises also wreaked havoc on my immediate and extended family. The first kid in my immediate neighborhood was shot and killed before I finished the eighth grade (gun violence east of Thirty-First Street has been an unfortunate fixture of black life in Des Moines for the past three decades). My parents sent me—via bus—to middle and high schools more than forty blocks from my home in a predominantly white and affluent part of the city. Like many of my friends, I barely made it through high school. One of my best friends—with whom I failed to reconcile over a petty dispute—was murdered several blocks from my grandparent's home on Sixteenth Street on September 8, 1994. This book is dedicated to Steve's memory.

I owe a great debt to Julian Bond—his caustic response to my question drove me to ask better questions about the shortfalls of the civil rights movement. I owe an even greater debt to "the hood" and the family, friends, and scholars who have helped inform the ideas and research in this book. Writing this book, despite the fact that it appears to be authored by one person, was a community endeavor. I sincerely hope that these acknowledgments give everyone the credit they deserve.

This effort would not have been possible without carefully crafted family and scholarly guidance. I would first like to thank immediate and extended family members and friends. I never understood the power of unconditional love until the first moment I saw my daughter's face. Evelyn has motivated this book in ways that she cannot fully understand yet, and so I dedicate it to her. I have been married to Cate Engel for nearly eight years. Although I have known Cate since high school, we do not know marriage apart from this book. My wife's patience, support, and tolerance made this book possible. I have loved her since "the first time ever I saw [her] face." I would have never made it through college and graduate school without the love and support of Kevin and Norma Hayter—I am eternally grateful for all that they have given me! My father passed away just before this book went to print. My dad's love of history has profoundly influenced my life—this effort is dedicated to his memory. Rest in peace, Dad. I would also like to thank Vernon Ashford, Veronica Amucha, Kelly Bonwell, Marguerite Cook, Rick and

Cathy Engel (and company), Evelyn Frazier, Fonda Frazier (and company), Tom Frazier, Bertie and Bryon Hayter, Montez Hayter, Nicole Hayter, Patricia Hayter, Tam Hayter, Dorothy Maness, and Uncle Barney (journey well).

Many friends have in various ways contributed to this effort. I have known many of these people for decades, and I met a few of them in college and graduate school. They all represent the power of unconditional companionship, and a few of them were essential to this book's research. Thanks to Clint Buckner, Brent Cebul, Christy Chapin, Robin Hamlyn, John Holveck, Matt Hupton, Alex Isaacson, Amy Jacobs, Matt Jeter, Chris Loomis (and Amanda), Scott Matthews, Justin Miller, Martin Miller, Rosetta Pearson, Adria Scharf, Courtney and Aaron Quinn, Erwin Thomas, George Van Cleve, Travis and Ling Weaver, and my good friends at Flintridge Preparatory School.

Brian Balogh has been a surrogate father to this book and me. I could not have asked for a better mentor and friend. His dedication to his students' growth as thinkers and historians is remarkable. He always kept me on course and refused to go easy on me. This book is a direct product of his dedication to my growth as a scholar and a man. I thank him for recognizing my potential and for being a good person.

I would be remiss if I did not mention the handful of historians and scholars who also made this effort possible. There is not a chapter in this book that Claudrena Harold did not influence. I thank her for guiding me through graduate school, pushing me to make this a better book, and just being the remarkable person and scholar she is. Ed Ayers also deserves profound thanks, especially for passing my research along to Thad Williamson at the University of Richmond and for the continued to support/mentorship. Thanks go to Michael F. Holt, who taught me more about the craft of history than he knows. He demanded that I respect the discipline—I wish I would have shown it at the time, but I am grateful for his guidance. Charles Jeffreys Jr. is still the most outstanding teacher I have ever encountered—he piqued a curiosity in me that runs throughout this effort. Thanks also to Bert Ashe, Al Black, Larry Blique, Bob Crutchfield, Risa Goluboff, Pippa Holloway, Amy Howard, Bob Kane, John Kneebone, Carl Livingston, Guian Mckee, Charles McCurdy, Ernest McGowen, Joe Miller, John Moeser, Nicole Sackley, Quintard Taylor,

Eric Yellin, and the folks at Thriving Cities (who helped me understand contemporary Richmond).

The University of Richmond's Jepson School of Leadership Studies, where I am currently one of three historians, also deserves particular praise. I could not have finished this book without Jepson's tremendous institutional and financial support. As it relates directly to this book, I would specifically like to thank my mentor, Al Goethals, for reading and giving comments, and Thad Williamson, who read this manuscript innumerable times. Thanks to everyone at Jepson—that means everyone! They all contributed to this book in one way or another. For the record, Lucretia McCulley, our library liaison, saved this book! I thank her for the link to historical newspapers and for lending her expertise to me over the past five years. Last, thanks to Elizabeth DeBusk-Maslanka for her work on this book's outstanding photos.

This book found the right home. I owe a great debt to Mark Kornbluh and the other good people at the University Press of Kentucky, in particular Anne Dean Dotson, Patrick O'Dowd, and the editors of the series "Civil Rights and the Struggle for Black Equality in the Twentieth Century." I thank them for their continued interest in this project and for guiding it through the early publication stages. And I cannot extend enough gratitude to the anonymous readers, who were not only prompt but also thorough in their comments on the manuscript. The quality of their comments and suggestions has made for a decidedly better book.

Last, I am profoundly indebted to Richmond, Virginia. While living there, I came to realize that many of the tragedies that beset the neighborhood I grew up in were not unique to Des Moines. Indeed, as I read through secondary and primary sources on modern American history and the civil rights struggle, it became clear to me that there was nothing specifically southern about Richmond after the civil rights era. In fact, I found striking similarities between Richmond and my experiences growing up in Des Moines. The research in this book, like so much recent scholarship on urban history, grapples with a fundamental question: How do we square "the movement" with the urban decline that plagued an appalling number of black communities in the waning years of the twentieth century and continues to plague them? I trust that the pages in this book demonstrate that Richmond, Virginia, had a strong legacy of African American civic engagement. It also contained large numbers of economically vulnerable black Americans who were no better off after the civil rights movement than before it. I hope this book does justice to the memory of Richmond's struggle for racial equality and the people who dedicated their lives to that struggle.

Actual Richmonders provided many of the photos, archival material, and primary sources in this book. I extend a special thanks to the *Richmond Times-Dispatch,* Ray Bonis at Virginia Commonwealth University, the Valentine Museum, the Virginia Historical Society, the Richmond Public Library, the Library of Virginia, and the Richmond Crusade for Voters. I thank Ray Boone, Willie Dell, William Ferguson Reid, Chuck Richardson, Preston Yancy, and many others for speaking with me about their experiences. I also thank Regie Ford, Tina Griego, Lauranette Lee, Bill Obrochta, Christy Sheppard, Michael Paul Williams, the folks at *Style Weekly,* and Leadership Metro Richmond.

Notes

Introduction

Portions of this introduction are drawn from Julian Maxwell Hayter, "From Intent to Effect: Richmond, Virginia, and the Protracted Struggle for Voting Rights, 1965–1977," *Journal of Policy History* 26, no. 4 (2014): 534–67.

1. Ron Harris, "Richmond: Former Confederate Capital Finally Falls to Blacks," *Ebony*, June 1980, 44–52. On Virginia's centrality to slave trading and tobacco production, see Midori Takagi, *Rearing Wolves to Our Own Destruction: Slavery in Richmond, Virginia, 1782–1865* (Charlottesville: University Press of Virginia, 1999), and Edward E. Baptist, *The Half Has Never Been Told: Slavery and the Making of American Capitalism* (New York: Basic Books, 2014).

2. In at-large election systems, voters fill all contested seats on governing bodies. These candidates must run throughout an entire jurisdiction. In single-member district systems, cities are divided into geographical districts. Voters in each district cast votes for candidates in their respective districts. On majority–minority district systems, see Alexander Keyssar, *The Right to Vote: The Contested History of Democracy in the United States* (New York: Basic Books, 2000), and Ruth P. Morgan, *Governance by Decree: The Impact of the Voting Rights Act in Dallas* (Lawrence: University Press of Kansas, 2004).

3. Harris, "Richmond," 45. Harris repeatedly misspelled Holt's name in the article, referring to Holt as "Hope." On historical memory, public history, and Monument Avenue, see Matthew Mace Barbee, *Race and Masculinity in Southern Memory: History of Richmond, Virginia's Monument Avenue, 1948–1996* (New York: Lexington Books, 2013). The other twelve cities were Chicago; Philadelphia; Washington, D.C.; New Orleans; Atlanta; Newark, New Jersey; Oakland, California; Birmingham, Alabama; Gary, Indiana; Hartford, Connecticut; and Portsmouth, Virginia (Adolph Reed, *Stirrings in the Jug: Black Politics in the Post-segregation Era* [Minneapolis: University of Minnesota Press, 1999], 79, 253–54).

4. On Richmond's early history, see Benjamin Campbell, *Richmond's Unhealed History* (Richmond, Va.: Brandylane, 2012); Harris, "Richmond," 50; Julian Maxwell Hayter, *City Profile of Richmond: Thriving Cities* (Richmond: Institute for Advanced Studies in Culture, University of Virginia, 2015); Takagi, *Rearing Wolves to Our Own Destruction*, chap. 1; and Edmund Morgan, *American Slavery, American Freedom: The Ordeal of Colonial Virginia* (New York: Norton, 1975), 5.

5. On industrial production and antebellum economics in Richmond, see Peter Rachleff, *Black Labor in Richmond, 1865–1890* (Urbana: University of Illinois Press, 1989). Also, the University of Richmond's Digital Scholarship Lab recently produced videos that depict Richmond's slave market (at http://dsl. richmond.edu/richmond3d/). On industrial slave labor in Richmond, see Takagi, *Rearing Wolves to Our Own Destruction*, 1–4. On domestic slave trading and Virginia, see Baptist, *The Half Has Never Been Told*, and Rachleff, *Black Labor in Richmond*, 13 (quote). Virginia's Constitution of 1901 was a panic reaction to the interracial politics that briefly emerged during the late nineteenth century. William Mahone (a former Confederate general) led an interracial coalition known as the Readjuster Party, which sought to break the power of Virginia's wealthy planter elites by promoting interracial cooperation, education, and universal manhood suffrage. They were defeated by white supremacists in the early 1880s. On the legacy of poll taxes, see *Harper v. Virginia Board of Elections*, 383 U.S. 663 (1966). On the Readjuster Party, see Rachleff, *Black Labor in Richmond*, chap. 6, and Harris, "Richmond," 50.

6. On early phases of the suffrage crusades before the VRA, see Steven F. Lawson, *Black Ballots: Voting Rights in the South, 1944–1969* (New York: Columbia University Press, 1976), chap. 5. Bader Ginsberg's comment is in *Shelby County v. Holder* 570 U.S. (2013), at 5.

7. J. Todd Moye, *Let the People Decide: Black Freedom and White Resistance Movements in Sunflower County, Mississippi, 1945–1986* (Chapel Hill: University of North Carolina Press, 2004), 23. On black mayors in majority–minority cities, see Clarence N. Stone, *Regime Politics: Governing Atlanta, 1946–1988* (Lawrence: University Press of Kansas, 1989), 6–9. On the hollow-prize problem, see H. Paul Friesema, "Black Control of Central Cities: The Hollow Prize," *American Institute of Planners Journal* 35, no. 2 (1969): 75–79; Neil Kraus and Todd Swanstrom, "Minority Mayors and the Hollow Prize Problem," *PS: Political Science and Politics* 34, no. 1 (2001): 99–105; and Reed, *Stirrings in the Jug*, 98.

8. This book defines politics generally, incorporating, like most political histories, print-media culture, voting rights mobilization, electoral politics, litigation, and so on. It also demonstrates how everyday people, federal officials, politicians, and policy makers engaged these institutions on state, local, and federal levels to define and redefine black citizenship. On early bottom-up approaches to the civil rights movement, see John Dittmer, *Local People: The Struggle for Civil Rights in Mississippi* (Urbana: University of Illinois Press, 1995); Charles M. Payne, *I've Got the Light of Freedom: The Organizing Tradition and the Mississippi Freedom Struggle* (Berkeley: University of California Press, 1995); Emilye Crosby, "Introduction: The Politics of Writing and Teaching Movement History," in *Civil Rights History from the Ground Up: Local Struggles, a National Movement*, ed. Emilye Crosby (Athens: University of Georgia Press, 2011), 6, emphasis in original; *Brown v. Board of Education of Topeka*, 347 U.S. 483

(1954); Tomiko Brown-Nagin, *Courage to Dissent: Atlanta and the Long History of the Civil Rights Movement* (New York: Oxford University Press, 2011), 8. For the relationship between the Cold War and the American civil rights movement, see Mary L. Dudziak, *Cold War Civil Rights: Race and the Image of America Democracy* (Princeton, N.J.: Prince University Press, 2000). On the relationship between African Americans and Africans during the civil rights movement, see James Hunter Meriwether, *Proudly We Can Be Africans: Black Americans and Africa, 1935–1961* (Chapel Hill: University of North Carolina Press, 2002).

9. On early-twentieth-century civil rights struggles in Richmond and black gradualism, see Blair Murphy Kelley, *Right to Ride: Streetcar Boycotts and African American Citizenship in the Era of* Plessy v. Ferguson (Chapel Hill: University of North Carolina Press, 2010); Raymond Gavins, *The Perils and Prospects of Southern Black Leadership: Gordon Blaine Hancock, 1884–1970* (Durham, N.C.: Duke University Press, 1993). For race relations in Virginia and Norfolk, see Earl Lewis, *In Their Own Interests: Race, Class, and Power in Twentieth-Century Norfolk, Virginia* (Berkeley: University of California Press, 1991). On Virginia's brand of paternalism—that is, the process of restricting and granting freedoms on whites' terms—see J. Douglas Smith, *Managing White Supremacy: Race, Politics, and Citizenship in Jim Crow Virginia* (Chapel Hill: University of North Carolina Press, 2002), 8–9, 14. On Richmond's centrality to the omnibus *Brown v. Board of Education* case, see Jill Ogline Titus, *Brown's Battleground: Students, Segregationists, and the Struggle for Justice in Prince Edward County, Virginia* (Chapel Hill: University Press of North Carolina, 2011), and Robert A. Pratt, *The Color of Their Skin: Education and Race in Richmond, Virginia, 1954–1989* (Charlottesville: University Press of Virginia, 1993).

10. Steven F. Lawson, *Running for Freedom: Civil Rights and Black Politics in America since 1941* (New York: Wiley, 2014), 70; John A. Hannah, *Voting: 1961 Commission on Civil Rights Report* (Washington, D.C.: U.S. Commission on Civil Rights, February 1961), 22. As historians and scholars shift the lens from developments in national voting rights to the local arena, they have discovered that local people were instrumental not just to the ratification of the VRA but to developments in voting rights law after 1965. On these local studies, see Brown-Nagin, *Courage to Dissent;* Chris Danielson, *After Freedom Summer: How Race Realigned Mississippi Politics, 1965–1986* (Gainesville: University of Florida Press, 2011); Brett V. Gadsden, *Between North and South: Delaware, Desegregation, and the Myth of American Sectionalism* (Philadelphia: University of Pennsylvania Press, 2013); Tracy Elaine K'Meyer, *Civil Rights in the Gateway to the South: Louisville, Kentucky, 1945–1980* (Lexington: University Press of Kentucky, 2009); Laughlin McDonald, *A Voting Rights Odyssey: Black Enfranchisement in Georgia* (Cambridge: Cambridge University Press, 2003); Moye, *Let the People Decide;* and J. Mills Thornton, *Dividing Lines: Municipal Politics and the Struggle for Civil Rights in Montgomery, Birmingham, and Selma* (Tuscaloosa: Univer-

sity of Alabama Press, 2002). A handful of voting rights and civil rights scholars
have written about these political initiatives for decades—especially in the wake of
the Civil Rights Act of 1957. On that act, see Richard M. Valelly, *The Two Reconstructions: The Struggle for Black Enfranchisement* (Chicago: University of Chicago Press, 2004), 183–89.

11. John H. Bracey Jr. and August Meier, eds., *Supplement to Part 4, Voting
Rights, General Office Files, 1956–1965*, 1995, in Papers of the National Associ-
ation for the Advancement of Colored People, Group III, Box 266, Library of
Congress, Washington, D.C. On Selma, see David J. Garrow, *Protest at Selma:
Martin Luther King, Jr., and the Voting Rights Act of 1965*, rev. ed. (New Haven,
Conn.: Yale University Press, 2015).

12. William A. Thornton, "History of the Crusade: Report of the Historian:
1953–1995," Richmond Crusade for Voters Collection, 1955–1995, M306,
Cabell Black Collection, M306, James Branch Cabell Library, Virginia Com-
monwealth University, Richmond; Charles W. McKinney Jr., "Finding Fannie
Corbett: Black Women, Gender, and the 'Politics of Protection,'" in Crosby,
Civil Rights History from the Ground Up, 82–83. Bruce Glasrud and Merline
Pitre masterfully catalog several recent local studies that emphasize women's cen-
trality to civil rights activism in "African American Women in the Virginia Civil
Rights Movement," in *Southern Black Women in the Modern Civil Rights Move-
ment*, ed. Bruce A. Glasrud and Merline Pitre (College Station: Texas A&M Uni-
versity Press, 2013), 4–5. See also Bettye Collier-Thomas and V. P. Franklin, eds.,
*Sisters in the Struggle: African American Women in the Civil Rights–Black Power
Movement* (New York: New York University Press, 2001); Shannon L. Frystak,
*Our Minds on Freedom: Women and the Struggle for Black Equality in Louisi-
ana, 1924–1967* (Baton Rouge: Louisiana State University Press, 2009); Cynthia
Griggs Fleming, *In the Shadow of Selma: The Continuing Struggle for Civil Rights
in the Rural South* (New York: Rowman and Littlefield, 2004); Payne, *I've Got
the Light of Freedom;* Belinda Robnett, *How Long? How Long? African-American Women in the Struggle for Civil Rights* (New York: Oxford University Press,
1997); Titus, Brown's *Battleground*. On black women and civil rights, see Caroline Emmons, "A Tremendous Job to Be Done: African American Women in the
Virginia Civil Rights Movement," in Glasrud and Pitre, *Southern Black Women
in the Modern Civil Rights Movement*, 15–28; and Lewis A. Randolph and Gayle
T. Tate, *Rights for a Season: The Politics of Race, Class, and Gender in Richmond,
Virginia* (Knoxville: University Press of Tennessee, 2003), 156, 171–80.

13. On Barbara Johns, see Titus, Brown's *Battleground*. On Maggie Walker,
see Gertrude Woodruff Marlowe, *A Right Worthy Grand Mission: Maggie Lena
Walker and the Quest for Black Economic Empowerment* (Washington, D.C.: How-
ard University Press, 2003). For the quote from Ransby, see Barbara Ransby, *Ella
Baker and the Black Freedom Movement: A Radical Democratic Vision* (Chapel
Hill: The University of North Carolina Press, 2003), 184. On women's roles

in the movement, see M. Bahati Kuumba, *Gender and Social Movements* (Walnut Creek, Calif.: AltaMira Press, 2001), 80–87, and Belinda Robnett, "African-American Women in the Civil Rights Movement, 1954–1965: Gender, Leadership, and Micromobilization," *American Journal of Sociology* 101, no. 6 (1996): 1661–93. On Green's discussion of "bridge leaders," see Laurie B. Green, "Challenging the Civil Rights Narrative: Women, Gender, and the 'Politics of Protection,'" in Crosby, *Civil Rights from the Ground Up*, 57. On leaders and "center-women," see Robnett, "African American Women in the Civil Rights Movement,", and Karen Brodkin Sacks, "Gender and Grassroots Leadership," in *Women and the Politics of Empowerment*, ed. Ann Bookman and Sandra Morgan (Philadelphia: Temple University Press, 1988), 77–94.

14. Julian Maxwell Hayter, "From Intent to Effect: Richmond, Virginia and the Protracted Struggle for Voting Rights, 1965–1977," *Journal of Policy History* 26, no. 4 (2014): 534–67, esp. 540–41. On racist civility, see Smith, *Managing White Supremacy*, 4–10. The best account of civil rights activism in other Virginia cities is still Earl Lewis's book *In Their Own Interests*.

15. *Harper v. Virginia Board of Elections* 383 U.S. 663 (1966).

16. On the legacy of Burger Court and civil rights, see Earl M. Maltz, *The Chief Justiceship of Warren Burger, 1969–1986* (Columbia: University of South Carolina Press, 2000), and Bernard Schwartz, ed., *The Burger Court: Counter-Revolution or Confirmation?* (New York: Oxford University Press, 1998). On the transformation of voting rights from intent to effect, see Hayter, "From Intent to Effect"; Morgan Kousser, *Colorblind Injustice: Minority Voting Rights and the Undoing of the Second Reconstruction* (Chapel Hill: University of North Carolina Press, 1999); and *Griggs v. Duke Power Company*, 401 U.S. 424 (1971). On *Griggs*, see Derrick Bell, "The Burger Court's Place on the Bell Curve of Racial Jurisprudence," in Schwartz, *The Burger Court*, 61–62. On the antidilution litigation, see Hayter, "From Intent to Effect," 552, and Valelly, *Two Reconstructions*, 215.

17. Tova Andrea Wang, *The Politics of Voter Suppression: Defending and Expanding Americans' Right to Vote* (Ithaca, N.Y.: Cornell University Press, 2012), xiv. On the politics of the civil rights bills in Washington, see the seminal text by Steven F. Lawson, *In Pursuit of Power: Southern Blacks and Electoral Politics, 1965–1982* (New York: Columbia University Press, 1985); Frank R. Parker, *Black Votes Count: Political Empowerment in Mississippi after 1965* (Chapel Hill: University of North Carolina Press, 1990); *Shaw v. Reno*, 509 U.S. 630 (1993); *Shelby v. Holder;* Charles S. Bullock III, Ronald Keith Gaddie, and Justin J. Wert, eds., *The Rise and Fall of the Voting Rights Act* (Norman: University of Oklahoma Press, 2016); and Jacquelyn Dowd Hall, "The Long Civil Rights Movement and the Political Uses of the Past," *Journal of American History* 91, no. 4 (2005): 1238 (quote). The first seminal voting rights texts, in particular *Black Ballots* by Lawson, published in the mid-1970s, recognized the VRA's ratifica-

tion as a watershed in U.S. political history. Lawson focused on how federal actors removed the remaining legal barriers to the franchise. During the 1980s and 1990s, voting rights scholarship emphasized increased attacks on the VRA and on antidilution litigation after 1965. These studies only occasionally used local cases to illustrate how the courts, Congress, and policy makers continued to focus on electoral-results standards and the spirit of equal opportunity. Hugh Davis Graham and Abigail Thernstrom were, for different reasons, much more critical of bureaucrats' involvement in the strengthening of the civil rights bills. On the initial voting rights/civil rights, policy-oriented studies, see Hugh Davis Graham, *The Civil Rights Era: Origins and Development of National Policy, 1960–1972* (New York: Oxford University Press, 1990); Lawson, *Black Ballots* and *In Pursuit of Power;* and Abigail Thernstrom, *Whose Votes Count? Affirmative Action and Minority Voting Rights* (Cambridge, Mass.: Harvard University Press, 1987).

18. On broad and comparative voting rights scholarship, see Jack Bass and Walter De Vries, *The Transformation of Southern Politics: Social Change and Political Consequence since 1945* (reprint, Athens: University of Georgia Press, 1995); Chandler Davidson and Bernard Grofman, eds., *Quiet Revolution in the South: The Impact of the Voting Rights Act, 1965–1990* (Princeton, N.J.: Princeton University Press, 1994); Kousser, *Colorblind Injustice;* Valelly, *Two Reconstructions;* and Bayard Rustin, "From Protest to Politics: The Future of the Civil Rights Movement," *Commentary* 39, no. 2 (1965), at https://www.commentarymagazine.com/articles/from-protest-to-politics-the-future-of-the-civil-rights-movement/. Karen Orren and Stephen Skowronek argue, "Political development is a durable shift in governing authority. By 'governing authority' we mean the exercise of control over persons or things that is designated and enforceable by the state. By 'shift' we have in mind a change in the locus or direction of control, resulting in a new distribution of authority among persons or organizations within the polity at large or between them and the counterparts outside. . . . [T]he term durable acknowledges that the distribution of authority is not fixed, . . . [and] any given historical instance must be regarded as contingent" (*The Search for American Political Development* [New York: Cambridge University Press, 2004], 123).

19. Thomas Sugrue, *Sweet Land of Liberty: The Forgotten Struggle for Civil Rights in the North* (New York: Random House, 2008), 357, 497. On Johnson's equality-of-results standard, see Lyndon B. Johnson, "To Fulfill These Rights," commencement address at Howard University, June 4, 1965, at http://www.lbjlib.utexas.edu/johnson/archives.hom/speeches.hom/650604.asp. The reemergence of legalistic strategies took place throughout the United States (Danielson, *After Freedom Summer,* 3). The Great Society created a framework that allowed blacks to formally contest institutional discrimination and racism. Extrainstitutional forms of uplift were often purposefully absorbed (or co-opted) by liberal political coalitions as a way to temper radicalism. The appeal of electoral

politics often consumed the struggle for basic civil and human rights. On black Americans and brokerage politics, see Devin Fergus, *Liberalism, Black Power, and the Making of American Politics, 1965–1980* (Athens: University of Georgia Press, 2009), 1–13; Hasan Kwame Jeffries, *Bloody Lowndes: Civil Rights and Black Power in Alabama's Black Belt* (New York: New York University Press, 2009); and Cedric Johnson, *Revolutionaries to Race Leaders: Black Power and the Making of African American Politics* (Minneapolis: University of Minnesota Press, 2007), xxiii. On the transition away from extrainstitutional forms of community mobilization, see Hayter, "From Intent to Effect," 538.

20. Matthew D. Lassiter, *The Silent Majority: Suburban Politics in the Sunbelt South* (Princeton, N.J.: Princeton University Press, 2006), 3. On struggle over white resistance to black voter power and municipal politics in the North, see Martha Biondi, *To Stand and Fight: The Struggle for Civil Rights in Postwar New York City* (Cambridge, Mass.: Harvard University Press, 2003); Matthew J. Countryman, *Up South: Civil Rights and Black Power in Philadelphia* (Philadelphia: University of Pennsylvania Press, 2006); Guian A. McKee, *The Problem of Jobs: Liberalism, Race, and Deindustrialization in Philadelphia* (Chicago: University of Chicago Press, 2008); and Sugrue, *Sweet Land of Liberty.* On the tension between black elected officials and white detractors, see Reed, *Stirrings in the Jug,* 95, and Peyton McCrary and Steven F. Lawson, "Race and Reapportionment, 1962: The Case of Georgia Senate Redistricting," *Journal of Policy History* 12, no. 3 (2000): 293.

21. Hall, "The Long Civil Rights Movement." On studies of Richmond's political history, see Michelle D. Byng, "Choice, Interests, and Black Political Actors: The Dilemmas of Inclusion," *Sociological Forum* 11, no. 1 (1996): 75–95; Michelle D. Byng, "The Clash of Government Structure and Racial Politics in *The City of Richmond v. J. A. Croson,*" *Race and Society* 1, no. 1 (1998): 77–91; Lassiter, *Silent Majority;* John V. Moeser and Rutledge M. Dennis, *The Politics of Annexation: Oligarchic Power in a Southern City* (Cambridge, Mass.: Schenkman, 1982); Christopher Silver, *Twentieth Century Richmond: Planning, Politics, and Race* (Knoxville: University of Tennessee Press, 1984); Christopher Silver and John V. Moeser, *The Separate City: Black Communities in the Urban South, 1940–1968* (Lexington: University Press of Kentucky, 1995); and Randolph and Tate, *Rights for a Season.*

22. On urban redevelopment across twentieth-century America, see Howard Gillette Jr., *Between Justice and Beauty: Race, Planning, and the Failure of Urban Policy in Washington, D.C.* (Philadelphia: University of Pennsylvania Press, 2006); Thomas W. Hanchett, *Sorting Out the New South City: Race, Class, and Urban Development in Charlotte, 1875–1975* (Chapel Hill: University of North Carolina Press, 1998); Arnold R. Hirsch, *Making the Second Ghetto: Race and Housing in Chicago, 1940–1960* (Chicago: University of Chicago Press, 1998); McKee, *The Problem of Jobs;* and Robert O. Self, *American Babylon: Race and the Struggle for*

Postwar Oakland (Princeton, N.J.: Princeton University Press, 2005). On the movement from tenements to housing projects and public-housing policies, see Edward G. Goetz, *New Deal Ruins: Race, Economic Justice, and Public Housing Policy* (Ithaca, N.Y.: Cornell University Press, 2013), and Campbell, *Richmond's Unhealed History*, 152–57. On the Richmond public schools, see James E. Ryan, *Five Miles Away, a World Apart: One City, Two Schools, and the Story of Educational Opportunity in Modern America* (Oxford: Oxford University Press, 2010).

23. On the legacy of urban renewal in America, see Lawrence J. Vale, *Purging the Poorest: Public Housing and the Design Politics of Twice-Cleared Communities* (Chicago: University of Chicago Press, 2013). Robert Moses was the preeminent urban planner of the twentieth century. On Robert Moses, see Samuel Zipp, *Manhattan Projects: The Rise and Fall of Urban Renewal in Cold War New York* (New York: Oxford University Press, 2010). For the poverty rate of blacks in Richmond, see U.S Bureau of the Census, "Poverty Status for Black Families" and "Educational Attainment for Black Population 25 Years Old and Over," Social Explorer, tables, http://www.socialexplorer.com/tables/C1970/R11289731, accessed November 11, 2016.

24. Reed, *Stirrings in the Jug*, 95. On how local governments are by tradition more constrained than their state and national counterparts and how informal arrangements between public and private groups are paramount, see Reed, *Stirrings in the Jug*, chap. 3, and Stone, *Regime Politics*, 1–3, 97.

25. Self, *American Babylon*, 4.

26. Stone, *Regime Politics*, ix–xii. On Dillon's Rule, see Gary T. Schwartz, "Reviewing and Revising Dillon's Rule," *University of Virginia Law School of Law, John M. Olin Foundation: Symposium on Law and Economics of Local Government*, 67, no. 3 (1991): 1025–32. On the rise of the Republican Party in Virginia and the South, see Earl Black and Merle Black, *The Rise of Southern Republicans* (Cambridge, Mass.: Belknap Press of Harvard University Press, 2002), 98–102. On the reddening of the South, see M. V. Hood III, Quentin Kidd, and Irwin L. Morris, *The Rational Southerner: Black Mobilization, Republican Growth, and the Partisan Transformation of the American South* (New York: Oxford University Press, 2012); Kevin Michael Kruse, *White Flight: Atlanta and the Making of Modern Conservatism* (Princeton, N.J.: Princeton University Press, 2005); and Lassiter, *Silent Majority*. On the moratorium on annexations, see Andrew V. Sorrell and Bruce A. Vlk, "Virginia's Never-Ending Moratorium on City–County Annexations," *Virginia News-Letter* 88, no. 1 (2012): 1–9. For the best account on transition from civil rights mayors to the black technocratic elite, see J. Phillip Thompson, *Double Trouble: Black Mayors, Black Communities, and the Call for a Deep Democracy* (New York: Oxford University Press, 2006). For more on the problems of black politics and dying cities, see Sugrue, *Sweet Land of Liberty*. On New Federalism and contemporary scholars' analysis of the Reagan rollbacks, see Demetrios Caraley and Yvette R. Schlussel, "Congress and Reagan's New Feder-

alism," *Publius* 16, no. 1 (1986): 49–79. On historical accounts of New Federalism, see James T. Patterson, *Restless Giant: The United States from Watergate to Bush v. Gore* (New York: Oxford University Press, 2005).

27. N. D. B. Connolly, "Black Appointees, Political Legitimacy, and the American Presidency," in *Recapturing the Oval Office: New Historical Approaches to the American Presidency,* ed. Brian Balogh and Bruce J. Schulman (Ithaca, N.Y.: Cornell University Press, 2015), 137; Sugrue, *Sweet Land of Liberty,* 357; Thompson, *Double Trouble,* 131–34; Eric S. Brown, *The Black Professional Middle Class: Race, Class, and Community in the Post–Civil Rights Era* (New York: Routledge, 2014), 121. On interracial politics, see Thompson, *Double Trouble,* chap. 4; Frank D. Gilliam Jr., "Exploring Minority Empowerment: Symbolic Politics, Governing Coalitions, and Traces of Political Style in Los Angeles," *American Journal of Political Science* 40, no. 1 (1966): 56–81; and McKee, *The Problem of Jobs.* On Coleman Young and Detroit, see Sugrue, *Sweet Land of Liberty,* 499–504.

28. Green, "Challenging the Civil Rights Narrative," 52–80, esp. 59 (on the "politics of protection"); Brown, *The Black Professional Middle Class,* 2. Ecological fallacy assumes that individual members of a group have the characteristics of the group at large. Despite the fact that no methodology exists to deduce how individuals might vote in elections or how representatives might vote when they get in office, policy makers assumed that African Americans would defend supposedly black agendas. On this issue, see Gary King, *A Solution to the Ecological Inference Problem: Reconstructing Individual Behavior from Aggregate Data* (Princeton, N.J.: Princeton University Press, 1997).

1. Strictly Political

1. *Richmond Afro-American & Planet* (hereafter, *Richmond Afro-American*), March 27, 1948, 1–2 (quote from Hill); Tova Andrea Wang, *The Politics of Voter Suppression: Defending and Expanding Americans' Right to Vote* (Ithaca, N.Y.: Cornell University Press, 2012), xv; Charles M. Payne, *I've Got the Light of Freedom: The Organizing Tradition and the Mississippi Freedom Struggle* (Berkeley: University of California Press, 1995), 3; J. Mills Thornton, *Dividing Lines: Municipal Politics and the Struggle for Civil Rights in Montgomery, Birmingham, and Selma* (Tuscaloosa: University of Alabama Press, 2002), 9.

2. Blair Murphy Kelley, *Right to Ride: Streetcar Boycotts and African American Citizenship in the Era of* Plessy v. Ferguson (Chapel Hill: University of North Carolina Press, 2010), 9, chap. 5 (on class tensions).

3. On interracial politics in Virginia before the General Assembly passed the Walton Act in 1894, see Jane Dailey, *Before Jim Crow: The Politics of Race in Postemancipation Virginia,* (Chapel Hill: University of North Carolina Press, 2000), 160–61. On Maggie L. Walker, see Gertrude Woodruff Marlowe, *A Right Wor-*

thy Grand Mission: Maggie Lena Walker and the Quest for Black Economic Empowerment (Washington, D.C.: Howard University Press, 2003). On John Mitchell, see Ann Field Alexander, *Race Man: The Rise and Fall of the "Fighting Editor," John Mitchell, Jr.* (Charlottesville: University of Virginia Press, 2002). On Virginia's culture of racist civility and gentility, see J. Douglas Smith, *Managing White Supremacy: Race, Politics, and Citizenship in Jim Crow Virginia* (Chapel Hill: University of North Carolina Press, 2002).

4. Kelley, *Right to Ride,* chaps. 5 and 6, esp. 118, 121–22; *Plessy v. Ferguson,* 163 U.S. 537 (1896).

5. *Buchanan v. Warley,* 245 U.S. 60 (1917); Amy E. Hillier, "Residential Security Maps and Neighborhood Appraisals: The Home Owners' Loan Corporation and the Case of Philadelphia," *Social Science History* 29, no. 2 (2005): 207–33; Redlining Richmond (webpage), http://dsl.richmond.edu/holc/pages/home; Jonathan K. Stubbs, "America's Enduring Legacy: Segregated Housing and Segregated Schools," *Minority Trial Lawyer,* Winter 2008, 1, 8.

6.Christopher Silver and John V. Moeser, *The Separate City: Black Communities in the Urban South, 1940–1968* (Lexington: University Press of Kentucky, 1995), 34; Christopher Silver, *Twentieth-Century Richmond: Planning, Politics, and Race* (Knoxville: University of Tennessee Press, 1984), 122. The formation of Jackson Ward turned out to be a Progressive Era ruse to dilute the voting power of recently emancipated freedpersons (U.S. Bureau of the Census, "Black Census Tracts, 1940," Social Explorer, table http://www.socialexplorer.com/tables/C1940TractDS/R11285355, accessed March 13, 2015).

7. Raymond Gavins, *The Perils and Prospects of Southern Black Leadership: Gordon Blaine Hancock, 1884–1970* (Durham, N.C.: Duke University Press, 1993), 5; Dwight Carter Holton, "Power to the People: The Struggle for Black Political Power in Richmond, Virginia," BA thesis, Brown University, 1987; Lewis A. Randolph and Gayle T. Tate, *Rights for a Season: The Politics of Race, Class, and Gender in Richmond, Virginia* (Knoxville: University of Tennessee Press, 2003), 75.

8. Raymond Gavins, "Gordon Blaine Hancock: A Black Profile from the New South," *Journal of Negro History* 59, no. 3 (1974): 214, 221–22.

9. Ibid., 214.

10. Smith, *Managing White Supremacy,* 4, 5, 8, 14, 248. On P. B. Young and civil rights in Norfolk, Virginia, see Earl Lewis, *In Their Own Interests: Race, Class, and Power in Twentieth-Century Norfolk, Virginia* (Berkeley: University of California Press, 1991).

11. David L. Lewis, *W. E. B. DuBois: The Fight for Equality and the American Century 1919–1963* (New York: Holt, 2000), 489; Gordon Blaine Hancock, "Southern Conference on Race Relations: Statement of Purpose," 6, 12–13, https://archive.org/details/southernconferen00sout. On the New Deal and African American aspirations, see Matthew J. Countryman, *Up South: Civil*

Rights and Black Power in Philadelphia (Philadelphia: University of Pennsylvania Press, 2006), 4–5.

12. *Baltimore Afro-American & Planet,* June 27, 1942, page number unavailable; Hancock, "Southern Conference on Race Relations Press Comments," 15–16; "The Conservative Course in Race Relations," editorial, *Richmond Times-Dispatch,* November 21, 1943, 48.

13. Robert B. Edgerton, *Hidden Heroism: Black Soldiers in America's Wars* (New York: Basic Books, 2002), 129; Pippa Holloway, *Sexuality, Politics, and Social Control in Virginia, 1920–1945* (Chapel Hill: University of North Carolina Press, 2006), 147.

14. John A. Hannah, *Voting: 1961 Commission on Civil Rights Report* (Washington, D.C.: U.S. Commission on Civil Rights, February 1962), 22; John A. Hannah, *Political Participation: A Study of the Participation by Negroes in the Electoral and Political Processes in 10 Southern States since Passage of the Voting Rights Act of 1965* (Washington, D.C.: U.S. Commission on Civil Rights, May 1968), 8; *Smith v. Allwright,* 321 U.S. 649 (1944); Charles E. Wilson, *To Secure These Rights: The Report of the President's Committee on Civil Rights* (New York: Simon and Schuster, 1947), 4.

15. Tomiko Brown-Nagin, *Courage to Dissent: Atlanta and the Long History of the Civil Rights Movement* (Oxford: Oxford University Press, 2011), 8; Julian M. Pleasants, *The Political Career of W. Kerr Scott: The Squire from Haw River* (Lexington: University Press of Kentucky, 2014), 4; Michael J. Klarman, "How Brown Changed Race Relations: The Backlash Thesis," *Journal of American History* 81, no. 1 (1994): 94; William H. Chafe, *Civilities and Civil Rights: Greensboro, North Carolina, and the Black Struggle for Freedom* (New York: Oxford University Press, 1980).

16. On William Byrd and Richmond's colonial history, see Midori Takagi, *Rearing Wolves to Our Own Destruction: Slavery in Richmond, Virginia, 1782–1865* (Charlottesville: University Press of Virginia, 1999), chap. 1. On the Byrd organization, see Ronald L. Heinemann, *Harry Byrd of Virginia* (Charlottesville: University Press of Virginia, 1996), 12, 44–45. Virginia lynched eighty-six blacks between 1880 and 1930 (twenty-three blacks were lynched between 1900 and 1930), which was a relatively low number compared to the number committed in other southern states. The predominantly coal-mining region of southwestern Virginia led the way. Scholars accredit higher lynching rates in the southwestern portion of the state to labor disputes. Whites lynched twelve African Americans in the commonwealth's Tidewater Region between 1880 and 1930. On lynching, see W. Fitzhugh Brundage, *Lynching in the New South: Georgia and Virginia, 1880–1930* (Urbana: University of Illinois Press, 1993), chap. 1. This region embraced elements of technological modernity in agricultural and industrial production during the first half of the twentieth century, and as labor-saving devices put people out of work and most African Americans migrated to the Tidewater's

cities, lynching decreased dramatically. In the early 1940s, the NAACP publicly confirmed that episodes of open violence were rarely the key barrier to black Virginians' upwardly mobile aspirations. See Benjamin Muse, *Virginia's Massive Resistance* (Glouchester, Mass.: Peter Smith, 1969), 3, and King Salim Khalfani, "Virginia Maintains a Disturbing Death Penalty Legacy," *Richmond Times-Dispatch,* January 29, 2012, at http://www.richmond.com/news/article_8fcf0eb4-24b7-5aa6-a16a-17c8f17e4968.html.

17. Abigail M. Thernstrom, *Whose Votes Count? Affirmative Action and Minority Voting Rights* (Cambridge, Mass.: Harvard University Press, 1987). On one hand, Virginia's poll tax was a panic reaction by white elites to the interracial politics of the late 1870s. William Mahone—a former Confederate general—and his interracial Readjuster Party sought to break the planter elite's ascendancy over state politics by promoting broad-based educational reforms. On the Readjuster Party, see Dailey, *Before Jim Crow;* Heinemann, *Harry Byrd of Virginia,* 12; and Robbins Gates, *The Making of Massive Resistance: Virginia's Politics of Public School Desegregation, 1954–1956* (Chapel Hill: University of North Carolina Press, 1964), 22. Although the issue of interracial education led to the Readjuster's demise in 1883, Virginia's policy makers passed literacy tests under the Walton Act of 1894 (Peter Rachleff, *Black Labor in Richmond, 1865–1890* [Urbana: University of Illinois Press, 1989], chaps. 6 and 12).

18. Randolph and Tate, *Rights for a Season,* 114; U.S. Bureau of the Census, *Census of Population and Housing* (Washington, D.C.: U.S. Bureau of the Census, 1930), and *Census of Population and Housing* (Washington, D.C.: U.S. Bureau of the Census, 1950); *The Crisis* (New York), February 1939, 55. First Baptist Church was also known for antebellum interracial cooperation. One of the church's most esteemed white preachers, Robert Ryland, had a reputation for being relatively moderate on the race question. Although Ryland strongly supported the slave system, he, in what was a revolutionary maneuver for the era, often allowed African Americans to preach from the *actual* pulpit. Ryland was also the first president of what is now the University of Richmond. The Commonwealth of Virginia mandated that white ministers lead all black assemblies, and the all-white First Baptist Church had authority over the African American church (Takagi, *Rearing Wolves to Our Own Destruction,* 104–5).

19. John V. Moeser and Rutledge M. Dennis, *The Politics of Annexation: Oligarchic Power in a Southern City* (Cambridge, Mass.: Schenkman, 1982), 32.

20. *Richmond Times-Dispatch,* November 1947, 1; Silver, *Twentieth Century Richmond,* 178–79.

21. *Richmond Afro-American,* March 27, 1948, 1; *Richmond Times-Dispatch,* April 18, 1948, 1. Oliver Hill and Spotswood Robinson, according to Richard Kluger, resolved to make Virginia pay the true price of genuinely unequal and still separate institutions. Both men relentlessly pursued litigation aimed at chipping away at Jim Crow by equalizing black teachers' salaries. These salaries

were monumentally lower than the salaries for their white counterparts despite the fact that many African American teachers had multiple degrees (*Simple Justice: The History of* Brown v. Board of Education *and Black America's Struggle for Equality* [New York: Vintage, 2004], 472).

22. *Richmond Afro-American,* June 12, 1984, 1, and June 19, 1948, 1.

23. *Brown v. Board of Education of Topeka,* 347 U.S. 483 (1954); *Plessy v. Ferguson,* at 537.

24. James Latimer, "Stanley Gets Big Array of Segregation Powers: School Package Contains More Than Governor Asked," *Richmond Times-Dispatch,* September, 1956, 1. On the Gray Plan, see Robert A. Pratt, *The Color of Their Skin: Education and Race in Richmond, Virginia, 1954–1989* (Charlottesville: University Press of Virginia, 1993), 4–6.

25. Silver, *Twentieth-Century Richmond,* 122; Pratt, *Color of Their Skin,* 4; *Brown v. Board of Education (II),* 349 U.S. 294 (1955). The commonwealth also began to pay the price for policies that codified scientific racism and the eugenics movement during the 1920s. The Racial Integrity Act of 1924 (Senate Bill 219) and the Sterilization Act of 1924 (Senate Bill 281) dictated the types of services Virginians did and did not provide to the mentally ill and physically impaired. These laws, on top of prohibiting interracial marriage, used mental-health facilities to sterilize and quarantine scores of Virginians. By the mid-1950s, the Old Dominion's mental- and physical-health facilities were in utter disarray. On Virginia's legacy of eugenics and scientific racism, see Smith, *Managing White Supremacy,* 87–89, and Heinemann, *Harry Byrd of Virginia,* 317–18.

26. Matthew D. Lassiter, *The Silent Majority: Suburban Politics in the Sunbelt South* (Princeton, N.J.: Princeton University Press, 2006), 32; *Richmond News-Leader,* February 2, 1955, 50.

27. James Latimer, "Anti-Integration Course Is Charted by Assembly: Accord on Placement Plan Ends Session at 2:11 A.M.," *Richmond Times-Dispatch,* September 22, 1956, 1, 2.

28. *Richmond Times-Dispatch,* September 22, 1956, 1. On the anti-NAACP laws throughout the South, see Richard Valelly, *The Two Reconstructions: The Struggle for Black Enfranchisement* (Chicago: University of Chicago Press, 2004), 180–81.

29. Smith, *Managing White Supremacy,* 2–5; *Richmond Afro-American,* August 11, 1951, 2, and June 14, 1952, 1.

30. Andrew Buni, *The Negro in Virginia Politics, 1902–1965* (Charlottesville: University Press of Virginia, 1967), 125. The election in 1952 turned into a veritable showdown between Ransome and an insurance salesman, David C. Deans. For Richmond's African Americans during the early 1950s, one of the most important issues concerning the community was the paradox between an integrated army in Korea and segregated public schools at home. Although neither Deans nor Ransome won a seat on the city council in 1952, three factors

contributed to the eventual demise of Richmond's gradualist ministers before the *Brown* decision: Hill endorsed Dean; the *Richmond Afro-American* smeared Ransome; and Ransome was accused of receiving money from white racial conservatives during this campaign (Randolph and Tate, *Rights for a Season,*131; *Richmond Times-Dispatch,* June 8, 1952, 4).

31. Kluger, *Simple Justice,* 475; Jill Ogline Titus, Brown*'s Battleground: Students, Segregationists, and the Struggle for Justice in Prince Edward County, Virginia* (Chapel Hill: University of North Carolina Press, 2011), 1; *Richmond Afro-American,* August 19, 1950, 1–2, and October 14, 1951, 2. On how *Dorothy E. Davis v. County School Board of Prince Edward County* (103 F. Supp. 337 [1952]) became part of *Brown,* see Titus, Brown*'s Battleground.*

32. Steven F. Lawson, *Running for Freedom: Civil Rights and Black Politics in America since 1941* (New York: Wiley, 2014), 49; Valelly, *Two Reconstructions,* 179; Harry Nash, "NAACP Speaker Attacks Negroes Refusing to Join," *Richmond Times-Dispatch,* October 5, 1957, 3. On Virginia's fight against the Stanley and Gray Plans, see Pratt, *Color of Their Skin,* 31–39. On the NAACP and the Supreme Court's fight against anti-NAACP laws, see Lucas A. Powe Jr., *The Warren Court and American Politics* (Cambridge, Mass.: Belknap Press of Harvard University Press, 2000).

33. Julian Hayter, "Strictly Political: The Rise of Black Political Participation in Richmond, Virginia, 1960–1970," MA thesis, University of Virginia, 2005; William A. Thornton, "History of the Crusade: Report of the Historian: 1953–1995, " Richmond Crusade for Voters Collection, 1955–1995, M306, Cabell Black Collection, M306, James Branch Cabell Library, Virginia Commonwealth University, Richmond; Moeser and Dennis, *Politics of Annexation,* 34–35; *Richmond Times-Dispatch,* March 7, 1966, 12; Caroline Emmons, "A Tremendous Job to Be Done: African American Women in the Virginia Civil Rights Movement," in *Southern Black Women in the Modern Civil Rights Movement,* ed. Bruce A. Glasrud and Merline Pitre (College Station: Texas A&M University Press, 2013), 22–23; Randolph and Tate, *Rights for a Season,* 154, 156, 158. Armstrong High School was, in fact, the first high school in Richmond exclusively set aside for African Americans. It was located on Richmond's lower east side, a predominantly black neighborhood.

34. Louise Ellyson, "The Negro Woman in Virginia: Women's Attitudes Range from Tolerance to Anger," *Richmond Times-Dispatch,* November 24, 1965, 21; Emmons, "A Tremendous Job to Be Done," 22.

35. *Richmond Times-Dispatch,* March 7, 1966, 12; Charles W. McKinney Jr., "Finding Fannie Corbett: Black Women, Gender, and the 'Politics of Protection,'" in *Civil Rights History from the Ground Up,* ed. Emilye Crosby (Athens: University of Georgia Press, 2011), 83; Emmons, "A Tremendous Job to Be Done," 22. In a series of pieces about black women in Virginia, Louise Ellyson of the *Richmond Times-Dispatch* reported that 54 percent of Richmond's women

were farm laborers, and another 41 percent were service workers. Forty-four percent of black women in 1960 had less than eight years of formal education. See Louise Ellyson, "The Negro Women in Virginia: Many Changes Are Reflected in Jobs, Schools, and Voting," *Richmond Times-Dispatch,* November 21, 1965, 4H, and "The Negro Women in Virginia: Middle Class Expands Rapidly," *Richmond Times-Dispatch,* November 23, 1965, 23.

36. Randolph and Tate, *Rights for a Season,* 143; William Ferguson Reid, interviewed by the author, Richmond, April 1, 2005; Thornton, "History of the Crusade"; Julian Maxwell Hayter, "From Intent to Effect: Richmond, Virginia, and the Protracted Struggle for Voting Rights, 1965–1977," *Journal of Policy History* 26, no. 4 (2014): 540; Robert A. Rankin, "The Richmond Crusade for Voters: The Quest for Black Power," *University of Virginia Newsletter* 51, no. 1 (1974): 1–7.

37. Rankin, "Richmond Crusade for Voters," 1–7.

38. Silver and Moeser, *Separate City,* 74; *Richmond Afro-American,* February 25, 1961, 1–2, February 11, 1962, 1, and February 4, 1961, 1; James Latimer, "Negro Voters' Ranks Here Increase 25%: Year's Tally Shows Drop in Whites," *Richmond Times-Dispatch,* June 14, 1959, 25.

39. Thomas J. Sugrue, *Sweet Land of Liberty: The Forgotten Struggle for Civil Rights in the North* (New York: Random House, 2008), 357.

40. Bracey and Meier, *Supplement to Part 4, Voting Rights,* Papers of the NAACP, Group III, Box 266. On the Civil Rights Act of 1957 and its shortcomings, see Valelly, *Two Reconstructions,* 187–88.

41. Bracey and Meier, *Supplement to Part 4, Voting Rights,* Papers of the NAACP, Group III, Box 266.

42. Valelly, *Two Reconstructions,* 177–78; Hannah, *Voting,* 22; Brooks's report is in Bracey and Meier, *Supplement to Part 4, Voting Rights,* Papers of the NAACP, Folders 1–3. Brooks initiated or built on various voting rights organizations throughout the South. He helped locals organize a registration drive in Memphis, Tennessee, between May 9 and July 18, 1958. The drive, under the name "Volunteer Committee of Memphis," raised the number of black registrants from 43,000 to 56,476. The Memphis state branch of the NAACP created a permanent coordinating group, and local organizations were an integral part of the movement—they had registered thousands of voters before Brooks's arrival. Memphis's African Americans nearly elected an African American attorney, Russell B. Sugarmon, to the position of public-works commissioner. Sugarmon was the first African American to run for a major city office in Memphis in the twentieth century (Bracey and Meier, *Supplement to Part 4, Voting Rights,* Papers of the NAACP, Folders 1–3).

43. Gloster B. Current, "Extend the Voting Rights Act: We Won't Go Back," *The Crisis,* February 1982, 13; Bracey and Meier, *Supplement to Part 4, Voting Rights,* Papers of the NAACP, Folders 1, 3, and 5. In 1959, John Stewart was elected to the Durham City Council; voters elected J. O. Falls to the Gastonia

City Council; Felton J. Capel garnered enough votes to win a seat on the Pine City Council; Rev. R. Manley was elected to the Chapel Hill Board of Education; Rev. W. R. Crawford became alderman of Winston-Salem; Waldo Falkener was elected to the Greensboro City Council; and John Stewart, who had won a city council seat in Durham in 1951, was reelected in 1957.

44. Hannah, *Voting*, 22, also 67–68 and 102–3 on registration purges; Valelly, *Two Reconstructions*, 185; Hugh Davis Graham, *Civil Rights and the Presidency: Race and Gender in American Politics, 1960–1972* (New York: Oxford University Press, 1992), 92.

45. Michael Harrington, *The Other America: Poverty in the United States* (New York: Macmillan, 1962), 63, 65; John A. Hannah, *Mobility in the Negro Community* (Washington, D.C.: U.S. Commission on Civil Rights, 1968), 5–6; U.S. Bureau of the Census, "Household Income (Tracts Only), 1960," Social Explorer, table, http://www.socialexplorer.com/tables/C1960TractDS/R11289393, accessed November 20, 2016; U.S. Bureau of the Census, *Census of Population and Housing* (Washington, D.C.: U.S. Bureau of the Census, 1960); Silver, *Twentieth-Century Richmond*, 122.

46. Hannah, *Mobility in the Negro Community*, 5–6; Richmond Annexation Files, 1942–1976, M183, Cabell Black Collection, M306; U.S. Bureau of the Census, *Census of Population and Housing* (1960); Silver, *Twentieth-Century Richmond*, 122.

47. *Richmond Times-Dispatch*, December 29, 1985, A11, and February 22, 1955, 1; John Murden, "High on the Hill," *Style Weekly*, September 24, 2013; Robert M. Andrews, "Movement for Restoration of Houses in Church Hill is Gaining Momentum," *Richmond Times-Dispatch*, January 26, 1958, 56; Michael Q. Rogers, "Remembering the Controversy of the Richmond-Petersburg Turnpike: Politics, Rhetoric, and Visions of Progress," senior thesis, University of Richmond, 2011.

48. Silver and Moeser, *Separate City*, 212; Benjamin P. Campbell, *Richmond's Unhealed History* (Richmond, Va.: Brandylane, 2012), 152–57.

49. All quotes from Ed Grimsley, "Clearing of Slums Involves Economics and Politics," *Richmond Times-Dispatch*, January 11, 1959, 25.

50. Harry Kollatz Jr., "The Curve around the Station," *Richmond Magazine*, December 23, 2013, at http://richmondmagazine.com/news/richmond-history/I-95-cross-into-Shockoe/.

51. William L. Martin and J. E. Buchholtz, "Annexation—Virginia's Dilemma," *Washington and Lee Law Review* 24, no. 2 (1967): 241–67 (on Virginia's county and city divide and Dillon's Rule); L. M. Wright Jr., "Route Is Fixed for Intercity Superhighway: Toll Road Will Cut in Half Driving Time on Stretch," *Richmond Times-Dispatch*, August 2, 1955, 1; Kollatz, "The Curve around the Station."

52. Ed Grimsley, "Land, Money Lacking: Problems Delay Anti-slum Efforts," *Richmond Times-Dispatch*, March 17, 1959, 1–2; U.S. Bureau of the Census, report, 1960, Richmond Annexation Files, 1942–1973, M183, Cabell

Black Collection, M306; Campbell, *Richmond's Unhealed History*, 152–57. The process of doubling-up generally meant that residents, homeowners, and landlords transformed single-family homes into multiple-family homes—for example, converting large and moderate-size homes into duplexes or multiple-dwelling apartments (Selden Richardson, *Built by Blacks: African American Architecture and Neighborhoods in Richmond* [Charleston, S.C.: History Press, 2008], 114).

53. Silver, *Twentieth-Century Richmond*, 195–96; *Richmond Times-Dispatch*, September 5, 1959, 1.

54. Campbell, *Richmond's Unhealed History*, 157; Countryman, *Up South*, 51–54; Tracy Elaine K'Meyer, *Civil Rights in the Gateway to the South: Louisville, Kentucky, 1945–1980* (Lexington: University Press of Kentucky, 2009), chap. 2; Thomas J. Sugrue, *Origins of the Urban Crisis: Race and Inequality in Postwar Detroit* (Princeton, N.J.: Princeton University Press, 2005), chap. 2.

55. Thornton, "History of the Crusade"; *Richmond Afro-American*, June 11, 1960, 1, January 1, 1960, 1, and April 30, 1960, 1; Moeser and Dennis, *Politics of Annexation*, 45–46.

56. *Richmond Afro-American*, June 11, 1960, 1, 6 (including quote from Thornton).

57. Richard Wilson, "Crusade for Voters Estimates 8,500 Negroes Voted Tuesday," *Richmond Times-Dispatch*, June 16, 1960, 1; *Richmond Afro-American*, June 18, 1960, 1; Silver and Moeser, *Separate City*, 75.

58. *Richmond Afro-American*, April 2, 1962, 1, and June 2, 1962, 1–2.

59. *Richmond Afro-American*, June 2, 1962, 1–2.

60. *Richmond Afro-American*, September 17, 1964, 1; June 6, 1964, 1–2; and February 23, 1963, 1.

61. *Richmond Afro-American*, March 14, 1964, 1–2; Ed Grimsley, "Negroes to Back Full Slate," *Richmond Times-Dispatch*, March 4, 1964, 1. Wilder initially stated that he intended to work in combination with the Crusade, but Eggleston and Charity eventually criticized Crusaders because the latter failed to endorse their campaigns.

62. Silver and Moeser, *Separate City*, 75; Randolph and Tate, *Rights for a Season*, 219; Moeser and Dennis, *Politics of Annexation*, 48–49.

63. Thornton, "History of the Crusade."

64. Bracey and Meier, *Supplement to Part 4, Voting Rights*, Papers of the NAACP, Group III, Box, A265, p. 59; Pratt, *Color of Their Skin*, 36; *Richmond Afro-American*, June 13, 1964, 1; *Richmond Times-Dispatch*, June 10, 1964, 1, 4.

2. Systematically Done In

Portions of this chapter are drawn from Julian Maxwell Hayter, "From Intent to Effect: Richmond, Virginia, and the Protracted Struggle for Voting Rights, 1965–1977," *Journal of Policy History* 26, no. 4 (2014): 534–67.

1. "The Vice Mayor of Richmond: Winfred Mundle, Insurance Executive Scored a Major Breakthrough in Dixie," *Ebony*, November 1966, 176–77.

2. On the Great Society, see Lyndon B. Johnson, "To Fulfill These Rights," commencement address at Howard University, June 4, 1965, at http://www.lbjlib.utexas.edu/johnson/archives.hom/speeches.hom/650604.asp. On the ways white workers thought about the New Deal and the ushering in of an era of moral capitalism, see Lizabeth Cohen, *Making a New Deal: Industrial Workers in Chicago, 1919–1939* (Cambridge: Cambridge University Press, 1990). On the ways the New Deal actually raised whites' standard of living, see Alan Brinkley, *The End of Reform: New Deal Liberalism in Recession and War* (New York: Vintage, 1996).

3. The VRA did not emerge out of thin air. Martin Luther King Jr. and the SCLC's voter registration demonstration in Selma, Alabama, provided the urgency Washington needed to push a voting rights bill through Congress. However, the heart of the VRA's provisions emerged from the Commission on Civil Rights data-collection efforts and the hundreds of voter registration drives that emerged in the South before Selma. Avoiding violence was central to the Kennedy administration's approach to the civil rights movement. Less is known (outside of a handful of voting rights scholars), however, about Kennedy's attempts to mollify the Congress for Racial Equality's direct-action tactics by proposing mass voter registration drives throughout the South. Referred to by voting rights experts as the "voter registration pact of 1961," the Kennedy administration helped pump millions of dollars into southern voter registration drives after 1961. On Selma, see David J. Garrow, *Protest at Selma: Martin Luther King, Jr., and the Voting Rights Act of 1965,* rev. ed. (New Haven, Conn.: Yale University Press, 2015). On Kennedy's response to the Freedom Rides, see David Niven, *The Politics of Injustice: The Kennedys, the Freedom Rides, and the Electoral Consequences of a Moral Compromise* (Knoxville: University of Tennessee Press, 2003). On the Voter Education Project, see Claybourne Carson King's Papers Project at http://mlk-kpp01.stanford.edu/index.php/encyclopedia/encyclopedia/enc_voter_education_project/. On the Civil Rights Acts of 1957 and 1960, see Frank Parker, *Black Votes Count: Political Empowerment in Mississippi after 1965* (Chapel Hill: University of North Carolina Press, 1990), and Richard M. Valelly, *The Two Reconstructions: The Struggle for Black Enfranchisement* (Chicago: University Chicago Press, 2004), 185–87, 190.

4. Lyndon Johnson, "And We Shall Overcome," speech before Congress on voting rights, March 15, 1965, at http://historymatters.gmu.edu/d/6336/; *Richmond Times-Dispatch,* August 8, 1965, 19.

5. Abigail M. Thernstrom, *Whose Votes Count? Affirmative Action and Minority Voting Rights* (Cambridge, Mass.: Harvard University Press, 1987), 15; Hugh Davis Graham, *Civil Rights and the Presidency: Race and Gender in American Politics, 1960–1972* (New York: Oxford University Press, 1992), 90–91. On

the interworkings of Congress and the passing of the VRA, see Steven F. Lawson, *Black Ballots: Voting Rights in the South, 1944–1969* (New York: Columbia University Press, 1976), 307–21.

6. Steven F. Lawson, *Running for Freedom: Civil Rights and Black Politics since 1941* (New York: Wiley, 2014), 94; Charles S. Bullock III, Ronald Keith Gaddie, and Justin J. Wert, eds., *The Rise and Fall of the Voting Rights Act* (Norman: University of Oklahoma Press, 2016), 18–20. The VRA covered Alabama, Alaska, Arizona, Georgia, Louisiana, Mississippi, South Carolina, Texas, and Virginia.

7. All figures are from John Hannah, *Political Participation: A Study of the Participation by Negroes in the Electoral and Political Processes in 10 Southern States since Passage of the Voting Rights Act of 1965* (Washington, D.C.: U.S. Commission on Civil Rights, May 1968), 12–15.

8. Bayard Rustin, "From Protest to Politics: The Future of the Civil Rights Movement," *Commentary* 39, no. 2 (1965), at https://www.commentary-magazine.com/articles/from-protest-to-politics-the-future-of-the-civil-rights-movement/; Dale M. Brumfield, *Richmond Independent Press: A History of the Underground Zine Scene* (Charleston, S.C.: History Press, 2013), 33; W. Avon Drake and Robert D. Holsworth, *Affirmative Action and the Stalled Quest for Black Progress* (Urbana: University of Illinois Press, 1996), 48. Although Boone was eventually promoted to vice president and editor of all thirteen papers put out by the Afro-American Company, he stayed with Richmond's edition until the early 1980s.

9. *Richmond Afro-American*, March 27, 1965, 4, and August 14, 1965, 1.

10. William S. White, "Much in Voting Act Up to White Moderates," *Richmond Times-Dispatch*, August 14, 1965, 7.

11. *Richmond Times-Dispatch*, August 15, 1965, 38; Kevin Michael Kruse, *White Flight: Atlanta and the Making of Modern Conservatism* (Princeton, N.J.: Princeton University Press, 2005), 9; Chandler Davidson and Bernard Grofman, *Quiet Revolution in the South: The Impact of the Voting Rights Act, 1965–1990* (Princeton, N.J.: Princeton University Press, 1994), 276; "Virginia to Challenge Voting Act in Court," *Richmond Times-Dispatch*, August 13, 1965, 1.

12. In *South Carolina v. Katzenbach* (383 U.S. 301 [1966]), Chief Justice Warren argued that the VRA was a legitimate response to the "insidious and pervasive evil" forces of disenfranchisement (at 310).

13. *Harper v. Virginia Board of Elections*, 383 U.S. 663 (1966), at 383; Lucas A. Powe, Jr., *The Warren Court and American Politics* (Cambridge, Mass.: Belknap Press of Harvard University, 2000), 265–66.

14. *Richmond Times-Dispatch*, March 25, 1966, 1; *Richmond Afro-American*, April 2, 1966, 1, 2, and April 9, 1966, 1; John V. Moeser and Rutledge M. Dennis, *The Politics of Annexation: Oligarchic Power in a Southern City* (Cambridge, Mass.: Schenckman, 1982), 60.

15. *Richmond Times-Dispatch,* date unknown; March 27, 1966, 38; and March 25, 1966, 1.

16. James E. Ryan, *Five Miles Away, a World Apart: One City, Two Schools, and the Story of Educational Opportunity in Modern America* (New York: Oxford University Press, 2010), 21–23; *Green v. County School Board of New Kent County,* 391 U.S. 430 (1968); *Reynolds v. Sims,* 377 U.S. 533 (1964). On the demise of the Byrd machine, see Ronald L. Heinemann, *Harry Byrd of Virginia* (Charlottesville: University Press of Virginia, 1996), 409–10. By 1968, white flight and the rise of private schools had taken its toll on RPS—the system was almost entirely African American in 1968.

17. Hannah, *Political Participation,* 13; Earl Black and Merle Black, *The Rise of Southern Republicans* (Cambridge, Mass.: Belknap Press of Harvard University Press, 2002), 98–102 (on the rise of antiestablishment Democrats and the rise of Virginia's Republican Party); James Kilpatrick, "Political Changes: Virginia Election Shows Dixie Politicians' Dilemma," *Richmond News-Leader,* November 12, 1965, page number unavailable.

18. Julian Maxwell Hayter, "From Intent to Effect: Richmond, Virginia, and the Protracted Struggle for Voting Rights, 1965–1977," *Journal of Policy History* 26, no. 4 (2014): 539; Hannah, *Political Participation,* 19–32.

19. Moeser and Dennis, *Politics of Annexation,* 60.

20. Hayter, "From Intent to Effect," 542–43.

21. *Richmond City Charter and Staggered Terms,* Richmond Annexation Files, 1942–1976, M183, Cabell Black Collection, M306, James Branch Cabell Library, Virginia Commonwealth University, Richmond; *Richmond Times-Dispatch,* January 29, 1966, 3.

22. *Richmond Times-Dispatch,* January 10, 1966, 10; RF campaign memo, Eleanor P. Sheppard Papers, 1924–1978, M277, Cabell Black Collection, M306; *Richmond News-Leader,* May 31, 1966, in Richmond Annexation Files, 1942–1976, M183, Cabell Black Collection, M306.

23. Moeser and Dennis, *Politics of Annexation,* 62; *Richmond Afro-American,* April 9, 1966, 1. Julian Sargeant Reynolds burst onto Virginia's and Richmond's political scene in 1965 after being elected to the state legislature. Reynolds, in his late twenties, represented Richmond's Thirty-Ninth District and the state Senate. Nearly half a million Virginians elected Reynolds lieutenant governor in 1969. While in the General Assembly, Reynolds helped establish Virginia's community colleges system. While lieutenant governor at the age of thirty-four, he died suddenly of a brain tumor in 1971. On Reynolds, see Andrew P. Miller, "J. Sargeant Reynolds: What He Was Not, Not What He Might Have Been," *Virginia Law Review* 57, no. 8 (1971): 1312–14, and Michael P. Gleason and Andrew McCutcheon, *Sarge Reynolds: In the Time of His Life* (Gwynn, Va.: Gleason, 1996).

24. *Richmond Times-Dispatch,* September 28, 1965, 16; *Ebony,* November 1966, 177.

25. *Richmond News-Leader,* June 17, 1966, page number unavailable; Moeser and Dennis, *Politics of Annexation,* 67. In 1966, Crusaders believed that allowing RF to co-opt two black candidates was a sign of weakness and might compromise their legitimacy with Richmond's black electorate. So they supported Mundle and Cephas to keep it from looking as if RF had snatched their candidates.

26. *Richmond Times-Dispatch,* June 15, 1966, 22.

27. *Richmond Afro-American,* June 17, 1966, 2; Leonard B. Moore, *Carl B. Stokes and the Rise of Black Political Power* (Urbana: University of Illinois Press, 2003), 1, see also chap. 4. On Julian Bond, white resistance to his election, his criticism of the war in Vietnam, and the Supreme Court's role in resolving the conflict, see Laughlin McDonald, *A Voting Rights Odyssey: Black Enfranchisement in Georgia* (Cambridge: Cambridge University Press, 2003); *Bond v. Floyd,* 385 U.S. 116 (1966); and William H. Chafe, *Civilities and Civil Rights: Greensboro, North Carolina, and the Black Struggle for Freedom* (New York: Oxford University Press, 1980), 214. Thirty-eight percent of the whites who participated in the November 1967 Richmond City Council election voted for William Reid (*Richmond Afro-American,* November 11, 1967, 2; see also Julian Maxwell Hayter, "Strictly Political: The Rise of Black Political Participation in Richmond, Virginia, 1960–1970," MA thesis, University of Virginia, 2005). H. E. Fountleroy won a council seat in Petersburg, and Rev. Lawrence A. Davie won a seat at Fredericksburg (*Richmond Afro-American,* June 25, 1966, 1).

28. Lawson, *Running for Freedom,* 119–29.

29. Jim Nolan and Andrew Cain, "Marsh Retiring After 22 Years in Virginia Senate," *Richmond Times-Dispatch,* July 1, 2014, http://www.richmond.com/news/virginia/article_b8132b0e-0146-11e4-8a5f-0017a43b2370.html; Mark V. Tushnet, *The NAACP's Legal Strategy against Segregated Education, 1925–1950* (Chapel Hill: University of North Carolina Press, 1987), 34–49; *Quarles v. Philip Morris, Inc.,* 279 F.Supp. 505 (1968); *Brewer v. School Board of City of Norfolk,* 397 F.2d 37 (1968); *Richmond Times-Dispatch,* July 25, 1966, 5. Marsh litigated more than twenty-five school cases after the *Brewer* decision.

30. *Richmond News-Leader,* June 15, 1969, 10.

31. Elliot M. Rudwick, "The Negro Policeman in the South," *Journal of Criminal Law, Criminology, and Police Science* 51, no. 2 (1960): 275; *Richmond Afro-American,* August 6, 1966, 1, and August 13, 1966, 7.

32. *Richmond Afro-American,* September 17, 1966, 1–2; *Richmond Times-Dispatch,* July 11, 1966, 1.

33. *Richmond Afro-American,* October 1, 1966, 1–2.

34. Christopher Silver, *Twentieth-Century Richmond: Planning, Politics, and Race* (Knoxville: University of Tennessee Press, 1984), 287; James E. Davis, "Expressway Plan Routes Disclosed: Cost Estimated at $95 Million," *Richmond Times-Dispatch,* October 23, 1966, 1, 6. For more on the plan and engineering

construction firm that designed the expressway system—Howard, Needles, Tommen, and Bergendoff—and the document on the expressway that the firm produced, see Eleanor P. Sheppard Papers, M277, Cabell Black Collection, M306.

35. *Richmond News-Leader,* December 10, 1966, 1; *Richmond Times-Dispatch,* November 12, 1966, 1, 3. The Downtown Expressway also happened at the same time the Community Renewal Program began to place greater emphasis on so-called neighborhood conservation and slum clearance. In 1966, Richmond unveiled a citywide housing and neighborhood assault on slums that coincided with Washington's growing scrutiny of urban-renewal efforts on a national scale. On urban renewal in Richmond, see Silver, *Twentieth-Century Richmond,* 285–88.

36. U.S. Bureau of the Census, "Annual Income, Property Values, and Population," Social Explorer, table, http://www.socialexplorer.com/tables/C1960TractDS/R11288116, accessed March 11, 2015; *Richmond News-Leader,* December 2, 1966, page number unavailable; *Richmond Afro-American,* December 3, 1966, 2, 6, and December 10, 1966, page number unavailable.

37. *Richmond Afro-American,* August 12, 1967, 1–2; *Richmond Times-Dispatch,* August 6, 1967, 1, and June 29, 1980, B2; *Richmond News-Leader,* April 24, 1966, page number unavailable.

38. Matthew D. Lassiter, *The Silent Majority: Suburban Politics in the Sunbelt South* (Princeton, N.J.: Princeton University Press, 2006), 289; Andrew V. Sorrell and Bruce A. Vlk, "Virginia's Never-Ending Moratorium on City–County Annexations," *Virginia News-Letter* 88, no. 1 (2012): 1–2; U.S. Bureau of the Census, *Census of Population and Housing* (Washington, D.C.: U.S. Bureau of the Census, 1950), *Census of Population and Housing* (Washington, D.C.: U.S. Bureau of the Census, 1960), and *Census of Population and Housing* (Washington, D.C.: U.S. Bureau of the Census, 1970). Like Chesterfield County in the late 1960s and early 1970s, Henrico County—located on the city's northern boundaries—resisted annexation. It appealed Richmond's petition (Moeser and Dennis, *Politics of Annexation,* 52–53).

39. Moeser and Dennis, *Politics of Annexation,* 70–76.

40. Ibid.; *Richmond Afro-American,* June 17, 1967, 2, and February 4, 1967, 2.

41. *Richmond Afro-American,* February 11, 1966, 3; February 18, 1967, 3; and July 8, 1968, 4.

42. *Richmond Times-Dispatch,* July 19, 1966, 1, 4; *Richmond Afro-American,* June 17, 1967, 1.

43. Thomas Jackson, *From Civil Rights to Human Rights: Martin Luther King, Jr., and the Struggle for Economic Justice* (Philadelphia: University of Pennsylvania Press, 2007); *Milwaukee Star,* March 30, 1968, 13; *City of Richmond v. United States,* 422 U.S. 358 (1975), Plaintiff's Exhibit 5(b), at 106–7; *Richmond Times-Dispatch,* June 6, 1968, 27, and June 9, 1968, 1; Moeser and Den-

nis, *Politics of Annexation*, 81. On the Poor People's Campaign, see Amy Nathan Wright, "The 1968 Poor People's Campaign, Marks, Mississippi, and the Mule Train: Fighting Poverty Locally, Representing Power Nationally," in *Civil Rights History from the Ground Up: Local Struggles, a National Movement*, ed. Emilye Crosby (Athens: University of Georgia Press, 2011), 109–46.

44. *Richmond Times-Dispatch*, April 13, 1968, 1; Robert Holland, "City Council Candidates Are Queried on Main Issues," *Richmond Times-Dispatch*, May 14, 1968, 19.

45. Moeser and Dennis, *Politics of Annexation*, 81–82; *Richmond Afro-American*, June 8, 1968, 5.

46. *City of Richmond v. United States*, Plaintiff's Exhibit 5(b), at 70; *Richmond Afro-American*, June 22, 1968, 1.

47. N. D. B. Connolly, "Black Appointees, Political Legitimacy, and the American Presidency," in *Recapturing the Oval Office: New Historical Approaches to the American Presidency*, ed. Brian Balogh and Bruce J. Schulman (Ithaca, N.Y.: Cornell University Press, 2015), 137; *Richmond Afro-American*, July 9, 1966, 1; *Ebony*, November 1966, 176–83.

48. Graham, *Civil Rights and the Presidency*, 99; *Richmond Afro-American*, October 1, 1966, 1–2; Thomas J. Sugrue, *Sweet Land of Liberty: The Forgotten Struggle for Civil Rights in the North* (New York: Random House, 2008), 325–26.

49. William H. Chafe, *The Unfinished Journey: America since World War II* (New York: Oxford University Press, 1999), 343, 379; William S. White, "The Poor March Is a Fraud," *Richmond Times-Dispatch*, May 20, 1968, 14.

50. Hannah, *Political Participation*, 19; Moeser and Dennis, *Politics of Annexation*, 77, 82; Connolly, "Black Appointees," 137.

51. William L. Van Deburg, *New Day in Babylon: The Black Power Movement and American Culture, 1965–1975* (Chicago: University of Chicago Press, 1992), 65; *Richmond Times-Dispatch*, February 23, 1960, 4, and February 28, 1960, 4; Yohuru Williams, *Rethinking the Black Freedom Movement* (New York: Routledge, Taylor & Francis Group, 2015). On Charles Sherrod, see Peter Wallenstein, *Blue Laws and Black Codes: Conflict, Courts, and Change in Twentieth Century Virginia* (Charlottesville: University of Virginia Press, 2004) and "Excesses in Rights Drive Are Listed by U.S. Official," *Richmond Times-Dispatch*, August 22, 1965, 13.

52. Connolly, "Black Appointees," 137; *Richmond News-Leader*, April 24, 1966, page number unavailable; *Richmond Afro-American*, October 1, 1966, 5. Pluralists concentrated their attention on what William L. Van DeBurg calls "community control." These proponents of Black Power sought to use educational, economic, and political institutions to alleviate de facto segregation (*New Day in Babylon*, 112–16). For robust delineation of what Black Power was and was not, see Jeffrey Ogbonna Green Ogbar, *Black Power: Radical Politics and African American Identity* (Baltimore: Johns Hopkins University Press, 2005).

53. *Richmond Afro-American,* October 1, 1966, 5; *City of Richmond v. United States,* Plaintiff's Exhibit 5(b), at 106.

54. Roger Biles, *The Human Tradition in Urban America* (New York: Roman and Littlefield, 2002), 188; *Richmond News-Leader,* September 7, 1966, B4; Lassiter, *Silent Majority,* 284.

55. U.S. Bureau of the Census, "Race by Census Tract, 1960," Social Explorer, table, http://www.socialexplorer.com/tables/C1960TractDS/R11288126, accessed March 11, 2015; U.S. Bureau of the Census, interconsal estimates prepared by the Bureau of Population and Economic Research, University of Virginia, Richmond Annexation Files, 1942–1976, M183, Cabell Black Collection, M306; U.S. Bureau of the Census, *Census of Population and Housing* (1970).

56. Irvin Horner, affidavit, Richmond Annexation Files, 1942–1976, M183, Cabell Black Collection, M306; *Richmond Times-Dispatch,* June 2, 1969, A10.

57. *Richmond Times-Dispatch,* June 2, 1969, A10, and July 1, 1969, A1; *City of Richmond v. United States; Richmond Afro-American,* September 27, 1969, 1.

58. Thomas Muller and Grace Dawson, *The Impact of Annexation on City Finances: A Case Study in Richmond, Virginia,* Richmond Annexation Files, 1942–1976, M183, Cabell Black Collection, M306; Hayter, "From Intent to Effect," 545; Moeser and Dennis, *Politics of Annexation,* 124; Lassiter, *Silent Majority,* 283; *City of Richmond v. United States,* Plaintiff's Exhibit 5(b), at 40; *Richmond Times-Dispatch,* December 5, 1969, A2; City of Richmond, Virginia, *City Budget—Fiscal Year, 1970–71: General Fund Budget Summary,* S2, in City of Richmond, annual budgets, Richmond Public Library, Main Branch, Richmond, Va.

59. Muller and Dawson, *The Impact of Annexation on City Finances;* Hayter, "From Intent to Effect," 545; Moeser and Dennis, *Politics of Annexation,* 124; Lassiter, *Silent Majority,* 283; *City of Richmond v. United States,* Plaintiff's Exhibit 5(b), at 40; *Richmond Times-Dispatch,* December 5, 1969, A2.

60. *Richmond Times-Dispatch,* June 26, 1969, A10, and May 14, 1970, 39; *Richmond Afro-American,* March 15, 1969, 1.

3. From Intent to Effect

Portions of this chapter are drawn from Julian Maxwell Hayter, "From Intent to Effect: Richmond, Virginia, and the Protracted Struggle for Voting Rights, 1965–1977," *Journal of Policy History* 26, no. 4 (2014): 534–67.

1. *Richmond News-Leader,* July 1, 1969, 1; *Allen v. Virginia State Board of Elections,* 393 U.S. 544 (1969), at 565; President Lyndon B. Johnson, "To Fulfill These Rights," commencement address at Howard University, June 4, 1965, at http://www.lbjlib.utexas.edu/johnson/archives.hom/speeches.hom/650604.asp.

2. John A. Hannah, *Political Participation: A Study of the Participation by Negroes in the Electoral and Political Processes in 10 Southern States since Passage of the Voting Rights Act of 1965* (Washington, D.C.: U.S. Commission on Civil Rights, May 1968), iii; Arthur S. Flemming, *The Voting Rights Act: Ten Years After* (Washington, D.C.: U.S. Commission on Civil Rights, January 1975), 2; Richard M. Valelly, *The Two Reconstructions: The Struggle for Black Enfranchisement* (Chicago: University of Chicago Press, 2004), 213.

3. After a departmental reorganization, the CRD reduced the number of lawyers on its staff to twenty-seven on March 13, 1968 (Hannah, *Political Participation,* 169). On the confusion about section 5 throughout the DOJ, see Hannah, *Political Participation,* 163–66.

4. Kevin Michael Kruse, *White Flight: Atlanta and the Making of Modern Conservatism* (Princeton, N.J.: Princeton University Press, 2005), 19–41 (on Atlanta being "too busy to hate"); Matthew D. Lassiter, *The Silent Majority: Suburban Politics in the Sunbelt South* (Princeton, N.J.: Princeton University Press, 2006), 128–29 (on the "Charlotte Way"); Clarence N. Stone, *Regime Politics: Governing Atlanta, 1946–1988* (Lawrence: University Press of Kansas, 1989), 77. Atlanta's black city council members and Maynard Jackson not only carried the momentum of reform of the civil rights movement but also met firm resistance from whites (much like Henry Marsh's BMC during the late 1970s). Jackson, under criticism from whites about his commissioner of administrative services, Emma Darnelle, and her attempts to hire black staff, capitulated to criticism by firing Darnelle. Jackson most notably also fired 1,000 predominantly black sanitation workers who went on strike for a $500 annual increase in salary. These workers made less than $7,000 per year. On Atlanta municipal politics during the late 1960s and the 1970s, see Stone, *Regime Politics,* chap. 5, and J. Phillip Thompson, *Double Trouble: Black Mayors, Black Communities, and the Call for a Deep Democracy* (New York: Oxford University Press, 2006), 58–59.

5. U.S. Bureau of the Census, "Census 1970," Social Explorer, table, http://www.socialexplorer.com/tables/C1970/R11288131, accessed November 20, 2016; Lassiter, *Silent Majority,* 208–9, 180–83, 214–15.

6. William A. Thornton, "History of the Crusade: Report of the Historian: 1953–1995," Richmond Crusade for Voters Collection, 1955–1995, M306, Cabell Black Collection, M306, James Branch Cabell Library, Virginia Commonwealth University, Richmond; *Richmond Times-Dispatch,* January 17, 1970, B1, and August 11, 1986, B2; Lewis A. Randolph and Gayle T. Tate, *Rights for a Season: The Politics of Race, Class, and Gender in Richmond, Virginia* (Knoxville: University of Tennessee Press, 2003), 161.

7. Thornton, "History of the Crusade."

8. John V. Moeser and Rutledge M. Dennis, *The Politics of Annexation: Oligarchic Power in a Southern City* (Cambridge, Mass.: Schenkman, 1982),

126–37; *Richmond Afro-American,* January 10, 1970, 1; *Richmond Times-Dispatch,* March 3, 1970, A15.

9. Moeser and Dennis, *Politics of Annexation,* 15, 137; *Richmond Times-Dispatch,* March 3, 1970, A15; *Holt v. City of Richmond,* 344 F.Supp. 228 (1972), at 66, 85.

10. "School Plan Alters Negro-White Ratios," *Richmond Times-Dispatch,* May 13, 1970, B3; "The Richmond Plan," *Richmond Times-Dispatch,* May 13, 1970, editorial page; Lassiter, *Silent Majority,* 290; Frank Walin, "HEW Omits Busing in," *Richmond Times-Dispatch,* May 12, 1970, 1, 17. On the "pairing system," see Robert A. Pratt, *The Color of Their Skin: Education and Race in Richmond, Virginia, 1954–1989* (Charlottesville: University Press of Virginia, 1993), 46–47. By 1970, African Americans made up 64 percent of the RPS system, whereas Chesterfield County schools were more than 90 percent white. Approximately 52,000 students were enrolled in RPS system. Of the seven high schools, three were 100 percent African American; another was 99.3 percent white; one was 92 percent white; the sixth was 81 percent white; and the seventh was 68 percent black. On the breakdown of middle schools and elementary schools, see Pratt, *Color of Their Skin,* 46–49.

11. *Richmond Afro-American,* May 30, 1970, 1.

12. *Richmond Afro-American,* June 13, 1970, 1.

13. *Richmond Afro-American,* February 6, 1971, 2, and June 20, 1970, 1.

14. Thomas Muller and Grace Dawson, *The Impact of Annexation on City Finances: A Case Study in Richmond, Virginia,* 9–10, Richmond Annexation Files, 1942–1976, M183, Cabell Black Collection, M306, Box 6; City of Richmond, Virginia, *City Budget—Fiscal Year, 1970–71: General Fund Budget Summary,* S2, in City of Richmond, annual budgets, Richmond Public Library, Main Branch, Richmond, Va. In 1969, the poverty threshold for an urban family of four was $3,743 (U.S. Census, *Census of Population and Housing* [Washington, D.C.: U.S. Bureau of the Census, 1970], Richmond, Virginia, SMSA, P-45; see also U.S Bureau of the Census, *Census of Population and Housing* [Washington, D.C.: U.S. Bureau of the Census, 1960]). *Green v. County School Board of New Kent* (391 U.S. 430 [1968]) specified that New Kent County's freedom-of-choice plan did not constitute compliance with admissions to public schools on a nonracial basis. The Court mandated that Richmond needed to implement more effective measures to integrate public schools.

15. Sidney M. Milkis, "The Modern Presidency, Social Movements, and the Administrative State: Lyndon Johnson and the Civil Rights Movement," in *Race and American Political Development,* ed. Joseph E. Lowndes, Julie Novkov, and Dorian Tod Warren (New York: Routledge, 2008), 259; *Richmond Times-Dispatch,* August 21, 1966, H16, and May 26, 1970, B3.

16. William L. Van Deburg, *New Day in Babylon: The Black Power Movement and American Culture, 1965–1975* (Chicago: University of Chicago Press,

1992), 64–74; Peter Guralnick, *Sweet Soul Music: Rhythm and Blues and the Southern Dream of Freedom* (New York: Back Bay Books, 1999); *Jet*, April 17, 1975, 4.

17. Dan Berger, *The Hidden 1970s: Histories of Radicalism* (New Brunswick, N.J.: Rutgers University Press, 2010), 75; *Richmond Times-Dispatch*, November A3, 1970, B1, February 11, 1971, C1, and September 3, 1971, B8; Ned Oliver, "Rearview Mirror," *Style Weekly*, July 16, 2013, http://www.styleweekly.com/richmond/rearview-mirror/Content?oid=1920347.

18. *Richmond Times-Dispatch*, April 27, 1966, A22; Curtis Holt Sr., campaign flier, 1970, Howard Carwile Collection, M294, James Branch Cabell Library, Virginia Commonwealth University, Richmond; *Richmond Afro-American*, February 6, 1971, 1, September 17, 1968, 1, and September 24, 1968, 3.

19. *Richmond Times-Dispatch*, November 3, 1969, B8, and August 1, 1971, D1.

20. Randolph and Tate, *Rights for a Season*, 233; *Perkins v. Matthews*, 400 U.S. 379 (1971); Moeser and Dennis, *Politics of Annexation*, 144. In the early 1970s, the Supreme Court began to recognize that southerners were diluting black voter strength by using at-large elections and annexations simultaneously.

21. Moeser and Dennis, *Politics of Annexation*, 144–45. Section 1 of the Fifteenth Amendment contends that citizens' rights to vote "shall not be denied or abridged by the United States or by any State on account of race, color, or previous condition of servitude." After Judge Abbott's initial ruling to annex Chesterfield County, white suburbanites formed steering committees that unsuccessfully tried to appeal annexation. Abbott and the three-judge annexation court rushed through annexation faster than these anti-annexation contingents could appeal the court's decision before January 1, 1970.

22. *Richmond Times-Dispatch*, July 1, 1969, A1.

23. Lassiter, *Silent Majority*, 290; Robert R. Merhige Jr., "A Judge Remembers Richmond in the Post-*Brown* Years," *Washington and Lee Law Review* 49, no. 23 (1992): 28. Richmonders exploded over Merhige's decision. Roughly 4,000 white students boycotted the bus plan, and nearly two-thirds of reassigned white pupils refused to attend black schools in Richmond's East End. The Supreme Court later overturned Merhige's ruling and invalidated city–county busing in a five-to-four vote in *Bradley v. School Board of Richmond*, 416 U.S. 696 (1974); see also Pratt, *Color of Their Skin*, 54.

24. Merhige, "A Judge Remembers Richmond," 23, 28; Moeser and Dennis, *Politics of Annexation*, 149.

25. Chris Danielson, *After Freedom Summer: How Race Realigned Mississippi Politics, 1965–1985* (Gainesville: University Press of Florida, 2011), 3; Hugh Davis Graham, "The Origins of Affirmative Action: Civil Rights and the Regulatory State," *Annals of the American Academy of Political and Social Science* 523, no. 1 (1992): 50–62. The Warren Court dived into issues of minor-

ity voting rights in the case *Gomillion v. Lightfoot* (364 U.S. 339 [1960]). The Alabama legislature redrew Tuskegee's boundaries after African Americans registered enough voters to challenge white control. The twenty-eight-sided figure drawn up effectively made it impossible for blacks to elect a candidate in Tuskegee. The Court ruled that the Tuskegee's electoral district boundaries violated the Fifteenth Amendment. Unlike in later cases, in this case Justice Frankfurter argued that states are protected from judicial review when they have exercised power within "the domain of the state." There was no "countervailing municipal function" that justified such boundaries in Alabama, however, so the Court ruled that these boundaries were designed to dilute blacks' votes. This was one of the first voting rights cases that dealt exclusively with issues of discriminatory intent and effect. See also J. Morgan Kousser, *Colorblind Injustice: Minority Voting Rights and the Undoing of the Second Reconstruction* (Chapel Hill: University of North Carolina Press, 1999), 54; Peyton McCrary and Steven F. Lawson, "Race and Reapportionment, 1962: The Case of Georgia Senate Redistricting," *Journal of Policy History* 12, no. 3 (2000): 293–320.

Although the Court had previously ruled that in terms of vote dilution the intent of discrimination could be proven solely on the grounds of effect, two cases, one in 1962 and the other in 1964, had tremendous implications for reapportionment guidelines, the VRA, and section 5 of that act. In *Baker v. Carr* (369 U.S. 186 [1962]), the Court ruled six to three that under the Equal Protection Clause issues of reapportionment were justiciable. More specifically, Charles W. Baker alleged that Tennessee officials had virtually ignored a statute of 1901 to equally apportion the state's General Assembly. Not only had Tennessee officials' apportionment plans ignored significant population growth (particularly in increasingly black urban areas), but many of the state's urban jurisdictions, in comparison to rural counties, were also severely underrepresented. In *Baker v. Carr*, the Court questioned whether it had jurisdiction over state-based legislative apportionment. In the end, Warren's Court contended that the Fourteenth Amendment's Equal Protection Clause gave the Court the right to correct violations of state administrations. More importantly, it concluded that Baker had the right to raise apportionment questions for judicial evaluation.

The Court went further in regulating malapportionment in *Reynolds v. Sims* (377 U.S. 533 [1964]). Alabama's legislative districts, by the mid–twentieth century, were still representative of the 1900 census: although Alabama's cities had grown tremendously since the turn of the century (in large part due to African American migration from rural areas), each county, according to the state's constitution, was entitled to at least one representative. As such, urban counties with higher and denser populations were decidedly underrepresented. The Court, in an eight-to-one decision, contended that the Equal Protection Clause required "no less than substantially equal state legislative" representation for all citizens (at 377). *Reynolds* required that states establish equally populated districts to protect against dilution under the principle of what became known as "one person, one vote."

26. *Allen v. Virginia State Board of Elections;* Julian Maxwell Hayter, "From Intent to Effect: Richmond, Virginia, and the Protracted Struggle for Voting Rights, 1965–1977," *Journal of Policy History* 26, no. 4 (2014): 542–43; Kousser, *Colorblind Injustice,* 54–56; Hugh Davis Graham, *Civil Rights and the Presidency: Race and Gender in American Politics, 1960–1972* (New York: Oxford University Press, 1992), 174–76; Valelly, *Two Reconstructions,* 214–15.

27. Hugh Davis Graham, *The Civil Rights Era: Origins and Development of National Policy, 1960–1972* (New York: Oxford University Press, 1990), 357; *Reynolds v. Sims,* at 555. White southerners viewed section 5 to be the most invasive of the VRA's provisions. They believed that preclearance impinged on states' prerogatives and their ability to govern themselves. According to Steven F. Lawson, this ruling "gave Justice Department lawyers . . . a fresh opportunity to pursue a promising avenue of suffrage enforcement" (*In Pursuit of Power: Southern Blacks and Electoral Politics, 1965–1982* [New York: Columbia University Press, 1985], 162). Of note, says Lawson, many of these lawyers were members of the adjunct CRD and liberal holdovers from Johnson's "Great Society" administration. Also, in *Fortson v. Dorsey* (379 U.S. 433 [1965]), the Court concluded that multimember districts used in Georgia's senatorial elections might possibly be unconstitutional in some places if they were used to cancel out or minimize blacks' voting strength. Justice John M. Harlan, who had dissented in *Allen,* strongly disagreed with the notion that judges should expand the scope of VRA section 5 to examine electoral outcomes. He also strongly disagreed that it was the Court's job to decide who preferred at-large systems to district-based systems. He contended that the VRA was fundamentally concerned with procedures that impinged upon blacks' rights to vote. Changes in electoral systems, Harlan argued, did not require voters to comply with anything at all. For him, the VRA was fundamentally regulatory. Harlan, according to Hugh Davis Graham, supported section 5, but he understood that section to be part of a complex regulatory scheme that the Court's majority had ignored in *Allen.* Harlan believed that section 4 was the VRA's most important section because it opened the door to black voting (Graham, *Civil Rights and the Presidency,* 176–78).

28. Nixon's strategies to roll back the VRA not only backfired but also led to the formation of a bipartisan, pro-suffragist congressional coalition. The conservative agenda to deregionalize the VRA and to limit the scope of section 5 inflamed Congress's civil rights coalition for two reasons: first, southerners were blatantly ignoring recent contention over vote dilution mechanisms that cancelled out blacks' voting strength; and, second, the Court's recent ruling in *Allen* extended the DOJ's ability to seek preclearance. Nixon's southern coalition also alienated moderate-to-liberal Republican senators who constituted nearly a third of the Republican Party's bloc of forty-three senators. These men, like their liberal

allies, had been influenced by recent reports on emergent vote dilution. Long-standing lawyer-bureaucrats in the CRD and the congressional committees that sponsored and benefited politically from liberal constituencies' were also ideologically hostile to the Nixon administration's sphere of conservative social politics. On the renewal of the VRA, see Graham, *Civil Rights Era,* 360–66, and Lawson, *In Pursuit of Power,* 168–70. Congress and the Supreme Court were extremely successful at selling the extension of the VRA. In fact, outside of a handful of conservative dissenters, the only real question was whether to extend the bill for five or ten years. On the ratification of the Twenty-Ninth Amendment, see Rowland Evans and Robert D. Novak, *Nixon in the White House: The Frustration of Power* (New York: Vintage, 1973), and Graham, *Civil Rights Era,* 357–65.

29. Hannah, *Political Participation,* 168–70; Lawson, *In Pursuit of Power,* 160–64.

30. Lawson, *In Pursuit of Power,* 163; Earl M. Maltz, The *Chief Justiceship of Warren Burger, 1969–1986* (Columbia: University of South Carolina Press, 2000), 7–8, 4–30, 31–57, 114; Derrick Bell, "The Burger Court's Place on the Bell Curve of Racial Jurisprudence," in *The Burger Court: Counter-Revolution or Confirmation?* ed. Bernard Schwartz (New York: Oxford University Press, 1998), 61; Bernard Schwartz, "The Burger Court in Action," in Schwartz, *The Burger Court,* 263; Hayter, "From Intent to Effect," 547. On the Southern Strategy, see Kevin P. Phillips, *The Emerging Republican Majority* (New Rochelle, N.Y.: Arlington House, 1969). According to Earl Black and Merle Black, the compression of black voters into exclusively urban enclaves expedited the rise of the Republican South. Over time, reapportionment and redistricting for congressional districts led to almost exclusively Republican districts in the South's suburbs. Although African Americans often held district majorities in the South's urban enclaves, congressional districts in effect became "safe" Republican districts (*The Rise of Southern Republicans* [Cambridge, Mass.: Belknap Press of Harvard University Press, 2002], 331–37). Not all racial redistricting took place at the municipal level. In fact, by the early 1970s congressional redistricting at the state and federal level had profound implications for representation in Washington and states congresses. In fact, large numbers of African Americans, who lived largely in southern cities, were concentrated into a small number of southern districts. This concentration, according to Black and Black, eventually solidified a small, African American Democratic southern base but also created additional safe districts—especially in suburbs—comprising mostly white voters who voted Republican.

The Burger Court eventually stemmed the tide on vote dilution cases in a case called *City of Mobile v. Bolden* (446 U.S. 55 [1980]). The Court pondered the question of whether at-large voting systems violated the Fourteenth and Fifteenth Amendments. The justices eventually held that the Fifteenth Amendment did not give blacks the right to elect black candidates. They also concluded that vote dilution should be mitigated with constitutional remedies. Facially neutral actions such as annexations were unconstitutional only if they were motivated by discriminatory intent. This decision turned the tide on Warren's holding in *Reynolds* and Burger's decisions in *White v. Regester*, 412 U.S. 755 (1973), and *Zimmer v. McKeithen*, 485 F.2d 1297 (1973). On *Bolden*, see Maltz, *Chief Justiceship of Warren Burger*, 194.

31. *Griggs v. Duke Power Company*, 401 U.S. 424 (1971); Hayter, "From Intent to Effect," 548.

32. *Griggs v. Duke Power Company*, at 401; Hayter, "From Intent to Effect," 548. On Supreme Court logic in *Brown*, see Graham, *Civil Rights Era*, 377–90. The *Griggs* decision held that aptitude tests violated Title VII of the Civil Rights Act of 1964, which prohibits employment-based discrimination on the basis of race, color, religion, sex, or national origin. It also prohibits discrimination based on employees' interracial associations. It applies to companies with a specific number of employees—fifteen at time of ratification. On Title VII, see Graham, *Civil Rights Era*, 136–40.

33. *Perkins v. Matthews*; *City of Richmond v. United States*, 422 U.S. 358 (1975); Hayter, "From Intent to Effect," 548.

34. When the Court recognized similarities between vote denial and vote dilution, it found it hard to provide a simple standard for vote dilution. The justices eventually came to rely on what they called a "totality of circumstances." The Court measured vote dilution not by annexations or at-large elections alone but rather by the effect these election-based schemes had on the outcome of minority votes combined. The Court did not hold that minority vote dilution was unconstitutional until *White v. Regester* in 1973. After *White*, minorities challenged the constitutionality of at-large election schemes at least forty times.

35. Kousser, *Colorblind Injustice*, 2; *Richmond Times-Dispatch*, October 18, 1972, A21.

36. *Richmond Afro-American*, February 26, 1977, 5, and May 22, 1971, 1; *Whitcomb v. Chavis*, 403 U.S. 124 (1971).

37. *Richmond Times-Dispatch*, January 15, 1971, A1; *City of Richmond v. United States*, Plaintiff's Exhibit 5(b), at 16; Hayter, "From Intent to Effect," 550–51.

38. *Connor v. Johnson*, 402 U.S. 690 (1971), at 402 (Justices Hugo Black, John Harlan, and Warren Burger dissented); Hayter, "From Intent to Effect," 550–51.

39. *Richmond Afro-American*, May 22, 1971, 1; *Richmond Afro-American*, May 29, 1971, 1; Moeser and Dennis, *Politics of Annexation*, 145–73.

40. Moeser and Dennis, *Politics of Annexation*, 151–52; *Richmond Afro-American*, June 17, 1967, 7.

41. *Richmond Afro-American*, October 2, 1971, 1–2; Moeser and Dennis, *Politics of Annexation*, 158; *City of Richmond v. United States*, at 168; Hayter,

"From Intent to Effect," 552. Merhige released his official decision regarding annexation on November 23, 1971.

42. *Holt v. City of Richmond*, 344 F.Supp. 228 (1972); *Holt v. City of Richmond*, 459 F.2d 1093 (1972); Moeser and Dennis, *Politics of Annexation*, 159; *Richmond Afro-American*, April 29, 1972, 1; Hayter, "From Intent to Effect," 552. Given the evidence of institutionalized discrimination, the Court stressed that Richmond was not an appropriate case to ignore the precedent established by the VRA.

43. In *Whitcomb v. Chavis* in 1971, the Court ruled that the use of multi-member state legislative districts is not per se unconstitutional under the Equal Protection Clause but may be "subject to challenge" where the circumstances of a particular case may "operate to minimize or cancel out the voting strength of racial or political elements of the voting population" (at 143). See also *City of Richmond v. United States*, at 30–31, and Moeser and Dennis, *Politics of Annexation*, 162.

44. Moeser and Dennis, *Politics of Annexation*, 163–64; *City of Petersburg v. United States*, 93 S.Ct. 1441 (1973), at 1029; *Richmond Times-Dispatch*, March 16, 1973, A21.

45. *White v. Regester*; Ruth P. Morgan, *Governance by Decree: The Impact of the Voting Rights Act in Dallas* (Lawrence: University Press of Kansas, 2004), 41–56; Kousser, *Colorblind Injustice*, 336; Valelly, *Two Reconstructions*, 215; *Zimmer v. McKeithen;* Gary A. Keith, *Rotten Boroughs, Political Thickets, and Legislative Donnybrooks: Redistricting in Texas* (Austin: University of Texas Press, 2013), 80.

46. Moeser and Dennis, *Politics of Annexation*, 165, 170; *City of Richmond v. United States*. Upon William Daniel's death in the summer of 2010, Henry Marsh remembered him as one of the few whites on the city council who was dedicated to racial justice (*Richmond Times-Dispatch*, July 8, 2010, page number unavailable).

47. *Richmond Times-Dispatch*, January 22, 1974, A5, February 9, 1974, 1, and March 19, 1974, 7; Moeser and Dennis, *Politics of Annexation*, 167. Members of Chesterfield County, the Crusade, the Richmond City Council (including Mayor Thomas Bliley), and TOP were called as witnesses in the city's suit.

48. All quotes from *City of Richmond v. United States*, audio recording of the oral argument, Oyez Project at IIT Chicago–Kent College of Law, at http://legacy.oyez.org/cases/1970-1979/1974/1974_74_201, accessed June 25, 2013.

49. Ibid.; Pratt, *Color of Their Skin*, 48.

50. *Richmond News-Leader*, August 10, 1976, page number unavailable.

51. *Richmond Afro-American*, August 7, 1976, 1, and February 26, 1977, 1, 5.

52. "Power to the People," *Richmond Afro-American*, March 2, 1977, 1; *Richmond Times-Dispatch*, March 2, 1977, A1. In February 2000, Mayor Tim

Kaine and Councilman Sa'ad El-Amin cosponsored a resolution to rename a number of Richmond's bridges. The Richmond City Council honored Curtis Holt Sr.'s memory by renaming the Stonewall Jackson Memorial Bridge, over the Fifth Street Viaduct, the Curtis Holt Sr. Memorial Bridge.

53. Flemming, *The Voting Rights Act,* 11, 43; Margaret Edds, "The Path of Black Political Power," 1985, at http://aliciapatterson.org/stories/path-black-political-power; H. W. "Chuck" Richardson, interviewed by the author, Richmond, fall 2012.

54. Andrew V. Sorrell and Bruce A. Vlk, "Virginia's Never-Ending Moratorium on City–County Annexations," *Virginia News-Letter* 88, no. 1 (2012): 1–2.

55. Ibid.

4. "The Dream Is Lost"

1. "Letters to the *Afro,*" *Richmond Afro-American,* March 12, 1977, 1, 3; Shelley Rolfe, "Afro's Raymond Boone: Challenger of the Establishment," *Richmond Times-Dispatch,* May 15, 1977, G2; William A. Thornton, "History of the Crusade: Report of the Historian, 1953–1995," Richmond Crusade for Voters Collection, 1955–1995, M306, Cabell Black Collection, M306, James Branch Cabell Library, Virginia Commonwealth University, Richmond.

2. On the transformation from protest to politics, see Thomas J. Sugrue, *Sweet Land of Liberty: The Forgotten Struggle for Civil Rights in the North* (New York: Random House, 2008), 497–99, 503; Steven F. Lawson, *In Pursuit of Power: Southern Blacks and Electoral Politics, 1965–1982* (New York: Columbia University Press, 1985); Arthur S. Flemming, *The Voting Rights Act: Ten Years Later* (Washington, D.C.: U.S. Commission on Civil Rights, January 1975), 49; Arthur S. Flemming, *The Voting Rights Act: Unfulfilled Goals* (Washington, D.C.: U.S. Commission on Civil Rights, September 1981), 64–70, 90. On Carl Stokes, see Leonard N. Moore, *Carl B. Stokes and the Rise of Black Political Power* (Urbana: University of Illinois Press, 2003). On Richard Hatcher, see Jon C. Teaford, "'King Richard' Hatcher: Mayor of Gary," *Journal of Negro History* 77, no. 3 (1992): 126–40. On Kenneth Gibson, see Andra Gillespie, *The New Black Politician: Cory Booker, Newark, and Post-racial America* (New York: New York University Press, 2013). On Tom Bradley, see Frank D. Gilliam Jr., "Exploring Minority Empowerment: Symbolic Politics, Governing Coalitions, and Traces of Political Style in Los Angeles," *American Journal of Political Science* 40, no. 1 (1966): 56–81.

3. Sugrue, *Sweet Land of Liberty,* 497; Frank R. Parker, *Black Votes Count: Political Empowerment in Mississippi after 1965* (Chapel Hill: University of North Carolina Press, 1990), 103; Flemming, *The Voting Rights Act: Unfulfilled Goals,* 64–70.

4. On residential segregation in American cities, see Arthur S. Flemming,

Equal Opportunity in Suburbia (Washington, D.C.: U.S. Commission on Civil Rights, July 1974), 9–10; the figures on income and the racial makeup of each census tract come from U.S. Bureau of the Census, *Census of Population and Housing* (Washington, D.C.: U.S. Bureau of the Census, 1980).

5. U.S. Bureau of the Census, *Census of Population and Housing* (Washington, D.C.: U.S. Bureau of the Census, 1970); U.S. Department of Commerce, *Current Population Reports, Consumer Income: Characteristics of Low-Income Population, 1970* (Washington, D.C.: U.S. Department of Commerce, 1970), 3; City of Richmond, *Budget: Fiscal Year 1977–78*, 27–28, in City of Richmond, annual budgets, Richmond Public Library, Main Branch, Richmond, Va.

6. *Richmond Times-Dispatch*, February 3, 1977, B7; *Richmond Afro-American*, March 5, 1977, 1, March 9, 1977, 14, and March 19, 1977, 1, 7.

7. *Richmond Afro-American*, May 15, 1982, 7; Glenn Frankel, "Richmond's Quiet Mayor: Low-Key First Black Chief of City Uses Political Connections to Get Results," *Washington Post*, June 24, 1979, at https://www.washingtonpost.com/archive/local/1979/06/24/richmonds-quiet-mayor-low-key-first-black-chief-of-city-uses-political-connections-to-get-results/99298c6e-0820-4c0b-a2d8-2e60b4d9d40a/.

8. *Richmond Times-Dispatch*, April 30, 1972, G1; June 4, 1972, G5; July 6, 1973, B4; June 7, 1973, B9; June 7, 1972, B9. See also Shelley Rolfe, "Power of Crusade Earns It Respect," *Richmond Times-Dispatch*, June 29, 1980, B2. On "bridge leaders," see Belinda Robnett, "African American Women in the Civil Rights Movement, 1954–1965: Gender, Leadership, and Micromobilization," *American Journal of Sociology* 101, no. 6 (1996): 1661–93; Laurie B. Green, "Challenging the Civil Rights Narrative: Women, Gender, and the 'Politics of Protection,'" in *Civil Rights from the Ground Up: Local Struggles, a National Movement*, ed. Emilye Crosby (Athens: University of Georgia Press, 2011), 57.

9. Green, "Challenging the Civil Rights Narrative," 55–56; *Richmond Times-Dispatch*, June 4, 1972, G5, and April 30, 1972, G1; *Richmond Afro-American*, July 17, 1982, 7, and June 17, 1982, 7; Lewis A. Randolph and Gayle T. Tate, *Rights for a Season: The Politics of Race, Class, and Gender in Richmond, Virginia* (Knoxville: University of Tennessee Press, 2003), 262–64.

10. Shelley Rolfe, "Afro's Ray Boone: Challenger of the Establishment," *Richmond Afro-American*, May 15, 1977, G2; Bill Miller, "Richmond's Silent Decision Makers," *Richmond Times-Dispatch*, February 26, 1978, B1; Bill Miller, "Ballot Wins Spur Visions for Crusade," *Richmond Times-Dispatch*, June 26, 1977, A1, A2; Shelley Rolfe, "A New Crusade," *Richmond Times-Dispatch*, April 25, 1979, B1.

11. Matthew Countryman, *Up South: Civil Rights and Black Power in Philadelphia* (Philadelphia: University of Pennsylvania Press, 2006), 296.

12. Miller, "Richmond's Silent Decision Makers," B1.

13. Ibid.

14. Ron Harris, "Richmond: Former Confederate Capital Finally Falls to Blacks," *Ebony*, June 1980, 50; *Richmond Times-Dispatch*, April 17, 1977, A1, A8, and February 26, 1978, B1, B3; Margaret Edds, "The Path of Black Political Power," 1985, at http://aliciapatterson.org/stories/path-black-political-power; Clarence N. Stone, *Regime Politics: Governing Atlanta, 1946–1988* (Lawrence: University Press of Kansas, 1989), ix–xii.

15. Harris, "Richmond," 48–50.

16. Bruce J. Schulman, *The Seventies: The Great Shift in American Culture, Society, and Politics* (New York: Free Press, 2001), 56, 39–42, 123–26 (on the larger economic trends in the United States during the 1970s); Bill Miller, "Job Losses Not as Bleak as Indicated," *Richmond Times-Dispatch*, July 30, 1978, B1, B2; Tim Wheeler, "Hanover Told of Industry Lag," *Richmond Times-Dispatch*, October 28, 1976, B5.

17. U.S. Bureau of the Census, *Census of Population and Housing* (1970); Miller, "Job Losses Not as Bleak," B2; *Richmond Times-Dispatch*, December 21, 1977, A5.

18. *Richmond Times-Dispatch*, March 9, 1977, A14; Randolph and Tate, *Rights for a Season*, 251. On the importance of public and private relationships and municipal governments' limited authority, see Stone, *Regime Politics*, ix–xii.

19. "Letters to the Afro," *Richmond Afro-American*, March 12, 1977, 1, 3; J. Phillip Thompson, *Double Trouble: Black Mayors, Black Communities, and the Call for Deep Democracy* (New York: Oxford University Press, 2006), 124; Flemming, *The Voting Rights Act: Ten Years After*, 173; Edds, "The Path of Black Political Power."

20. Moore, *Carl B. Stokes*; Jimmie Lewis Franklin, *Back to Birmingham: Richard Arrington, Jr. and His Times* (Tuscaloosa: University of Alabama Press, 1989); J. Mills Thornton, *Dividing Lines: Municipal Politics and the Struggle for Civil Rights in Montgomery, Birmingham, and Selma* (Tuscaloosa: University of Alabama Press, 2002); Edds, "The Path of Black Political Power"; "Tom Bradley Elected First Black Mayor of Los Angeles," *Chicago Metro-News*, June 2, 1972, 1; Adolph Reed, *Stirrings in the Jug: Black Politics in the Post-segregation Era* (Minneapolis: University of Minnesota Press, 1999), 96.

21. *Richmond Times-Dispatch*, May 3, 1978, A6; April 30, 1978, N1; and August 22, 1978, A1.

22. *Richmond Times-Dispatch*, May 3, 1978, A1, A6; April 29, 1975, B1; May 4, 1978, C10. For election results, see *Richmond Times-Dispatch*, May 7, 1978, editorial page.

23. Christopher Silver, *Twentieth-Century Richmond: Planning, Politics, and Race* (Knoxville: University of Tennessee Press, 1984), 317. On the Kanawha Square plaza construction, see Virginia Churn, "City Seeking Riverfront Plan," *Richmond Times-Dispatch*, July 11, 1976, D1.

24. Glenn Frankel, "Richmond's Quiet Mayor," *Washington Post*, June

24, 1979, at https://www.washingtonpost.com/archive/local/1979/06/24/richmonds-quiet-mayor-low-key-first-black-chief-of-city-uses-political-connections-to-get-results/99298c6e-0820-4c0b-a2d8-2e60b4d9d40a/; *Richmond Times-Dispatch*, August 7, 1978, A4; Paul G. Edwards, "Black Councilmen vs. White City Manager, *Washington Post*, August 29, 1978, at https://www.washingtonpost.com/archive/politics/1978/08/29/black-councilmen-vs-white-manager/6032af97-a9dc-4813-a031-78520c12490c/.

25. Bill Miller, "Five on Council Ask Leidinger to Resign," *Richmond Times-Dispatch*, August 7, 1978, A1; Preston Yancy, "Let's Be Fair with Leidinger," *Richmond Afro-American*, August 12, 1978, editorial page; *Richmond Times-Dispatch*, August 16, 1978, editorial page; H. W. "Chuck" Richardson, interviewed by the author, Richmond, fall 2012; Ray Filegar, "Jinkins Raps Bid to Oust Leidinger," *Richmond Times-Dispatch*, August 10, 1978, B1.

26. Shelley Rolfe, "A Fiscal Conservative," *Richmond Times-Dispatch*, January 24, 1979, B1; *Richmond Times-Dispatch*, May 3, 1978, A6, and August 16, 1978, editorial page; *Richmond News-Leader*, August 28, 1978, 10; Frankel, "Richmond's Quiet Mayor."

27. Randolph and Tate, *Rights for a Season*, 252; *Richmond Afro-American*, February 3, 1979, 1.

28. On black-led cities, atrophying tax bases, and silver-bullet strategies, see Sugrue, *Sweet Land of Liberty*, 503–4; Thompson, *Double Trouble*, 4–6; and Reed, *Stirrings in the Jug*, 90–95.

29. *Richmond Times-Dispatch*, October 23, 1977, B5, and December 21, 1977, A5; *Richmond Afro-American*, October 2, 1982, 1. For more on the Richmond Coliseum, see Harry Kollatz Jr., "Give 'em Hell, Howard," *Richmond Magazine*, March 29, 2016, http://richmondmagazine.com/news/richmond-history/give-em-hell-howard/.

30. Edds, "The Path of Black Political Power"; Randolph and Tate, *Rights for a Season*, 254–55; Dan Moreau, "Right for 8 Years, Rennie Says," *Richmond Times-Dispatch*, July 19, 1979, C1.

31. Bill Miller, "Richmond's Embattled Ship Survived the Shells of 1978," *Richmond Times-Dispatch*, January 1, 1979, B1; Edds, "The Path of Black Political Power"; Dan Moreau, "Mayor Termed Empire Builder," *Richmond Times-Dispatch*, May 23, 1979, B1; *Richmond Times-Dispatch*, April 14, 1980, editorial page, and October 17, 1978, B4; Bill Wasson, "Either . . . or: Mayor's Actions Draw Strong, Differing Opinions," *Richmond News-Leader*, March 26, 1980, 1; *Richmond News-Leader*, June 20, 1980, 12.

32. Ruth P. Morgan, *Governance by Decree: The Impact of the Voting Rights Act in Dallas* (Lawrence: University Press of Kansas, 2004), 273; *Richmond Times-Dispatch*, October 24, 1978, B4; Dan Moreau, "Blacks in Slight Majority in City," *Richmond Times-Dispatch*, August 22, 1979, A1.

33. Dan Moreau, "Redistricting Timetable Set," *Richmond Times-Dispatch*,

October 4, 1979, D1, D10; *Richmond Times-Dispatch,* September 18, 1979, A10. On "Marshgate" and racial animus on the city council during the early 1980s, see Michael Isikoff, "Virginia Tradition," *Washington Post,* September 19, 1982, https://www.washingtonpost.com/archive/politics/1982/09/19/virginia-tradition/54f49892-5cf8-47dc-9e01-7882d293db57/; "Marshgate," *Richmond News-Leader,* August 30, 1979, 10; and "Marshgate II," *Richmond News-Leader,* September 5, 1979, 11.

34. Dan Moreau, "Redistricting Plan Halted by Court," *Richmond Times-Dispatch,* October 11, 1979, A1.

35. *Richmond Times-Dispatch,* July 8, 1979, C4, October 16, 1979, B1, and September 23, 1981, A5; *Richmond News-Leader,* October 9, 1979, 14; Dan Moreau, "End of Name Calling Asked," *Richmond Times-Dispatch,* August 28, 1979, A1; Yancy, "Let's Be Fair with Leidinger"; *Richmond Afro-American,* May 7, 1980, A7.

36. "The Last Chance," *Richmond Times-Dispatch,* April 14, 1980, editorial page.

37. *Richmond Times-Dispatch,* May 4, 1980, L1; Shelley Rolfe, "Council Election Baedeker," *Richmond Times-Dispatch,* April 26, 1980, B1; *Richmond Times-Dispatch,* May 7, 1980, A1, and May 4, 1980, L1.

38. *Richmond Times-Dispatch,* May 4, 1980, L1, and May 2, 1980, editorial page; Shelley Rolfe, "Power of Crusade Has Earned It Respect," *Richmond-Times Dispatch,* June 29, 1980, B2.

39. *Richmond Afro-American,* May 15, 1982, 7; Frankel, "Richmond's Quiet Mayor"; Tom Campbell, "Jackson Ward: Downtown's Back Porch Is High on Priority List," *Richmond Times-Dispatch,* December 19, 1976, M1, M2.

40. Rolfe, "Power of Crusade Has Earned It Respect," B1; *Richmond Times-Dispatch,* September 24, 1981, A6.

41. Rolfe, "Power of Crusade Has Earned It Respect," B1; *Richmond Times-Dispatch,* September 24, 1981, A6; U.S. Bureau of the Census, *Census of Population and Housing* (1970); U.S. Bureau of the Census, *Census of Population and Housing* (1980); Harris, "Richmond," 51; *Richmond News-Leader,* January 21, 1981, 1; Stanley Pierre-Louis, "The Politics of Influence: Recognizing Influence in Dilution Claims under Section 2 of the Voting Rights Act," *University of Chicago Law Review* 62, no. 3 (1995): 1215.

42. *Richmond Times-Dispatch,* June 4, 1981, A10; *Richmond News-Leader,* June 6, 1981, page number unavailable.

43. Morgan, *Governance by Decree,* 52; *Richmond-Times Dispatch,* June 10, 1981, B3, and June 6, 1981, A1, A11 (on the inner workings of the redistricting schemes in 1981); *Richmond News-Leader,* June 6, 1981, 11. Packing, according to political scientists, refers to the concentration of a minority group into one district in order to dilute opportunities of influence (in Richmond's case, a breakup of the BMC) in other districts.

44. Morgan, *Governance by Decree,* 52; *Richmond News-Leader,* June 6, 1981, 1; *Richmond Times-Dispatch,* June 6, 1981, A11; *Richmond News-Leader,* June 6, 1981, 1. "Cracking" is the opposite of "packing." Cracking refers to the fracturing of a homogenous minority group among several voting districts to dilute that group's—in this case blacks'—voting strength.

45. *Richmond News-Leader,* June 3, 1981, page number unavailable; *Richmond Afro-American,* July 1, 1981, 1; Dan Moreau, "Real Issue Clear, Says Hill," *Richmond Times-Dispatch,* June 24, 1981, C1, C2; *Richmond Times-Dispatch,* June 24, 1981, A6. In the early 1980s, Professor J. John Palen and Richard D. Morrison examined the numbers of blacks in administrative positions in local public and private spheres. Despite black Richmonders' approximately twenty-five-year involvement in politics, they had been systematically frozen out of boardrooms, executive suites, administrative offices, and so on. By 1982, of Richmond's 1,535 corporate officers, only 9 were black; of Richmond's 4,482 decision-making positions (e.g., board members, judges, administrators, corporate officers, etc.), blacks, despite making up more than half of the city's population, held only 474 ("Numbers Don't Lie," *Richmond Afro-American,* May 15, 1982, editorial page).

46. *City of Richmond v. United States,* 422 U.S. 358 (1975); *Richmond News-Leader,* June 2, 1981, 10, and June 3, 1981, 8; *Richmond Times-Dispatch,* January 23, 1981, B3; "Let It Die," *Richmond Times-Dispatch,* April 21, 1981, editorial page; *Richmond Afro-American,* July 1, 1981, 1. Whites, in essence, questioned *City of Richmond v. United States.* In *Richmond,* the Court concluded that when a city alters its external boundaries and uses at-large elections simultaneously, minorities are entitled to representation in proportion to their population strength. Whites in Richmond argued that the law was moot because blacks now outnumbered whites.

47. Dan Moreau, "Districting of City Plan Approved," *Richmond Times-Dispatch,* September 1, 1981, A1, A5; *Richmond Times-Dispatch,* June 6, 1981, A1.

48. Morgan, *Governance by Decree,* 23–24; *Richmond Afro-American,* February 5, 1982, 5. On the "Senate factors," section 2, and the VRA's extension in the 1980s, see Thomas M. Boyd and Stephen J. Markman, "The 1982 Amendments to the Voting Rights Act: A Legislative History," *Washington and Lee Law Review* 40, no. 4 (1983): 1347–1428, esp. 1378, and Richard M. Valelly, *The Two Reconstructions: The Struggle for Black Enfranchisement* (Chicago: University of Chicago Press, 2004), 240. On the arguments against majority–minority districts during the 1980s, see Abigail Thernstrom, *Whose Votes Count? Affirmative Action and Minority Voting Rights* (Cambridge, Mass.: Harvard University Press, 1989). *City of Mobile v. Bolden* (446 U.S. 55 [1980]) held that the Fifteenth Amendment (and, as a result, section 2 of the VRA) prohibited only direct interference with the right to vote and did not reach voting dilution claims

based on a results test. A proposed electoral change based on quantifiable electoral results rather than on intent to discriminate was easier to prove. In fact, *Bolden* represented a retreat from earlier notions of vote dilution. In 1981, the U.S. House of Representatives passed a bill (H.R. 3112) to amend the section 2 of the VRA to prohibit laws and practices that *resulted* in a denial or abridgement of the right to vote on account of race.

49. George S. Kemp to Gordon L. Crenshaw, Universal Leaf Tobacco Company, July 13, 1981, George Stevenson Kemp Papers, 1965–1984, M240, Cabell Black Collection, M306; *Richmond Times-Dispatch,* July 15, 1981, editorial page. Congress not only eventually counteracted the Supreme Court ruling in *Mobile v. Bolden* (446 U.S. 55 [1980]), which held that the Fifteenth Amendment did not secure blacks' rights to elect candidates, but also eventually expanded section 2, arguing that it was no longer necessary for minorities to prove racial intent.

50. William Gardner Jr., Hampton Gardens Association president, to James P. Turner, acting assistant attorney general, July 17, 1981, George Stevenson Kemp Papers, M240, Cabell Black Collection, M306; *Richmond Times-Dispatch,* September 7, 1978, editorial page; *Richmond Afro-American,* August 29, 1981, 2.

51. *Richmond Times-Dispatch,* March 2, 1982, B4.

52. *Richmond Times-Dispatch,* November 20, 1978, B4; Tom Campbell, "Opponents of West's Transfer to Seek Board Hearing Today," *Richmond Times-Dispatch,* June 19, 1980, C4; Shelley Rolfe, "Autocratic, Democratic," *Richmond Times-Dispatch,* May 8, 1982, B1; Edds, "The Path of Black Political Power."

53. *Richmond Afro-American,* July 10, 1982, 4; "Roy West for Council" campaign pamphlet, Richmond Crusade for Voters Collection, M306, Cabell Black Collection, M306; *Richmond Times-Dispatch,* April 28, 1982, B2.

54. Tom Campbell, "Contest between Blacks in District C Is Watched," *Richmond Times-Dispatch,* April 27, 1982, B1, B2. According to a segment of the Highland Park constituency, Dell was a "sapphire." The sapphire caricature, perpetuated in Jim Crow minstrelsy and late-nineteenth- and early-twentieth-century American popular culture, portrays African American women as rude, stubborn, and often overbearing. Sapphires are often depicted as angry black women (Randolph and Tate, *Rights for a Season,* 274–27; Preston Yancy, interviewed by the author, Richmond, February 2008; Willie Dell, interviewed by the author, Richmond, 2012).

55. Alison Griffin, "The Minister's Wife: Color Her Anything but Gray," *Richmond Times-Dispatch,* April 30, 1972, G1; *Richmond Afro-American,* July 17, 1982, 7; Randolph and Tate, *Rights for a Season,* 268.

56. Thompson, *Double Trouble,* 4; *Richmond Times-Dispatch,* June 4, 1972, G5, June 19, 1973, B1, and April 27, 1982, B4.

57. *Richmond Times-Dispatch,* April 27, 1982, B4, and May 5, 1981, A1.

5. "All He Gave Me Was a Foot"

1. Tom Campbell, "Gillespie Becomes Vice Mayor," *Richmond Times-Dispatch,* July 2, 1982, A1; Shelley Rolfe, "No Comment and No Comment," *Richmond Times-Dispatch,* March 5, 1983, B1.

2. Tom Campbell and Monte Young, "City Council Election May Signal Political Renaissance," *Richmond Times-Dispatch,* May 9, 1982, C1.

3. Michelle D. Byng, "Choice, Interests, and Black Political Actors: The Dilemmas of Inclusion," *Sociological Forum* 11, no. 1 (1996): 76; Eric S. Brown, *The Black Professional Middle Class: Race, Class, and Community in the Post–Civil Rights Era* (New York: Routledge, 2014), 121, 137.

4. Campbell and Young, "City Council Election May Signal Political Renaissance," C1; *Jet,* June 19, 1982, 6.

5. On technocratic black mayors, see J. Phillip Thompson, *Double Trouble: Black Mayors, Black Communities, and the Call for Deep Democracy* (New York: Oxford University Press, 2006), 4–15.

6. Thomas J. Sugrue, *Sweet Land of Liberty: The Forgotten Struggle of Civil Rights in the North* (New York: Random House, 2008), 522–23; Steven M. Gillon and Cathy D. Matson, *The American Experiment: A History of the United States,* 2nd ed. (Boston: Houghton Mifflin, 2006), chap. 31; James Patterson, *The Restless Giant: The United States from Watergate to Bush v. Gore* (reprint, New York: Oxford University Press, 2007), 157; Demetrios Caraley and Yvette R. Schlussel, "Congress and Reagan's New Federalism," *Publius* 16, no. 1 (1986): 49–50.

7. Patterson, *Restless Giant,* 157; Sugrue, *Sweet Land of Liberty,* 522–23; *Richmond News-Leader,* February 12, 1982, 4.

8. *Richmond Times-Dispatch,* March 14, 1982, B4; Bonnie V. Winston, "We're Going There to Reason," *Richmond Times-Dispatch,* March 1, 1981, B1; Sugrue, *Sweet Land of Liberty,* 524; Donald F. Kettl, "The Uncertain Brides: Regulatory Reform in Reagan's New Federalism," *Publius* 12 (1983): 19–21.

9. Kettl, "The Uncertain Brides," 19–20; *Richmond Afro-American,* March 5, 1983, 4.

10. Michael L. Clemons and Charles E. Jones, "African American Legislative Politics in Virginia," *Journal of Black Studies* 30, no. 6 (2000): 747–53; Andrew V. Sorrell and Bruce A. Vlk, "Virginia's Never-Ending Moratorium on City–County Annexations," *Virginia News-Letter* 88, no. 1 (2012): 3; Eric Sundquist, "Violence Rules in Group Rest of U.S. Left Behind," *Richmond Times-Dispatch,* June 15, 1986, A8. On the reddening of suburban politics throughout America and the rise of Republicans, see Earl Black and Merle Black, *The Rise of Southern Republicans* (Cambridge, Mass.: Belknap Press of Harvard University Press, 2002), and Matthew Lassiter, *The Silent Majority: Suburban Politics in the Sunbelt South* (Princeton, N.J.: Princeton University Press, 2006).

11. Bonnie Winston and Monte Young, "Black-White Economic Gulf is Termed Vast," *Richmond Times-Dispatch*, August 28, 1983, G1, G3; U.S. Bureau of the Census, *Census of Population and Housing* (Washington, D.C.: U.S. Bureau of the Census, 1980); Sundquist, "Violence Rules in Group Rest of U.S. Left Behind," A8.

12. U.S. Bureau of the Census, *Census of Population and Housing* (1980); *Richmond Times-Dispatch*, December 29, 1986, A11; John V. Moeser and Christopher Silver, "Race, Social Stratification, and Politics: The Case of Atlanta, Memphis, and Richmond," *Virginia Magazine of History and Biography* 102, no. 4 (1994): 530.

13. Sundquist, "Violence Rules in Group Rest of U.S. Left Behind," A1, A8; City of Richmond, *City Budget: Fiscal Year 1981–1982*, 27-10, and *City Budget: Fiscal Year 1985–86*, 22-14, in City of Richmond, annual budgets, Richmond Public Library, Main Branch, Richmond, Va.; *Richmond News-Leader*, December 12, 1982, page number unavailable; Christopher Silver and John V. Moeser, *The Separate City: Black Communities in the Urban South, 1940–1968* (Lexington: University Press of Kentucky, 1995), 167–68.

14. Sundquist, "Violence Rules in Group Rest of U.S. Left Behind," A1, A8.

15. Gil Klein, "Safety Net of City Called Full of Holes," *Richmond Times-Dispatch*, April 19, 1986, A1, A15; Martha R. Burt and Karen J. Pittman, *Testing the Social Safety Net: The Impact of Changes in Support Programs during the Reagan Administration* (Washington, D.C.: Urban Institute, 1986), 46, 161; City of Richmond, *City Budget: Fiscal Year 1981–82*, 4 and 5, in City of Richmond, annual budgets, Richmond Public Library.

16. *Richmond Times-Dispatch*, March 7, 1983, B4; Kevin Michael Kruse, *White Flight: Atlanta and the Making of Modern Conservatism* (Princeton, N.J.: Princeton University Press, 2006), 8; Lassiter, *Silent Majority*; *Milliken v. Bradley*, 418 U.S. 717 (1974); Steve Goldberg, "Study Terms Area Busing Best Solution," *Richmond Times-Dispatch*, January 25, 1983, B4; *Richmond Times-Dispatch*, September 17, 1982, editorial page. On *Milliken*, see James E. Ryan, *Five Miles Away, a World Apart: One City, Two Schools, and the Story of Educational Opportunity in Modern America* (Oxford: Oxford University Press, 2010), 138–39.

17. *Richmond Times-Dispatch*, November 1, 1980, B4; *Richmond Afro-American*, February 25, 1984, 7.

18. Moeser and Silver, "Race, Social Stratification, and Politics," 540; Manuel Deese, "New Federalism Brings New Pressures to Central Cities and Black Managers," *Public Management* 64 (1982): 10; *Richmond Afro-American*, February 12, 1982, 4, and August 21, 1982, 1–2.

19. Tina Griego, "The Former Capital of the Confederacy's All-Out Plan to Fight Poverty—and Confront Its Past," *Washington Post*, September 2, 2014; Neil Kraus and Todd Swanstrom, "Minority Mayors and the Hollow-Prize Prob-

lem," *PS: Political Science and Politics* 34, no. 1 (2001): 99; City of Richmond, *City Budget: Fiscal Year of 1981–82*, 2 (Deese quote), and *City Budget: Fiscal Year of 1985–86*, 3 (Todd quote), in City of Richmond, annual budgets, Richmond Public Library.

20. *Richmond Afro-American*, August 21, 1982, 1.

21. *Richmond Afro-American*, July 17, 1982, 1; December 12, 1982, 1, 7; and June 14, 1982, 12. See also *Richmond Afro-American*, August 25, 1984, 11, and Tom Campbell, "New Rules Adopted by Council," *Richmond Times-Dispatch*, July 27, 1982, B1, B3.

22. Shelley Rolfe, "Power of Crusade Has Earned It Respect," *Richmond Times-Dispatch*, June 29, 1980, B2.

23. William A. Thornton, "History of the Crusade: Report of the Historian, 1953–1995," Richmond Crusade for Voters Collection, 1955–1995, M306, Cabell Black Collection, M306, James Branch Cabell Library, Virginia Commonwealth University, Richmond.

24. "Black Backed by Whites Is Richmond Mayor," *New York Times*, July 3, 1982, at http://www.nytimes.com/1982/07/04/us/black-backed-by-whites-is-richmond-mayor.html; *Jet*, June 6, 1983, 18; *Wall Street Journal*, November 2, 1983, 60; *Richmond Afro-American*, August 7, 1982, 1.

25. *Richmond Times-Dispatch*, August 1, 1982, C6; *Richmond Afro-American*, August 7, 1982, 1, and June 25, 1983, 7.

26. *Richmond Afro-American*, April 16, 1983, 1; "Minority Firm Wins Marriot Job," *Richmond Times-Dispatch*, February 4, 1983, C4; *Richmond Times-Dispatch*, March 30, 1984, A1; Byng, "Choice, Interests, and Black Political Actors," 80.

27. *Richmond Afro-American*, April 16, 1983, 1, and April 21, 1984, 9; Byng, "Choice, Interests, and Black Political Actors," 83; Margaret Edds, "The Path of Black Political Power," http://aliciapatterson.org/stories/path-black-political-power; Rob Walker, "Minority Firms Plan Is Legal, Merhige Rules," *Richmond Times-Dispatch*, December 5, 1984, B1.

28. Tom Campbell, "Mrs. Dell, Newcomer Plan to Run," *Richmond Times-Dispatch*, August 20, 1983, B1; Sa'ad El-Amin, "Images: West and Dell," *Richmond Afro-American*, April 7, 1984, 4.

29. Thompson, *Double Trouble*, 131; Brown, *Black Professional Middle Class*, 121; *Richmond Times-Dispatch*, April 25, 1984, A10.

30. Tom Campbell, "City Renaissance Plan," *Richmond Times-Dispatch*, March 25, 1982, A1.

31. Amy Biegelsen, "Requiem for a Dream: The Last Days of 6th Street Marketplace," *Style Weekly*, June 27, 2007, at http://www.styleweekly.com/richmond/requiem-for-a-dream/Content?oid=1372301; *Richmond Times-Dispatch*, April 12, 1983, editorial page; *Free Lance-Star* (Fredericksburg, Va.), March 24, 1992, page number unavailable.

32. Cindy Creasy, "Trend Puts Women, Children at Poverty Level," *Richmond Times-Dispatch*, May 15, 1984, B5; Sa'ad El-Amin, no title, *Richmond Afro-American*, April 21, 1984, 9.

33. Monte Young, "Four Incumbents, 2 Challengers Endorsed by Crusade for Council," *Richmond Times-Dispatch*, April 4, 1984, B1; *Richmond Times-Dispatch*, April 22, 1984, C6.

34. *Richmond Times-Dispatch*, April 22, 1984, C6.

35. *Richmond Afro-American*, April 28, 1984, 1; Tom Campbell, "Ministers' Group Urges Return of City's Faithful Five to Power," *Richmond Times-Dispatch*, April 16, 1984, B1; Monte Young, "Housing Views Offered by 11 in Council Races," *Richmond Times-Dispatch*, April 20, 1984, B1.

36. William Ruberry, "Mrs. Dell, West Draw Distinctions," *Richmond Times-Dispatch*, April 9, 1984, B1, B4.

37. *Richmond Times-Dispatch*, April 25, 1984, A9, and June 1, 1984, B4; Lewis A. Randolph and Gayle T. Tate, *Rights for a Season: The Politics of Race, Class, and Gender in Richmond, Virginia* (Knoxville: University of Tennessee Press, 2003) 290–91.

38. Cindy Creasy, "Teen Pregnancy, Child Care, Jobs Linked to Poverty," *Richmond Times-Dispatch*, March 25, 1985, B4; *Richmond Times-Dispatch*, October 24, 1982, K7. On Fannie Lou Hamer, see Chana Kai Lee, *For Freedom's Sake: The Life of Fannie Lou Hamer* (Urbana: University of Illinois Press, 1999).

39. *Richmond Times-Dispatch*, December 29, 1986, A1; April 17, 1984, B3; and April 26, 1984, B6.

40. *Richmond Times-Dispatch*, May 1, 1984, A9, A10, and May 2, 1984, A10; *Richmond Afro-American*, May 5, 1984, 1.

41. Tom Campbell, "City Politics Now Seen as More Diverse," *Richmond Times-Dispatch*, May 6, 1984, C9; *Richmond Times-Dispatch*, June 1, 1984, B4.

42. Monte Young, "Glad He Defied Order, Gravely Says," *Richmond Times-Dispatch*, January 6, 1985, D1, D8; *Richmond Times-Dispatch*, May 9, 1984, 1.

43. Sundquist, "Violence Rules in Group Rest of U.S. Left Behind," A1, A8; Bruce J. Schulman, *The Seventies: The Great Shift in American Culture, Society, and Politics* (New York: Free Press, 2001), 58.

44. Silver and Moeser, *Separate City*, 180; *Richmond Times-Dispatch*, April 20, 2010, page number unavailable; *Richmond Afro-American*, November 10, 1983, 1.

45. *Richmond Times-Dispatch*, September 24, 1983, A1; El-Amin, "Images: West and Dell," 4; Sa'ad El Amin, "Is Mayor West a Traitor?" *Richmond Afro-American*, February 19, 1983, editorial page ; "Who Are Black Leaders," *Richmond Afro-American*, June 25, 1983, editorial page; *Richmond Afro-American*, October 13, 1984, 1.

46. Roxanne Stenson, "How Can We Fight Crime?" *Richmond Afro-American*, November 16, 1985, 1; Sa'ad El-Amin, "Richmond Ranks 3rd in Nation,"

Richmond Afro-American, October 19, 1985, 7; *Richmond Afro-American,* May 11, 1985, 14; Mark Smith, "City May Have Nation's Second-Highest Murder Rate," *Richmond Times-Dispatch,* February 3, 1986, B1, B4; *Richmond Times-Dispatch,* December 29, 1985, A11.

47. Jerry Turner, "Citizens Anti-crime Efforts Nothing New," *Richmond Afro-American,* February 2, 1985, 1; *Richmond Afro-American,* August 3, 1985, 1.

48. Tom Campbell, "Housing Selection Stirs Fight," *Richmond Times-Dispatch,* August 27, 1985, B1, B2; Mark Smith, "Crime Report's Authors Worked for Five Months," *Richmond Times-Dispatch,* February 14, 1986, D1; City of Richmond, *City Budget: Fiscal Year, 1984–85,* 15, in City of Richmond, annual budgets, Richmond Public Library.

49. Tom Campbell, "Crime Commission to Offer 82 Measures," *Richmond Times-Dispatch,* February 13, 1986, A1, A15.

50. Sugrue, *Sweet Land of Liberty,* 512; *Richmond Times-Dispatch,* April 11, 1985, B6; Shelley Rolfe, "West's Vision of Retribution," *Richmond Times-Dispatch,* August 10, 1985, B1; *Richmond Afro-American,* September 14, 1985, 1. On the "tough on crime" approach to policing, see Michelle Alexander, *The New Jim Crow: Mass Incarceration in the Age of Colorblindness* (New York: New Press, 2012).

51. *Richmond Times-Dispatch,* September 14, 1984, A5, and March 23, 1984, editorial page.

52. *Richmond Times-Dispatch,* October 30, 1985, B1; *Richmond Afro-American,* November 9, 1985, 1, 2; Tom Campbell, "Deese Believed It Was Time to Move On," *Richmond Times-Dispatch,* November 19, 1985, A7; *Richmond Times-Dispatch,* June 13, 1984, B1, and November 19, 1985, A1.

53. Thompson, *Double Trouble,* 4.

54. Shelley Rolfe, "The Crusade's Blunted Lance," *Richmond Times-Dispatch,* May 14, 1986, B1; Rolfe, "Power of Crusade Has Earned It Respect," B2.

55. Bill Miller, "'80s Critical Stage for Blacks," *Richmond Times-Dispatch,* May 15, 1981, G4; Rolfe, "The Crusade's Blunted Lance," B1.

Conclusion

1. William Ruberry, "Court Told to Look Again at Minority Business Plan," *Richmond Times-Dispatch,* July 8, 1986, A1, A2; *Richmond v. J. A. Croson Co.,* 488 U.S. 469 (1989); Michelle Byng, "The Clash of Government Structure and Racial Politics in *The City of Richmond v. J. A. Croson,*" *Race and Society* 1, no. 1 (1998): 77–91.

2. Emilye Crosby, "The Politics of Writing and Teaching Movement History," in *Civil Rights from the Ground Up: Local Struggles, a National Movement,* ed. Emilye Crosby (Athens: University of Georgia Press, 2011), 15; *Griggs v.*

Duke Power Company, 401 U.S. 424 (1971); *Allen v. Virginia State Board of Elections,* 393 U.S. 544 (1969); *Brown v. Board of Education of Topeka,* 347 U.S. 483 (1954); *City of Richmond v. United States,* 422 U.S. 358 (1975).

3. *City of Richmond v. J. A. Croson,* at 724 and 725; *Shaw v. Reno,* 509 U.S. 630 (1993). On *Croson,* see also Gregg Ivers and Karen O'Connor, "Minority Set-Aside Programs in the States after *City of Richmond v. J. A. Croson Co.,*" *Publius* 20, no. 3 (1990): 72; on *Shaw v. Reno,* see J. Morgan Kousser, *Colorblind Injustice: Minority Voting Rights and the Undoing of the Second Reconstruction* (Chapel Hill: University of North Carolina Press, 1999), 344–45.

4. Julian Maxwell Hayter, *City Profile of Richmond: Thriving Cities* (Richmond: Institute for Advanced Studies in Culture, University of Virginia, 2015), 8. On Richmond's current problems with poverty, schools, and transportation, see City of Richmond, *Mayor's Anti-poverty Commission Report,* January 18, 2013, at http://www.richmondgov.com/CommissionAntiPoverty/documents/Antipovertycommissionfinal1_17_2013c--printready.pdf.

5. Amy Biegelsen, "Wild West," *Style Weekly,* July 11, 2007, at http://www.styleweekly.com/richmond/wild-west/Content?oid=1361719.   Experts argue that Wilder had expressed no interest in the mayoralty while putting this bill forward. See Thad Williamson, "The Relationship to Democracy, Leadership, and Justice in Urban America: A View from Richmond," in *Good Democratic Leadership: On Prudence and Judgment in Modern Democracies,* ed. John Kane and Haig Patapan (New York: Oxford University Press, 2014), 39.

6. Hayter, *City Profile of Richmond,* 14, 16, 17; Ned Oliver, "Richmond Outpaces Counties in Population Growth, Census Estimates Say," *Richmond Times-Dispatch,* December 3, 2015, at http://www.richmond.com/news/local/article_4a83b372-c3a9-5bb0-aeb8-e977f6fd941d.html.

7. Michael Paul Williams, "Wide Disparities between Richmond and Henrico School Project Funding," *Richmond Times-Dispatch,* May 26, 2016, at   http://www.richmond.com/news/local/michael-paul-williams/article_e1097176-8ea3-50c5-b5fa-10bdffe10ab1.html; City of Richmond, *Mayor's Anti-poverty Commission Report,* 1, 5, 16, 17–24.

8. Hayter, *City Profile of Richmond,* 7, 10, 87; Williams, "Wide Disparities"; Leah Small, "Richmond Group Tackling Dilapidated Schools," *Style Weekly,* December 28, 2015, at http://www.styleweekly.com/ScrumBlog/archives/2015/12/26/local-group-wants-to-tackle-issue-of-packed-and-dilapidated-city-schools; City of Richmond, *Mayor's Anti-poverty Commission Report,* 1, 5, 16, 17–24.

Bibliography

Archival Collections

Brooks, John Mitchell, Collection. M296. Cabell Black Collection, M306. James Branch Cabell Library. Virginia Commonwealth University, Richmond.

Cabell Black Collection. M306. James Branch Cabell Library. Virginia Commonwealth University, Richmond.

Carwile, Howard H., Collection. M294. James Branch Cabell Library. Virginia Commonwealth University, Richmond.

City of Richmond. Annual budgets. Richmond Public Library, Main Branch, Richmond, Va.

Kemp, George Stevenson, Papers, 1965–1984. M240. Cabell Black Collection, M306. James Branch Cabell Library. Virginia Commonwealth University, Richmond.

Papers of the National Association for the Advancement of Colored People (NAACP). Library of Congress, Washington, D.C.

Richmond Annexation Files, 1942–1976. M183. Cabell Black Collection, M306. James Branch Cabell Library. Virginia Commonwealth University, Richmond.

Richmond Crusade for Voters Collection, 1955–1995. M306. Cabell Black Collection, M306. James Branch Cabell Library. Virginia Commonwealth University, Richmond.

Sheppard, Eleanor P., Papers, 1924–1978. M277. Cabell Black Collection, M306. James Branch Cabell Library. Virginia Commonwealth University, Richmond.

Newspapers and Magazines

Baltimore Afro-American & Planet
Chicago Metro-News
The Crisis (New York)
Freelance Star (Fredericksburg, Virginia)
Ebony magazine
Jet magazine
New York Times
Richmond Afro-American & Planet

Richmond Magazine
Richmond News-Leader
Richmond Times-Dispatch
Style Weekly
Wall Street Journal
Washington Post

Government Documents

Flemming, Arthur S. *Equal Opportunity in Suburbia.* Washington, D.C.: U.S. Commission on Civil Rights, July 1974.
————. *The Voting Rights Act: Ten Years After.* Washington, D.C.: U.S. Commission on Civil Rights, January 1975.
————. *The Voting Rights Act: Unfulfilled Goals.* Washington, D.C.: U.S. Commission on Civil Rights, September 1981.
Hannah, John. *Mobility in the Negro Community.* Washington, D.C.: U.S. Commission on Civil Rights, 1968.
————. *Political Participation: A Study of the Participation by Negroes in the Electoral and Political Processes in 10 Southern States since Passage of the Voting Rights Act of 1965.* Washington, D.C.: U.S. Commission on Civil Rights, May 1968.
————. *Voting: 1961 Commission on Civil Rights Report.* Washington, D.C.: U.S. Commission on Civil Rights, February 1961.
U.S. Bureau of the Census. *Census of Population and Housing.* Washington, D.C.: U.S. Bureau of the Census, 1930.
————. *Census of Population and Housing.* Washington, D.C.: U.S. Bureau of the Census, 1940.
————. *Census of Population and Housing.* Washington, D.C.: U.S. Bureau of the Census, 1950.
————. *Census of Population and Housing.* Washington, D.C.: U.S. Bureau of the Census, 1960.
————. *Census of Population and Housing.* Washington, D.C.: U.S. Bureau of the Census, 1970.
————. *Census of Population and Housing.* Washington, D.C.: U.S. Bureau of the Census, 1980.
U.S. Department of Commerce. *Current Population Reports, Consumer Income: Characteristics of Low-Income Populations, 1970.* Washington, D.C.: U.S. Department of Commerce, 1970.
Wilson, Charles E. *To Secure These Rights: The Report of the President's Committee on Civil Rights.* New York: Simon and Schuster, 1947.

Federal Court Cases

Allen v. Virginia State Board of Elections. 393 U.S. 544 (1969).

Avery v. Midland County Texas. 390 U.S. 474 (1967).

Baker v. Carr. 369 U.S. 186 (1962).

Bond v. Floyd. 385 U.S. 115 (1966).

Bradley v. School Board of Richmond. 416 U.S. 696 (1974).

Brewer v. School Board of City of Norfolk. 397 F.2d 37 (1968).

Brown v. Board of Education of Topeka. 347 U.S. 483 (1954).

Brown v. Board of Education (II). 349 U.S. 294 (1955).

Buchanan v. Warley. 245 U.S. 60 (1917).

Burns v. Richardson. 384 U.S. 73 (1966).

City of Mobile v. Bolden. 446 U.S. 55 (1980).

City of Petersburg v. United States. 93 S.Ct. 1441 (1973).

City of Richmond v. United States. 422 U.S. 358 (1975).

Colegrove v. Green. 328 U.S. 549 (1946).

Connor v. Johnson. 402 U.S. 690 (1971).

Dorothy E. Davis v. County School Board of Prince Edward County. 103 F. Supp. 337 (1952).

Fortson v. Dorsey. 379 U.S. 433 (1965).

Gomillion v. Lightfoot. 364 U.S. 339 (1960).

Green v. County School Board of New Kent County. 391 U.S. 430 (1968).

Griggs v. Duke Power Company. 401 U.S. 424 (1971).

Harper v. Virginia Board of Elections. 383 U.S. 663 (1966).

Holt v. City of Richmond. 344 F.Supp. 228 (1972).

Holt v. City of Richmond. 459 F.2d 1093 (1972).

Milliken v. Bradley. 418 U.S. 717 (1974).

Perkins v. Matthews. 400 U.S. 379 (1971).

Plessy v. Ferguson. 163 U.S. 537 (1896).

Quarles v. Philip Morris, Inc. 279 F.Supp 505 (1968).

Regents of the University of California v. Bakke. 438 U.S. 265 (1978).

Reynolds v. Sims. 377 U.S. 533 (1964).

Richmond v. J. A. Croson Co. 488 U.S. 469 (1989).

Shaw v. Reno. 509 U.S. 630 (1993).

Shelby County v. Holder. 570 U.S. _____ (2013).

Smith v. Allwright. 321 U.S. 649 (1944).

South Carolina v. Katzenbach. 383 U.S. 301 (1966).

Whitcomb v. Chavis. 403 U.S. 124 (1971).

White v. Regester. 412 U.S. 755 (1973).

Zimmer v. McKeithen. 485 F.2d 1297 (1973).

Interviews by Julian Maxwell Hayter

Boone, Raymond. Richmond, Va., July 6, 2008.
Dell, Willie. Richmond, Va., fall 2012.
Moeser, John V. Richmond, Va., April 10, 2008.
Reid, William Ferguson. Richmond, Va., April 1 and July 21, 2005.
Richardson, H. W. "Chuck." Richmond, Va., Fall 2013.
Yancy, Preston. Richmond, Va., February 15, 2008.

Books, Articles, and Other Published Materials

Alexander, Ann Field. *Race Man: The Rise and Fall of the "Fighting Editor," John Mitchell, Jr.* Charlottesville: University of Virginia Press, 2002.
Alexander, Michelle. *The New Jim Crow: Mass Incarceration in the Age of Colorblindness.* New York: New Press, 2012.
Balogh, Brian, and Bruce J. Schulman, eds. *Recapturing the Oval Office: New Historical Approaches to the American Presidency.* Ithaca, N.Y.: Cornell University Press, 2015.
Baptist, Edward E. *The Half Has Never Been Told: Slavery and the Making of American Capitalism.* New York: Basic Books, 2014.
Barbee, Matthew Mace. *Race and Masculinity in Southern Memory: History of Richmond, Virginia's Monument Avenue, 1948–1996.* New York: Lexington Books, 2013.
Bass, Jack, and Walter De Vries. *The Transformation of Southern Politics: Social Change and Political Consequence since 1945.* Reprint. Athens: University of Georgia Press, 1995.
Berger, Dan. *The Hidden 1970s: Histories of Radicalism.* New Brunswick, N.J.: Rutgers University Press, 2010.
Biles, Roger. *The Human Tradition in Urban America.* New York: Roman and Littlefield, 2002.
Biondi, Martha. *To Stand and Fight: The Struggle for Civil Rights in Postwar New York City.* Cambridge, Mass.: Harvard University Press, 2003.
Black, Earl, and Merle Black. *The Rise of Southern Republicans.* Cambridge, Mass.: Belknap Press of Harvard University Press, 2002.
Bookman, Ann, and Sandra Morgen. *Women and the Politics of Empowerment.* Philadelphia: Temple University Press, 1988.
Boyd, Thomas M., and Stephen J. Markman. "The 1982 Amendments to the Voting Rights Act: A Legislative History." *Washington and Lee Law Review* 40, no. 4 (1983): 1347–1428.
Branch, Taylor. *At Canaan's Edge: America in the King Years, 1965–68.* New York: Simon and Schuster Paperbacks, 2006.
———. *Parting the Waters: America in the King Years, 1954–63.* New York: Simon and Schuster Paperbacks, 1988.

————. *Pillar of Fire: America in the King Years, 1963–1965.* New York: Simon and Schuster Paperbacks, 1998.

Brinkley, Alan. *The End of Reform: New Deal Liberalism in Recession and War.* New York: Vintage, 1996.

Brown, Eric S. *The Black Professional Middle Class: Race, Class, and Community in the Post–Civil Rights Era.* New York: Routledge, 2014.

Brown-Nagin, Tomiko. *Courage to Dissent: Atlanta and the Long History of the Civil Rights Movement.* Oxford: Oxford University Press, 2011.

Brumfield, Dale M. *Richmond Independent Press: A History of the Underground Zine Scene.* Charleston, S.C.: History Press, 2013.

Brundage, W. Fitzhugh. *Lynching in the New South: Georgia and Virginia, 1880–1930.* Urbana: University of Illinois Press, 1993.

Bullock, Charles S., III, Ronald Keith Gaddie, and Justin J. Wert, eds. *The Rise and Fall of the Voting Rights Act.* Norman: University of Oklahoma Press, 2016.

Buni, Andrew. *The Negro in Virginia Politics 1902–1965.* Charlottesville: University Press of Virginia, 1967.

Burt, Martha R., and Karen J. Pittman. *Testing the Social Safety Net: The Impact of Changes in Support Programs during the Reagan Administration.* Washington, D.C.: Urban Institute, 1986.

Byng, Michelle D. "Choice, Interests, and Black Political Actors: The Dilemmas of Inclusion." *Sociological Forum* 11, no. 1 (1996): 75–95. DOI:10.1007/bf02408302.

————. "The Clash of Government Structure and Racial Politics in *The City of Richmond v. J. A. Croson.*" *Race and Society* 1, no. 1 (1998): 77–91. DOI:10.1016/s1090-9524(99)80187-9.

Callahan, James J., Jr. Review of *Testing the Social Safety Net* by Martha R. Burt and Karen J. Pittman. *Social Service Review* 61, no. 4 (1987): 675–76. DOI:10.1086/644488.

Campbell, Benjamin P. *Richmond's Unhealed History.* Richmond, Va.: Brandylane, 2012.

Caraley, Demetrios, and Yvette R. Schlussel. "Congress and Reagan's New Federalism." *Publius* 16, no. 1 (1986): 49–79. DOI:10.2307/3330176.

Chafe, William H. *Civilities and Civil Rights: Greensboro, North Carolina, and the Black Struggle for Freedom.* New York: Oxford University Press, 1980.

————. *The Unfinished Journey: America since World War II.* New York: Oxford University Press, 1999.

Clemons, Michael L., and Charles E. Jones. "African American Legislative Politics in Virginia." *Journal of Black Studies* 30, no. 6 (2000): 744–67. DOI:10.1177/002193470003000603.

Cohen, Lizabeth. *Making a New Deal: Industrial Workers in Chicago, 1919–1939.* Cambridge: Cambridge University Press, 1990.

Collier-Thomas, Bettye, and V. P. Franklin, eds. *Sisters in the Struggle: African*

American Women in the Civil Rights–Black Power Movement. New York: New York University Press, 2001.

Countryman, Matthew J. *Up South: Civil Rights and Black Power in Philadelphia.* Philadelphia: University of Pennsylvania Press, 2006.

Crosby, Emilye, ed. *Civil Rights History from the Ground Up: Local Struggles, a National Movement.* Athens: University of Georgia Press, 2011.

Dabney, Virginius. *Richmond: The Story of a City.* Garden City, N.Y.: Doubleday, 1976.

Dailey, Jane Elizabeth. *Before Jim Crow: The Politics of Race in Postemancipation Virginia.* Chapel Hill: University of North Carolina Press, 2000.

Danielson, Chris. *After Freedom Summer: How Race Realigned Mississippi Politics, 1965–1986.* Gainesville: University Press of Florida, 2011.

Davidson, Chandler. *Minority Vote Dilution.* Washington, D.C.: Howard University Press, 1984.

Davidson, Chandler, and Bernard Grofman. *Quiet Revolution in the South: The Impact of the Voting Rights Act, 1965–1990.* Princeton, N.J.: Princeton University Press, 1994.

Dittmer, John. *Local People: The Struggle for Civil Rights in Mississippi.* Urbana: University of Illinois Press, 1995.

Drake, W. Avon, and Robert D. Holsworth. *Affirmative Action and the Stalled Quest for Black Progress.* Urbana: University of Illinois Press, 1996.

Dudziak, Mary L. *Cold War Civil Rights: Race and the Image of American Democracy.* Princeton, N.J.: Princeton University Press, 2000.

Durr, Virginia Foster. *Outside the Magic Circle: The Autobiography of Virginia Foster Durr.* Tuscaloosa: University of Alabama Press, 1985.

Edds, Margaret. "The Path of Black Political Power." 1985. At http://aliciapatterson.org/stories/path-black-political-power.

Edgerton, Robert B. *Hidden Heroism: Black Soldiers in America's Wars.* New York: Basic Books, 2002.

Evans, Rowland, and Robert D. Novak. *Nixon in the White House: The Frustration of Power.* New York: Vintage, 1973.

Fergus, Devin. *Liberalism, Black Power, and the Making of American Politics, 1965–1980.* Athens: University of Georgia Press, 2009.

Fleming, Cynthia Griggs. *In the Shadow of Selma: The Continuing Struggle for Civil Rights in the Rural South.* Lanham, Md.: Rowman and Littlefield, 2004.

Franklin, Jimmie Lewis. *Back to Birmingham: Richard Arrington, Jr., and His Times.* Tuscaloosa: University of Alabama Press, 1989.

Friesema, H. Paul. "Black Control of Central Cities: The Hollow Prize." *Journal of the American Institute of Planners* 35, no. 2 (1969): 75–79. DOI:10.1080/01944366908977576.

Frystak, Shannon L. *Our Minds on Freedom: Women and the Struggle for Black*

Equality in Louisiana, 1924–1967. Baton Rouge: Louisiana State University Press, 2009.

Gadsden, Brett V. *Between North and South: Delaware, Desegregation, and the Myth of American Sectionalism.* Philadelphia: University of Pennsylvania Press, 2013.

Garrow, David J. *Protest at Selma: Martin Luther King, Jr., and the Voting Rights Act of 1965.* Rev. ed. New Haven, Conn.: Yale University Press, 2015.

Gates, Robbins L. *The Making of Massive Resistance: Virginia's Politics and Public School Desegregation, 1954–1956.* Chapel Hill: University of North Carolina Press, 1964.

Gavins, Raymond. "Gordon Blaine Hancock: A Black Profile from the New South." *Journal of Negro History* 59, no. 3 (1974): 207–27. DOI:10.2307/2716763.

———. *The Perils and Prospects of Southern Black Leadership: Gordon Blaine Hancock, 1884–1970.* Durham, N.C.: Duke University Press, 1993.

Gillespie, Andra. *The New Black Politician: Cory Booker, Newark, and Post-racial America.* New York: New York University Press, 2013.

Gillette, Howard, Jr. *Between Justice and Beauty: Race, Planning, and the Failure of Urban Policy in Washington, D.C.* Philadelphia: University of Pennsylvania Press, 2006.

Gilliam, Frank D., Jr. "Exploring Minority Empowerment: Symbolic Politics, Governing Coalitions, and Traces of Political Style in Los Angeles." *American Journal of Political Science* 40, no. 1 (1996): 56–81. DOI:10.2307/2111694.

Gillon, Steven M., and Cathy D. Matson. *The American Experiment: A History of the United States.* 2nd ed. Boston: Houghton Mifflin, 2006.

Glasrud, Bruce A., and Merline Pitre, eds. *Southern Black Women in the Modern Civil Rights Movement.* College Station: Texas A&M University Press, 2013.

Gleason, Michael P., and Andrew McCutcheon. *Sarge Reynolds: In the Time of His Life.* Gwynn, Va.: Gleason, 1996.

Goetz, Edward G. *New Deal Ruins: Race, Economic Justice, and Public Housing Policy.* Ithaca, N.Y.: Cornell University Press, 2013.

Goluboff, Risa Lauren. *The Lost Promise of Civil Rights.* Cambridge, Mass.: Harvard University Press, 2007.

Graham, Hugh Davis. *Civil Rights and the Presidency: Race and Gender in American Politics, 1960–1972.* New York: Oxford University Press, 1992.

———. *The Civil Rights Era: Origins and Development of National Policy, 1960–1972.* New York: Oxford University Press, 1990.

———. "The Origins of Affirmative Action: Civil Rights and the Regulatory State." *Annals of the American Academy of Political and Social Science* 523, no. 1 (1992): 50–62. DOI:10.1177/0002716292523001006.

Guralnick, Peter. *Sweet Soul Music: Rhythm and Blues and the Southern Dream of Freedom*. New York: Back Bay Books, 1999.

Hall, Jacquelyn Dowd. "The Long Civil Rights Movement and the Political Uses of the Past." *Journal of American History* 91, no. 4 (2005): 1233–63. DOI:10.2307/3660172.

Hanchett, Thomas W. *Sorting Out the New South City: Race, Class, and Urban Development in Charlotte, 1875–1975*. Chapel Hill: University of North Carolina Press, 1998.

Harrington, Michael. *The Other America: Poverty in the United States*. New York: Macmillan, 1962.

Hayter, Julian Maxwell. *City Profile of Richmond: Thriving Cities*. Richmond: Institute for Advanced Studies in Culture, University of Virginia, 2015.

———. "From Intent to Effect: Richmond, Virginia, and the Protracted Struggle for Voting Rights, 1965–1977." *Journal of Policy History* 26, no. 4 (2014): 534–67. DOI:10.1017/s0898030614000256.

Heinemann, Ronald L. *Harry Byrd of Virginia*. Charlottesville: University Press of Virginia, 1996.

Hillier, Amy E. "Residential Security Maps and Neighborhood Appraisals: The Home Owners' Loan Corporation and the Case of Philadelphia." *Social Science History* 29, no. 2 (2005): 207–33. DOI:10.1017/s014555320001292x.

Hirsch, Arnold R. *Making the Second Ghetto: Race and Housing in Chicago, 1940–1960*. Chicago: University of Chicago Press, 1998.

Holloway, Pippa. *Sexuality, Politics, and Social Control in Virginia, 1920–1945*. Chapel Hill: University of North Carolina Press, 2006.

Hood, M. V., III, Quentin Kidd, and Irwin L. Morris. *The Rational Southerner: Black Mobilization, Republican Growth, and the Partisan Transformation of the American South*. Oxford: Oxford University Press, 2012.

Hustwit, William P. *James J. Kilpatrick: Salesman for Segregation*. Chapel Hill: University of North Carolina Press, 2013.

Ivers, Gregg, and Karen O'Connor. "Minority Set-Aside Programs in the States after *City of Richmond v. J. A. Croson Co.*" *Publius* 20, no. 3 (1990): 63–78. DOI:10.2307/3330215.

Jackson, Thomas F. *From Civil Rights to Human Rights: Martin Luther King, Jr., and the Struggle for Economic Justice*. Philadelphia: University of Pennsylvania Press, 2007.

Jeffries, Hasan Kwame. *Bloody Lowndes: Civil Rights and Black Power in Alabama's Black Belt*. New York: New York University Press, 2009.

Johnson, Cedric. *Revolutionaries to Race Leaders: Black Power and the Making of African American Politics*. Minneapolis: University of Minnesota Press, 2007.

Kane, John, and Haig Patapan. *Good Democratic Leadership: On Prudence and Judgment in Modern Democracies*. New York: Oxford University Press, 2014.

Keith, Gary. *Rotten Boroughs, Political Thickets, and Legislative Donnybrooks: Redistricting in Texas.* Austin: University of Texas Press, 2013.

Kelley, Blair Murphy. *Right to Ride: Streetcar Boycotts and African American Citizenship in the Era of* Plessy v. Ferguson. Chapel Hill: University of North Carolina Press, 2010.

Kettl, Donald F. "The Uncertain Brides: Regulatory Reform in Reagan's New Federalism." *Publius* 12 (1983): 19–34. DOI:10.2307/3329877.

Keyssar, Alexander. *The Right to Vote: The Contested History of Democracy in the United States.* New York: Basic Books, 2000.

King, Gary. *A Solution to the Ecological Inference Problem: Reconstructing Individual Behavior from Aggregate Data.* Princeton, N.J.: Princeton University Press, 1997.

Klarman, Michael J. *From Jim Crow to Civil Rights: The Supreme Court and the Struggle for Racial Equality.* Oxford: Oxford University Press, 2004.

———. "How Brown Changed Race Relations: The Backlash Thesis." *Journal of American History* 81, no. 1 (1994): 81–118. DOI:10.2307/2080994.

Kluger, Richard. *Simple Justice: The History of* Brown v. Board of Education *and Black America's Struggle for Equality.* New York: Vintage, 2004.

K'Meyer, Tracy Elaine. *Civil Rights in the Gateway to the South: Louisville, Kentucky, 1945–1980.* Lexington: University Press of Kentucky, 2009.

Kollatz, Harry. *Richmond in Ragtime: Socialists, Suffragists, Sex, & Murder.* Charleston, S.C.: History Press, 2008.

Kousser, J. Morgan. *Colorblind Injustice: Minority Voting Rights and the Undoing of the Second Reconstruction.* Chapel Hill: University of North Carolina Press, 1999.

Kraus, Neil, and Todd Swanstrom. "Minority Mayors and the Hollow-Prize Problem." *PS: Political Science and Politics* 34, no. 1 (2001): 99–105. DOI:10.1017/s1049096501000154.

Kruse, Kevin Michael. *White Flight: Atlanta and the Making of Modern Conservatism.* Princeton, N.J.: Princeton University Press, 2005.

Kuumba, M. Bahati. *Gender and Social Movements.* Walnut Creek, Calif.: AltaMira Press, 2001.

Lassiter, Matthew D. *The Silent Majority: Suburban Politics in the Sunbelt South.* Princeton, N.J.: Princeton University Press, 2006.

Lawson, Steven F. *Black Ballots: Voting Rights in the South, 1944–1969.* New York: Columbia University Press, 1976.

———. "Freedom Then, Freedom Now: The Historiography of the Civil Rights Movement." *American Historical Review* 96, no. 2 (1991): 456–71. DOI:10.2307/2163219.

———. *In Pursuit of Power: Southern Blacks and Electoral Politics, 1965–1982.* New York: Columbia University Press, 1985.

———. *Running for Freedom: Civil Rights and Black Politics in America since 1941.* New York: Wiley, 2014.

Lee, Chana Kai. *For Freedom's Sake: The Life of Fannie Lou Hamer.* Urbana: University of Illinois Press, 1999.

Lewis, David L. *W. E. B. DuBois: The Fight for Equality and the American Century, 1919–1963.* New York: Holt, 2000.

Lewis, Earl. *In Their Own Interests: Race, Class, and Power in Twentieth-Century Norfolk, Virginia.* Berkeley: University of California Press, 1991.

Lowndes, Joseph E., Julie Novkov, and Dorian Tod Warren. *Race and American Political Development.* New York: Routledge, 2008.

Maltz, Earl M. *The Chief Justiceship of Warren Burger, 1969–1986.* Columbia: University of South Carolina Press, 2000.

Marlowe, Gertrude Woodruff. *A Right Worthy Grand Mission: Maggie Lena Walker and the Quest for Black Economic Empowerment.* Washington, D.C.: Howard University Press, 2003.

Martin, William L., and J. E. Buchholtz. "Annexation—Virginia's Dilemma." *Washington and Lee Review* 24, no. 2 (1967): 241–67.

McCrary, Peyton, and Steven F. Lawson. "Race and Reapportionment, 1962: The Case of Georgia Senate Redistricting." *Journal of Policy History* 12, no. 3 (2000): 293–320. DOI:10.1353/jph.2000.0018.

McDonald, Laughlin. *A Voting Rights Odyssey: Black Enfranchisement in Georgia.* Cambridge: Cambridge University Press, 2003.

McKee, Guian A. *The Problem of Jobs: Liberalism, Race, and Deindustrialization in Philadelphia.* Chicago: University of Chicago Press, 2008.

Merhige, Robert R., Jr. "A Judge Remembers Richmond in the Post-*Brown* Years." *Washington and Lee Review* 49, no. 23 (1992): 23–30.

Meriwether, James Hunter. *Proudly We Can Be Africans: Black Americans and Africa, 1935–1961.* Chapel Hill: University of North Carolina Press, 2002.

Miller, Andrew P. "J. Sargeant Reynolds: What He Was Not, Not What He Might Have Been." *Virginia Law Review* 57, no. 8 (1971): 1312–14.

Moeser, John V., and Rutledge M. Dennis. *The Politics of Annexation: Oligarchic Power in a Southern City.* Cambridge, Mass.: Schenkman, 1982.

Moeser, John V., and Christopher Silver. "Race, Social Stratification, and Politics: The Case of Atlanta, Memphis, and Richmond." *Virginia Magazine of History and Biography* 102, no. 4 (1994): 519–50.

Moore, Leonard N. *Carl B. Stokes and the Rise of Black Political Power.* Urbana: University of Illinois Press, 2003.

Morgan, Edmund S. *American Slavery, American Freedom: The Ordeal of Colonial Virginia.* New York: Norton, 1975.

Morgan, Ruth P. *Governance by Decree: The Impact of the Voting Rights Act in Dallas.* Lawrence: University Press of Kansas, 2004.

Moye, J. Todd. *Let the People Decide: Black Freedom and White Resistance Movements in Sunflower County, Mississippi, 1945–1986.* Chapel Hill: University of North Carolina Press, 2004.

Muse, Benjamin. *Virginia's Massive Resistance.* Gloucester, Mass.: Peter Smith, 1969.

Niven, David. *The Politics of Injustice: The Kennedys, the Freedom Rides, and the Electoral Consequences of a Moral Compromise.* Knoxville: University of Tennessee Press, 2003.

Ogbar, Jeffrey Ogbonna Green. *Black Power: Radical Politics and African American Identity.* Baltimore: Johns Hopkins University Press, 2004.

Orren, Karen, and Stephen Skowronek. *The Search for American Political Development.* Cambridge: Cambridge University Press, 2004.

Ownby, Ted, ed. *The Civil Rights Movement in Mississippi.* Jackson: University Press of Mississippi, 2013.

Parker, Frank R. *Black Votes Count: Political Empowerment in Mississippi after 1965.* Chapel Hill: University of North Carolina Press, 1990.

Patterson, James T. *Restless Giant: The United States from Watergate to Bush v. Gore.* Reprint. New York: Oxford University Press, 2007.

Payne, Charles M. *I've Got the Light of Freedom: The Organizing Tradition and the Mississippi Freedom Struggle.* Berkeley: University of California Press, 1995.

Payne, Charles M., and Adam Green. *Time Longer Than Rope: A Century of African American Activism, 1850–1950.* New York: New York University Press, 2003.

Phillips, Kevin. *The Emerging Republican Majority.* New Rochelle, N.Y.: Arlington House, 1969.

Pierre-Louis, Stanley. "The Politics of Influence: Recognizing Influence in Dilution Claims under Section 2 of the Voting Rights Act." *University of Chicago Law Review* 62, no. 3 (1995): 1215–41. DOI:10.2307/1600060.

Pleasants, Julian M. *The Political Career of W. Kerr Scott: The Squire from Haw River.* Lexington: University Press of Kentucky, 2014.

Powe, Lucas A., Jr. *The Warren Court and American Politics.* Cambridge, Mass.: Belknap Press of Harvard University Press, 2000.

Pratt, Robert A. *The Color of Their Skin: Education and Race in Richmond, Virginia, 1954–1989.* Charlottesville: University Press of Virginia, 1993.

Rachleff, Peter J. *Black Labor in Richmond, 1865–1890.* Urbana: University of Illinois Press, 1989.

Randolph, Lewis A., and Gayle T. Tate. *Rights for a Season: The Politics of Race, Class, and Gender in Richmond, Virginia.* Knoxville: University of Tennessee Press, 2003.

Rankin, Robert A. "The Richmond Crusade for Voters: The Quest for Black Power." *University of Virginia Newsletter* 51, no. 1 (1974): 1–7.

Ransby, Barbara. *Ella Baker and the Black Freedom Movement: A Radical Democratic Vision.* Chapel Hill: University of North Carolina Press, 2003.

Reed, Adolph L. *Stirrings in the Jug: Black Politics in the Post-segregation Era.* Minneapolis: University of Minnesota Press, 1999.

Richardson, Selden. *Built by Blacks: African American Architecture and Neighborhoods in Richmond*. Charleston, S.C.: History Press, 2008.

Robnett, Belinda. "African-American Women in the Civil Rights Movement, 1954–1965: Gender, Leadership, and Micromobilization." *American Journal of Sociology* 101, no. 6 (1996): 1661–93. DOI:10.1086/230870.

———. *How Long? How Long? African-American Women in the Struggle for Civil Rights*. New York: Oxford University Press, 1997.

Rudwick, Elliott M. "The Negro Policeman in the South." *Journal of Criminal Law, Criminology, and Police Science* 51, no. 2 (1960): 273–76. DOI:10.2307/1141205.

Rustin, Bayard. "From Protest to Politics: The Future of the Civil Rights Movement." *Commentary* 39, no. 2 (1965). At https://www.commentarymagazine.com/articles/from-protest-to-politics-the-future-of-the-civil-rights-movement/.

Ryan, James E. *Five Miles Away, a World Apart: One City, Two Schools, and the Story of Educational Opportunity in Modern America*. Oxford: Oxford University Press, 2010.

Ryan, Yvonne. *Roy Wilkins: The Quiet Revolutionary and the NAACP*. Lexington: University Press of Kentucky, 2014.

Schulman, Bruce J. *The Seventies: The Great Shift in American Culture, Society, and Politics*. New York: Free Press, 2001.

Schwartz, Bernard, ed. *The Burger Court: Counter-Revolution or Confirmation?* New York: Oxford University Press, 1998.

Schwartz, Gary T. "Reviewing and Revising Dillon's Rule." *University of Virginia Law School of Law, John M. Olin Foundation: Symposium on Law and Economics of Local Government* 67, no. 3 (1991): 1025–32.

Self, Robert O. *American Babylon: Race and the Struggle for Postwar Oakland*. Princeton, N.J.: Princeton University Press, 2005.

Silver, Christopher. *Twentieth-Century Richmond: Planning, Politics, and Race*. Knoxville: University of Tennessee Press, 1984.

Silver, Christopher, and John V. Moeser. *The Separate City: Black Communities in the Urban South, 1940–1968*. Lexington: University Press of Kentucky, 1995.

Smith, J. Douglas. *Managing White Supremacy: Race, Politics, and Citizenship in Jim Crow Virginia*. Chapel Hill: University of North Carolina Press, 2002.

Sorrell, Andrew V., and Bruce A. Vlk. "Virginian's Never-Ending Moratorium on City–County Annexations." *Virginia News-Letter* 88, no. 1 (2012): 1–9.

Stone, Clarence N. *Regime Politics: Governing Atlanta, 1946–1988*. Lawrence: University Press of Kansas, 1989.

Stubbs, Jonathan K. "America's Enduring Legacy: Segregated Housing and Segregated Schools." *Minority Trial Lawyer*, Winter 2008, 1, 8.

Sugrue, Thomas J. *The Origins of the Urban Crisis: Race and Inequality in Postwar Detroit*. Princeton, N.J.: Princeton University Press, 1996.

————. *Sweet Land of Liberty: The Forgotten Struggle for Civil Rights in the North*. New York: Random House, 2008.

Takagi, Midori. *Rearing Wolves to Our Own Destruction: Slavery in Richmond, Virginia, 1782–1865*. Charlottesville: University Press of Virginia, 1999.

Teaford, Jon C. "'King Richard' Hatcher: Mayor of Gary." *Journal of Negro History* 77, no. 3 (1992): 126–40. DOI:10.2307/2717557.

Thernstrom, Abigail M. *Whose Votes Count? Affirmative Action and Minority Voting Rights*. Cambridge, Mass.: Harvard University Press, 1987.

Thompson, J. Phillip. *Double Trouble: Black Mayors, Black Communities, and the Call for a Deep Democracy*. New York: Oxford University Press, 2006.

Thornton, J. Mills. *Dividing Lines: Municipal Politics and the Struggle for Civil Rights in Montgomery, Birmingham, and Selma*. Tuscaloosa: University of Alabama Press, 2002.

Titus, Jill Ogline. Brown's *Battleground: Students, Segregationists, and the Struggle for Justice in Prince Edward County, Virginia*. Chapel Hill: University of North Carolina Press, 2011.

Tocqueville, Alexis de. *Old Regime and the Revolution*. New York: Harper and Brothers, 1856.

Tushnet, Mark V. *The NAACP's Legal Strategy against Segregated Education, 1925–1950*. Chapel Hill: University of North Carolina Press, 1987.

Vale, Lawrence J. *Purging the Poorest: Public Housing and the Design Politics of Twice-Cleared Communities*. Chicago: University of Chicago Press, 2013.

Valelly, Richard M. *The Two Reconstructions: The Struggle for Black Enfranchisement*. Chicago: University of Chicago Press, 2004.

Van Deburg, William L. *New Day in Babylon: The Black Power Movement and American Culture, 1965–1975*. Chicago: University of Chicago Press, 1992.

Wallenstein, Peter. *Blue Laws and Black Codes: Conflict, Courts, and the Change in Twentieth Century Virginia*. Charlottesville: University of Virginia Press, 2004.

Wang, Tova Andrea. *The Politics of Voter Suppression: Defending and Expanding Americans' Right to Vote*. Ithaca, N.Y.: Cornell University Press, 2012.

Williams, Yohuru R. *Rethinking the Black Freedom Movement*. New York: Routledge, Taylor & Francis Group, 2015.

Zipp, Samuel. *Manhattan Projects: The Rise and Fall of Urban Renewal in Cold War New York*. New York: Oxford University Press, 2010.

Dissertations and Theses

Fergus, Devin. "The Ordeal of Liberalism and Black Nationalism in an American Southern State, 1965–1980." Ph.D. diss., Columbia University, 2002.

Hayter, Julian Maxwell. "Strictly Political: The Rise of Black Political Participation in Richmond, Virginia, 1960–1970." MA thesis, University of Virginia, 2005.

———. "We've Been Overcome: Black Voter Mobilization and White Resistance in Richmond, Virginia 1954–1985." Ph.D. diss., University of Virginia, 2010.

Holton, Dwight Carter. "Power to the People: The Struggle for Black Political Power in Richmond, Virginia." BA thesis, Brown University, 1987.

Jones, Michele Davis. "The Rules of the Game and Who Governs: Municipal Reform and Re-reform in Norfolk, Virginia." Ph.D. diss., University of Virginia, 2006.

Rogers, Michael Q. "Remembering the Controversy of the Richmond–Petersburg Turnpike: Politics, Rhetoric, and Visions of Progress." Senior thesis, University of Richmond, 2011.

Websites

Carson, Clayborn. "King Papers Project." At http://mlk-kpp01.stanford.edu/index.php/encyclopedia/documentsentry.

Social Explorer. Tables at http://www.socialexplorer.com/tables.

Index

Community Development Block
Grants, 14, 199–200, 218
Comprehensive Education and
Training Act (CETA), 199–200,
223
Congress of Racial Equality, 49
Connor v. Johnson, 138–39
Conquest, Edwin P., 61
Creighton Court, 2, 125–26, 157,
205; creation of, 52
Creighton Court Civic Association,
85, 125–26, 157
Crowe, Morrill M., 60, 63, 84, 96,
98; city council election results,
249–51; during the annexation
era, 104; role in staggering
elections, 75, 79
Crusade for Citizenship, 49

Dabney, Virginius, 25, 184
Daniel, William V., 117, 121–22,
144; city council election results,
252
Davis, Earl, 45
Deese, Manuel "Manny," 171–
73, 207; crime during early
1980s, 232, 234; minority set-
asides, 214–15; reaction to
New Federalism, 206, 208–10;
resignation from city hall, 235;
role in sixth Street Market, 218
Dell, Willie J., 9; appointment to
city council, 144; campaigns
for council, 167, 175, 190–93,
196–97; career in social work,
43; city council election results,
253–55; controversy with the
NAACP, 226; end of council
tenure, 219–22, 223, 225, 242;
leadership of, 185, 226; member

of the black majority-council,
148, 156–58, 212; reaction to
poverty, 18, 123, 180, 227; role
in and reaction to redistricting,
183, 189; role in community
development, 157; role of
sexism, 191, 194
Derfner, Armand, 135, 145–46,
182–83
Detroit, Michigan, 18, 19, 152,
171, 198; crime, 231; *Testing the
Social Safety Net* in, 206
Dillon's Rule, 16, 54, 90–92, 149,
244
direct-action, 49, 64, 80, 101
disparate impact, 11, 134–35
"don't buy where you can't work," 24
*Dorothy E. Davis v. County School
Board of Prince Edward County*,
39
"double-duty dollar," 24
Downtown Development
Commission, 168
Downtown Expressway, 98,
161, 200. *See also* expressway
construction
DuBois, W. E. B., 24
Durham Manifesto, 25–28

East End, 22, 77, 88, 122, 156,
223; crime in, 231; influence of
poverty, 52, 56, 203, 224, 244;
public housing in, 155; public
schools in, 118
Ebenezer Baptist Church, 23
Eggleston Hotel, 60
Eggleston, Neverett A., 53, 61–62
Eisenhower, Dwight D., 46
El-Amin, Sa'ad (Jeroyd Greene),
17, 101, 152, 242; critique of

Richmond Planning Commission, 58, 60

Richmond Police Department (RPD), 83, 235; instances of police brutality, 84–85, 101, 125; response to crime in, 231–34

Richmond Professional Institute, 85, 86. *See also* Virginia Commonwealth University

Richmond Public Schools. *See* public schools

Richmond Public Works Department, 234–36

Richmond Redevelopment and Housing Authority, 52, 55–56, 88, 125, 126, 157, 180

Richmond Renaissance, 16, 214, 217–18, 220, 224, 243

Richmond 34, 101

Richmond Times-Dispatch: backlash to black voters, 77, 178, 193; criticism of districts in, 114, 177, 185, 188; paternalism in, 25, 26, 99; poverty in, 52, 227–28; on power of Crusade in, 58, 79, 212, 236–37; on Richmond leadership in, 160–61, 173; resistance to VRA in, 69; support for Hill, Oliver W., 33; support for Roy West, 197, 223; weighing in on annexation in, 145

Richmond v. J. A. Croson, 239–40

Robertson, A. Willis, 36, 70, 73

Robinson, Norvell, 158–59, 173, 184–85, 227

Robinson, Spotswood, 25, 33–34, 38, 42

Rolfe, Shelley, 159, 180, 212, 236–37

Rouse, James, 218

Royall, Raymond, 144, 167; city council election results, 253–54

Rustin, Bayard, 68

Rust Belt, 162

Scott, Hugh, 132

Scott, W. Kerr, 28

Second Reconstruction, 12, 136

segregation, 2; before 1965, 6, 9–10, 14, 19–20, 28; challenges to, 33–34, 38–39, 40, 49, 67, 125; Crusade challenges to, 57, 78; defense of, 70, 72, 83; during the Progressive Era, 8, 21–22; following the VRA, 63, 73, 113; legacy of, 239–40, 241, 243; role of de facto segregation and poverty, 126, 150, 154, 182, 203–4, 207, 216; role of de jure segregation and poverty, 3–4, 15, 17, 45–46, 52–56, 103–4, 208, 224, 227, 233; role in gradualism, 24–27; role in massive resistance, 36–37; role in municipal employment, 58–59, 235; role in public schools, 35, 62, 82, 108, 117, 128, 134–35; role in World War II, 28

Selma, Alabama: nature of protest, 7, 280n3

"Senate factors," 187

separation by consent, 25

service industry, 26, 42, 202. *See also* professionalization of work

Shaw University, 101

Shaw v. Reno, 240

Shelby County v. Holder, 4

Sheppard, Eleanor P., 60; city council election results, 248–50;

student movement, 100–1; white benefaction, 186
"Virginia Way," 6, 9, 25, 32
vote dilution: annexations, 153; definition of, 1; fight against, 116, 127, 130–31, 134–36, 138–40, 146, 174, 289n25, 292n30; nature of, 11, 93, 109, 113; prevalence of, 12; in recent years, 240, 267n17; renewal of VRA, 187; role in staggering elections, 75–78; role in "totality of circumstances" test, 143, 293n34. *See also* majority-minority districts
voter mobilization/registration: immediately following the VRA, 67–68, 112; prior to VRA, 64, 27, 48; role of the Crusade, 44, 45, 71–72; role of local people, 60, 80; role of NAACP, 46–49; role of Selma, Alabama, 280n3
Voter Registration Committee (of the NAACP), 47–48
Voter Registration Project, 280n3
Voters' Voice, 60–61
Voting Rights Act of 1965 (VRA), 1; and annexation in Richmond, 102–9, 115; backlash to, 7, 10–11, 69–70, 74, 75, 99, 112, 132, 188–89, 193, 196; creation of, 65–67; impact of, 2, 3, 64, 67–68, 129–30, 148, 153, 165; renewal, 132, 180–81; role of local people and, 4, 7, 46, 49, 64–65, 241; role in poll taxes, 63, 68, 71–72, 73; role of redistricting in Richmond, 11, 186–89; Section 2, 66, 187, 300n48; Section 4, 66, 132,

291n27; Section 5, 1, 67, 112–13, 130–33, 135–38, 141–42, 153, 186, 188; Section 10, 67; strengthening of, 12, 111; unintended consequences of, 4, 10, 12, 81, 113

Wainwright, Richard G., 167; city council election results, 254
Wake, Carolyn, 170; city council election results, 175, 254–55; resistance to BMC, 174, 176, 185, 195, 210; role in district system, 175, 179, 181, 183
Walden, W. T., 47
Walker, Maggie Lena, 8, 20–21, 41, 43
War on Drugs, 233
War on Poverty, 13, 130, 199, 200
Warren, Earl, 10, 34, 70, 72, 130–31, 133–34. *See also* Supreme Court
West, Dr. Roy, 16–17, 18, 189–90, 235; anti-Marsh sentiment of, 151–52, 229; black opposition to, 211–12; city council election results, 255; election of 1984, 219–21, 225–26; leadership of, 171, 192, 196–98, 210–11, 213–14, 215–16, 217, 219, 222–23; legacy of, 239, 242; relationship to middle-class voters, 154, 204, 222, 228, 237; relationship with the Crusade (1984), 226–27, 230, 236; resistance to BMC, 190, 193, 194, 195; role in public schools, 211; role in set-asides, 214–15; stance on crime, 232–34; white support for, 217

CIVIL RIGHTS AND THE STRUGGLE FOR BLACK EQUALITY
IN THE TWENTIETH CENTURY

SERIES EDITORS: Steven F. Lawson, Rutgers University
Cynthia Griggs Fleming, University of Tennessee
Hasan Kwame Jeffries, Ohio State University

Freedom's Main Line: The Journey of Reconciliation and the Freedom Rides
Derek Charles Catsam

Gateway to Equality: Black Women and the Struggle for Economic Justice in St. Louis
Keona K. Ervin

The Chicago Freedom Movement: Martin Luther King Jr. and Civil Rights Activism in the North
edited by Mary Lou Finley, Bernard LaFayette Jr., James R. Ralph Jr., and Pam Smith

The Struggle Is Eternal: Gloria Richardson and Black Liberation
Joseph R. Fitzgerald

Subversive Southerner: Anne Braden and the Struggle for Racial Justice in the Cold War South
Catherine Fosl

Constructing Affirmative Action: The Struggle for Equal Employment Opportunity
David Hamilton Golland

An Unseen Light: Black Struggles for Freedom in Memphis, Tennessee
edited by Aram Goudsouzian and Charles W. McKinney Jr.

River of Hope: Black Politics and the Memphis Freedom Movement, 1865–1954
Elizabeth Gritter

The Dream Is Lost: Voting Rights and the Politics of Race in Richmond, Virginia
Julian Maxwell Hayter

Sidelined: How American Sports Challenged the Black Freedom Struggle
Simon Henderson

Becoming King: Martin Luther King Jr. and the Making of a National Leader
Troy Jackson

Civil Rights in the Gateway to the South: Louisville, Kentucky, 1945–1980
Tracy E. K'Meyer

John Hervey Wheeler, Black Banking, and the Economic Struggle for Civil Rights
Brandon K. Winford

Art for Equality: The NAACP's Cultural Campaign for Civil Rights
Jenny Woodley

For Jobs and Freedom: Race and Labor in America since 1865
Robert H. Zieger

Lightning Source UK Ltd.
Milton Keynes UK
UKHW012157291219
355969UK00015B/128/P